*ARAB FOLK EPIC AND IDENTITY*

# ARAB FOLK EPIC AND IDENTITY

Bridget Connelly

UNIVERSITY OF CALIFORNIA PRESS
Berkeley Los Angeles London

University of California Press
Berkeley and Los Angeles, California

University of California Press, Ltd.
London, England



Library of Congress Cataloging in Publication Data

Connelly, Bridget.
Arab folk epic and identity.

Bibliography: p.
1. Sīrat Banī Hilāl. 2. Story-telling—Egypt.
3. Folklore—Egypt. I. Title.
PJ7580.S55C66 1986 892'7103'09 86–884
ISBN 0–520–05536–5 (alk. paper)

Printed in the United States of America

1 2 3 4 5 6 7 8 9

*To Hank, Kate, and James*

# CONTENTS

## PART IV. SĪRA AND EPIC AND THE ORAL WAY OF KNOWING

# ACKNOWLEDGMENTS

This book is primarily an interpretive study of one Arab epic tradition, *Sīrat Banī Hilāl.*

Its methods and goals derive from the humanistic fields of Comparative Literature and Rhetoric. For their generous financial support, I thank the Social Science Research Council, the American Philosophical Society, and the McLeod Lewis Memorial Foundation. The research effort that went into this book is in many ways a dialogue with many people. I should like to recognize the debt my work owes to my mentor and teacher in Egypt, ʿAbd al-Raḥmān al-Abnoudy. To a great extent this book is about this famous poet-scholar and his relationship with the Hilālī folk epic tradition in Egypt. It is to Abnoudy and his wife, the filmmaker Atiat Abnoudy, that I owe my education in the *sīra* and the truth purveyed by Abū Zayd. I especially thank the poets Shamandī and Farūq for the many hours they spent with me. My work in Tunisia owes much to the help of Sarah and Mohamed Moussa and the Ezzine family. I should also particularly like to thank my American teachers and mentors: Phillip Damon, who introduced me to comparative literature and oral-epic critical theory; the late Tawfiq Sayigh, who encouraged me in my pursuit of that "difficult muse," Arabic letters; and above all I should like to recognize the intellectual debt this work owes to years of on-going dialogue with my former teacher and present colleague, James T. Monroe, with whom I share so many critical perspectives and excitement about Arabic literature.

I particularly thank Kristina Nelson and Humphrey Davies for their assistance and support during my 1978 research in Egypt. I also thank Malak Wassef for her unstinting service as my research assistant, translator, and interpreter while in Egypt, and my other research assistants: Benjamin Brinner for his collaboration in transcribing and describing the musicality of the performed tradition, Aisha Hassan and her husband Abd al-Salam for their friendship and assistance, and Michael Chyet for his careful editorial work and transcription of texts into final form. A particular thank-you also to Diana Lorentz for her word processing of my manuscript and to Josie Adler for her very special assistance.

Many of the working questions and the methodology of this rhetorical study of the argumentative strategies and cultural polemics involved in the Arab epic tradition derive directly from my dialogue with the faculty of the University of California, Berkeley, Department of Rhetoric. I particularly thank Robert Beloof, Leonard Nathan, Daniel Melia, Arthur Quinn, and William Brandt. I also thank my colleague Ibrahim Muhawi for sharing his knowledge of the Palestinian folk tradition with me and for his conversations about the "dialectic of the inside and the outside" in Arabic folktales. I thank too William Hickman, George Lakoff, Giovanni Canova, Micheline Galley, Gene Irschick, ʿAbd al-Hamīd Hawwās, Anita Baker, Carolyn Burke, Edmund Burke, Janet Stevens Jebali and especially Ferial Ghaźoul and Juliane Monroe. I thank Pierre Cachia, Samuel Armistead, Micheline Galley, and Theodore Anderson for their careful readings and helpful comments on my manuscript. I should also like to acknowledge the intellectual debt I owe to my husband, Henry Massie, whose comments on the heroic pattern pushed me to greater comprehension of the meaning of the epic tale in its human, developmental context as a "felt-history" of its folks.

Serious collection and fieldwork on the living Arab epic tradition in Egypt today is only beginning. Many talented researchers and folklorists in the last five years or so have begun to turn their efforts to systematic observation of the performance tradition. One looks forward particularly to the complete published work of ʿAbd al-Raḥmān al-Abnoudy (who holds the most extensive oral archive), to the work of Micheline Galley, Arlette Roth, Rosalyn Grech, Abderrahman Ayoub, the continued publications of Giovanni Canova, and the texts and performance data collected by Lucienne Saada, Susan Slyomovics, Dwight Reynolds and others who are discovering the world of Abū Zayd.

Berkeley, California
March 31, 1984

Bridget Connelly

# PART I
# Cultural Polemics and the Arab Epic Tradition

# 1
# IN DEFENSE OF *AL-SĪRA*

Western historians of Arabic literature generally agree that there is no Arab epic—certainly none that in any way rivals the *Iliad* or the *Odyssey,* the *Song of Roland,* or *Beowulf,* or the *Shahnameh.* This view represents not only a misconception of the workings of Indo-European epic narrative and a literate overevaluation of it but also an incomplete view of Arabic culture and its verbal artistry. Von Grunebaum, in a 1970 article entitled "The Hero in Medieval Arabic Prose,"[1] ably summarized the Western literary historian's position:

> On the strictly literary or standard or educated level, Medieval Arabic literature does not possess an epic narrative. There are popular epics . . . so these would fall under the specifications of this paper. But I am afraid I shall have to take the point of view of the Medieval Arab littérateur, which is another way of saying that those lengthy and repetitious tales lack the dignity that would qualify them for my notice, the Arabic being overly simple not to say defective, their images vulgar, and their composition disheveled. I must admit, as many a contemporary Arab and every Western historian would, that these epic narratives offer many facets to interest scholarship, literary and otherwise. (One should not think of Homer or the *Chanson de Roland* but rather of an almost endless sequence of episodes kept in place by one or two more or less historical figures—avoid the word hero—and retailed without surcease to edify and to stimulate religious feeling and political antagonisms among the untutored.) But I shall exclude these narratives from this presentation . . . narratives which led a lively existence in coffeehouses and other places down to perhaps thirty or forty years ago, yet never qualified as full members of literature in the eyes of their public.[2]

Von Grunebaum is not alone in his assessment of Arab "popular epics" as inferior, somehow in the shadow both of Homer and of "educated standards" of literature. The Arab man of letters (*adīb*), whose opinion von Grunebaum cites, scorns Arabic literature for its lack of a great "epic" from the golden age. Mūsá Sulaymān, in his 1956 book on Arabic story tradition, reflected the stance typical of the Arab adīb when he denounced the vulgar, "not-to-say-defective" epics of which von Grunebaum speaks. Sulaymān terms the *siyar* (sg. *sīra*), as they are called, "coarse vulgarities, ignorant of authorship, anonymous, wretched in language and style, a register of the conditions of the vulgar, deprived of color and literary splendor. . . . Had these events or this epic found an Arab poet of finer sentiment, of elevated sensations and profound imagination, the Arabs would have had an epic poem not inferior to those of the West."[3]

However invidious the comparison, it looms large in mentions of Arabic vernacular narrative tradition. These "defective" would-be epics to which von Grunebaum and Sulaymān refer are the legendary biographies called *al-sīra* (pl. *siyar*) in Arabic. These stories, recited and sung in coffeehouses for generations, include *Sīrat ʿAntar,* which champions the pre-Islamic poet-warrior ʿAntar ibn Shaddād and makes him a romantic Bedouin knight of old, powerful over all odds. They also include from later periods *Sīrat al-Ẓāhir Baybars, Sīrat al-Amīra Dhāt al-Himma* (also called *Dhū al-Himma* or *Delhemma*), *Sīrat Sayf ibn Dhī Yazan,* and *Sīrat Banī Hilāl. Baybars* chronicles the wars of the Mamluk sultan Baybars (1246–1277) against the Mongols, Persians, and Christian crusaders. *Dhāt al-Himma* recounts deeds of the Arabs in wars against the Byzantine crusaders and the ensuing Islamic struggles against the Franks. *Sīrat Sayf ibn Dhī Yazan* changes Sayf (the Himyarite prince of history who expelled the Abyssinians from southern Arabia in pre-Islamic times) into a precursor of the Prophet Muḥammad fighting battles in the name of Islam against pagan Abyssinians and Negroes. And *Sīrat Banī Hilāl* glorifies the migratory trek undertaken by that tribe in the tenth and eleventh centuries out of famine-stricken Arabia through the Levant to Egypt, the Sudan, and the Maghrib. The different siyar have had currency in the various parts of the Arab Middle East. *ʿAntar,* for example, was popular in Syria and Iraq, the *Hilāliyya* popular in Egypt and North Africa. In Tunisia, a popular epic was *Futūḥ*

*Ifrīqiyya* (The Conquest of North Africa), which sets forth the adventures of a local hero, ʿAbd Allāh ibn Jaʿfar, and the conquest of Tūnis by the Arab armies.

Professional *rāwīs* (reciters, storytellers) and poets (*shuʿarāʾ;* sg. *shāʿir*) performed these siyar in coffeehouses throughout the nineteenth century. References to oral performance of heroic tales and romances (siyar) document the existence of a rich oral, vernacular narrative tradition from the early days of the Islamic conquests. Most frequently, these references take the form of negative judgments, like Sulaymān's, made by learned men steeped in the religious or literate Classical tradition. The Egyptian historian, al-Kurtī, mentions *Aḥādīth al-Baṭṭāl* (Stories of al-Baṭṭāl from *Sīrat al-Amīra Dhāt al-Himma*) as known already in 1160. Samaw'al b. Yahyá al-Maghribī, a Jewish convert to Islam, writes of the pleasure he took in stories, romances, and collections of legendary histories like *Dīwān Akhbār ʿAntara* and *Dīwān Delhemma wa'l-Baṭṭāl* [*sic*] in 1163. In 1279, a Maghribī *shaykh* is said to have heard *al-Baṭṭāl* recited in Fatimid Cairo.[4] More recent testimony of the continuing existence of the sīra tradition may be found in the work of writers such as Ṭāhā Ḥusayn, who fondly recollects in his biography recitals of the sīra among the Egyptian fellahin.[5]

Western travelers and colonial administrators also recount their observations of poets and storytellers performing oral narratives. Villoteau describes *rabāb* (or *rabāba,* a one-stringed viol) poets singing the Abū Zayd epic in Cairo cafés.[6] Other nineteenth-century travelers observed such poets as well. Lamartine, while visiting Lebanon, heard Bedouin poets sing the exploits of ʿAntar.[7] Sir Wilfred and Lady Anne Blunt mention the "Arabian Turolds" they listened to in the Egyptian countryside.[8] Colonial visitors to North Africa, like Vaissière, Desparmet, Largeau, and Guin, observed and collected specimens of the songs and tales that Algerian café poets (the *maddāḥ* and *guwwāl*) were singing in the days of the French Protectorate.[9] Berque much later noted the maddāḥ in Sirs (Egypt) who chronicle current events and recent history in their ballads.[10] Both Villoteau and Lane observed poets and rhapsodists performing during the nineteenth century in public cafés and at private parties or festivals to celebrate a birth or a marriage or to entertain guests in a wealthy home. Villoteau, writing in the Napoleonic French expeditionary force's monumental *Description de l'Egypte* mentioned two types of performer: the improviser, called shāʿir, and reciters or rhapsodists, called *muḥaddithīn*. The former used a rabāba to provide a humming support for the singing voice, which declaimed its narrative in a measure that, although regular and cadenced, was nevertheless ornamented and modulated. The reciters performed tales of the ancient Arabs. Some read and some recited by heart. Those who recited without a book generally celebrated the exploits of a single hero and were designated by his name: the *Ẓāhiriyya* sang about the heroism of the prince Baybars, the *ʿAntariyya* vaunted ʿAntar ibn Shaddād, and the *Zanātiyya,* the *Abū-Zaydiyya,* the *Zughbī,* and the *Hilāliyya* improvised narrative poems about the tribal confederations and heroes related to *Sīrat Banī Hilāl.*[11]

Commenting on the same scene some thirty years later, Lane, in *Manners and Customs of the Modern Egyptians,* tells of the Cairene musician-poet-storyteller who, seated on a stool on the front step of a café, would animatedly regale his coffee-drinking, all-male audience with tales chanted and sung on the rabāba. The narratives alternated prose and verse. According to Lane, Cairene professional entertainers of his day belonged to three categories: (1) the "Shuʿarā'" or "Abū-Zaydiyya," who numbered about fifty and related the *Sīrat Abū Zayd;* (2) the "Muḥaddithīn" who numbered approximately thirty and narrated exclusively the "Sīrat al-Ẓāhir" or *Baybars;* and (3) the "ʿAntariyya" who numbered only about six, and unlike the other two bards, used a printed text and no musical accompaniment during performance. The latter recited from various printed romances such as *Sīrat Delhemeh* [*sic*] and *Sīrat Sayf al-Yazan,* as well as from *Alf Layla wa Layla.*[12]

The subject matter of these siyar, along with the *Alf Layla wa Layla* (The Thousand and One Nights), circulated not only in Egypt but throughout the Arab countries, told in varying form and manner by amateurs in Arabian desert tents,[13] in Algerian cafés,[14] on Tunisian street corners,[15] and in Nigerian Shuwa Arab tribal compounds.[16] Professionals in Fez intoned the tales to the rhythm not of the rabāb but of a square tambourine,[17] while Jordanian rabāb minstrels much like those in Egypt sang the Banī Hilāl saga to the troops as recently as the 1950s.[18] One or two *ḥakawātīs* (public storytellers) still recite Hilālī stories in Damascus and Baghdad cafés today.[19]

In Tunisia, up until World War II, the *fdāwī* (storyteller) was a familiar figure in the community.[20] Plying his trade in various ways, he sometimes traveled from door to door to spin tales for the women and children of the households, often holding forth in the marketplaces and neighborhood squares before a mixed audience, or performing in cafés for a strictly male audience. The fḍāwīs had a large and varied repertoire of tales structured to suit the nature of their noisy, fluid audience. Their episodic tales were designed to capture and retain the attention of an audience thoroughly familiar with the subject and to entertain them sufficiently to earn a living. The primary means of obtaining money was to build suspense gradually as the crowd grew; then, with the hero almost at the sword of his enemy (and the crowd at its numerical peak), the fḍāwī would stop the narration and collect a few millièmes before going on. If the crowd was small or the contributions niggardly, the storyteller would pack up and move to another neighborhood, leaving his hero and story behind in midaction. The storyteller ensured a constant audience over a long period of time (and thus a steady income) by presenting a serial-like continuation of particular tales at special times and places each day over several months, or for as long as he could maintain the interest of a steady and sizable crowd and continue to embellish the various episodes of a given tale. In the case of some narratives, such as *ʿAntar* or the Hilālī tales, a skilled storyteller well versed in his tradition could stretch the episodes out over a year, while maintaining an interested and paying audience.

The audience, often as large as two hundred, depending on the season and time of day, was primarily composed of poor, usually illiterate or semiliterate people who had memorized the Koran at *Kuttāb* (Koranic school). In this stratum of society, the fḍāwī represented a loved and respected personage, an important figure in the community. The lure of the storyteller, however, attracted children of all classes. Street urchins flocked about their hero, while better-dressed children of the more educated classes were unceremoniously pulled away by parents who greeted the vagabond storyteller with suspicion and scorn, treating him like a disreputable beggar.

In addition to such oral manifestations of the sīra tradition, sources indicate that these heroic narratives also circulated in written manuscript versions. Ḥamzah al-Iṣfahānī, in the first half of the tenth century, states that seventy books of such "entertainment" were widely read. Ibn al-Nadīm tells us that *asmār* (nightly recitals and story-telling sessions) and *khurāfāt* (legendary tales, fairy tales) were extremely popular in the Abbasid period; booksellers and copyists had a large market for which to reproduce old stories and collect new ones in writing.[21] Even with such early references to vernacular narrative fiction, only fairly recent manuscripts exist. One of the earliest sīra manuscripts appears to be a 500-page sixteenth-century Vatican manuscript of *Sīrat Baybars*.[22] Most manuscripts of *Baybars,* however, date from the eighteenth century, and those of *Sīrat ʿAntar* and *Sīrat Banī Hilāl* from the nineteenth century.

Printed versions of the popular story matter also exist. Cheap *kutub ṣafrā'* (called "yellow books" for their low-grade paper that easily discolors) lie about bookstalls throughout the Middle East and may be found in private homes and in libraries. Exhibiting the same episodic narrative features as the oral compositions of the popular poets who declaim the tales in public squares, in coffeehouses, or at Ramadan soirees, these pulp editions are written in various colloquial tongues, most often in a sort of "Middle Arabic,"[23] or a popular dialect corrected (often hypercorrected) so as to approach the Classical idiom. Their language is replete with coined words, nonsense words, anachronistic and archaic words, and the grossest solecisms. The printed editions appear in varied forms, which include the multivolume, episodic siyar and shorter *qiṣaṣ* (stories; sg. *qiṣṣa*) or *ḥikāyāt* (sg. *ḥikāya*) written in prose and verse in proportions varying with the edition and particular tradition; long *qaṣīda*-like poems (monorhymed odes); songs in the style of the *zajal* and *muwashshaḥa* (strophic forms); and long narratives in either rhymed or simple prose.

The authorship and the date of these works are generally obscure, although within the texts themselves, such works are often attributed to various well-known scholars, grammarians, and authors of the Classical tradition, such as Abū ʿUbayda and al-Aṣmaʿī. For example, the *Taghrībat Banī Hilāl ilá Bilād al-Gharb* and the *Kitāb al-Riyāḍa al-Bahiyya wa-Mā Jará lil-Amīr Abū Zayd wa-al ʿArab al-Hilāliyya,* found in the University of California, Berkeley, Library, give no indication of authorship. The former, published in Beirut by the Maktabat al-Turqī, gives no date of publication; the latter, published in 1282AH/1865AD, gives no notice as to the publisher or place of publication. The

Beirut publisher of the *Kitāb ʿAntara ibn Shaddād* solves the problem of authorship, in the 1883 and 1901 editions, by claiming it as its own work based on the tales of others. As Heller says in his *Encyclopaedia of Islam* essay, internal comments in *Sīrat ʿAntar* on its origin suggest there is a "regular romance regarding the origin of the romance." It professes to be the work of al-Aṣmaʿī in the time of Hārūn al-Rashīd in Baghdad. Al-Aṣmaʿī seems to have lived 670 years—400 during the Jahiliyya (pre-Islamic days) when he personally knew ʿAntar and began his compositions, which he completed in 1080.

The obscurity of attribution the reader finds in the written editions of the various siyar merely parallels their netherworld existence in the total culture and underscores the ambivalent status of the vernacular narratives, on the margins between folk and learned society, between oral and literate culture. The view expressed in most Western literary histories of the Arabs—that there is no epic and indeed no indigenous tradition of fiction—may result from a profound value dichotomy in Arabic-speaking countries. Scholars of von Grunebaum's generation and earlier knew Arabic culture and literature through its *texts,* that is, through its high, literary court aesthetic. Most literary histories written by English, French, or other European scholars chronicle the Classical literature of the high court tradition as a restricted aesthetic, an almost exclusive cult of poetry. Fiction, it is said, is Arabic literature's adopted stepsister, borrowed from European languages; prior to the modern period, no story tradition as such exists in Arabic, nor do the mimetic forms of drama and epic. Von Grunebaum wonders about this lack of imagination, this highly restricted aesthetic of the Arabs, and always in his extensive writings somehow compares Arabic literature unfavorably with Greek and Western tradition.[24]

In his self-confessed adoption of the stance of the medieval Arab littérateur, von Grunebaum (and some other Western critics who approach Arabic culture) views story tradition through an elitist prism. Such a prism, while legitimate perhaps in its reflection of audience taste and values for the literate tradition, distorts folk culture and vernacular narrative traditions. It also mistakes the narratives' audience and their implicit aesthetic and moral value in the community for which their makers intended them. In adopting the perspective and prescriptions of literate, Classical aesthetics, the foreign critic-scholar misjudges the audience of popular coffeehouse epics and thus their status in the society as a whole. Even an early field-worker like Lane perforce adopted a tone of subtle disparagement in his treatment of sīra performance in nineteenth-century Cairo, since many of his informants were wealthy men educated in the Classical tradition of letters.

Traditionally, the Arab philologist, critic, and man of letters (adīb) has looked down on written versions of the siyar and on the oral performances of illiterate folk poets as something outside the realm of Arabic literature proper. From the earliest days of Arabic literary criticism, a prejudice against fiction in general, and against orally disseminated narrative, poetry, and song in particular, emerged. This prejudice existed despite (indeed, perhaps because of) the fact that the Koran and *Ḥadīth* and the pre-Islamic poetic corpus are the products of a long oral tradition. In European tradition, the oral world of Merlin the Magician and the *chansons de geste* were soon incorporated into written discourse; epic and romance became generically part of the developing fictive voice of the roman or novel.[25] In the Arab Islamic culture, things developed quite differently, for early Islam feared the oral mimetic mode and recognized, much as Plato did, the power of the rhapsodist over the minds of young men sitting at their feet.[26] Islam thus co-opted, as Weber asserts religions always attempt to, the means of expression in its quest to tell the one true story—or History.[27] The newly developing religion managed to assume all the functions of the oral arts in a traditional society: to educate, to elucidate, to entertain, and to edify the souls of men. Literacy also became its exclusive domain.

Indeed, the first written document in Arabic literature appears to be the Koran. As Ṭāhā Ḥusayn announced, "pre-Islamic" poetry actually postdates the Muslim Holy Book as a written tradition;[28] so-called pre-Islamic poetry was in fact collected much after the advent of Islam by philologist-folklorists of the schools of Baṣra and Kūfa from the mouths of Bedouin poet-transmitters in order to elucidate obscure Koranic idioms. The Koranic text, which was itself established from an orally preserved and transmitted text in the first century of Islam, contained many phrases and terms difficult for the faithful to understand. In the interest of Koranic exegesis, theologians thus became folklore collectors and philologists. The Bedouin bards' poetic declamations assisted the scholars in establishing the Koranic text and in understanding obscurities of its idiom, which was that of the old oral poetic koine, rapidly becoming obscure in the urban empire.[29]

Theologians-turned-grammarians thus created an official language of letters as the vehicle of court, state, and religious discourse, and as the poetic idiom of the educated, literate elite. Written discourse was established out of the need to protect the Word of God and his Prophet for the newly expanding nation of Islam. What might have provided the material of myth, epic, and story, thus became, as the Italian scholars Bausani and Canova argue, history and legend written down in the official literary language of the new empire. Islam converted that which might have become epic into either history or legend, either preempting as its own truth any potential epic material or dismissing it as lies. As Bausani puts it, "The literal-minded early, monotheistic, Muslim culture, with its drive toward demythologization, consequently categorized the epic tales of the Muslim conquest not as literary works, but as annals of sacred history, or as folk literature or semi-folk literature which has long been looked down upon by the official Arab literary establishment."[30]

Stories of the deeds of Muḥammad, his sayings, and the oral poetry composed by some of his companions to celebrate his military exploits, revile his enemies, and praise his friends became part of the accepted, official biography of the Prophet. *Sīrat al-Nabī*, as the epic chronicle of early Islam, thus seems unique of its kind in Arabic literature. Similar competing heroic narratives (siyar), no doubt produced in the same kind of professional oral poetic story-telling milieu as the legends and stories surrounding the deeds of the Prophet, remained largely in the province of oral tradition. Their late folk redactions into manuscripts and yellow books exist in a poetic, linguistic register closer to the evolving dialects than to the more fixed, linguistic idiom of the official, literate mode of discourse, the language of Classical Arabic literature.

Arabic oral tradition and fiction thus have been obscured by an aura of mystique, on the one hand, and by an attitude of disdain and neglect, on the other. While the pre-Islamic qaṣīdas are viewed as great lyrical effusions of the Arab soul, and the Koran and Ḥadīth as the Word of God and the Prophet, such vernacular narratives as *Sīrat ʿAntar, Sīrat al-Amīra Dhāt al-Himma, Sīrat*

*Baybars, Sīrat Sayf ibn Dhī Yazan,* and the like, have long been, as the official view was expressed in 988 by Ibn al-Nadīm, but "vulgar and insipid works not meriting serious consideration."[31] Critically, these epic tales of heroism and high adventure did not exist. Theirs was the language of "nonliterature," or "illiterature"; their subjects at once frivolous lies that threatened the proper Muslim and a sign of unlettered poverty, the purview of beggars and peasants—certainly in no way fitting entertainment for a serious person. The professed adīb's artistic sensibility could only respond to the highly developed genius of literate Arab poets writing in the inflected literary language. Arabic poetry became a highly conventional art, until the twentieth century restricted to the sixteen meters of pre-Islamic poetry as described by Khalīl b. Aḥmad in the eighth century. So too, the themes, motifs, and format of the earliest Arabian poetry became codified as the standard for all subsequent poetry, the frame on which generations of literate court poets would embroider. That this poetry of the high canon was based on an original oral poetry remains an anomaly of Arabic letters which may in large part explain much about medieval aesthetics and poetics.

By and large, the literarily adept recoiled from anything that departed from the Classical canon. Ibn Khaldūn, virtually alone among medieval Arab scholars, commented on the anomalous situation of oral poetry in the dialects. In his al-*Muqaddima* (Introduction to History), he defended "the poems of the Arab Bedouins" as "true poetry," and denounced pedantic scholars and philologists who recoil from oral, vernacular poetry, disdaining it for its lack of case endings.[32] Most other medieval references to vernacular lore are negative. Arab officialdom has long suppressed the representational arts, suspicious of fiction, story, music, and painting on religious, political, social, and economic grounds. Scholars, as guardians of the official culture, have long condemned vernacular poetry and story traditions. ʿAbd al-Wahhāb al-Subkī (d. 1370) writes that "copyists should abstain from transcribing books God doesn't need, like *Sīrat ʿAntar.*" Ibn Kathīr (d. 1373) says the *Sīrat al-Amīra Dhāt al-Himma* is naught but a tissue of lies, like the *Sīrat ʿAntar* or al-Bakri's sīra on the Prophet, and calls the siyar foolish elaborations, ignorantly full of disgusting groping. Al-Suyūṭī (d. 1505) also condemns qiṣaṣ (tales), quoting

Ibn Hanbal (d. 855), who maintained that *malāḥim* (epics) and *maghāzī* (military campaign stories) have no foundation.[33] The sixteenth-century jurist al-Wansharishī, in *Miʿyār al-Maghrib,* reports that it was illegal to sell or possess historical romances such as *ʿAntar* and *Dhū al-Himma* or to listen to recitations of them.[34]

The alterity of oral story tradition as seen through the Muslim definition of "art" and "culture" was such as to have the force of taboo. The continuing oral, traditional poetic performance tradition was roundly condemned in what was to become an ongoing cultural polemic. Only the religiously condoned oral recitation was permissible. Much of the polemic surrounding recitation stems from the fact that the central text of the culture itself is a "recitation"; indeed, the word *Qur'ān* means recitation. As Nelson puts it in her work on the oral Koran, to Muslims the Koran is the Word of God in Arabic, the last of God's revelations to mankind, transmitted to His Prophet Muḥammad through the intermediary of the Angel Gabriel. The command to recite was one of the earliest revelations: "Recite, in the name of the Lord" (Koran 96,1). Over twenty years, until Muḥammad's death in A.D. 632, the Angel Gabriel orally transmitted the recitation of the Heavenly Book preserved in the divine realm on tablets (Koran 85,21–22) to the illiterate Muḥammad who transmitted it in recitations to his illiterate people. The teachings were only written down after the Prophet's death to assure the existence of one complete text. The Koran, as revealed in seven *aḥruf* (dialects or versions), is presumed to be fluid. The Heavenly Book, to quote Nelson again,

> exists not as a single linearly ordered original from which emanate subsequent versions, but as one transcendent phenomenon embracing a number of manifestations, oral and written. . . . The written text exists not to preserve against change; it is taken for granted that oral tradition does that. Nor is the written text the ultimate referent of the oral. Oral tradition has served as the final arbitrator of the written traditions; only those fragments written down in the presence of the Prophet were accepted as material for the written text, and any differences in the fragments were settled by oral tradition. Muḥammad spread the message by sending out reciters, not texts.[35]

Early Muslims thus evinced a profound distrust of "writing" and a trust of "orality," a confidence in the authority of personal, face-to-face speech acts. Muslim accounts of their Scripture's genesis and transmission stress the illiteracy of the Prophet so as to lend authenticity to his teachings as the direct, inimitable Word(s) of God—which the Prophet and Believers would endlessly repeat and recite. Rhyme, rhythm, and assonance emerge as central in the oral Koranic recitation. The poetic language and style of the Koran make it inimitable. Its sounds conveyed to the listener have both a divine source and significance. In the very act of recitation, the Believer partakes in the transmission of the living Book of Sounds and recapitulates the Ur-rhetorical act whereby Muḥammad received the Word of God, the Qur'ān—the "recitation" that became the "reading" and the Divine Scripture.[36]

The ongoing polemic concerning listening to poetry, music, song, and story which permeates the culture thus seeks to separate the secular, vain arts, which distract ears from God's Word, from divinely revealed Truth and divinely emanating Sounds. Almost as a leitmotiv, condemnation of vain talk (*laghw* and *lahw al-ḥadīth*) runs through the Muslim Holy Book. Al-Nuwayrī (d. 1332),[37] for example, culled the following lines from the Koran as condemnation of *samāʿ* (listening):

| | |
|---|---|
| 23,1–3 | "The believers who are humble in their prayers and who turn away from vain talk (*laghw*) are prosperous." |
| 25,72 | "And those who do not bear false witness, and when they pass idle talk (*laghw*), pass honorably." |
| 28,55 | "And when they hear vain talk (*laghw*) they turn away from it." |
| 31,5 | "And among men are those who buy sportive talk (*lahwa al-ḥadīth*) to lead astray from Allah's Path without knowledge and make a mock of it. Those will have a shameful punishment." |
| 17,64 | "And excite those of them whom you can with your voice." |
| 53,60–61 | "Do you wonder at this talk? And do you laugh and not work while you are amusing yourselves?" |

Such suspicion of "talk" reveals itself in other verses of the Koran as suspicion of stories. Ibn ʿAbd Rabbihi (d. 940), in his *ʿIqd al-Farīd,* cites Sura 16,117, which forbids lies against Allah; he maintains that this sūra refers to the stories of *Ayyām al-ʿArab* (Battle Days of the Arabs), which are all vanity and lies.[38] Sūra 31,6 is more explicit: "And of mankind are those who purchase a ludicrous story, in order that they may lead astray from the path of Allah without knowledge and take it for mockery." According to the interpretation of Ibn ʿAbd Rabbihi, this verse refers to people who buy storybooks containing the biographies and tales of the ancients, compare them to the Koran, and deem them superior to the Holy Book.[39]

The Prophet was at particular pains to separate himself and his divinely revealed "Recitation" or "Oral Reading" (i.e., Qur'ān) from the diviners, soothsayers, and professional poets of the traditional milieu of oral culture, of which he was a part. In a world where the word had the power to heal or to wound and where the poet (shāʿir, feeler or kenner) possessed extraordinary knowledge of things hidden to the ordinary person, poetry became suspect, an ambivalent force for good or evil in its dual modes of *hijā'* and *madīḥ* (blame and praise). The Prophet's ambivalence on the subject is well known, for he made full use of poets, Ḥasan ibn Thābit in particular, to spread and defend his Word and to defame his enemies. But whether the Prophet of God was an oral poet or not, the Muslim Good Book strongly condemns lies and fictions, and by extension, story telling in any form. Accusations that he was a poet caused the Prophet Muḥammad to take a particular stand against poets and their audience in Sura 26, 224–6 which suggests that the poets are liars and those who follow them have gone astray.[40]

Subsequent Muslim scholars and critics reinforce their Prophet's ambivalence on the subject of poetry. In the early decades and centuries of Islam, a rift grew between story and history, lies and truth, between heroic tales of the pagan past and heroic accounts of Islamic martyrs, between the Jāhiliyya (the pre-Islamic Age of Ignorance) and Islam. Throughout the history of Arabic literature and poetry, as the Egyptian folklorist Ghālī Shukrī puts it, there is a thin line between the two views: on one hand, poetry was divinely inspired rhetoric; on the other, poetry was Satan's Koran and the poet was possessed by a *shayṭān* (devil).[41] Throughout Arab history, various sources have condemned and attempted to suppress the vernacular folk arts. As we have seen, the several levels of prejudice include (1) religious, founded on Koranic injunctions against story, poetry, and, by implication, music; (2) scholarly, founded on the development out of Koranic studies of grammar and philology as sciences; (3) social and economic, founded on the attitude of the literate elite classes that professional poets and musicians are beggars and their stories lies; (4) political, founded on a fear that vernacular lore would destroy political and cultural unity among Arab nations and thus intensify regional differences; and (5) official, founded on all the previous factors and resulting in government interdictions.

Linguistic and literary diglossia[42] exists today as a cultural phenomenon that dichotomizes Arab society along several lines: oral and written, literate and illiterate, private and public, male and female, religious and secular, high and low, rich and poor, learned and popular. As Saad Sowayan, a Saudi Arabian folklorist, has said, the Classical Arabic established by grammarians has come to be revered as the language of the Koran. As the language of daily prayers and the public media, it is viewed as a force that unites speakers of Arabic into one large community. Any encouragement of vernacular arts has been suspected as some kind of covert attempt to encourage political discord and cultural disintegration among the Arab people. Such attitudes, Sowayan continues, have effectively hampered research, but they have not silenced the people, who continue to compose poetry in the local dialect.[43]

Faiq Amin Mukhlis, an Iraqi scholar, speaks of the difficulties he encountered doing fieldwork in North Africa in 1963 because scholars and librarians regarded his study of folk literature as a waste of time. People in the Tunisian countryside even refused to believe he was serious in his inquiries.[44]

The virtual taboo against narrative poetry, particularly al-sīra, continues into the present century. As Sowayan's comments imply, great cultural divisiveness also continues to surround the issue of vernacular story and poetry traditions. The Egyptian sociologist, Hamed Ammar, for example, summarizes the attitudes of the literate, religious people of Silwa in the Aswan province during the 1950s to story telling of all kinds: "Stories, as seen through the puritanic eyes of adults, are considered to be demonic and of no practical value." Story telling is thus viewed as "dissipated leisure" (*lahwa*), which a strictly religious community does not accept as one of the commendable spheres of indulgence in a pious life. Fiction is viewed as "unreal" and of "no immediate value," or as imaginative frivolities from which children must be weaned as quickly as possible. The children of Silwa, a village presumably typical of Upper Egyptian life, instead of listening to stories, are encouraged to learn didactic literature such as proverbs and wise sayings which will enable them as men to cope with the "realistic and matter-of-fact affairs of life." Only in this sort of "serious" oral literature, accounts of the sayings and reported deeds of socially or religiously prestigious men, can the boy and man find wisdom.[45]

Another Egyptian commentator, writing in 1946, mentions the nefarious influence of one recited sīra in particular on its audiences. According to ʿAbd al-Laṭīf, *Sīrat Banī Hilāl* inspired Bedouins and other rural folk to steal and kill. Aḥmad Ḥasan al-Zayyāt also comments, in 1935, on the disruptive influence of the poet who recited the sīra to provincial Egyptian audiences; he asserts that the words of the rāwī influenced men's ears and resulted in fights based on old tribal alliances among members of the assembled audience.[46]

If official suppression and disdain dominated past attitudes toward oral narrative tradition, perhaps official recognition of the folk arts today replaces that suspicion. The folklore researcher in Egypt, for example, may observe government-sponsored "folk-singers" performing their propagandistic praise-songs side-by-side with genuine folk artists.[47] One man I interviewed during my research in Tunisia in 1972–1973 talked with me about what he considered to be a kind of "fakelore" that had replaced the old street culture of the world in which he had grown up. Now in his fifties, the man told me about growing up in Sfax, about the rich oral street culture that had intrigued him as a boy. The ambulant musicians, poets, and storytellers of his boyhood had been officially discouraged by the government after the Independence, as signs of backwardness and illiteracy that the newly emergent nation sought to eradicate. Police treated ambulant poets and musicians, as well as the book vendors who sold cheap folk narratives, as vagrants. They suppressed their performance on street corners and public squares. Such remnants of the oral culture as one might find in Tunisia today on radio and television are carefully edited and revised by literate dramaturgies. The recitations one hears at government-sponsored folk poetry contests, which are annual events in Tunisia, amount to little more than propagandistic praise of the political regime sponsoring the cash-prize events. According to this particular aficionado of the old ways, such modern manifestations of the old street culture are a travesty of the living art and craft of the fḍāwī and other folk poets and musicians whose performances he recalls.

Despite government suppression and attempts to infiltrate and control it, despite religious suspicion and scholarly contempt, vernacular narrative poetry has a long and continuous history in the Arab countries. While the professed adīb could not condescend to the narration of a story merely for the sake of a story, story telling in one form or another has been a craft and a trade throughout Arab history and Arab lands.

In their sojourns in Arab countries, European scholars, travelers, and colonialists have encountered Arabic folk literature in both its oral and written forms. They greeted it with the fervent enthusiasm of the romantic amateur as well as with the captious and contradictory criticism of Arabists. The "spell of the Orient," transmitted through its folktales, enraptured the European reading public from the very moment Galland's first translations of *Mille et Une Nuit* [*sic*] appeared in 1704. Although less widely known than the *Arabian Nights*, the *Romance of ʿAntar* was available to eighteenth- and nineteenth-century European readers in Terrick Hamilton's four-volume English adaptation as well as in many French translations that appeared in the *Journal asiatique*.[48] Non-Arabists—such as Lamartine, who traveled in Lebanon and heard Bedouin poets singing the exploits of ʿAntar—often carried translations and manuscripts home with them. Lamartine's description of *ʿAntar* is typical of the romantic's vision of the Orient; it exemplifies the quest of nineteenth century criticism for national epic literature expressing the "soul" of a people. In his historical work *Vie des grands hommes*,[49] Lamartine compares the author to Homer and the hero to Roland, Achilles, and Siegfried, and he praises the narrative as one of the great works of world literature.[50] In addition, the stories of Abū Zayd of the Banī Hilāl, Baybars, and Sayf were also known, but to a much lesser extent and primarily by Arabists who wrote and read articles in professional journals. Tales of these heroes are all mentioned in nineteenth-century dictionaries of world literature as *chansons de geste arabes*.[51]

While the amateur and the general European reading public admiringly accepted Arabic folk literature in the translations available to them,[52] Western students of Arabic literature, aware of the official Arab attitude toward this body of "nonliterature," have consistently taken an ambivalent stance: they are tempted to accept the compositions as a great epic literature in the tradition of, for example, Homer and Turold, yet they are aware of the linguistic and formal discrepancies between this literature and what the Arabs consider to be great literature. They almost consistently err on both sides. They judge the works by formalistic criteria applicable only to Classical Arabic literature, or they engage in the sort of rationalistic criticism employed by nineteenth-century Homeric scholars. Perhaps, however, the romantic traveler's élan, his leap to epic analogies and high praise, were preferable and indeed more precise than the more "scientific," presumably more detached studies of many Arabists. Such studies often have sought the date and authorship of a text as though it were originally a literate composition and attempt to make the text conform to Classical thematic and prosodic rules; their authors always disparage and dismiss al-sīra for its colloquial, vulgar language, for its repetition, its lack of historicity, and its unlimited fantasy and hyperbole.

A critical—indeed a polemically captious—look at the articles on Arab oral narrative tradition in the two editions of the *Encyclopaedia of Islam* indicates the failure of Western criticism to come to grips with the essential nature of this genre. These articles are successful only when the intrinsic social, historical, and cultural interest of the texts is discussed; when the authors attempt to treat the works' aesthetic merits and techniques, their discussions become confused, flawed by imprecise and ill-defined terminology. Much confusion seems to stem from the knowledge that the tales exist not only in libraries as written texts but also among the people as living "oral tradition." Unable to conceive of stories as existing without some preexisting, definitive written text, the scholar is perplexed about the relationship between the written texts, between the book and its oral manifestations, and between the original "author" and "original version" of a given story.

This inability to conceive of composition without the aid of writing, or of oral composition by illiterate people, results in a variety of theories designed to explain away seeming anomalies of style, language, and content. In articles in the *Encyclopaedia of*

*Islam,* MacDonald, Paret, and Pellat (as well as ʿAbdel-Meguid in a general article that surveys Arabic story literature) each suggest, whether implicitly or explicitly, that the siyar were at some time written for the common people by an educated, self-conscious literary artist who, by his very language, contrived to address himself to them.[53] MacDonald maintains that in their structure the stories exhibit "a technical skill beyond any public reciter," and that respectable authors wrote the tales but left them anonymous since they "did not dare own to them."[54] This is in contradiction, however, to his earlier statement that the professed littérateur has never condescended to a narrative of fictitious facts and events for its own sake, leaving such undertakings "to professional entertainers, buffoons, and the vulgar in general." ʿAbdel-Meguid likewise indicates that the "romances" were written in simple language, which made it possible for the common people to understand, recite, and enjoy them and to retain them in the "folk memory."[55]

Paret, discussing *Sayf* and *Baybars* in separate *Encyclopaedia* articles, attributes the preponderance of pagan, magical elements in the former and the crude jokes, puns, and situations in the latter to the authors' attempt to appeal to the uncultured taste of listeners in works that were "composed and put into circulation" and "meant to be recited not read."[56] These *Encyclopaedia* articles exhibit the typical confusion and contradictions inherent in past approaches to Arabic folk literature. While Paret emphasizes the primary merit of *Baybars* and *Sayf* as faithful depictions of the popular mind in Muslim Egypt at the end of the Middle Ages, and while he indicates that many of the notions must have originated in the "unlimited fancy of the narrators," he nonetheless assumes that the siyar were originally books, composed for the people.[57] The contradictions as well as the implications in his statement are obvious: if, as Paret concedes, the "narrators" had an "unlimited fancy," if the sīra is a representation of the popular mind, if, furthermore, the language is that of the people, perhaps it might follow that the sīra is also the composition of a nonliterate, popular artist working within the confines of a traditional medium whose technique can best be discerned through close examination of the specific sīra in its various manifestations, whether oral or written. Paret also finally indicates that the history and development of the sīra would be much clearer if the various manuscripts were classified and compared; he questions, however, "whether it would be worth the time involved." Similarly, Pellat suggests that the popular tales in the cycle of the *Thousand and One Nights* and the "great romances of chivalry" collected up to now, and those still to be collected, should be investigated.[58]

Consistent with presuppositions that the stories first appeared in written form are theories concerning the existence of a definitive, datable, original text attributable to a single literate author—a text that was given over to the "folk" and "relapsed into oral tradition,"[59] and once corrupted, its original conformance to rules of prosody and its original thematic unity[60] were distorted by popular "transmitters." The creation or "authorship" of a tale is never, in this view, attributed to the fḍāwī or rāwī or shāʿir (whatever his local appellation) who tells the story: he is merely a transmitter who passes on the original story with forgeries, fabrications, and distortions.

Amid the notions of "oral tradition" in Western studies dealing with Arabic folk literature there also recur analogies between the sīra and the chanson de geste or the Homeric epic. Critics refer to the sīra variously as "romances of chivalry,"[61] gestes,[62] or epics,[63] and frequently point out the presence in the sīra of all the "commonplaces of the epic."[64] Like Lamartine, scholars are struck by the apparent similarity between Western epic and the sīra. Such scholars point particularly to al-sīra's heroic themes of adventure, mass migration, and earthshaking battles waged by armed knights, its use of repetition and parallelisms, its epithets and clichés, its catalogs, its frequent confusion and contradiction of incidents, its historicity, and its manner of performance. Comparison with the epic, whether on the thematic or stylistic level, is superficial; it never, in any measure, delves into the essence of either form as a basis of comparison. Until only recently, critics of al-sīra have consistently gone the same road as nineteenth-century Homeric and Old French scholars: they have endeavored to discover formal, logical, sequential unity in literature where it may well not exist. In this quest, they interpolate episodes to present a more "coherent" narrative in answer to their demands for "unity," or they rationalize inconsistencies in the narrative. They never accept and study a tale in the form in which it exists, but they always hypothesize and try to reestablish through textual legerdemain a preexisting magnum opus that has suffered at the hands of the "folk."

I am aware, of course, that the *Encyclopaedia* articles I criticize are out-of-date. I take up a polemic with them by virtue of their ease of access to the uninitiated in Arabic folk traditions and the force of authority that such encyclopedia-ized essays often enjoy in the formation of major premises and assumptions about an area of learning. I also point to their failings because even works on the siyar published as recently as 1980 contain many of the same "literate" fallacies in their consideration of what I believe to be primarily and essentially a folk genre, orally composed, orally transmitted and disseminated, and even redacted into writing by "folks" of marginal literacy.[65]

The legitimacy of the folk in recent decades has gained a new respect among certain Arab intellectuals. A Maghribī writer, Abdallah Laroui, suggests that the intelligentsia today can view folkloric works in a more detached vein, with less emotional investment, because of their educational background and intellectual formation. Thus, no longer must folklore be the exclusive reserve of foreign scholars; today the Arab national community has detached itself sufficiently from its own past to begin to be able to appreciate its old traditions.[66] Egyptian intellectuals appear less distanced from the folk, less identified with the West in their defense of folk narrative, and a growing force is beginning to make itself felt against the sort of invidious distaste Mūsá Sulaymān expressed for the siyar. ʿAbd al-Ḥamīd Yūnis, for example, in 1973 wrote *Defense of Folklore,*[67] which was directly addressed to Shawqī Ḍayf and other learned men who continued the age-old polemic against the popular, vernacular story arts.

Nationalists and leftists in both Egypt and Tunisia have become newly aware of their indigenous folk heritage and seek in it their national "roots" or national identity. In a similar vein to Laroui, Ghālī Shukrī, assessing the newly possible appreciation of folk traditions by the educated in Egypt, mentions four predominant factors: (1) nationalism, which is causing a reevaluation of traditional patrimony; (2) anticolonialistic sentiment, which rejects vehemently any imposed, outside cultural values and views; (3) cognizance of the relative fragility of oral culture in a rapidly changing social and economic environment, which stresses the urgency of preserving folk traditions; and (4) a current trend in the social sciences to study the "common" man in the context of his own environment and tradition.[68] Aḥmad Rushdī Ṣāliḥ, for example, in his pioneering works of the 1950s on Arabic folklore, insists on placing folkloric items in their appropriate social, historical, political, and cultural context. He views folk literature as the life lived by the people through their various evolutions and cultural strata.[69] He distinguishes between written and oral versions of the tradition, granting each its own integrity and characteristic features.

Serious Arab scholarship in the discipline of folklore only began in the 1950s. Since then, the work in Egypt of such professional folklorists as Rushdī Ṣāliḥ and Yūnis has slowly made headway and entered a defense of the folk in the ongoing cultural polemic. Egypt, Iraq, and Tunisia have set up folklore centers in an effort to collect and systematically study the oral patrimony of the individual countries. In Egypt, the University of Cairo established a chair of folklore studies for the pioneering scholar Yūnis, who, along with Rushdī Ṣālih, may be called the father of Arab folklore studies.[70] Only slowly, as Canova pointed out in a groundbreaking 1977 bibliographic essay on Arabic popular epic,[71] have the old prejudices begun to erode, as a few Egyptian, Iraqi, and Tunisian scholars are beginning to consider a conception of the world that diverges from the dominant, official one. In their quest for national "authenticity" (*aṣāla*), intellectuals are now beginning to discover folk values, to accept the local dialect of Arabic as the vehicle of this "other" culture, and to find a new relationship with the folk classes—the illiterate peasants and poor working people who comprise the majority of the population of the Arab Middle East.

The field of Arabic oral tradition and folk literature is immense. It provides a vast array of genres and subjects and a unique case study of the mechanism and function of traditional arts in popular society. This study focuses on the genre al-sīra, one of the most loved and most despised of all the folk forms; its specific focus is *Sīrat Banī Hilāl,* the saga of the adventures of the Hilālī tribe in the early centuries of Islam and their migrations, from the eleventh to the thirteenth century, out of Arabia, across North Africa via the Levant and Egypt, to Tunisia and as far south and west as Nigeria. Various clans and subclans of the tribe settled along the migration route, and wherever they traveled or settled, we can find today, if not a full-blown tradition, at least remnants of songs and stories celebrating the migratory exploits, glorifying the heroic deeds of a bygone age of trial and tribulation, of magnificence, wealth, and triumph over adversity.

Historians depict the Hilālī as a renegade tribe of outlaws whose pestilential force was unleashed by the Fatimid caliph against the Berber tribes of North Africa in the eleventh and twelfth centuries. Ibn Khaldūn is the source for much of this notoriety, for his was the metaphor from which much scholarly controversy today stems: he labeled the Bedouin tribes "locusts" who destroyed North Africa's sedentary agricultural economy. At the same time, however, he also considered them "restorers of social energy, the necessary cement of Maghribī society."[72] Whether agents of catastrophic economic phenomena or the heroes of a golden age of military glory, the Banī Hilāl present a study in contrasts and ambivalence. While historians, religious and secular authorities, literary scholars, philologists, and grammarians, along with the educated classes in general, denounce and despise the tradition and legislate and inveigh against it, *Sīrat Banī Hilāl* has long been the orally recounted chronicle of their times and deeds. For the vast majority of people inhabiting the villages and countryside of Egypt and the rooftops and stairwells of crowded Cairo, it is the story of their cultural identity. These people view the sīra as history and venerate it alongside the Koran and the tales of the Prophet as an oral performance tradition of recitation.

*Sīrat Banī Hilāl* offers a tradition particularly amenable to study, since it manifests itself in a plethora of forms—written and oral, professional and amateur, prose and poetry—spread over a broad geographic expanse. Written documents first date from Ibn Khaldūn's transcription of some fourteenth-century Hilālī poetry. The bulk of the written versions spans the nineteenth century and exists today as manuscripts in European libraries and as cheap, printed, pulp editions sold in bookstalls throughout the Middle East. In Egypt today, rabāb poets, much like those Lane observed performing in nineteenth-century Cairo cafés, still sing the old epic, and the tradition continues to flourish throughout the countryside, particularly in Upper Egypt. In Tunisia, under the French Protectorate, the fḍāwī recounted the tale in his travels from door to door, while poet-musicians crafted songs, and painters in Sfax folk artisan workshops depicted Hilālī heroes and heroines in reverse-glass paintings. A similar tradition exists in Syria and Iraq where café owners used to commission a glass painting to celebrate the particularly beautiful rendition of the epic song on their premises. Throughout the Sudan, as far southwest as Lake Chad, the tale is told as part of tribal historical lore.

Both as history and story, the Hilālī tradition is a vital one. Unlike *Sīrat ʿAntar, Sīrat Baybars, Sīrat Sayf ibn Dhī Yazan,* or similar siyar, it is not fixed or stable but remains a living, fluid tradition. The scholarly aficionado can not only read it but see it and hear it performed; for this reason, this study treats *Sīrat Banī Hilāl* in its effort to begin to comprehend the Arabic folk genre al-sīra as a whole, from the point of view and aesthetic tastes of its intended audience.

# 2
# *SĪRAT BANĪ HILĀL,* A DECAYED EPIC?

Ibn Khaldūn was the first to collect Banī Hilāl poetry. When he heard Bedouin poets singing narratives about the Hilālī heroine al-Jāziyya and the battles waged in her name by the tribal heroes Abū Zayd and Diyāb against the Zanātī Khalīfa, the Berber ruler of Tunis and the Maghrib, he recorded some of them and eleven Hilālī poems come down to us in his writings. The fourteenth-century North African historian devoted an entire chapter of his *Muqaddima* to the subject of Bedouin oral poetry. Always aware of the dichotomies and tensions implicit in Arab society (whether Bedouin versus sedentary groups or high versus low linguistic register), Ibn Khaldūn presented a clear defense of vernacular poetry. Addressing himself to scholarly pedants whose aesthetic sense recoiled from oral, dialect poetry with its lack of Classical language case endings, he argues vigorously that the poetry of the Arab Bedouins "shows all the methods and forms of true poetry," that oral poems composed in the vernacular tongue demonstrate "sound eloquence" having nothing to do with the rules of grammarians. His comments merit quoting in full:

> Most contemporary scholars, philologists in particular, disapprove of these types of poems when they hear them, and refuse to consider them poetry when they are recited. They believe their literary taste recoils from them, because they are linguistically incorrect and lack vowel endings. This, however, is merely the result of the loss of the habit of using vowel endings in the dialect of the Arabs. . . . These poems are eloquent, provided their own natural dispositions and point of view were not distorted. Vowel endings have nothing to do with eloquence. . . . If the indicated meaning is in conformity with what one wants to express and with the require-

ments of the situation, we have sound eloquence. The rules of the grammarians have nothing to do with that. The poems of the Arabs show all the methods and forms of true poetry.[1]

Ibn Khaldūn is very definite in his approach to poetry in the various dialects. His admonitions are at odds with prejudices that still prevail today, for he accepts the vernacular poetry he collected as poetry composed by the Bedouin tribal poets. He never hypothesizes some preexisting written opus; he does not view Hilālī poetry as a degenerative form. In this, he is virtually unique among Banī Hilāl collectors, striking a throughly modern note.

After the few lines of Hilālī poetry taken down in the fourteenth century by Ibn Khaldūn, there is a lacuna of at least five centuries. The collecting and writing down of the songs and narratives has, for the most part, been sporadic and its history obscure. Many written versions do exist, however, both in manuscript and printed editions. The Ahlwardt catalog of Arabic manuscripts in the Berlin Museum alone lists and summarizes 173 Banī Hilāl texts.[2] According to Abderrahman Ayoub, in his critical reappraisal of the classification of the manuscripts in Ahlwardt's catalog,[3] the West Berlin Staatsbibliothek today contains 189 manuscripts that date from 1785 to 1854 and comprise some eight thousand pages. The manuscripts are written in both poetry and prose in the approximate ratio of 30 percent prose to 70 percent poetry. Their Egyptian and Syrian dialectal features suggest that the manuscripts originated in these countries. Scattered manuscripts also reside in the libraries of Gotha, Cambridge, London, Tübingen, Oxford, and Milan. The British Library and the John Rylands Library of the University of Manchester each contain an early nineteenth-century manuscript.[4] Manuscript holdings in Arab libraries seem to be largely uncataloged, although the National Library of Tunis[5] contains a manuscript dated 1840 which Ahmad Pasha, the bey of Tunis, commissioned. The Egyptian Library[6] lists two Hilālī manuscripts, while the recently published catalog of the National Library of Bahrain[7] lists three.

Printed editions, which are often very similar to the manuscript versions, also exist. Ellis's *Catalogue of Arabic Books in the British Museum* enumerates many editions printed in Cairo and Beirut on cheap, pulp paper.[8] Chauvin, in *Bibliographie des ouvrages arabes*, and Brockelmann, in *Geschichte der arabischen Lit-*

*teratur,* give editions and partial editions not found in the British Museum catalog.[9] These bibliographies taken together indicate the existence of hundreds of printed versions of the Hilālī matter, ranging from an 1885 Cairene partial edition through numerous other Cairo and Beirut editions printed from approximately 1864 to 1889 to editions published in Damascus in 1922 and 1927. Many of the Egyptian editions of *Sīrat Banī Hilāl* available in Arab countries today were reprinted (and often abridged) by ʿAbd al-Ḥamīd Ḥanafī in 1948 and, after 1952, by Maktabat al-Jumhūriyya in Cairo. The University of Utah has collected approximately twelve of the Jumhūriyya editions. It is mostly these editions that the investigator may find scattered in bookstalls throughout the Middle East. I recently purchased, for example, nine or ten exemplars from booksellers in the Azbakiyya Gardens of Cairo. The total number of different editions, versions, and episodes of the tale is impossible to estimate, especially since editions overlap and frequently represent reprintings of the same version.

A recent study by Mukhlis[10] attempts to collate 86 Hilālī manuscripts from the Tübingen and Cambridge collections and 23 printed editions according to their story matter. Mukhlis categorizes the tales into three cycles, following the old *Encyclopaedia of Islam* article by Schliefer and an 1898 monograph by Hartmann.[11] The locale of the story provides the basis for a three-cycle division: (1) the history of the Banī Hilāl in Bilād al-Sarw wa-ʿUbāda, the birth of Abū Zayd, and his conquest of the fire worshipers in the land of Badhakka in India; (2) the migration of the Banī Hilāl to the land of Nejd after a severe famine and their encounters with Diyāb ibn Ghānim; and (3) the migration of the Hilālī to the west and the wars of the renegade tribe with the Zanātī Khalīfa in Tūnis.

The circumstances surrounding the redaction of these folk editions into written form generally remain a mystery; for example, *Taghrībat Banī Hilāl ilá Bilād al-Gharb* (Westward Migrations of the Banī Hilāl to the Land of the West), published in Beirut and later in a post-1452 abridged Cairo edition, and *Kitāb al-Riyāḍa al-Bahiyya* (The Book of the Magnificent Journey), published in 1865, are anonymous. Very often, printed editions give neither the date nor the place of publication. Less mysterious as to how, when, where, and even why they were put into written form are the various ḥikāyāt, poems, and songs collected from oral tradition. Others besides Ibn Khaldūn have noted folk poets and singers performing episodes of the long tale of migratory exploits. A 1978 bibliographic essay by Breteau et al. summarizes the source material for the *Hilāliyya* which may be termed oral.[12] The authors cite documents taken down from oral tradition in Algeria, Morocco, Egypt, Tunisia, and the Sudan. Such authentically oral texts range from Féraud's 1865 collection of an Algerian narrative about al-Jāziyya's hatred for the Hilālī enemy, the Zanātī Khalīfa, to very recent electronically recorded sound versions of Libyan, Tunisian, Jordanian, and Egyptian tales and poems.[13]

While the work of the first generation of Hilālī scholars was cast in the captious, ambivalent tone encapsulated in *Encyclopaedia of Islam* essays, that of the second generation, present-day students, takes a more positivistic, empirical approach. The early generation analyzed manuscripts as listed in library catalog content summaries and compared printed editions with manuscript inventories and versions taken down from oral renditions. Always the early students attempted to place the *Hilāliyya* oral "fragment" within the larger sīra "text" in an effort to discover (or recover) the entire "original text" in its "integrity." The second generation, while continuing to assemble and collate the manuscripts and printed tradition, is focusing its attention on collecting from oral tradition. Questions of "original" texts have given way to concern with "versions" and "episodes."

The first significant study of the Banī Hilāl matter, an 1885 article by Basset entitled "Un épisode d'une chanson de geste arabe,"[14] considers the Algerian al-Jāziyya legend as it appears in the poem "Rouba," collected and presented "sous une forme élégante" by Guin,[15] and in a version collected by Largeau in *Flore saharienne.*[16] Basset discusses the oral poems by comparing them to the "chanson de geste des Arabes antérieure au XV$^{e}$ siecle," from which he believes the Guin texts as well as Ibn Khaldūn's versions of the same legend to be episodes. Outlining in detail portions of a Būlāq printed edition of the "Roman d'Abou Zeyd et des Bani Hilal," pertinent to the al-Jāziyya story, he quotes relevant parts to show how the shorter poems contain "confusions," "interpolations," "variants," and "alternations" from the "original" versions of the "geste" from which the more lately collected poems are most certainly derived. Although aware that

Largeau and Guin collected the poems from the oral tradition of Algerian tribes and having himself listened in Algerian cafés to the maddāḥ and the guwwāl singing and telling the tale of "Abū Hilāl,"[17] Basset presupposes a single literary work as the origin of the popular oral versions rife throughout Algeria.

Inspired by Basset's article and based in large measure on it is Bel's 1902–1903 publication in the *Journal asiatique* of yet another version of the Algerian al-Jāziyya poem.[18] A student of Basset and a professor at the Tlemcen *madrasa,* he presents the most fully documented and annotated Banī Hilāl text available as well as one of the most linguistically authentic. Bel, as a student of North African dialects, makes no attempt at "correcting" the language in which three poems were dictated to him by different *ṭalbas* in the area of Tlemcen. The Arabic text, the linguistic notes, and his translations are thus sound linguistic documents. Bel recognizes the necessity of knowing something about the cultural matrix to which the poems refer, and he appends notes of social, cultural, and historical interest to the translation, thereby making his text accessible not only to linguists and Arabists but also to anthropologists and students of folklore.

Bel's attitude toward the songs he has collected, however, is representative of many Western scholars' peculiar ambivalence toward Arabic vernacular literature, and its consequent interference on texts. Although he avoids the pitfalls many plunge into in their acceptance of the Arab critic's disdain for the language of the popular arts, Bel reveals an attitude at once that of the superior, condescending colonialist and that of one who has discovered a great Arab epic comparable to the *Iliad* or the *Roland.* Throughout his monograph, Bel employs terms fraught with invidious connotation, viewing the people to whom the Banī Hilāl tales belong as "nos sujets algériens . . . comme tous les gens d'esprit simple fort amateur de contes merveilleux, de récits fantastiques, de légendes extraordinaires." He cites "La Djazya" as "un specimen de la corruption que peut subir l'histoire par la transmission populaire," and goes on to say that the "corruption" may well be involuntary, a concomitant of the ignorance of the transmitters, who undoubtedly suppressed or transposed certain words or verses they did not understand. It is just thus, he further maintains, that we do not possess any of the Banī Hilāl poems, the *Iliad,* the *Odyssey,* the pre-Islamic qaṣīda "dans leur intégrité." Having thus concerned himself with the "integrity" of a popular composition, Bel indicates how he has attempted to reconstitute a "definitive," coherent text by juggling the three "variants" of the poems he has collected.

Vaissière, a French colonial officer in the Sahara who translated and published the partial Arabic text of a prose and verse tale about al-Jāziyya in an ethnographic survey of the Walad Rashaish, displays the same condescending attitude to the material as Bel.[19] Interested in the tale to the extent that it demonstrates the mentality and manners of the Arabs, their concepts of love, chivalric loyalty, the epic struggles of their heroic age, scenes from everyday pastoral and nomadic life, Vaissière remarks in a footnote that the refined chivalric ideals of the "épopée" must certainly be due to "notre influence" on Arabic poetry. He asserts that the scenes of single combat, the great respect for women, and the concept of love in the tale must certainly be French in origin. More important, however, than the text and his commentary is the background information he provides about the people's attitude toward the tale. The story, in "vulgar" prose, mixed with rhythmical pieces of verse, was known by most of the Rashaishi tribe and was frequently recited by "rhapsodists" around the evening campfire. Vaissière indicates that all the ṭalbas could recite it in its entirety. The verses were generally fixed and known to all the listeners, while the terms of the prose parts were more fluid. The details of a given episode were, however, immutable.

The discussion of public recitations in Lane's *Manners and Customs of the Modern Egyptians* also incorporates many stereotypical notions about the origin and nature of the material "recited" by the "Aboo-Ẓeydeeyeh." Lane's account, however, contains much valuable information as to the role of the stories and storytellers in society. His colorful description of a Cairene café wherein the poet with viol would chant the deeds of the Hilālī tribe provides information that is nowhere else available about the nature of the compositions, how they were performed, and their musical accompaniment. As suggested above (chap. 1), Lane bases many of his assumptions about the performance tradition he observed on the opinions of some of the erudite in Cairo; he states that the works recited by the café poets have "little merit" as literary composition, at least "in their present state," and that the verses originally conformed to the prescribed measures of poetry but were "altered by copyists." His account is based on the assumption that only one version of the Banī Hilāl story exists. In addition, Lane assumes the café poet was a literate person who read and memorized the long sīra so that he could recite it publicly.

Commentaries such as those of Bel, Lane, Vaissière, and Basset are primarily of value for their information, often incidental to the main argument, about the Arab tradition of popular vernacular arts. Although their presuppositions often affect the very recording of a text and distort critical appreciation, these students have observed and reported the recurring phenomenon of oral performances of the Banī Hilāl story matter across North Africa. The very perplexities they express when confronted with multiple versions of the same story in the mouths of unlearned people are enlightening as to the nature of the tradition, just as the prejudicial views they adopt, both for their own ethnocentric reasons and in imitation of Arab scholars, are reflective of the position of popular compositions in the total society.

Critics and collectors of the Banī Hilāl matter have for the most part interested themselves in its historical and cultural aspects and only incidentally treated the texts as literature. Hartmann cites the great linguistic, cultural, historical, and folkloric value of this "most important work" whose degree of historicity he would like to establish.[20] His article, similar to Basset's and inspired by it, is largely devoted to a list of the titles of the "Books" that make up a Beirut edition[21] of the *Sīrat Banī Hilāl*. Hartmann summarizes the contents of these booklets and compares them with Ahlwardt's list of Berlin manuscripts as well as three other Lebanese and four Egyptian printed editions. He then attempts to indicate the correspondence of characters and events in the story with historical ones. The chief value of the article, however, lies in some of the questions raised incidental to its main objectives. Aware of the multiplicity of versions, having himself taken down some stories dictated by Bedouin poets in Egypt and Libya, Hartmann never presupposes either implicitly or explicitly the existence of a single version from which all others derive; neither does he employ prejudicial, subjective, or condescending terminology. While he does not endeavor to come to grips with the Banī Hilāl matter as a whole within the scope of the article, he indicates the desirability of a comprehensive study to determine the *treibende Kräfte* that have created the forms coming down to us under the name of *Sīrat Banī Hilāl*.[22] Along with his willingness to look at the various forms and to let the genre, its mechanism of transmission, and its major features define themselves, Hartmann also takes a sensibly cautious stance with regard to labeling the genre. He neither proclaims the different forms epics or romances nor engages in invidious comparisons to works such as *Roland;* rather, he suggests that perhaps Basset's term "chanson de geste" would be "more adequate" than Ahlwardt's catalog title "grosse Romans." He also hints at major structural features of the sīra in his discussion of the fluctuating relationship of the three parts (or cycles) of the tales and indicates how the three parts to some extent flow into and become confused with one another in the various narratives, even though the sequence of events was relatively fixed by tradition quite early.[23]

More contemporary students of *Sīrat Banī Hilāl* have taken up the question of the work's structure directly. Two Czechs and a Russian are among the few scholars who have attempted to answer Hartmann's call to uncover the "treibende Kräfte" of the sīra genre. Petráček, Pantuček, and Onaeva[24] each analyze printed editions of the *Hilāliyya,* comparing the edition in hand to the Ahlwardt Index classifications of the Berlin manuscripts. Each is aware of the oral existence of the *Hilāliyya* and each posits the primary orality of the written manuscript and editions. While Petráček strives to prove the oral version precedes and forms the written version on purely linguistic grounds, Pantuček and Onaeva attempt more literary critical approaches. Pantuček indexes the motifs present in the printed edition he is analyzing and discusses the sīra genre as a "folk-conceived historiography" whose intention is to entertain its listeners. He sees the *Hilāliyya* as a "Volksroman,"[25] as a forerunner of the historical novel. The best European term for it, in his estimation, is epic, that is, verse narrative sung by rhapsodists, a preliterate poetry with communal themes, formulas, and many repetitions. Onaeva attempts a structural analysis of the *Hilāliyya*'s printed versions which takes up what the author calls the "serial cyclicalization" of episodes and leads to a "genealogical cyclicalization" of the entire narrative in an attempt to make the sīra a biography of Abū Zayd. Both Onaeva and Pantuček limit their analyses to the syntagmatic level of plot construction; in their discussion of linear plot development, they appear to be little aware of other rhetorical constraints on oral narrative.

Curiously, two studies that treat the *Hilāliyya* in fairly serious depth as one of the major works of world literature are written by non-Arabists: J. W. MacKail[26] and C. M. Bowra.[27] Both based their comments on a translation presented by Sir Wilfred Scawen and Lady Anne Blunt to the late-nineteenth-century English reading public.[28] In 1892, the Blunts had published an admirable verse and prose translation of an episode from the first part of the *Sīrat Banī Hilāl* which they entitled *The Romance of the Stealing of the Mare*. In their introductory comments, they claim to have discovered an "Arabian Turold" in "a remote area of Egypt." They fail to indicate, however, exactly where they heard the tale, how they obtained the text for translation and adaptation, or even whether an Arabic manuscript exists.[29] The reader is left to infer that they took down the tale directly from the lips of their "Turold" in the remote Egyptian countryside. They do state authoritatively, however, that "Abu Obeyd" is the tenth-century composer of this grand epic.

The quality of the Blunts' translation makes up for any shortcomings they may have had as observers, collectors, and scholars. On the basis of their translation, MacKail, who held the chair of poetry at Oxford, delivered a lecture in 1911 in which he posited a comparative theory of epic development and growth. Although aware that the poem is "little known" even among Arab scholars, he propounded a theory of an inchoate Arab epic, to which he brings all the turn-of-the-century ideas about the Homeric question and oral literature in general. He speaks of a work transmitted orally through centuries by illiterate storytellers who "corrupted" both its versification and language, a work that was, however, of such an essentially excellent construction that it resisted "decay" and became "neither greatly debased nor badly mutilated."[30] Concerned with the problem of the transmission and corruption of this "epic," he theorized that it originally existed in the shape of a continuous poem. He saw the interstitial prose as the alteration work of rhapsodists and professional storytellers who, reciting portions of the "lays" of the original poem, used them only incidentally here and there in the course of telling the original poem as a prose story. He saw traces of the mechanism of an epic poem-in-the-making, and hazarded guesses as to the possible genetic relationship of this particular Hilālī poem to the form and content of the Old French epics. In his enthusiasm for the Banī Hilāl epic, MacKail took his comparison with European epic to such an extent that he hypothesized the chansons de geste derived their end-assonating *laisse* structure from the Arabic epic's monorhymed poetic narrative.

Such endeavors in comparative literature frequently demonstrate the limitations of genetic comparisons more than they offer any real understanding of generic origins and derivation. More productive a comparative approach than either MacKail's genetic one or the "decayed epic theory" to which so many Hilālī scholars and collectors have subscribed is Bowra's use of "oral epic theory." In his *Heroic Poetry,* a work greatly influenced by the pioneering research in oral epic by the Chadwicks[31] and Parry,[32] Bowra treats the *Hilāliyya* in its Blunt translation as "sophisticated epic poetry" and cites it beside the Homeric poems, Serbo-Croatian *guslar* poetry, and all the great epics of the world. He uses the *Stealing of the Mare* to demonstrate what heroic epic narrative is and how it works. For example, in his discussion of point of view and the use of a dramatic first-person narration in epic discourse, Bowra shows how a close identification between narrator and hero occurs even in "sophisticated poetry like the *Stealing of the Mare.*"[33]

He cites passages from the Blunt translation to demonstrate the various categories he sets up to qualify narration as heroic epic. According to Bowra, *Stealing of the Mare* shares the following characteristics with epic narrative: (1) dramatic first-person narration in speech form; (2) an action-packed story line; (3) a superlative hero, physically strong and endowed with craftiness; (4) a realistic background; (5) detailed descriptions of stock action and scenes that in themselves are trivial—like arrivals and departures, entrances and exits, rising in the morning and going to bed at night, mounting a horse, dressing, arming, disguising oneself, feasts, entertainments, and councils; (6) formulaic language and a thematic mode of narration; and (7) many repetitions and similes. Bowra quotes at length from the Blunt translation to demonstrate various techniques of epic narrative and finds that the poet of the Abū Zayd epic "uses stock themes with much brilliance and dash to secure a special effect."[34]

Bowra of course based his analysis on a translation. He knew virtually nothing about the culture outside the text and remained happily ignorant of the netherworld existence the Banī Hilāl tales have had in their own countries. Nevertheless, he describes the *Hilāliyya* more precisely and more adequately than any critic before him. How could he do this on the basis of a translation? How could he talk about "brilliance and dash" and other such textural matters without reading the work in its original tongue? He was able to do so because the Blunt translation closely follows both the story outline and the narrative style of the original, a British Museum copy of an 1865 Cairo lithograph edition of *Qiṣṣat Faras al-ʿUqaylī* (The Tale of Uqayli's Mare). The English text reads smoothly and even elegantly, albeit in an old-fashioned rhymed and metered line. For the purposes of English syntax and sense, the Blunts often transposed the order of lines and adapted the metaphor; for the most part, however, their translation retains the parallelisms, repetitions, catalog similes, pleonasms, and paratactic style of the original text.[35] In short, the Blunt translation reflects the art and craft of the oral poet behind the 1865 lithographic edition of the tale.

The first systematic study to suggest the primacy of the oral versions of *Sīrat Banī Hilāl* was published in 1956 by ʿAbd al-Ḥamīd Yūnis, a professor of folk literature at Cairo University.[36] He pointed out that on both internal and external evidence the Banī Hilāl epic is orally performed, sung poetry. He treats the tale as a malḥama (epic) on the basis of its themes of war and high heroic adventure cast in a realistic setting.[37] Yūnis sees fit to study the text out of the lips of a folk poet (shāʿir). He also describes the rabāba on which the musician-poet recites the words of his poetry. Yūnis further points out the constant mention within the sīra of *qāla al-rāwī* (the narrator said) before verse sections. He argues that this internal reference to the oral tradition proves that the poem has always been a sung recitation and that this sung poetry comprises the original part of the epic; he suggests that the poem passed from oral version to its written forms, rather than the reverse,[38] as the "decayed epic" theorists would have it. Yūnis condemns scholars who see the sīra genre as existing only in written versions when in fact it continues to this day to be orally diffused. Very recent Hilālī scholarship on written texts has attempted to prove oral transmission and composition of the epic on the basis of close reading and internal analysis. That the texts were originally and primarily oral seems to be suggested by several factors, which include: (1) the style and language of the poetry, (2) the episodic construction of themes, and (3) the existence of multiple versions.

Petráček argues very convincingly in his 1971 article[39] that the verse language of printed editions of the *Hilāliyya* and other Arabic "folk romances" is vernacular and that the verse forms are those of popular poetry and song. For Petráček the presence of colloquial language as the main linguistic register of the text suggests that the text itself is of oral genesis. My own study of various written editions of the *Hilāliyya* not only corroborates Petráček's assertion that the folk narratives are of oral provenance and "transmission" but goes on to suggest that they may be oral *compositions*. Comparative studies of oral epic the world over in the past century indicate that texts generated from oral tradition—from composition during oral performance by skilled bards schooled in the musical, improvisational technique of verse making—have particular features not found in texts composed by means of writing.[40]

Close reading and analysis of the style of randomly chosen verse passages from various editions of *Sīrat Banī Hilāl* reveal an oral poet at work, molecularly constructing the building blocks of his long, narrative song much in the way Parry and Lord describe the craft of the Yugoslav singer of tales. For example, the epic technique of the shāʿir al-rabāba is readily apparent from the opening lines of the 1865 Cairo lithograph edition of *Qiṣṣat Faras al-ʿUqaylī*,[41] which I cite alongside the Blunt adaptation:[42]

(Arabic Transliteration)
1 Anā awwal mā nibdī nṣallī ʿalā-n-nabī
  Nabī ʿArabī khaṭabūlu ʿalā-l-manābir
2 Yaqūl Abū Zayd al-Hilālī Salāmah
  Wa-nīrān qalbī zāyidāt al-majāmir
3 Anā kunt jālis yōm jumʿah maʿa-ḍ-ḍuḥā
  Rābiʿ thalāthah fī Hilāl ibn ʿĀmir
4 Naẓart bi-ʿaynī ilā wāsiʿ al-khalā
  Arā zawāl fī-l-khalā wa-l-ʿafāyir
5 Tabaddayt li-Abū-l-Qumṣān ʿabdī wa-qult luh
  Unkuf li-nā-l-akhbār in kunt shāṭir
6 Fa-ghāb Abū-l-Qumṣān wa-rtadd qāl lī
  Yā sīdī Abū Zayd hāt il-bashāyir
7 Ḥasībah atat ilā-ḍ-ḍaʿni ḍayfah
  Wa-lākinnahā tabkī bi-nkisār al-khawātir
8 Qalaʿ burnusu-l-asmar wa-aʿṭah luh jubbah

Wa-tabassam al-mansūb baʿdi mā kān kāshir
9 Tabaddā lahum Ḥasan al-Hilālī wa-qāl lahum
Bi-kalām yiḥākī-sh-shahdi wiyyā-l-ʿasākir
10 Anā Ḥasan sulṭān al-bawādī jamīʿihim
Baytī ahū maftūḥ li-man jāhu zāyir
11 Idhā hadāhā-ḷḷāh wa-jat yamm sāḥatī
La-aʿṭī lahā alfayn nāqatin ʿashāyir
12 Tabaddā Diyāb al-Khayl wa-alfat wa-qāl lahum
Anā aʿṭīhā alfayn wa-ʿasharah bawākir
13 Tabaddā-l-fatā al-qādī wa-qāla lahum
Mā ḥīlatī illā-l-waraq wa-d-dafātir
14 In hadāhā-r-Raḥmān wa-jat yamm manzilī
La-aʿṭīhā thalāthūn nāqatan ʿashāyir
15 Tabaddā Salāmah bi-l-jawāb wa-qāla lahum
Tirūnī mā yafʿal Allāh ṣābir
16 In hadāhā-r-Raḥmān wa-jat yamm sāḥatī
La-aʿṭī lahā min al-māl mā kunt qādir
17 Wa-aʿṭīhā mahmā turīduh wa-tuṭlubuh
Wa-law turīd al-ḥarb la-uṣbiḥ mubādir
18 Wa-law turīd ḥajah kabīrah muʿassarah
La-aqḍī lahā-l-maṭlūb wa-afikk al-maʿasir
19 Wa-law kānat ḥājatuhā fī bilād baʿīdah
La-ujahhiz lahā nafsī wa-uṣbiḥ musāfir
20 Wa-mā zālū bi-l-ʿuyūn yiṭṭallaʿū lahā
Li-waqti adhān aẓ-ẓuhr wa-l-jamʿu ḥādir

Then began the Narrator to sing:

Saith the hero Abu Zayd the Helali Salameh:
(Woe is me, my heart is a fire, a fire that burneth!)
On a Friday morning once, I sat with three companions,
I in my tent, the fourth of four, with the sons of Amer.
Sudden I raised my eyes and gazed at the breadth of the desert,
Searching the void afar, the empty hills and the valleys;
Lo, in the midmost waste a form, where the rainways sundered,
Wandering uncertain round in doubt, with steps of a stranger.

Turned I to Abul Komsan, my slave, and straightway I bade him,
"Ho, thou master of signs, expound to us this new comer."
Abul Komsan arose and went, and anon returning,
"Fortune fair," said he, "I bring and a noble token.
Oh my Lord Abu Zayd," he cried, and his lips were smiling,
"Here is a guest of renown for thee, a stranger, a lady,
One for the wounding of hearts, a dame of illustrious lineage,
One whose heart is on fire with grief, and sorely afflicted."
The dark one threw off his cloak to Abul Komsan in guerdon,
Even I, Abu Zayd Salameh, the while my companions
Rose with me all as I rose in my place, we four rejoicing,
Hasan and Abu Kheyl Diab, and the Kadi Faid.
And first of them Hasan spake and said, "Is my name not Hasan?
Sultan and chief and lord am I of the lords of the Bedu.
Shall not my tent stand free to all, to each guest that cometh?
So God send her to me, be they hers, two thousand camels."
And Abu Kheyl uprose, and with him the Kadi Faid.
"And I," said he, "no less will give to this dame two thousand."
Nor was the Kadi slow to speak: "Though this pen and paper
All my poor fortune be," said he, "I will name her thirty."
But I, Salameh, said, "By my faith, these gifts were little;
Mine be a larger vow." And I swore an oath and I promised
All that she would to bring, nay, all her soul demanded,
Even a service of fear, a thing from the land of danger.
and thus they sat in discourse till the hour of noon was upon them,
And the caller called to prayer, and the great ones prayed assembled;
And these too in their place, and they stood in prayer together.

And when they had made an end of praises and
prostrations,
Back to the tent came they, and still behold the lady
Wandering in doubt uncertain there with steps of a
stranger.

Immediately remarkable in the passage is the highly stylized quality of the verse language. Stock phrases, stereotyped diction, and repetitions abound. The noun-epithet phrases so frequent in epic narrative also leap out. The binary, paratactic hemistichs of the verse line each contain a complete thought. The expression, the thought never exceeds a given line and is often contained in just the space of the hemistich. The language is lexically economical; it does not seek elegant variation. A phrase will be repeated in exactly the same words to communicate a given essential idea within the rhythmic boundaries of the hemistich. For example, in the exchange of views by the Hilālī heroes in assembly, each new speaker is introduced with the virtually identical phrase, beginning with "Tabaddā" (see 11. 9, 12, 13, 15), and then the discourse of each speaker proceeds with remarkable similarity of phrasing, substituting only exactly what each hero will give the strange lady who is approaching the tent (see Arabic text, 11. 11, 12, 14, 16). Further, such parallel constructions ensue as line 17b introduces the *wa-law* construction that will form the pattern of the next verses.

While reading the nineteenth-century printed, manuscript, and lithograph editions of the *Hilāliyya,* we might usefully think back to the figure of the professional poet-musician, the Abū Zaydiyya of Lane's account of the Cairo storytellers of his day, contemporaneous with the earliest date of the *Hilāliyya* editions and manuscripts. Lane reports that the performer sang the verse portions of his tale to the accompaniment of the rabāba. If we take up Lane's cues and observations, it is instructive to think of the Abū Zaydiyya as the creating force behind these mostly anonymous written editions of the sīra. Once the shāʿir al-rabāba is conceived of as a musician improvising a song in performance, the story-song grounded firmly in traditional components just as any musical improvisatory art always is, the stock phrases, the epithets, the highly stylized diction, the repetitions and patterns of the Banī Hilāl narratives become easily understandable. They are the functional bones of the craft of the poet-musician, which provide ready-made, semantically, syntactically, and rhythmically appropriate utterances to the performing singer whose main goal is to narrate a traditional verse tale to an audience who knows it well. Such frequently used, useful phrases, as those observed in the above passage, allow the singer to advance the narrative by singing an automatic, prepared line of verse, while the next line forms itself in the singer's head on the pattern of lines just uttered.

This technique of verse making is that of oral epic song, defined by Lord and his teacher, Parry, as "narrative poetry composed in a manner evolved over many generations by singers of tales who did not know how to write. . . . it consists of the building of metrical lines and half-lines by means of formulas and formulaic expressions and the building of songs by the use of themes."[43] The most important elements in the technique are the basic patterns, the set, regular phrases that Parry and Lord called "formulas" and "formulaic systems." The traditional bard's manner of composition differs from that of writer, for the oral poet makes no conscious effort to break from the stereotyped phrases and incidents. His art, according to Lord, consists not so much in learning through repetition the timeworn formulas as in the ability to compose and recompose the phrases to express the idea of the moment on the pattern established by the basic formulas. The bard is not an iconoclast but a traditional creative artist. In the technique of composition that Parry and Lord describe from their fieldwork in Yugoslavia, oral learning, oral composition, and oral transmission merge as different facets of the same process. Melodic, metric, syntactic, and acoustic patterns form in the young singer's mind as he learns the formulaic language of traditional story-verse in an unconscious process of assimilation.

The living art of the epic bard leaves its peculiar stamp on songs and their texts. Consequently, the Parry-Lord theory of oral composition maintains that through textual analysis of style we can establish to a high degree of certainty whether a given text was originally the work of a traditional bard. Repeated phrases or formulas mark the style; that is, a given essential idea in a given rhythmic position of the verse line is always repeated in the same group of words. One immediately apparent earmark of an oral composition is its characteristic "adding style," the almost staccato way in which line is added to line paratactically, with a given line containing a complete thought. As Parry puts it, "Any one verse line either ends at the end of a sentence and the new verse begins a new sentence, or a verse can also end with a word group in such a way that the sentence, at the verse end, already gives a complete thought, although it goes on in the next verse adding ideas by new word groups." Scholars of oral poetry apply to the latter situation the term "non-periodic enjambement."[44] The total effect is cumulative: one element is added serially to another.

Parallelism and pleonasm are other characteristic signs of oral style. In fact, readers of the written editions of the *Hilāliyya* often experience tedium and irritation with texts that present such a high degree of repeated phrases and such extremely stylized diction and formulaically episodic plot construction. Critics and scholars of al-sīra have indeed long been at a loss when faced with so much repetition on the written page. While recognizing the *Hilāliyya* as a great epic in its verse narration of heroic exploit, mass migration, war, and upheaval of nations, its idealization of a past "heroic age" of the ancestors, and its concerns with national or tribal identity, scholars have been perplexed by its anomalies of style and language. They have faulted it for its repetitions and redundancies (both verbal and thematic), for its continual recapitulation of incidents with little or no variation, its confusion of incident, its lack of dramatic suspense, its revelation of the outcome of the story in the beginning, and its sameness of scene and character depiction.[45]

Ironically, these dilemmas may point to the "treibende Kräfte" of the genre, which, in 1898, Hartmann suggested scholars seek to discover.[46] Just what that force is, and, more important, what that craft is, we are only beginning to discover today. The very repetitions of both phrase and incident, the very cyclical composition that critics deplore as bad writing, as well as the very language of the text, point to a text that was originally composed orally by a traditional bard in performance.

As we understand oral epic narrative today, in light of the Parry-Lord work on south Slavic and Greek tradition as well as subsequent studies of such narrative around the world, orally composed epic poetry can perhaps be recognized on the basis of frequency of repeated phrases. The Parry-Lord theory provides a model and a method of analysis by which one can determine whether or not a given text is written or oral. The usual method employed is to take a sample passage of about 25 lines chosen at random from a given text and analyze it using the remaining poetic corpus as a referent body to discover the percentage of repeated passages. In the following 28-line excerpt from *Taghrībat Banī Hilāl ilá Bilād al-Gharb* (Beirut, n.d.), on the model of Parry and Lord,[47] those phrases which are repeated verbatim elsewhere in the corpus are underlined with a solid line and those which recur with lexical substitution are underlined with a broken line. Certain lines may be repeated in their entirety. These, accordingly, are underlined with a solid line. Other phrases of these same lines will be repeated in the same rhythmic position in other lines. Such partial repetition accounts for the instances in the excerpt where I have put more than one line beneath a given verse.[48]

1 Taqūl fatāt al-ḥayy Umm Muḥammad
Bi-damᶜ jarā fawq al-khudūd ghazzār
2 A-lā Malik Shamᶜūn ismaᶜ qiṣṣatī
Wa-ṣghā li-qawlī yā ḥumāt al-jār
3 Anā bint Sirḥān akhūy Abū ᶜAlī
Wa-hā'ulāᶜ yā malik ᶜabīdnā wa-jawār
4 Kunnā bi-Najd fī surūr wa-fī hanā
Namraḥ bi-hā fī layl thumma nahār
5 Atānā bihā maḥlan shadīdan wa-ḍurnā
Sabᶜah sinīn kāmilāt ᶜisār
6 Raḥilnā li-arḍ Qayrawān wa-Qābis
Atānā-z-Zanātī mithla shuᶜlat nār
7 Qatal minnā tisᶜīn qatīlan mujarraban
Bi-rās ramḥuh al-murhaf al-battār
8 Qatalahu Abū Waṭfā Diyāb ibn Ghānim
Bi-ᶜazm shadīd yufliq al-aḥjār
9 Malikna bi-qatlihi sāyir al-Gharb yā malik
Maliknā madāyinhā wa-kull dār
10 Arād Diyāb yamluk al-qaṣr waḥdahu
Wa-yaqᶜud bihi sulṭān yā mighwār

11 Ḥabasahu akhī sabᶜah sinīn kāmilah
Sabᶜah sinīn fī balā wa-kadār
12 Wa-aṭlaqahu Abū Zayd al-Hilālī ghaṣībah
Wa-hādhihi ḥīlah minhum ᶜalayhi dār
13 Maraḍ Ḥasan wa-l-wajh minhu mughayyaran
Wa-ᶜala wajhi baᶜḍ al-bayād sawār
14 Atūhu jamīᶜ al-qawm min kull jānib
Wa-jā'ū Ḥilāl kibārhum wa-ṣighār
15 Wa-jānā Diyāb maᶜ akābir qawmihi
Wa-qalbuhu aswad khāyinan ghaddār
16 Nāmū jamīᶜan laylatayn kawāmilan
Wa-thālith laylah qām Diyāb wa-dār
17 Dhabaḥa Ḥasan min fawq ᶜālī firāshihi
Wa-khallāhu yakhtabiṭ maymanah wa-yasār
18 Wa-rāḥ ᶜannā huwa wa-kull jumūᶜihi
Dakhal bilād az-Zanj wa-l-aqfār
19 Jābuh Abū Zayd ṭayyab bi-khāṭirihi
Wa-arsal lahu maktūb bi-l-iḥḍār (?)
20 Wa-jābuh ilā ᶜindihi sarīᶜan bilā baṭā
Wa-rajiᶜū aṣḥāb wa-rāḥat al-akdār
21 Wa-baᶜdahu atū li-ṣ-ṣayd fī ᶜizz maᶜ hanā
Wa-laᶜibū bi-l-jarīd kam mishwār
22 Fa-shāl Diyāb min taḥt bāṭihi li-Salāmah
Dabbūs ḥadīd fihi alf mismār
23 Ḍarabahu bihi armāhu mulqan ᶜalā-th-tharā
Ḍarābat Diyāb mā ᶜalayhā ᶜiyār
24 Wa-qāl Abū Zayd rūḥū bi-ahlikum
Ilā Malik Shamᶜūn ᶜizz al-jār
25 Wa-jīnā la-ᶜindak ṭalibīn makārimak
Yā Barmakī yā mukrim al-zuwwār
26 Diyāb qatal minnā-l-fawāris jamīᶜahā
Shabīh al-ghanam in jazzhā-l-jazzār

27 Wa-ʿāda Diyāb mālik al-Gharb kullihā
Wa-ṣār malik wa-l-ʿizz lahu ṣār
28 Hādhā jarā fīnā wa-hādhā aṣābanā
Wa-d-dahr dūlāb ʿalaynā dār

1 Umm Muḥammad, the girl of the camp, said,
With the abundant tears flowing down her cheek:
2 Oh King Shamʿūn, hear my story,
and heed what I have to say, of protectors of refugees
3 I am the daughter of Sirḥān, my brother is Abū ʿAlī,
And these, O King, are our servants and slavegirls
4 We were in Nejd, in happiness and contentment,
rejoicing there night and day
5 A severe famine befell us, and we starved
for seven full and difficult years
6 We journeyed to the land of Kairouan and Gabes [=Tunisia],
the Zanātī came upon us like a blaze of fire
7 They killed 90 of our most experienced warriors
with spearheads sharp and fine
8 Abū Waṭfā Diyāb ibn Ghānim killed him [=al-Zanātī
Khalīfah] with resolution strong enough to split boulders
9 By killing him, we gained possession of the rest of the West,
O King,
We captured its cities, and every house
10 Diyāb wanted to rule the palace alone
and sit in it as sultan, great raider
11 My brother held him captive for seven full years,
seven years in grief and sorrow
12 And Abū Zayd al-Hilāli set him free *by force?*
And this was a ruse from them, which turned against him
13 Ḥasan fell ill, and his face was changed,
And on his face, there was a ring around his whiteness[?]
14 The whole clan came to him from all sides,
the great and small of Hilāl came
15 Diyāb came to us with the elders of his clan,
his heart black, treacherous, deceitful
16 They slept altogether for two whole nights
And on the third night, Diyāb got up and turned
17 He slaughtered Ḥasan while atop his bed

and let him roll around right and left
18 Then he and all his company left us,
and entered the land of the Blacks and the desert
19 Abū Zayd went after him and placated him,
and sent him a letter asking him to come
20 They brought it into him quickly, without delay
and friends returned, and sorrow departed
21 Afterward they went hunting in joy and delight
and played a few horse games with blunt javelins
22 And Diyāb took out from under his arm for Salāmah
an iron mace with 1,000 nails in it.
23 He struck him with it, knocking him to the ground,
Diyāb's blows were innumerable.
24 And Abū Zayd said: Go with your families
to King Shamʿūn, our dear neighbor (protector)
25 So we've come to you to seek your favors
O Barmakī,* o honorer of guests
26 Diyāb has murdered all of our horsemen,
our sheep look as if a butcher sheared them
27 And Diyāb has taken possession of the entire West,
he has become king, and glory is his
28 This has happened to us and befallen us,
fate is a wheel which has turned on us.

Of the 54 hemistichs analyzed above, 51 are wholly or in part formulaic, that is, phrases are repeated several times in the same rhythmic position of the verse line throughout the corpus. On this basis, 94 percent of the hemistichs are wholly or in part formulaic. In his study of pre-Islamic oral poetry, M. Zwettler argues that Arabic formula analysis should be done on the basis of formulaic *words,* rather than hemistichs or lines. Calculated on a verbal basis, the percentage of formulaic words in the passage cited from the Hilāliyya would be 75.90 percent (387 words, 293 words identifiably formulaic).[49] Since I scanned about 4,500 verses as a referent body to verify semantically identical or nearly identical phrases, my statistics are necessarily approximate. Had I used a computer concordance and broadened the base of the referent

*The Barmakīs or Barmecides were a family of trusted viziers and confidants in the times of Hārūn al-Rashīd.

lines, the hemistichs would no doubt have been 100 percent or wholly formulaic.[50] Or, had I broadened my definition of formula, the same would have appeared. As it was, following Lord in the *Singer of Tales,*[51] I used a strictly semantic definition of the formula. Had I used a syntactic or structural definition of the formula as Zwettler and Monroe, respectively, do for the pre-Islamic material, again almost 100 percent of the words could have been identified as forming part of a formulaic phrase. The relative density of formulas in a given passage of a text has been found to be a fairly good basis for assuming that the total work from which it is drawn is wholly formulaic and thus represents true oral composition.[52]

The Parry-Lord theory of oral epic composition also illuminates the confusion scholars have expressed when faced with many different versions of a given episode of *Sīrat Banī Hilāl;* the theory elucidates the fluidity of the "text" which scholars puzzling over the Berlin manuscripts for the past sixty-five years or so have noted. For as Lord has demonstrated in the *Singer of Tales,* the act of composition and performance is at once a transmission and a creation, or re-creation, of the traditional tale. The singer learns his art orally by listening to his father or grandfather, or uncle. The south Slavic poet learns to play the gusle (a one-stringed, viol-like instrument with a square sounding box, very similar to the rabāb), while he gradually builds up a knowledge of the story themes and motifs, a body of formulas and stock expressions. With the aid of his gusle, the beginner learns to build lines and half-lines, and finally builds a whole song, choosing a theme and standard patterns of action adhering to that theme which he interweaves to form the total song.

Once the student has mastered the technique of line building and can interweave themes adroitly enough, he is ready for performance-composition. Thus, the performance of each song is different, depending, for example, on the circumstances of composition, the type of audience, the time allowed. Lord asserts that scholarly comprehension of this technique of composition suggests that he who is led in pursuit of the "original" pursues the will-o'-the-wisp and that critics are deluded by a mirage when they try to construct an ideal form of any given song. The song listened to, the song of a given moment which a singer may dictate to someone who knows how to write, is *the* song—the specific song and the generic song. Talk of originals and variants is meaningless within this kind of tradition.

The wealth of source materials, both oral and written, the multiplicity of versions and episodes of the Hilālī poem, and its language and poetic style all point to its primary orality. As Yūnis tells us, internal evidence suggests that the shāʿir al-rabāba (rebec poet) is the prime generator, creator, and transmitter of the 900-year-old tradition. Earliest samples of Hilālī poetry refer to the orality of the text(s). The poetry Ibn Khaldūn cites in his *Muqaddima* is sung poetry, and one of the poems mentions the rabāb and *qānūn*.[53] Subsequent written manuscripts and printed editions of the *Hilāliyya* all mention again and again, almost as a leitmotiv, the shāʿir al-rabāba. The Hilālī hero, Abū Zayd, for example, is himself a poet and frequently travels in disguise as an itinerant bard with rabāb. Written versions all refer to the lines of verse as spoken, declaimed, or sung. And all refer to the oral transmission of the text, constantly and consistently repeating "qāla al-rāwī" (the narrator-transmitter said). The Berlin manuscripts in fact generally name the poet who related the story to the scribe-compiler of the text.[54] The implied audience in all the written texts is an oral one comprised of listeners. The poet-speaker in the text repeats the formulaic phrase over and over which admonishes his audience to "*Ismaʿ kalāmī*" (hear my words) and "*iṣghā kalāmī wa ifhamuh*" (heed my words and understand them). The listener, not the reader, is constantly told to hear the tale and to heed the words.

Heeding the words of my text and mindful of Ibn Khaldūn's clear admonition to take the oral poetry in its own terms rather than as some degeneration of the Classical Poetic Tradition, I determined to study the art and craft of the Egyptian shāʿir al-rabāba. During fieldwork in Egypt in 1978, I sought out rabāb artists to learn what I could of the sīra tradition from them and from the people who made up their audience; I sought also to discover the extent to which the tradition of oral performances such as Lane described in the early nineteenth century still exists.

When I arrived in Cairo, the 900-year-old epic of the migratory exploits of the Banī Hilāl turned out to be very much alive in the imagination of the vast population inhabiting Cairo rooftops and stairwells. Every evening, cafés in the Husseyn area were filled to overflowing with men listening intently to Jābir Abū Ḥusayn reciting with rabāb the nightly episode of the *Hilāliyya*. Unlike Lane's nineteenth-century Cairo café scene, however, the poet was heard on the radio, as recorded and presented by ʿAbd al-Raḥmān al-Abnoudy. Every night, between 10:00 and 10:30, all coffee service stopped and the radio program dominated the café. The men of the *bawwāb* (doorkeeper) families in the apartment buildings in my neighborhood listened faithfully to the program. They told how they used to listen to "Abū Zayd" in their Upper Egyptian home villages while sitting around outdoors on benches as the poet performed on the doorstep. Taxi drivers throughout Cairo could not only narrate the content of the evening's episodic adventures, they could also recite lines of Jābir's poetry they had heard on the radio the night before. Every cabbie asked could recount "what happens next." In winter and spring 1978, Abnoudy presented Jābir's version of the *Hilāliyya* in ninety half-hour radio programs that interspersed Abnoudy's commentary with the rabāb poet's musical rendition of the sīra. On earlier occasions, Abnoudy had broadcasted other poets of the Hilāl tradition whom he had found in his travels throughout Upper Egypt in his quest for the *Hilāliyya*.

ʿAbd al-Raḥmān al-Abnoudy holds the most significant oral archive of Banī Hilāl poetry today. He began recording the epic in 1964, when he decided to record and collect what he considers to be *the* great Arab epic (malḥama) in the tradition of Homer. A very successful and well-known poet himself, Abnoudy writes in the colloquial Egyptian tongue, eschewing the high Classical language of the Cairo literary establishment. He grew up in the Upper Egyptian village of Abnoud. His father was Azharī educated, one of the few men of the village to learn to read and write. He was the local man of letters, the shaykh who wrote marriage and other legal contracts. He also wrote poetry in the Classical tradition. Abnoudy grew up hearing the oral poetry and song of the folk poets and musicians all around him, and, in his own words, rebelled against the artificial strictures of the language of his father: "I couldn't understand his poetry. I didn't like it. I could understand the singers and popular language poets."[55] So Abnoudy went to Cairo and made his fame as a poet, lyricist, and songwriter for such popular Egyptian recording stars as ʿAbd al-Ḥalīm Ḥāfiẓ. *Sīrat Banī Hilāl*, however, brought him back to learning. He went to the oral musician-poets he had heard all his life singing the old epic, and recorded as many versions and as many poets and narrators as he could find in his effort to weave together his own finished epic from the versions of all the others. Such work led him to become a scholar. He entered Cairo University in his thirties to study folklore under Dr. ʿAbd al-Ḥamīd Yūnis.

In his quest for the sīra, Abnoudy learned anew from the Egyptian oral poets many of the lessons taught Parry and Lord by the Serbo-Croatian singers of tales. When I studied with him in 1978, Abnoudy pointed out to me the language, the forms, the art and craft of the oral poets. The terms he used were those of the folk poets. One day as we sat listening to the sounds of a khuṭba (sermon) broadcast on loudspeakers over downtown Cairo for the funeral of a prominent government official, Abnoudy told me to listen to the rhythms and cadences of the preacher's speech, to hear how similar its phrasing, its musicality, and even much of its vocabulary was to the poetry of Jābir Abū Ḥusayn. Abnoudy in fact said, "Listen, he's copying Jābir."[56] And, indeed, I could recognize whole lines of Jābir's poetry in the religious sermon.

Abnoudy used the term miftāḥ (key) to refer to the essential, repeated ideas in fixed phrases which the poets (and the folk preacher as well) used to construct their long poetic narrative history. This term was precisely that used by the Tunisian rāwī interviewed by Saada.[57] This rāwī, M. H. Ḥsīnī, explained that coherence is provided by "keys" in the story which are a "kind of prison, they keep the listener hanging so that until the story ends, he remains hanging, waiting impatiently for the end of the story." The term appears to be used for both the small-scale molecules of verse line composition and for the larger elements of story construction, in Parry-Lord terminology, "formulas" and "themes."

Collectors and commentators from inside the tradition, like Abnoudy, point to a new way of looking at the sīra. Abnoudy, who grew up from childhood hearing the poets perform *Sīrat Banī Hilāl,* absorbed the tradition and is, indeed, part of it, both as a member of the audience and as a creative force and patron of the poets. He sees the oral versions as primary. To him, the written versions—the cheap, pulp-paper editions to be found in Cairo's Azbakiyya Garden bookstalls—are beneath contempt.[58] They do not represent the living vitality of the sīra as Abnoudy and any Egyptian peasant knows it in his heart and mind and as the poets sing it on their rabābas. According to this fervent aficionado of the Hilālī tradition, hack writers, impoverished Azharī students no doubt, composed the written versions to earn a few quick piasters. In Abnoudy's view, the only "decayed" epic is the written version of *Sīrat Banī Hilāl,* a poor, feeble rendering of the poetic vision and magnificence of the living poem in its orally performed versions.

PART II

# Listening to Egyptian Rabāb Poets

# 3
# THE POETS, THE PEOPLE, AND THE EPIC TRADITION

Foreigners to Egypt have witnessed the rhetorical scene of the shāʿir al-rabāba interpreting an episode of *Sīrat Banī Hilāl* to his gallābiyya-clad audience and have written various accounts of it, making it the subject of either highly romanticized fancy or scholarly disavowal. A certain sense of discomfiture mingles with attraction for the Westerner viewing the scene, for his romantic projections conflict with social and political realities of power and prestige. In the case of *Sīrat Banī Hilāl* and its like, the Orientalist, often without being aware of it, has participated in a cultural polemic between the classes of Arab society and has sometimes even participated ironically in the discursive, rhetorical scene as the butt of an ongoing polemic between the literate and the oral worlds, between the contained in-group of the oral poet's world and the dominant world against which the poet's oral discourse offers a masked aggression. For, as we shall discover in our attempt to enter ever deeper into the perceptual world of the Banī Hilāl epic, the perception the sīra tradition offers is essentially xenophobic; the poet's oral discourse addressed to his listening public offers powerful interpretive analogies that criticize Arabo-Muslim society both in its internal political and social dynamics and in its relations with foreign powers.

The foreign scholar and collector, as we have seen, often adopts elitist, literate attitudes when he approaches oral discourse. Caught in a myopic perspective, he has most often misconstrued and undervalued oral folk cultural compositions and transmission, both in their subject matter and their mechanisms. The oral poet, even more than most literate poets, works out of known conventions, patterns, stereotypical phrases, commonplaces of attitude and opinion. Close listening by the scholarly auditor reveals the poet's oral art as essentially metonymic and integrative. In the chiastic structures of his inherited story patterns, in the figures of speech buried in his formulaic language, and in the tropes and conceits of his rhymes, the Egyptian oral poet incorporates current reality into the past and the past into the present. His is a metonymic kind of representation, which "involves a contiguous link of part to whole, container to contained, penetration of subsequent by prior events,"[1] and which collapses tense and time. It incorporates the immediate into the past and inserts current event into the perceptual mold of the inherited poetic formulary.[2]

The oral poet's art is one that eschews originality and individuality. His public is a collective one; his poetry is a communal event and performance. The rhetorical transaction is not the private, solitary transaction of the isolated writing poet and the isolated reader of the written word, but a public transaction that is at once a transmission and a composition. The rhetorical scene thus affects the poetic "text" to a certain extent, as the poet adapts and adjusts his improvised saga of Hilāl and the lineage of its heroes to changing audience parameters. The foreigner, as collector, can, as we shall see, influence the narration both in its detail and in its implications, for the oral bard's figural representation of reality condenses and incorporates the outsider into an opinionated poetics.

A basic premise underlying this study of traditional epic song concerns the human quality of the tradition. I believe that behind every tradition are the people who make it, shape it, and craft it, and who pass it on to each other because it represents a reality they live. This study is posited on a view of the folk poet as a thinking, critical human being. Individuals make and carry on the tradition through collective effort and through collective dialogue. Consequently, my study of the Hilālī epic is in many ways the study of individual people I met during my research in Egypt and an account of my dialogue with them and my ongoing attempts as an ultimate outsider (a female, Irish-American scholar) to understand what is essentially a male, Arab-Egyptian performance tradition from within both the oral culture and the texts it generates.

The oral poetry researcher, upon his arrival in Egypt, can easily find poets eager to perform a commissioned session of the

*Hilāliyya* as well as an eager audience who will listen with enthusiasm and critical severity to the ad hoc performance. In the course of my research, the aesthetic pertaining to the traditional poetics emerged only slowly in the context of the performance. Through the interaction of poets and audiences which I observed, I learned experientially and inductively the rhetorical dynamic of the living performance art that is the *Hilāliyya.* This account of my initial experience in Egypt ferreting out the performance tradition and then recording a number of performances thus will be anecdotal and geometric[3] rather than abstractly analytic. It will attempt to bring the reader inside the tradition to discover experientially its communicative dynamic and its continuing relevance to the ethos of the community.[4] It will also reveal one poet's bad performance, which I suspect might have been conditioned by the performer's perception of his patron (the author) as an ignoramus outsider. Audience reaction to this "bad" performance taught me as much about the traditional art of the shāʿir al-rabāba as any "decent" performances I later witnessed, not as the major patron, but in the company of ʿAbd al-Raḥmān al-Abnoudy, who is acknowledged by poets and their public alike as the most famous patron of the Hilālī poet vending his verse wares. Let us begin in medias res and listen to various accounts of the tradition which instructed me on how, as an outsider, to approach the *Hilāliyya.*[5]

When I asked the family who cared for the Duqqī apartment building in which I was staying if they knew stories about Abū Zayd al-Hilālī, the white-haired grandfather replied, "How could I not know Abū Zayd al-Hilālī? I am from the Ṣaʿīd [Upper Egypt]." Later, as he sat in our living room at a party arranged to record one of a series of performances of "The Birth of Abū Zayd" (Mīlād Abū Zayd), the old man leaned back with his eyes closed in meditative rapture while he absorbed the words of the poet, Fārūq ʿAbd al-ʿAzīz. Alternatively, the old man would lean forward attentively, smile at the rabāb poet, and call "Yā Al̤l̤āh!" at the conclusion of particularly well-cast lines of sung verse. Also listening to the poet were the bawwāb, ʿAlī, and his poetry-loving brother, who had confided just prior to the performance, "I just love poetry so." Their bodies swayed. The rabāb wailed its old, familiar tune. The voice of Fārūq, hesitating and jerky at first, became steady as he found his tune and the rhythm of his lines. The two poetry lovers smiled as Fārūq sang, and they saluted "Yā marḥaban" between lines. ʿAlī gestured with his hand in rhythm to the music, pointing out the end-rhymed lines of the quatrains (*murabbaʿāt*) as Fārūq constructed his cross-rhymed verses.

Fārūq continued to sing as more people entered the room. He smiled, holding the two-stringed viol with his left hand on his left knee and bowing with his right hand. Sometimes he closed his eyes. His face and neck grew red, his neck strained as he sang intently and the story became intense. He was singing the history of the Banī Hilāl tribe as his father and grandfather had taught it to him many years earlier during his boyhood in Banī Ṣuwayf: "My father was like a sea—like Jābir—for knowing all the sīra."

From a family of poets and professional wandering folk musicians, Fārūq was born in Banī Ṣuwayf in 1938. ʿĀ'ida, the maid in our Duqqī household, also from Banī Ṣuwayf, had called me to the window to see him passing in the street with his rabāb under his arm. Fārūq reports that his brother, Fu'ād, can also perform portions of *Sīrat Banī Hilāl,* also called *Sīrat Abū Zayd* or *al-Hilāliyya.* Their grandfather had urged them when they were boys to learn all of the sīra, but neither of them really learned very much of it. Fārūq himself only learned to sing a few episodes of the heroic migratory epic—from the birth of the hero through one of his first adventures, the killing of Jāyil, and a couple others, such as "Malik Manṣūr." Both he and his brother found the shorter folk songs easier to learn as well as bigger money-makers in their perambulations with rabāb to entertain at weddings, festivals, and parties. Nowadays, Fārūq reports, the young people at wedding parties only want to hear *mawwāls* and the more popular folk tunes and ballads. Only at the end of a party do the old men ask to hear an episode of *al-Hilāliyya.*

Shamandī, another rabāb poet who recorded for me, says of Fārūq and other gypsylike poets who wander the streets in search of work, "Yes, there are quite a few of them. They go around, play maddāḥ, but they aren't very good. They learn a few songs, they copy from each other and go around trying to earn a living." The bawwāb, ʿAlī, concurred. "They're maddāḥs [praise singers]," he said. "They're gypsies [*ḥalabī*—Syrian, Aleppan]." Shamandī is perhaps Egypt's most famous rabāb artist, and comes from a family of renowned musicians. Born in 1918 in Karnak (Qinā), his National Identity Card lists his profession as itinerant poet (*shāʿir mutajawwil*). Fifteen years ago or so, he says, the government brought him and members of his family troupe to Cairo to appear in the National Orchestra of Folk Music at the National Folk Theater under the direction of ʿAbd al-Raḥmān al-Shāfiʿī. One and all consider Shamandī to be a virtuoso rabāb player.[6] He has traveled, he tells me, to Greece, Paris, and Tūnis. Whenever Egyptian folk musicians are sent on international tours, he is among them. He has recorded folk songs, and parts of the *Hilāliyya* for French and Italian companies. "It was," he confided, "very nice down south before the government brought us to Cairo. We went to private parties and traveled around and earned a good living." But now, Shamandī wears an expensive Seiko digital watch and has, as he pointed out, a wool *ʿabāya* (cloak) worth U.A.R. £100. His professional fee for private performances and recording sessions is high. After we arranged the fee, Shamandī agreed to come back six times to sing "The Story of Yūnis," from the third part of *Sīrat Banī Hilāl,* for my tape recorder and my friends and assembled household.

Shamandī learned the art of sīra poetry from his father and his paternal uncles, Mitqāl and Qināwī. He is from the Matāqīl family of Sudanese origin.[7] Shamandī himself tells that Mitqāl raised him from infancy and taught him the rabāb and a *shaʿbī* (folk) version of "Abū Zayd." He recounted various scenes from his boyhood when he was learning the art:

> "I was very young when I first played. I was young. I was with my father the first time. There was a person called Shaykh al-Mursī Abū 'l-ʿAbbās. He's a shaykh. He was a sainted man and could foretell the future. Wherever he went people followed him [i.e., became a follower of the Way of this saint]. They would let their beards grow. My father followed Sīdī al-Mursī Abū 'l-ʿAbbās, who was buried here in the cemetery when he came back from the Hijaz—his wife was from the Hijaz and bore him children. Well, that was the first time I held a rabāb. When I played, people liked me immediately. I got a reputation. Shamandī, Shamandī,

> Shamandī Mitqāl. This man [Shaykh al-Mursī Abū 'l-ᶜAbbās] had real *baraka.*[8] Praise be the Lord. And I continue to live with his blessings." (Oral Communication, Feb. 25, 1978)

Shamandī's account of how he learned to play the rabāb elliptically condenses past and present. He mentions the Spanish holy man, whose shrine may be found today in an Alexandria mosque, as if he were in personal contact with his (Shamandī's) father; the saint in fact lived over 700 years ago. Shamandī juxtaposes, in an implied causal relationship, learning the rabāba and his father's conversion to the Way of the holy man al-Mursī.

On another occasion, as Shamandī talked about learning the rabāb, he made it less a matter of "baraka" and more a matter of apprenticeship.[9]

> "My father at home, when we were sitting at home, taught me how to play. He did not send us either to the Kuttāb or to school. He said, 'Hold the rabāb!' So I held it. He said, 'Put your fingers here and do that and that.' This is how I learned. Slowly, slowly I learned. He would hit me. I liked it though, so I learned. My father when he went to places to play Abū Zayd used to take me with him. He used to say, 'When I play Abū Zayd, don't fall asleep!' I was about seven or eight years old. He would make me sit next to him. And whenever I fell asleep, he would wake me up and hit me on the head with his bow. So I heard the poem from him while he recited it, while he played. So I took it from him." (Oral communication, Feb. 27, 1978)

The instrument Shamandī now uses is not the one on which he learned. He tells a sad story about leaving that instrument in a taxi during a trip to Greece. His father's rabāb is in Luxor, hung in the family's house as a remembrance: "We call it the *rababit il-marḥūm*—the rabāb of the deceased."

The rabāb both Shamandī and Fārūq use to tell the epic tale is a viol-like instrument played with a bow. It has a neck, two strings, a sound box, and measures about ninety centimeters. Shamandī describes his rabāb's sound box as a coconut shell with fish skin stretched over it. The two strings are horsehair.[10] Canova[11] describes the rabāb in great detail in the notes accompanying his 1982 record for I Suoni di Musica di Tradizione Orale:

> The first string is the *qawwāl* or speaker; the second is the *raddād* or answerer. The neck (*sā'ed*) is made of ebony or *zān*, it is about 65 cm long, and on the upper part it has a notch where the pegs are inserted: these are called *ʿuṣfūrs* (little birds). The end of the neck has a carved ornament (*ma'dhanah*, minaret). The sound box consists of a coconut shell which has been perforated with a piece of hot iron. The *rababah shaʿer* (or rababah of the poet) is distinguished by a larger sound box and thicker strings which produce a lower and warmer tone. The *rababah* of the *mughanni* (singer) is smaller, part of its bottom is removed in order to produce more brilliant sound (S. Duwi). A skin of fish, gazelle, or rabbit is stretched across the opening and glued into the coconut. A bridge is fastened to the skin: it is called Kaʿb (dice). A metal rod passed through the sound box joins it to the neck of the instrument. The bow consists of a bamboo cane stretched with horsehair, and the tension is regulated using the same hand that the performer plays with. The tuning varies from poet to poet, according to the piece performed. The most common is in fourths (e-a), or in thirds. The ambitus of each string is about two octaves, but it is rare that more than one octave is used.

Fārūq ʿAbd al-ʿAzīz's rabāb is much simpler. Poorer, ambulant poet-musicians like Fārūq and Muḥammad Ḥasan, the "beggar-poet" described in the journal *al-Funūn al-Shaʿbiyya* (Baghdad, February 1977), use carved, wooden instruments fitted with wire strings which have a smaller sound box (see pl. 1).

In spite of Fārūq's simple, slightly shrill instrument, the audience preferred his rendition of the epic to Shamandī's. The criteria for judgment appear to be the story and the poetry, since no one could possibly fault Shamandī's mellow, resonant rabāb and voice. One day after Shamandī had left, ʿAlī commented, "il-giṣṣa mish hiyya" (the story is not right). Then he proceeded to narrate how the story really goes. ʿAlī further criticized Shamandī's *āyāt* (verses, a word normally used only for Koranic verses) as faulty. According to him, Fārūq's story, however, is quite good. ʿAlī listened to Fārūq's performances with great animation. As Fārūq began to sing, ʿAlī pinched his fingers together to indicate, "This is it, this is much better." His brother agreed. They listened passionately to Fārūq's āyāt, and pointed out to me the rhyme words of the murabbaʿāt.

Evidently, Shamandī was once a good poet of the sīra, but today his "memory is weak." Muḥammad ʿAmrān of the Cairo Folklore Center said that while Shamandī is possibly Egypt's best rabāb artist and used to be a good poet, he does not "memorize" (*ḥafiẓ*, i.e., preserve, retain in mind) the epic any more. Abnoudy, who put Shamandī on his evening radio show, said the audience clamored to tell him that Shamandī's story was wrong, that he should take him off the air. Shamandī himself said he prefers to sing folk songs, and he makes more money with the shorter, popular tunes in his cabaret career since coming to Cairo. Other rabāb poets echo this experience, and many have become almost exclusively nightclub entertainers after moving to Cairo.

The critical responses Shamandī and Fārūq received from ʿAlī, his brother, father, and uncles are typical audience reactions to interpretations of *Sīrat Banī Hilāl.* So are the severe criticisms Shamandī received for his radio performances. Abnoudy reports that he received diverse audience responses to the poets he put on the air, ranging from high praise to severe criticism.[12] The audience knows the story well and will not tolerate any serious deviation from the essential structural pattern or from the linear story sequence of events, as my experience in recording Shamandī's version of "The Story of Yūnis" taught me.

The audience will not listen for long to the poet who confuses episodes, characters, and places, or who repeats formulas aimlessly without forwarding the story action in a more or less dramatic way. When Shamandī sang of the scouting expedition to the "land of the West," Tunisia, by Abū Zayd's three nephews, he repeated lines over and over. He gave the audience the impression that he had somehow forgotten the story or did not care about bringing it to a climax. In one instance, the famous rabāb artist repeated "He took the sword in his hand" at least ten times. Such aimless repetition serves the oral bard little, and by audience standards appears to be a mockery of the lexically economical, functional repetition of the inherited formulaic language of improvisation in performance.

In this version performed by Shamandī, the words and story had become secondary to the music, which was ingeniously developed and varied. This twist was contrary to audience expectations, for they had come to hear the traditional tale told once more, not to hear a virtuoso instrumental performance with a pleasantly sung lyric refrain. Hence, ʿAlī, our doorkeeper and guardian-critic of the Hilālī tradition, informed me, "il-giṣṣa mish hiyya" (the story is not right), and did not return to hear any subsequent sessions Shamandī recorded for me.

Shamandī has since performed quite decent songs for other researchers; Canova, for example, recorded him in 1979 for his record anthology, *Egitto: Epica*. I suspect the famous rabāb artist gave an overly musical performance and a simplistically nonsensical rendition of the story because he perceived of me (his patron) as a foreign female outsider. Whatever the case, in my household, Shamandī soon lost his Egyptian male audience.

Later, when I recorded Fārūq, ʿAlī assembled many of the neighborhood men to hear the tale. Abnoudy too joined us to hear the poet I had "discovered." Fārūq was obviously pleased when Abnoudy became a member of his audience, and was even more honored when Abnoudy invited him to perform for a daylong session at his own house. Fārūq confided at one point that often when his audience was not appreciative or responsive, he would sing out just anything that came to his mind. With an important patron like Abnoudy present, Fārūq's performance demeanor was very serious, even a bit nervous.

In fall 1979, another member of the audience, Yūsuf Māzin, told Canova about the proper traditional performance decorum and the distinction reserved for the term *shāʿir*.[13] Many of the terms Māzin used, as well as his critical standards as to form, content, and manner of performance, coincide with those used by the people who taught me about the Hilālī tradition during my 1978 stay in Egypt.

> He [the poet] must follow the tradition: at the beginning, he must sing an éloge to the Prophet and mention the name of God. Only then can he start with Abū Zayd. Also at the end,

> he must conclude with the initial madīḥ. Every once in a while, he can stop to rest and drink a coffee or tea. When he starts again, he must begin with a madīḥ; the poet who starts the episode immediately is not a poet. Nor is the one who only sings praise to the Prophet—he's a maddāḥ and not a shāʿir. The shāʿir is the one who declaims the geste of the Arabs ("beyshʿar fī sīret el-ʿArab"), true poetry is only the *Sīrat Banī Hilāl.*[14]

The seventy-five-year-old Māzin talked to Canova in Luxor and told him how poets used to pass from village to village in Upper Egypt, sounding the rabāb around the houses of the countryside to gather people together for a *majlis* (assembly) in a village square; when everyone was sitting around on the ground, the poet would begin his exposition with a madīḥ (praise poem) to the Prophet and then sing an episode of the sīra. Sometimes another musician performed as well—the poet with the rabāb and an accompanist with tambourine. The audience would put money in the bowl placed in front of the poet. Māzin stressed the traditional performance decorum, he emphasizing that the poet cannot do whatever he wants. He then went on to talk about the tradition today:

> But times have changed. People nowadays want little songs and dances and silly things. There are poets with the rabāb or without it. They play in cafés, at wedding parties or circumcisions, at the *mūlids* [feast days]. The most famous cycle and the most loved one here in Egypt is that of Abū Zayd al-Hilālī. Other stories like ʿAntar ibn Shaddād or Dhāt el-Himmah are not poetry (*shoʿr*) but rather tales (*rewayat*) drawn from books. . . . Jābir Abū Huseyn is the greatest poet of Egypt. He is of peasant origin, from a place near Sohaj. A poet must have a beautiful voice, know (*yeḥfaẓ*) the poetry well, and execute the story well. He must above all know how to execute the poetry (shoʿr) in the exact order (*nizam*) and with good technique (*ada'*). He must know how to mount the words (*yrakkeb*) and make a conclusion in such a way that the listener will want to return the next evening to see how it will finish.[15]

As Māzin points out, in the world of Egyptian traditional folk song, the word *shāʿir* (poet) has historically been reserved only for the maker of *Sīrat Banī Hilāl.* Lane also tells us that in the early nineteenth century he listened to the various siyar in Cairo cafés. Only the Hilālī performer, who sang his song to the accompaniment of a one-stringed viol with a square sound box, was called a "poet." Other performers who recited the subject matter of other heroic tales were evidently called rāwīs (reciters, narrators) with more specific designation according to the sīra recited. Unlike the shāʿir (the Hilālī poet) who improvised his composition, the reciters of *Sīrat ʿAntar* performed with a book in front of them; they read prose sections "in the popular manner" and chanted the poetry.[16]

In his account, Lane highlights the shāʿir al-rabāba, and gives an etching of a Hilālī poet in performance before an audience. Lane's picture of the poet shows two men seated on steps at the threshold of a café. Each holds a large, square one-stringed rabāb, one playing, as the other, evidently the poet, looks up and gesticulates with his bow. These poets sang and chanted nothing but *Sīrat Banī Hilāl.* All were referred to as "Abū Zaydiyya," but were further distinguished as "Hilāliyya," or "Zughbiyya" or "Zanātiyya." The various titles denote the different categories of the shāʿir, who are named according to the particular episodes of the epic that they specialized in singing; each episode bears the name of a tribal group whose heroes dominate the action. One singer might chronicle the deeds of Abū Zayd, his father, Rizq, and their progeny, the Hilālī heroes; another might devote himself to tales of Diyāb son of Ghānim and the men of the Zughba tribe; yet another poet might recount tales focusing on the North African Berber enemy tribe, the Zanāta confederacy.[17]

Lane reports that the poet's listeners would gather around him on the café stoop, some sitting beside the performers, others sitting on benches outside the café, all smoking and drinking coffee. Still others would listen from the steps of houses across the narrow street. Members of the audience would sometimes offer the singer a few piasters, but the café owner generally paid the poet's fee.

Although the shāʿir al-rabāba cannot be seen today as Lane observed him performing in Cairo working-class cafés (his place now taken all too often by a radio or TV set), he still appears at village festivals throughout Egypt and as the central feature at private parties such as the one Critchfield describes in an Upper Egyptian village.[18] The itinerant poet-musician can also be found in Cairo, as he follows his audience to the city. Egyptian village men, peasant farmers, and displaced peasants now living in Cairo make up, for the most part, the poet's present-day audience. Some poets have left their home region to follow the huge waves of country people in their migration to Cairo. Today Cairo is crowded, with more people than it was ever intended to accommodate.[19] Migrants to the city live on roofs and in stairwells, and cluster by village in the various quarters.[20] These people recall hearing the epic song back in their villages. Sometimes the older men will request it at the end of a party as a special entertainment the young folks do not really care to hear.

The extent of the sīra tradition in Egypt today in terms of such spontaneous performances before traditional audiences in indigenous contexts remains an open question for the oral poetry scholar and folklorist. Reports by students who have done fieldwork since my visit in 1978 indicate that in certain villages the tradition still flourishes.[21] Critchfield, in his biography of an Upper Egyptian farmer, documented a village party in the early 1970s which featured the performance of a well-known rabāb poet, now dead, named Zakariyya al-Hijjawī. The actual extent of the audience today remains unknown. Canova suggests that it is very limited, that indeed the shāʿir al-rabāba today finds the *Hilāliyya* in little demand. He estimates the number of poets still performing the tradition at about a dozen.[22] ʿAbd al-Ḥamīd Hawwās of the Cairo Folklore Center and Abnoudy disagree with this estimate and suggest that active bearers of the tradition along with a genuine audience of passionate adherents may be found throughout Egypt.

Yūsuf Māzin's comments to Canova (above) suggest that at least the critical response Shamandī's and Fārūq's performances elicited in ʿAlī and his brother and uncles is not atypical; they also suggest the tradition may be very much alive. Abnoudy told me about collective letters he received from Upper Egyptian villagers—letters often penned by the single literate man in the town, written with the express purpose of letting Abnoudy know what was "true and not true" in the various versions of the

*Hilāliyya* performed by the different rabāb poets he had presented on the radio. Another example of the audience's zealous insistence on authenticity is provided by a milkman who came to Abnoudy's house to tell him that his village knew the history as told by Jābir, but they detest the way he sings a stall phrase, "Ya laylī, ya laylī" (O, my night, O my night), in between lines of poetry. Abnoudy explained to the man that the phrase is a pattern that enables the poet to rest his voice. But the milkman responded, "This is bad. This is a bad rest pattern because it is from outside the Hilālī tradition."[23]

Abnoudy believes the villagers know the sīra and lead the poet to truth with their criticism; the demanding, critical audience guards the tradition and keeps it alive by paying its poets to recite it for them. Māzin's comments cited above further suggest that what has kept listeners coming back evening after evening to hear how the poet will finish the well-known saga has something to do with poetic technique, with a proper adjustment of words, music, and story. Taking my cues from the poets' ever-critical real audience and from such ideal audience members as Māzin and Abnoudy, I determined to focus my research on Fārūq ʿAbd al-ʿAzīz and on two other poets widely admired throughout Egypt, Jābir Abū Ḥusayn and al-Sayyid al-Ḍūwī. Chapters 4 and 5 thus will present a "listening analysis" of one episode, "The Birth of Abū Zayd," performed by each of these three rabāb poets who are judged competent by their audiences on various levels.

Since all my resident critics implied that there is a right story and a wrong story, as well as a good poet and a bad poet, I decided in my subsequent analysis of the tape-recorded, performed texts to look at (or rather *listen* for) the relationship between the individual creating poet and the tradition, the relationship between story, poetic style, and musical technique in the three renditions of the opening episode of the sīra. I will seek to discover through a comparison of the three performed versions the basic conventions they have in common—the inherited traditional motifs and story sequence, and the other elements that must be present for the tale to be recognizable as *Sīrat Banī Hilāl*. I will examine the range of individual style, voice, and craft within the tradition—in short, what constitutes "good" and "bad" renditions, based on audience response. I will show from "close listening" with Egyptian audience members like ʿAlī's family and Abnoudy how end-rhyme formulas become an interpretive device, as well as a compositional-improvisational device, which guides listeners to an understanding of the meaning of sīra. The same elements that function as cognitive organizational devices for the poet "remembering" the *Hilāliyya* in oral composition-performance (formulas and motifs) will be seen to function also as canons of taste held artistic by the culture.

Inasmuch as folk aesthetics match the way a culture perceives itself and categorizes experience, Part III will attempt an understanding of Upper Egyptian culture from the folk perspective interpreted in the epic. I will discuss the place of the Hilālī tradition in Upper Egyptian culture and consider the meaning of the tradition within this society, the role of the rabāb poet, and the meaning given by individual poets in their re-creation and interpretation of the sīra tradition. My purpose throughout is to discover and examine through "close listening" (as opposed to reading) of representative performed texts the folk aesthetic and poetic of *Sīrat Banī Hilāl*.

# 4
# MUSICAL IMPROVISATION AND THE ORAL-FORMULAIC MODE

In listening to the performances of three Egyptian rabāb poets rendering "Mīlād Abū Zayd" (Birth of Abū Zayd), the opening episode of *Sīrat Banī Hilāl* as it is told in Egypt, the scholarly outsider quickly becomes aware of the generic decorum, of which Yūsuf Māzin spoke, and the rhetorical dynamic of prior expectation that shapes a performed version of the tradition. Although Egyptians speak of the sīra as recited (*qāla*), and often objected to my referring to the poets as singers or musicians, a performance by a shāʿir al-rabāba communicates itself as sung story.[1] The medium for the story is the interaction of the poet's singing voice and the rabāb accompaniment.

As one listens to different performers sing the same episode, certain patterns of sameness are immediately apparent. Yet from within these traditional, inherited similar components, there emerge certain individual features that mark the re-creation of the "text." Three rabāb poets I listened to in Cairo with an Egyptian audience (and have subsequently listened to again and again in their tape-recorded oral texts of "The Birth of Abū Zayd") all tell essentially the same story. In its larger story pattern and its cast of characters, the different versions of the tale are one and the same. The tale follows in large measure the hero pattern delineated by Raglan,[2] Rank,[3] Campbell,[4] and Dundes;[5] its language and diction are formulaic, full of the repeated phrases and fixed lines described by Parry and Lord.[6] It follows the epic laws of narration defined by Olrik and the epic "Departure-Devastation-Return" pattern outlined variously by Campbell, Nagler, Lord, and Connelly.[7] Its musical and prosodic form follow an identical pattern in the three renditions.

## PROSODIC AND MUSICAL FORM

Al-Sayyid al-Ḍūwī, Jābir Abū Ḥusayn, and Fārūq ʿAbd al-ʿAzīz each introduces his performance with a *taqsīm,* an instrumental prelude that demonstrates his skill as a rabāb artist and invites the audience to assemble to hear the old tale once again. Each poet begins the vocal section of the epic with a *ṣalāt* (prayer of praise to God and the Prophet Muḥammad), and then introduces the main characters of that particular episode and begins to narrate the story proper. Performances generally conclude with another prayer of thanks to God. The opening section (the ṣalāt and introduction of characters and subject matter) takes the form of either a mawwāl (ballad) or a qaṣīda (ode) followed by a brief section of rhymed prose (*sajʿ*) that summarizes the main theme of the episode to be related. The primary vehicle of story narration for all three poets is the murabbaʿ (quatrain rhymed *abab*). This organization and poetic structuring of a performance is standard for any rendition of *Sīrat Banī Hilāl* by Egyptian professional rabāb poets.[8]

All three performances of "Mīlād Abū Zayd" exhibit a small range musically and follow the same musical patterns.[9] Voice and rabāb interact; the instrument follows and echoes the voice. The rabāb may play an ornamented version of the melody being sung (heterophony), or it may be silent while the poet sings. In the latter case, an instrumental phrase follows the vocal phrase.

The performer relies on three or four basic melodic formulas: an initial melody, a final melody,[10] plus the "Abū Zayd" melody. All three poets use a tonal center—a single important pitch that is employed as a point of reference or as a home base to which almost every phrase returns. In these performances, the musical phrases end approximately on the note D. The "line" is the basic musical unit, just as it is the basic poetic unit. Poetic lines are paired musically as couplets. These paired musical phrases work around the tonal center: as the first line moves off the base pitch, the second line descends back to it, thus completing and resolving the musical phrase as a whole.

Rhythmically, a clear pulse usually grouped in twos can be heard. This duple metre reflects the binarism of the couplet structure.[11] The three rabāb poets all use rapid double bowing to highlight certain phrases. Rabāb interludes of various lengths occur:

(1) very short interludes that are only one phrase long and are not of sectional importance, and (2) longer ones that isolate one section of the narrative text from the next and mark off groups of quatrains by means of ornate versions of the preceding vocal melody or variations on the "Abū Zayd" melody. Change of speed along with use of the "final melody" also give musical shape to the sections of the text. In general, the music respects the form of the text and echoes it, while emphasizing and reinforcing the meaning. What I call the "Abū Zayd" melody recurs in the versions of all three poets as an instrumental section that is seldom sung.[12]

## FORMULAIC STYLE AND LANGUAGE

Just as the poets' musical vocabulary expresses itself within a limited range of set motifs, phrases, and repeated patterns, so does the language of his poetic text. The three rabāb poets build the story they sing out of traditional components: formulas of line or phrase and larger formulas of theme. The first lines of Jābir's opening prayer, a qaṣīda monorhymed in [ān], illustrate his paratactic style:

Lam yakhluqi-r-Raḥmānu mithla Muḥammadin
Nabīyu-l-hudā jānā bi-kulli ʾaman
Ṣalla ʿalayka-llāhu yā ʿalama-l-hudā
Ya nūri-l-ʿuyūni ya ṣafwati-r-Raḥmān

The Merciful One did not create the like of Muḥammad
The prophet of Right Guidance came to us in all peace
God Bless you, O, Banner of Right Guidance
O, Light of my eyes, O Choice of the Merciful

The lines, usually arranged in quatrains (murabbaʿāt), demonstrate the same paratactic, molecular style, which Parry called "adding style."[13]

Balaghanī-l-kibar ya ḍahrī wa-ḥanēt
Mina-llāh tiqḍā-l-maṣāliḥ
Bakēt ʿalā-l-balāwī wa-ḥannēt
Fī bētī mā fīsh ṭifli fāliḥ

I became old, O, my back was bent
From God we get our desires [lit., derives benefit]
I cried for my troubles and moaned
In my house there's no clever boy.

In this oral poetry, ideas are linked to each other additively, one juxtaposed to the other coordinately rather than subordinately, paratactically rather than hypotactically. In the examples cited, no full enjambement occurs between lines; each is end-stopped, the thought is complete at line's end. "Nonperiodic" enjambement, however, does occur in a few lines:

Balūj bi-ʿēnī yamīn wa-shimāl
ʿalā ṭifl ʿandī yilāghīnī

I look with my eyes right and left
for a boy to have to babble to me.

Here, the verse line itself constitutes a sentence or a complete thought, but the next verse amplifies this thought by adding an idea.[14] The narrative thus proceeds in a serial, adding style—one element is added to another cumulatively.

Such a molecular building style is typical of Jābir's, Sayyid's, and Fārūq's poetic technique. It is also one of the earmarks of oral epic style and of oral composition as delineated by Parry, Lord, and others in the study of oral epic poetry around the world. In addition, the parallelism and pleonasm that generally mark oral style recur as a salient stylistic feature in the poetry of these Egyptian rabāb poets. The poet states an idea and then repeats it pleonastically, with only a slight variation or elaboration. In the example cited above, Jābir sings "I became old," then adds a specific illustration to fill out the line: "and my back was bent." The next line takes up the metaphoric meaning of the second half of the preceding line, namely, the speaker's troubles; it works in a similar fashion: "I cried for my troubles" is immediately reiterated, "and I moaned."

In the opening qaṣīda (monorhymed ode) of Jābir's fourth session of the "Birth" episode, he summarizes the tale for the new member of his fluid audience. This qaṣīda illustrates the parallel construction oral poets typically use to recapitulate, to set a mood or background, or to retard action or forward it by incremental repetition. I translate:

> But not all who have been through trouble know the remedy
> But not all who have read the Book are faithful
> But not all who have brandished a sword have stabbed an enemy
> But not all who have antagonized are gentlemen
> But not all whom I tell a secret can keep it.

Sayyid's description of the childless Khaḍrā before she conceives the hero also demonstrates how the Egyptian rabāb poets use repetition with variation to construct the story:

> Days after this story happened
> By the life of the Lord of Creation
> Khaḍrā was sitting in misery and pain
> Listen to the order of the story/the lines of the analogy
>
> Ninety days after this story happened
> By the life of the Book of Right Guidance
> Khaḍrā was drinking bitter colocynth
> She saw the girls of Hilāyil
>
> She saw the 90 girls
> Pretty ones the Master formed them
> And they are going up to the Lake of the Birds
> They beseech their Master.
>
> She saw the girls walking
> Pretty ones the Master formed them
> And they are going up to the Lake of the Birds
> Saʿīda and Khaḍrā went up behind them.

Certain lines may be noted which are repeated in their entirety, others that are repeated with only slight variation. These repetitions and variations represent the "formulas" of the oral poet, the flexible patterns or paradigms on which he builds his improvised story-song during his performance—much as he improvises musically on the basis of a number of set melodic motifs. Abnoudy, as noted earlier, uses the Arabic term *miftāḥ* (key) to refer to these essential, repeated ideas which occur in fairly fixed phrases and by which the poets construct the lines of their verses.[15]

The rabāb poet never puts his proposition directly or singly. Sayyid will never say simply, "She went to the lake along with 90 girls because she was grief stricken at not having given her husband an heir." This is the sentence logic of written discourse. Rather, Sayyid refers to the ḥikāya (story): the scene just narrated in which Rizq reproaches his wife for not giving him a baby boy. Passage of time is expressed by a sort of incremental repetition. At the beginning of one quatrain, the poet says "Days after this story happened"; then in the next quatrain, he names the temporal sequence more exactly: "Ninety days after this story happened." Each of these temporal formulas is followed by an oath formula, and then by a line describing Khaḍrā's emotional state. First, she is sitting in misery and pain. Then, in the second quatrain of the passage, the pain is reiterated figurally, that is, as drinking the "bitter colocynth," the bitter apple whose brew, like onions, brings tears.

In this same incremental fashion, Sayyid tells his audience three times, "She saw the girls"; in each line, he varies the fact only slightly to describe the ninety Hilālī girls as they go out for a walk. The poet conveys the information not all at once but additively and incrementally over three quatrains: each subsequent rhyme word further specifies the girls and gradually builds up to the entire thought that ninety Hilālī girls were out walking. Such triple repetition of an action is typical of oral folk epic narration. Olrik terms such tripartite repetition one of the basic "epic laws" of folk narrative.[16]

Egyptian rabāb poets use the two main types of epic narration: (1) a distant third-person, impersonal descriptive narrative of events, combined with (2) a very direct, dramatic presentation of scene through direct discourse between two characters.[17] The rabāb poet in performance typically adds a third form of address to his narration: a second-person direct address by the poet himself to his real audience. The performer frequently greets, admonishes, and exhorts the audience; this sort of direct address brings the listener into the epic narrative scene to see, hear, feel, and act with the characters. The last line of the first quatrain cited above, for example, directly addresses the listener, admonishing him to "listen to the lines of the story." This whole formulaic line is one repeated frequently by all rabāb poets. They use it as a very direct signal to the audience, for such salutations to the audience commonly serve as signals for the listeners to offer the poet a tip for his efforts.[18] As we will hear in the course of our close-listening analysis in the following chapters, these formulas serve also to underscore central meaning and symbolically crucial junctures of the tale.

The larger part of the story narration unfolds as the direct discourse of characters—speeches either in the form of monologues or dialogues. These speeches are introduced by one of the statistically most frequent formulas in the language of epic poets the world over: "yaqūl al-fatā Rizq al-shujāʿ Ibn Nāyil" (Says the lad Rizq, the brave Ibn Nāyil). The formulaic mold or paradigm follows the pattern: *qāla* (he said) + name + epithet. The epithet is formed and deformed to fit the demands of the rhyme at line's end. A similar full-line fixed phrase formula used with great frequency to manipulate dialogue is:

> simaʿ dōlah galb il-fatā-nsarr
>
> he heard these words and the heart of the lad rejoiced.

The poet, of course, varies the basic pattern of the formula to fit different situations: simaʿ (he, she, etc., heard) + object + feeling of the hearer. Both of these formulas exemplify the flexible and ready-made phrases the poet uses to build his story-song. The rabāb poet will repeat a fixed, memorized phrase wherever it is useful in rapid, improvisational performance. He does not seek elegant variation per se; rather, his style is marked by lexical economy and redundancy.[19]

## STORY PATTERNS

The same contrastive structures, parallelisms, and set patterns repeated with slight variation and embellishment which mark the musical and small-scale textural features of the *Hilāliyya* also mark its larger constructional elements. Table 1 schematizes the

TABLE 1

"BIRTH OF ABŪ ZAYD" CHIASTIC STORY PATTERN

LACK (father's lamentation on lack of a son and heir)

LACK LIQUIDATED THROUGH DIVINE INTERVENTION (Mother's wish on bird, conception and birth of a black son)

BROKEN CONTRACT[1]
(Boy unrecognized, miracle unrecognized)
(False accusation of adultery and bastardy)
(Marriage contract annulled and property divided)

DEPARTURE (Khaḍrā's banishment from tribe)

CONFLICT[1] (Khaḍrā the Outcast versus ʿAṭwān the Outlaw)

RECONCILIATION[1] (Zaḥlān intervenes and Khaḍrā takes refuge with his tribe)

BROKEN CONTRACT[2] (Teacher repeats false accusations of adultery and bastardy)

CONFLICT[2] (Hero kills Koranic teacher in revenge)

TRIAL BY DUEL (Teacher's brother meets A.Z. in man-to-man combat)

RECONCILIATION[2] (Acquittal of hero, acclaim as hero of Zaḥlān)

BROKEN CONTRACT[3] (Zaḥlān refuse to pay Banī Hilāl the land tax)

CONFLICT[3] (Zaḥlān versus Banī Hilāl)

TRIAL BY DUEL (A.Z. vs. Rizq in man-to-man combat representing 2 groups)

RECOGNITION/LACK LIQUIDATED (Father and son recognize each other)

RECONCILIATION[3] (Battle thus averted as father claims son and heir Banī Hilāl and Zaḥlān tribes form a confederation)

RETURN (reunited family returns home)

bare bones of the story of the "Birth of Abū Zayd"; it represents the "morphology" of the tale as told in linear sequence. The poet balances various themes in a contrastive antithetical style. In the verbal balancing logic of the epic singer, a contract violated engenders conflict, a departure assumes a return; a conflict, a resolution; an insult, a revenge; a need presumes a quest and an eventual fulfillment; a rupture presupposes a reconciliation. These parallelisms of story sequence are charted in table 1; their chiastic arrangement is indicated with brackets. The story sung by all three rabāb poets follows the same basic pattern. Prince Rizq Ibn Nāyil of the Banī Hilāl tribe, although rich and powerful, grieves because he has failed to beget a son and heir from his marriage to the noble princess Khaḍrā, daughter of the Sharīf of Mecca. As anguished as her husband over this lack of a boy, Khaḍrā goes with the tribe's women on their annual fertility pilgrimage to the lake, where she sees many different colored birds fighting for supremacy. These women are the mothers-to-be of the future Hilālī heroes who will lead their tribe out of the drought and famine afflicting Nejd, their birthplace. The women pray to God and wish on the birds. Each woman vows to conceive a son like the colored bird she favors in the avian struggle. Khaḍrā makes her wish on the big black bird who routs all the others, and she conceives a son that very day. Her pregnancy causes great rejoicing. A boy is born—black. The tribe accuses Khaḍra of adultery with a black slave and her husband, Rizq, dishonored in the eyes of the tribe, banishes her. Their property is divided by lottery and she is sent away, headed in the direction of Mecca and her father.

All three poets tell of the outcast Khaḍrā's journey, how she meets ʿAṭwān the outlaw who guards the border lands between the tribes of Hilāl and Zaḥlān, and how Prince Fāḍil of the Zaḥlān rescues her and takes her in, recognizing her innocence and nobility. Each poet recounts the story of the boy's schooling in the Zaḥlān tribe, and the insults the Koranic schoolteacher levies against the boy's birth and his mother's honor as he teaches the black child the alphabet. The boy murders the schoolmaster as revenge. The poets all follow the same outline of events: the tribe tries the boy, and he battles the teacher's brother. The youth rises to fame and status as a warrior of the Zaḥlān. When the Banī Hilāl demand payment of the annual land tax and the Zaḥlān refuse to pay it, the boy Abū Zayd is sent forth in man-to-man combat as the representative of the Zaḥlān. Thus, the black hero Abū Zayd and Rizq the Hilālī hero meet on the battlefield; father and son recognize each other and reconcile. The two tribes reunite into a large confederation as the family of Rizq, Khaḍrā, and Abū Zayd return home.

The basic story pattern follows the structural rhythm of epic as outlined variously by Campbell, Lord, and Nagler: Departure-Adventure/Conflict-Return.[20] More specifically, the schema around which the Egyptian singers structure their versions of the "Birth of Abū Zayd" might be reduced to the following more or less Proppian[21] morphology:

> / LACK - CONTRACT - BROKEN CONTRACT -
> DEPARTURE - CONFLICT - RECONCILIATION -
> LACK·LIQUIDATED - RETURN /

Of course, what I call "Broken Contract" might, in more strictly Proppian terms, be viewed as some kind of Injunction, Interdiction, or Command and its subsequent Violation—the pattern that constitutes the onset of most folktales. In the "Birth" episode, the lack of a son and heir sets the story in motion. This initial need is almost immediately fulfilled by means of divine intervention at the tribe's annual fertility rite at the Lake of the Birds. God answers Khaḍrā's prayers for a son just like the fierce black bird on which she swears her oath. In fact, God grants her wish in very literal terms, for the boy is born black. The Hilālī tribe does not recognize the boy as legitimate, suspecting the mother of an adulterous affair with a black slave,[22] and thus violates a ritual contract with divine powers. A marriage contract is broken, a family ruptured by the false accusations of adultery and bastardy.

In the chiastic balancing logic of oral poets, the story narrative must put to rights these disrupted spheres, for both the familial group and the political group are thrown into disorder. The subsequent narration reworks this initial problem in the manner typical of folktale. Just as the oral poet constructs the musicopoetic line, so he constructs the larger elements of his tale. Just as he builds up an idea by means of repetitions, pleonastic constructions, and paratactically arranged thoughts with no temporal or logical subordinating connectives between them, so he arranges the sequence of events: three times a contract is broken, three times a conflict erupts, and three times a reconciliation occurs. The first Broken Contract subsumes the second two since a marriage contract of individuals is violated and a miraculous intervention goes unrecognized by the group. The second Broken Contract occurs when the Koranic schoolteacher insults Abū Zayd and his mother. The third variation on the theme takes the form of a confrontation between larger groups, as the Zaḥlān tribe, of which Abū Zayd and his mother are now a part, refuses to pay the Banī Hilāl the land tax due them. Each Broken Contract engenders a Conflict and an eventual Resolution. The individual hero, the young Abū Zayd, acquits his honor on the battlefield in his conflict with the schoolteacher; then, as a representative of the group, the Zaḥlān tribe, the boy meets his father, representing the Hilālī, in man-to-man combat. The recognition of father and son resolves at once the conflict between the two tribes and the initial dilemma generating the drama, the Lack of a son and heir. Recognition on the battlefield restores equilibrium and the status quo to both the larger tribal groups and the family. The episode thus ends with the family returning home, presumably to live happily ever after in the peace established by the confederacy of tribes—at least until famine or some other problem arises and engenders another cycle of Lack-Contract-Violation-Departure-Conflict-Reconciliation-Lack Liquidated-Return, and the next episode of the Hilālī saga.[23]

This is the story of the "Birth of Abū Zayd the Hilālī" as everyone knows it and as everyone in the poet's traditional audience expects to hear it by virtue of having heard it earlier on the occasion of different performances, either by the same or yet another poet. The dramatic presentation of the plot, to borrow from Gizellis's Aristotelian paraphrase of the Parry-Lord theory, is highly structured by virtue of the fact that both performer and audience have internalized it.[24] People infer that episodes follow a given sequence and that motifs within the episode also follow a given sequence. This pattern of prior expectation on the part of both poet and listener provides the schema around which the individual performer elaborates his interpretation of the traditional poem.[25] The smaller-scale formulaic phraseology or "language" the poet uses to construct his musically told tale is highly conventional. The poet eschews "originality" in the interests of authenticity and truth. Shamandī's performance was beyond the limits of the permissible because the famous nightclub artist innovated too much. His instrumentally elaborated interpretation violated the audience's sense of decorum. What he gave us was not "probable" within the boundaries of what is traditionally known as the *Hilāliyya*. The episode did not lead anywhere in the narrative sense. It formed the part of no greater whole, nor did it serve to interpret the meaning of the greater sīra. The poet's aimless repetition of formulaic refrains fitted into no greater story frame and thus the performance violated the audience's sense of the probable. Based on these violations of decorum, Shamandī, although a famous, respected rabāb artist whom the people recognized and were honored to meet, lost his audience in the context of singing the *Hilāliyya*.

Fārūq, in contrast, observed the expected decorum. Comparison of Fārūq's performance with those of two acknowledged masters of the tradition, however, indicates that even within the highly conventional, highly stylized formal patterns and chiastic structures and melodic phrases that emerge as stock features in a performance, each poet also has a distinct personal style. On hearing the poets, the listener is immediately struck by the individuality of interpretive style. Jābir, Sayyid, and Fārūq, for example, give quite different emphasis and interpretation to the story of the birth of the Hilālī leader. Each in his unique way exploits the argumentative potentialities of the traditional media of rabāb and voice, story and poetry. Each has mastered to varying degrees the traditional components of his oral, improvisatory art. Each has his own style of recasting the argumentative logic and textural embellishments of the formulaic language, story patterns, and melodic motifs.

Musical ornamentation is a mark of personal style and, as such, sets up an implicit contract with the audience. The listener immediately notices great differences among the poets on at least two levels, for each projects a distinct musical ethos or "energy" and each has his own performance mode. Al-Sayyid al-Ḍūwī, a forty-year-old professional musician of great fame throughout Egypt, performs the epic in the orchestral style typical of the Egyptian musical milieu,[26] while Jābir Abū Ḥasayn sings with his brother Ḥasan accompanying him on the rabāb and Fārūq ʿAbd al-ʿAzīz sings and plays solo.

The sīra tradition historically has always been a solo phenomenon. Eighteenth- and nineteenth-century accounts of the shāʿir al-rabāba in Egypt show him performing a solo, accompanying his own voice with *rabābat al-shāʿir* (poet's viol), a one-stringed, square sound box instrument.[27] The observer today finds the performance mode relatively changed. While nineteenth-century transcriptions of the melodic motifs and phrases from the Abū Zayd epic are the same heard today, the instrument itself is different. The poets I observed all use a two-stringed rabāb.[28] Jābir and Sayyid are accompanied by the horsehair string, coconut shell sound box rabāb described by Canova,[29] while Fārūq's instrument is a simple wooden affair with metal strings.

Fārūq, the forty-year-old itinerant musician, sang his version of the "Birth of Abū Zayd" in the more traditional solo mode. The first day he arrived in our living room from the street he had a tambourine player with him, and as he began his rendition of the epic, she accompanied him. He soon signaled her to be silent, however, and thereafter performed alone. Egyptian gypsy women frequently sing and dance professionally.[30] Fārūq earns more money playing popular music at weddings and parties, so he rarely anticipates singing the epic; thus the woman accompanied him until he indicated it was inappropriate. On subsequent days, he came alone to sing the sīra for our household. In performance, Fārūq often seemed remote, with his eyes closed, his face and neck straining with the effort; at other times, he seemed congenial, but for the most part slightly passive and distant.

Sayyid, in contrast, surrounded by three other rabāb artists and a drummer, presents himself as an energetic, zestful performer. He flourishes his rabāb as his eyes flash and maintain almost constant contact with his audience. His musical style is flashy, more decorated and varied than Fārūq's. It has the flavor of Cairo movie and nightclub popular music even though the poet uses the same three or four traditional Hilālī tunes Fārūq does. Sayyid and Fārūq both stay with one tonal center. Sayyid, however, varies his music more, frequently modifying his basic tunes or switching from one to another, thereby creating a greater liveliness.

Poets normally, as noted above, use three melodies to do their work for them: an initial, reciting, and final tune. Fārūq, however, has no initial melody. This may well account for the "sudden" quality of his narrative song—he seems to "plunge" in, and his opening lines are irregular from almost every point of view. In addition, he varies the pace or tempo very little: his song remains consistently rapid. In conjunction with frequent syncopations (rhythmic disruptions in which an accent falls on a normally unaccented beat or part of a beat), this rapidity gives a forward momentum to the performance. Fārūq really only warms up musically after about twenty lines. His opening quatrains use a single melodic pattern for each line—his "reciting" melody (see the Appendix for a musical transcription of his basic melodies). Only in line 20 does he use the final melody for the first time to mark a couplet. He settles into what will become his standard couplet format only in lines 28 to 39, that is, four quatrains, or a few minutes, into the narrative. With few exceptions, he often sings in couplets, occasionally repeating half the melody to accommodate an odd line. Once he has warmed up and found his stride, he repeats the "reciting" melody over and over, replacing it with a "final" melody for the last couplet of a section of quatrains. He shapes his performance and demarcates musical sections ranging in length from one quatrain to three or four quatrains with such use of the "final" melody along with rabāb interludes. The rabāb plays the same "reciting" and "final" melodies contained in the vocal, but uses the "Abū Zayd" tunes as the usual instrumental interlude.

Sayyid employs all three basic vocal melodies plus the "Abū Zayd" tune to give coherence and structure to his performance. His singing has a sureness and authority from the onset, as rabāb interacts with voice not only to mark off sections but also to underscore important meaning. Sayyid typically repeats the last line of quatrains. Jābir's performance, like Sayyid's, is marked by a great deal of variety. He too continually explores and exploits the musical resources of his media. A very old man who had recently been ill when he recorded this episode, Jābir had his brother Ḥasan accompany him in this performance. Jābir used to perform solo. His musical ethos is one of dignity and authority. Unlike the other two poets, he does not stay with a single pitch center throughout the performance. The initial tonal center established in the taqsīm provides a reference point to which Jābir always returns, but at least two other pitches serve for a while as tonal centers. The poet frequently varies the regularity, accentuation, and speed of the pulse. His brother's rabāb technique usually flows with unobtrusive bowing and moderate ornamentation. This main style alternates with at least two other clearly distinguishable styles: a detached style in which each note is clearly marked and which has little ornamentation; and a double-bowing technique that creates a more rapid pulsation. Voice and rabāb may be heterophonic—that is, performing approximately the same melody—or they may alternate, with a vocal phrase followed by an instrumental phrase. In spoken sections, Jābir's speech is punctuated with short rhythmic or melodic motifs of the rabāb; the vocal melody may also be supported by sustained rabāb pitches.

Jābir characteristically often alters one or more of the musical elements. For instance, he sings a given melodic formula several times with a gradual increase in speed and commensurate increase in accentuation of the pulse until a point is reached at which the speed suddenly decreases; then the pulse becomes irregular and the singer pauses before either starting the process over again or switching to a different melodic pattern. At such points, the tonal center as well as the relationship between voice and rabāb may be changed. In other words, Jābir frequently changes several of the musical elements at once in shaping his performance.

With few exceptions, every line of Jabīr's performance can be classified as a variant of one of a small number of melodic patterns. Each pattern or formula is one or two text lines long and is characterized by a specific pitch contour (pattern of ascending and descending melodic motion), pitch center, phrase length, rhythmic pattern, and instrumental interlude or tail played on the rabāb.

Significantly, Jābir does not combine these formulas in totally haphazard fashion. Rather, he repeats a given formula at least three or four times (sometimes many more times) before switching to another. Thus, sections are created by the musical unity of a repeated formula. Jābir's repetitions, however, are not mechanical, but always involve some variation ranging from minute alterations to rather extensive changes in duration, pitch, and so forth. The basic contour remains clear despite these changes.

The poet sings most of the text in a "standard" melody that is fast, syllabic, and fairly rhythmic. Long sections consist only of this melody with or without rabāb interludes. Such sections always seem to increase in intensity up to a certain point. Then the pace suddenly slows, Jābir may chant a few lines and revert to a slower melody, much freer rhythmically, with florid mellismas. This is his initial melody by which he introduced his first two quatrains and which echoes the melody of the Invocation. Melody type 3 seems to be a transitional melody and has a strikingly different rhythm. After it, he typically returns to the so-called standard melody.

The musical persona of the poet, the kind of energy and dynamism he projects in performance, as well as variations in personal musicianship and talent, produce distinctly different effects in performance, different reactions from the audience, and ultimately a different final product, a uniquely individual shaping and conception of the traditional poem. The total ethos of the singer in performance, his stance toward his audience and his subject matter—in short, his personality and presence as a performer—emerge to communicate a very personal vision of the epic tale. His intelligence and personal experience also shape the voice behind the interpretation given his particular re-creation of the tale.

It is this question of individual voice, tonality, craft, and vision which I will examine in three versions of the story of the birth of the Banī Hilāl leader and hero, Abū Zayd, recorded from oral performances. My intention is to hear and to interpret what the poet's audience was meant to hear and understand. My questions are: How do the poets intend their songs to be experienced? And how does each poet give his own unique shaping to the epic, at once musically, poetically, and dramatically? Within such a highly conventional medium as oral epic song, what is the potentiality for individual creativity and intention?[31] How does the poet's musical "presence" or ethos persuade audiences to hear and rehear time and again the immemorial verse of the sīra? In short, how does today's generation of individual poets transmit the traditional poetic history in such a way as to make it ever relevant to the moral and psychological concerns of the present community? How does a "collective text" sustain the communal ethos and thereby retain a twentieth-century audience?

To answer some of these questions, I propose a close listening analysis that will reveal (1) the individual shāʿir's opening contract with his audience, (2) his mode of story exposition, (3) his manipulation of point of view, (4) his use of formulas, and (5) his poetic texture and use of small-scale rhetorical features. As Bloch tells us in his analysis of medieval French *chansons de geste,* the farther back in the genealogy of the epic heroes an episodic cycle goes, the more recent is the genesis of the tale itself.[32] In light of this reverse chronology and in answer to some of my questions, I propose to listen to the "first" episodes of the *Hilāliyya,* the story of the birth and origins of the Hilālī heroes Abū Zayd, Diyāb, and Ḥasan.

Jabir Abū Ḥusayn
Typical melodies from first part of performance. (Before Murabba^c)

Jabir Abū Ḥusayn
Murabbaᶜ Melodies

Fārūq ᶜAbd al-ᶜAzīz
1. regular couplet ("reciting" melody)
ba-da-wī aṣ-ṣul-lah__ na-ḍī-fa
a-rūḥ fīn hu-wa ā-jū fīn______
2. concluding couplet ("final" melody)
da-sha-ka min ba-lā____ wī kha fī-feh
wi-luh dam ᶜi nā-zil ṣa-bā' īb
Sayyid al-Ḍuwī
Tune 1
ṣa lā tin__ na-bī ti-za-ww-id__ dir-rizq____
Tune 2
wi-m qā rib__ ᶜīd ra-ma ḍān___
Type 3
Type 3
qāl__ rab-bi-nā jād bi-rrizq la ᶜa mil fa-raḥ lil___ hi-lā-yel

# 5
# MUSICAL METAPHOR AND POETIC COMPETENCE

The opening is particularly important in orally performed narration, for it is there that the poet sets up his contract with the audience and orients himself. The instrumental taqsīm (introduction improvised on the rabāb) announces the presence of the performer and attracts attention to him, signaling in the tune he strikes up that he is about to begin singing the *Hilāliyya*. In the first five to ten minutes of the narration, the poet, whether explicitly or implicitly, consciously or unconsciously, establishes his purpose, states his intention, and tells his audience what they may expect from listening to his song. He sets up the pattern, the expectations that will be fulfilled on various levels. These contracts made with the listener may be overt announcements of intent or they may be subtler ones at the level of use of music or language, the poetic or musical diction of the performance, the cognitive style, the use of verse forms, figures of speech, or other salient stylistic and ornamental features. In the opening, the poet also establishes his stance toward both his subject matter and his audience, the ethos that will in large measure determine the voice he gives to the sīra, the larger understanding he will offer his listener of the 900-year-old traditional tale of the migration of the ancestors.

## CLOSE LISTENING ANALYSIS[1]

### *Fārūq ʿAbd al-ʿAzīz's Opening*

Fārūq begins his song with an eight-line mawwāl then quickly introduces two other types of verse—rhymed prose and quatrains rhymed *abab* (murabbaʿāt):

Khaḍrā begot the one whose uncle is Muṣṭafá
Rizq swore, "This boy is not mine.
He is not mine, and I won't keep him.
How many times did you drink, O Khaḍrā, from the bowl of bitterness my vinegar?"
She called to the tribe of Zaḥlān, and they came swiftly
She said to them; "I am a girl, and I have no status among the Arabs.
I have taken you, O Zaḥlān
to support the child in a noble upbringing, until he can ride horses

[rhymed prose]
Prince Rizq Ibn Nāyil on a feast day was sitting in King Sirḥān's tent
Every Bedouin had come, bringing along his own son by the hand and entering the tent
When Prince Rizq saw them, he became angry and he became irritated and worried,
For he was without a child. He kept on reciting, "Bless Ṭāhā the prophet."

[murabbaʿ]
After my éloge to the prophet
Aḥmad, the one whose path is clear,
Or I should say a Chosroes and continue
The Arabs remember before this

The sīra of the ancient Arabs,
They were people afraid of blame
Their leader is a strong and powerful lion.
He is called al-Hilālī Salāmah.

Praising the Prophet increased my zeal.
The Prophet is beautiful and has a strong light.
Hear these words of mine about the nobles.
Brave Rizq called Ibn Nāyil.

He has closed his tent since evening.
Difficulties made his load heavy.

This one complained from hidden distress.
He has tears pouring down.

He cries with tears of his eyes,
A Bedouin whose roots are clean.
"Where shall I go? Where do I come from?
And I am without an heir."

(Da) Khaḍara jābit ṭilb *yub'ā-l-Muṣṭafá* a) *Khallīh* [2x] or b) *Khāl līh*—(spoken) yub'ā Khālu
(= and Khaḍrā gave birth to Tilb, *may al-Muṣṭafá, i.e., Muḥammad, keep him alive and well;* or b) *al-Muṣṭafá, i.e., Muḥammad, is a maternal uncle to him.*)
Ḥilif Rizg il-walad da mā hū waladī
Mā hū waladī wa-lā-khallīh
Yā mā shiribtī yā Khaḍara min kās il-marār khallī
Da nadmit ᶜala-z-Zaḥlān bil-ᶜajal jāhā
Gālitlu: Anā wilīyyah wa-lā lī fil-ᶜArab jāh[a]
Anā khadtak yā Zaḥlān
Lil-walad jāhā fī rbāyit il-ᶜizzi lammā nirkab il-khilli

=
[rhymed prose]
(spoken sajᶜ)
Ammā-l-Amīr Rizg ibn Nāyil, kān yōm mawsam, wa-gaᶜad fi-ṣwān il-Malik Sarḥān /
Wa-kulli-wāḥad yījī mn-il-bawādī w-hūwa jāyib ibno f-'īdo w-dākhil aṣ-ṣwān /
Fa-lammā shāfhum il-Amir Rizg fa-ḥaṣal ᶜando ghēẓ wa-ḥaṣal ᶜando nakad wa-ziᶜil /
Innih kān galīl il-khalīfah, wa-mā zāl yinshid yagūl ṣallū ᶜalā Ṭāhā-r-rasūl

=
[murabbaᶜ]
Baᶜdi madīḥī fil-mukammal
Aḥmad abū darb-i sālik
Wi-lā-gūl "Kisrah" wa-kammil
ᶜArab yizkarū gabli zālik

Sīrit ʿArab agdamīyīn
Kānū nās yikhshū-l-malāmah
Ra'īs-hum asās sabʿi wi-matīn
Yisammā-l-Hilālī Salāmah

The poet announces his intention openly and directly after an abbreviated invocation. His contract with the audience is clear. He will tell them the sīra of the ancient Arabs as the Arabs have recalled it before. The audience is asked to listen to these words of the poet about the noble ones, about brave Rizq Ibn Nāyil specifically. Less explicit are the other understandings Fārūq makes with his listener by means of an unvaried musical pulse, the verse form, and the logic of his exposition of the subject, as well as his position vis-à-vis the subject, the position he invites his audience to take toward the subject, and his position toward the audience.

Fārūq's song begins abruptly, after a brief taqsīm. Instead of opening with an invocation praising the Prophet as is conventionally done by most singers, he thrusts immediately into the middle of the narrative. As we have mentioned, in contrast to most singers, he uses no initial melody. His narrative style thus parallels his musical style: music and verse have a fragmentary, disjointed quality that will be paralleled in the presentation of events. Throughout his 2,373-line version of the "Birth of Abū Zayd," the poet rarely varies the rapid pulse of the music he establishes at the onset. After Fārūq sings the opening mawwāl and declaims the rhymed prose, he produces a narrative that will progress unexceptionally in quatrains, rhymed *abab*. Fārūq's condensed presentation of the subject in the opening vignette assumes a great deal about the audience's prior knowledge of the sīra and of the coming episode.

The first line is difficult to understand. The crux of the action to come is contained in his first three lines—all the pain, all the tension that will make the story. Elliptically and referentially, the poet presents the hero, Abū Zayd, through the opening-line periphrasis, "The one whose uncle is Muṣṭafá." The hero's holy lineage, his descent from the Prophet, thus stands for the whole man. Khaḍrā, Rizq, and the Zaḥlān also crowd immediately in the fore. In the opening outburst of song and story, it is often difficult to know who is speaking to whom. Fārūq uses here, as he will throughout the brief tale, pronouns of pronomial suffixes contained in verbs with no clear antecedent. The sixth line of the poem uses the subject "she" as contained in the suffix of the verb *nadmit* (she regretted). "She," we understand implicitly, must be Khaḍrā, mentioned in the first line, though she is not speaking to Rizq, who gave voice to the second and possibly the fifth line, but to the Zaḥlān tribe. The audience must bring this knowledge to the poet's prologue.

After this dramatic but summary sketch of what is to come, the narrative backs up and fills in the specific detail of the scene prior to the prologue. The scene, declaimed in chanted rhymed prose, unfolds progressively. The verbs are participial forms. The poet puts Rizq before us as he is sitting in the king's tent on a feast day and the other men of the tribe are entering the tent, bringing their sons by the hand. The poet's voice declaiming the rhymed prose lines reinforces the unfolding, happening quality of the event; each phrase ends with a rising pitch that suspends the scene being built, suggesting to the ear that there is more to come. And there is. For the vocal rising pattern is broken and a declarative downward cadence substituted when Rizq sees the men with their male sons and his feelings of worry, anger, and irritation break through, to disrupt the ongoing scene. These feelings engender the story to follow. As the audience knows, Abū Zayd, the great hero of the Banī Hilāl tribe, will be born a black man, banished by his father as a bastard only to rise and lead his people from lands of famine and hunger to the promised land of the West.

Continuing into the murabbaᶜ verse form that the Egyptian rabāb poets use as the main narrative vehicle for the song, the poet uses mixed verb tenses; he employs both the complete and incomplete aspect. He thereby moves in and out of the scene: now an objective, slightly distant, third-person narrator of a past event and again a close participant immersed in a present, ongoing scene of words and acts.[2] Noun sentences, too, heighten the presence and immediacy of the scene. Fārūq also brings forward the scene he is building with his use of demonstrative pronouns that point directly to his subject: "this one complained" (*dī shakat*), "This one said (*dī gālit*), "hear these words of mine" (*'ismaᶜ gūlī dā*), or "this here boy" (*il-walad da*). He thus takes a familiar stance toward his audience. He makes himself one of them through his choice of everyday vernacular language, albeit in the verse and formulaic castings of the traditional way of telling the sīra.

### *Al-Sayyid al-Ḍūwī's Opening Contract with the Audience*

The forty-three-year-old professional musician, al-Sayyid al-Ḍūwī, establishes this same direct, close relationship with his audience. His diction level, too, is very colloquial. He uses, for example, as a frequent formulaic phrase beginning a line, the common Egyptian expression *yaʿnī* (you know, so then). The opening of his version of the story also places him, the narrator, along with the audience members, close to the action and scene. Sayyid and the three rabāb artists who make up the group of itinerant musicians with whom he performs, preface his rendition of the "Birth of Abū Zayd" with a taqsīm. In the midst of the improvised musical introduction, the poet calls out to his patron, ʿAbd al-Raḥmān al-Abnoudy, "What do you want to hear? Abū Zayd or Abū Hilāl?" Abnoudy responds, "The Birth of Abū Zayd."[3] And then the rabābas set the musical tempo of the ṣalāt (blessing):

[murabbaʿ]
The blessings of the Prophet of course increase the sustenance
 The burdens of the tribulation are not light
I compose my speech about King Rizq
 And his wife Khaḍrā the sharīfah (= direct descendant of the Prophet Muḥammad)
Rizq Ibn Nāyil was unhappy/dominant
 A man with light clothes
Eleven years he did not get a child
 But his wife was Khaḍrā the sharīfah

=

[prose]
Rizq Ibn Nāyil begot a girl, Shīḥa, early.
He spent eleven years without having a boy,
Waiting patiently for years and nights for the promise of the Merciful One.
Until the feast of Ramaḍān was drawing near.

=

[murabbaʿ]
And the feast of Ramaḍān drew near
His mind became aware of this

He put on his clothes, the Sultan,
And he entered the dīwān of al-Duraydi
ya ʿaynī . . .
And he entered the dīwān of al-Duraydi

[prose]
Rizq Ibn Nāyil, that is; so on the feast day he changed his clothes,
The man with the shawl to his summit tilting
And he rode his thoroughbred onto the heaps [of white cotton]
And he entered the dīwān of the king of the Halāyil.
This king is who? His brother calls him Sirḥān
And, of course, he is entering, and coming to wish a merry feast to the Arabs.
To wish a merry feast to the chiefs and the men and the four tribes
For it is the feast of ʿĪd al-Fiṭr, and it is his duty
The leader of the Arabs is he . . . and he entered the dīwān

=

[murabbaʿ]
On a floating [horse] that doesn't anchor
By the life of the Book of Right Guidance
Everyone of those sitting on chairs
Stood up for the son of Nāyil
ya ʿaynī . . .
stood up for the son of Nāyil

Ṣalāt in-nabī ṭabʿan tizawwid ir-rizq
Ḥumūl il-balā' mish khafīfeh
Awḍaʿ khiṭābī ʿalā-l-Malik Rizq
Wa-murātuh Khaḍrā-l-sharīfeh
Rizq ibni-Nāyil kān ṭaghyān
Rājil hidūmuh khafīfeh
Ḥidāshir sanah mā jābish ʿiyāl
Lākin murātuh Khaḍrā-l-sharīfeh

=

[prose]

Rizq ibni-Nāyil kān bakkar bi-Shīḥā
Wi-gaʿad ḥidāshir saneh wa-mā jābish ghulām
Wa-fī-s-sinīn wi-l-layālī wa-ṣābir ʿalā waʿd ir-Ruḥmān
Illā mu'ātī wi-mgārib ʿīd Ramaḍān

=

[murabbaʿ]

Wi-mgārib ʿīd Ramaḍān
Il-ʿagli minnuh dirē di
Wa-libis hidūmuh-s-sulṭān
Dakhal dīwān id-Dirēdī
  Yā ʿēnī yā ʿēnī yā ʿēnī āh [2x]
  Dākhil dīwān id-Dirēdī

[prose]

Yaʿnī Rizq ibni-Nāyil: wa-yōm il-ʿīd ghayyar il-malābīs
Abū shāl ʿal-garni māyil
Wa-rikib Kaḥēluh ʿalā-l-karābīs
Wa-dakhal fī dīwān malik il-Halāyil
Illī hūwa-l-malik mīn? Yisammī akhūh Sirḥān
Wa-ṭabʿan dākhil u-ḥādir yiʿayyid ʿal-ʿArab
Wa-akābruh wa-rijāluh wa-arbaʿ qabīlāt yiʿayyid ʿalēhum
Dā ʿĪd il-Fiṭr wa-yūjab ʿalēh
Zaʿīm il-ʿArab hūwa . . . wa-dakhal id-dīwān

=

[murabbaʿ]

ʿAlā ʿāyima-llī mā tirsī [2x]
Wa-ḥayāt Kitāb il-Dalāyil
ʿAdad min gāʿid-luh ʿalā kursī
Wagaf li-wald-in-Nāyil
  Ya ʿēnī yā ʿēnī yā ʿēnī āh [2x]
  Wagaf li-wald-in-Nāyil

Compared to Fārūq's, the music and verse of Sayyid's opening are extremely varied. Musically, for example, he repeats the last line of each quatrain with an interspersed nonsense line (ya ʿēnī . . .). Sayyid interprets the first eight-line poem (rhymed *abbabcbcb*) in a slow, stately rhythm and tone, as he announces his subject and his intention to "explain" his *khiṭāb* (public address) about King Rizq and his wife Khaḍrā. Four lines of unrhymed, rhythmic prose, declaimed in a rising voice pattern to the sustaining note of the rabāb, repeat what will be the dilemma that makes the tale. This prose fills in the background detail, recapitulating in the adding style typical of oral epic song, the sad fate of Prince Rizq, who has no son after eleven years of marriage.

The rabāb then moves into the tune that all three poets use to accompany quatrains, and the scene moves forward. Narrator and listener are participants in the scene, as present participles and nominal sentences foreground the figure of Rizq preparing to celebrate the feast of Ramaḍān. The poet fixes on Rizq's state for three lines, then shifts from incomplete to complete verb forms and moves the character into action. The rabāb signals with its sustaining motif more declaimed prose, and once again the poet brings the scene forward into the present; he repeats with additive variation the action of lines 16–20, elaborating the arrival of Rizq at his leader's tent. The present, ongoing quality of the scene depicted is doubly argued as the rabāb's sustaining note reinforces the rising, suspended pattern of the voice declaiming in active participles the state of the character.

Sayyid will continue his narration of the story in this same varied style, in which rabāb and voice highlight vivid and visually immediate, well-detailed scenes. The lucidity and amplitude of his presentation contrasts with Fārūq's rapid, condensed, and generally vague exposition of the same events. Fārūq's narrative develops in a monotonous, unvaried, unembellished instrumental style that parallels his unvaried use of quatrains as the main story-telling vehicle. As Sayyid has promised, he will explain, elucidate, and make clear to us his address. His logical exposition of the story typically argues from a general statement (such as "Rizq was unhappy") to specific causes (as "Eleven years he did not get a child"). In this progression from the abstract situation to concrete details of action, Sayyid's tone is never preaching, never moralizing. He maintains the position of the detached third-person, impersonal narrator observing the scene. The situation is always exposed clearly and fully to the listener in the paratactic adding style of his verses.

Fārūq, however, from his very opening lines employs abundant full-line epithets of a judgmental and evaluative quality, commenting on the character or the action, expressing his point of view and his values. Sayyid's logical development typically presents a general gnomic whole-line formulaic statement, such as "the burdens of tribulation are not light," then demonstrates it. Fārūq uses this same full-line formula over and over, almost as a refrain to pound home his idea. Sayyid's narrative permits the actions of the character to tell the tale. Fārūq generally gives a scene that is confused (as his opening is) and then attempts to clarify it with a pronouncement of a broad cultural truism.

The two poets implicitly contract with their audience to do very different things. Fārūq's listener must fill in a great deal of narrative detail; the poet's confused rush of thoughts tumbling out on the rapidly humming rabāb never really get sorted out in the exposition of the tale. Sayyid, in contrast, does not depend so heavily on the audience's prior knowledge of the story to provide the missing links in his logic or to comprehend the specific meaning of broad formulations. He specifies the details of the scene unfolding in music and words.

## *Jābir Abū Ḥusayn's Opening*

Jābir Abū Ḥusayn exploits to its fullest the potentiality of the medium of rabāb and voice telling a story.[4] He brings to his narration of the tale all the solid authority and dignity of his years. The nearly seventy-year-old singer opens his version in the leisurely, fully amplified style that the listener will come to expect of him at all levels of the performance—in music, both instrumental and vocal, in poetry, and in story development. After a lengthy taqsīm on the rabāb which strikes up the familiar theme of *Sīrat Banī Hilāl* and thereby announces to the audience the musician's intention to sing the sīra, Jābir begins his version in praise of God and the Prophet:

1 The Merciful One did not create the likes of Muḥammad
The Prophet of Right Guidance came to us in all peace
2 God bless you, O banner of Right Guidance
O light of the eyes, O purity of the Merciful One
3 I pray for the one who said: O Lord of my nation,
Ṭāhā, who honored the Banī ʿAdnān
4 The slave was disappointed who did not bless the prophet
Ṭāhā who brought the proof.
5 After my glorifying thc beauty of Muḥammad
Hear the words of my poetry and odes
6 Says the lad Rizq the brave son of Nāyil:
Outrage of nights, who has confused mankind
7 I trusted you, O Fate, and you cheated me
And I never expected time to be a cheat
8 Why do you cheat me, O Fate, breaking my bones?
My tears have been released, rending my eyelids
9 O slaves of God, O deviation of time
You see the delusive one's nature is cheating
10 I cry for separation and for what happened
My tears wet the ground as a flood
11 For what happened to me, O woe is my heart for what happened
I wonder if I will sit with my friends
12 I cry for the days with painful eye
Lack of an heir has crushed me in my place.
13 I am the one whom separation has afflicted, and distance
I complain to my Lord, the One, the Merciful
14 We were on high, but our time has laid us low [2x]
We became weak and the noble humiliated
15 Oh, how we laughed [3x] and crying was for others
And now today we cry and our enemy is happy
16 If the days of happiness and joy would return [2x]
I would ride on a filly and hurl a lance
17 And I would let the Bedouin girls let down their hair
And I would let our enemies' blood into a flooded canal
18 And I would beat the drums of happiness before our door
And I would say: a powerful and compassionate God has provided for me

[rhymed prose]
19 When the prince Rizq Ibn Nāyil finished his words
20 And completed the theme of his lines
21 And his sadness and his woe and his grief increased
22 For lack of an heir and children
23 He cried and his crying from troubles increased
24 And he began to chant and to say
25 Praise be to Ṭāhā the Prophet

[murabbaᶜ]
26 I became old and my back was bent
From God derives benefit
27 I cried for my troubles and felt sad
In my house there's no clever boy
28 (I search with my eyes) [2x] right and left
For a boy to entertain me / babble to me
29 Night came to me black, and disaster
You are able, O Lord, to give me

1 Lam yakhluqi-r-Raḥmānu misla Muḥammadin
Nabīyu-l-hudā jānā bi-kulli amān
2 Ṣallā ᶜalayka-ḷḷāhu yā ᶜalama-l-hudā
Yā nūri-l-ᶜuyūni yā Ṣafwati-r-Raḥmān
3 Aṣallī ᶜalā man qāla yā rabbi ummatī
Ṭāhā-lladhī sharraf Banī ᶜad(i)nān
4 Qad khāba ᶜabdun lā yuṣallī ᶜalā-n-nabī
Ṭāhā-lladhī qad(i) jā'a bi-l-burhān
5 Baᶜdi tamjīdī fī jamāli Muḥammad
Iṣghā kalām shiᶜrī maᶜ il-qiṣdān
6 Yaqūl il-fatā Rizq ish-shajīᶜ-ibni-Nāyil
Jūr il-layālī ḥayyar il-insān
7 Āmintu lak yā dahr wa-rajaᶜta khuntanī
Wa-lā kān ḥisābī innu-z-zamān khawwān
8 Bitkhūnnī lēh yā dahru tiksirnī fi-l-ᶜiẓām
Khallēt dumūᶜī mazzaqū-l-ajfān
9 A-lā yā ᶜibādi-ḷḷahi yā maylati-z-zamān
Tarīhā-l-gharūrah ṭabaᶜhā khawwān
(Yā yā ᶜēn, yā ᶜēn, āh)

10 Abkī ʿalā-l-furqah wa-ʿalā ḥēth mā jarā
Damʿī sarā balla-l-arāḍī ṭīfān
11 ʿAlā mā jarā lī yā wayḥa qalbī li-mā jarā
Yā hun tarā agʿud maʿa-l-ikhwān
(Yā lēl, yā lēl, āh)
12 Ab(i)kī ʿala-l-ayyām bi-ʿaynin wajīʿatin-āh
ʿAdam il-khalīfah haddinī fī makān
13 Anā-lladhī qad(i) ṣābanī-l-bēn wi-n-nāy
Ashkū li-rabbī wāḥidun raḥmān
(Yā lēl, yā lēl, āh yā lēlī, ana āh)
14 Kunnā bi-rifʿatin qad khafaḍnā zamānanā [2x]
Ṣabbaḥnā azillah wi-l-ʿazīz it'hān
(Yā lēl āh)
15 (Yā mā ḍaḥiknā) [3x] w-kān al-bukā ʿinda ghayrinā
W-ādī-l-yōm bakēnā w-khiṣminā farḥān
(Yā lēlāh)
16 In ʿādat il-iyyāmi bi-l-farḥi wa-l-hanā [2x]
Arkab ʿalā-l-muhrah w-aṭawwaḥ zān
17 W-akhallī banāt il-badū tirkhī shuʿūrahā
W-akhallī dimā-l-aʿdā qanā ṭīfān
18 W-adugg(i) ṭabl-il-farḥ giddām bābnā
W-agūl ʿaṭānī mugtadir raḥmān

=

[rhymed prose]
19 Fa-lammā faragh al-amīr Rizq ibni-Nāyil min kalāmo
20 Wa-tamma maʿnā niẓāmo
21 Wa-zāda bihi wa-ḥasrato wa-ghulbo wa-ālāmo
22 ʿAlā ʿadam il-khalīfah wi-l-awlād
23 Bakā wa-bukā'u fi-l-balāwī zād
24 Wa-ṣāra yanshidu wa-yaqūl
25 Ṣallū ʿalā Ṭāhā-r-rasūl

=

[murabbaʿ]
26 Balaghanī-l-kibar yā ḍahrī wi-ḥanet
Min Allāh tiqḍā-l-maṣāliḥ
27 Bakēt ʿalā-l-balāwī wa-ḥannēt
Fī bētī mā fīsh ṭifli fāliḥ

28 (Balūj bi-ᶜēnī) [2x] yamīn wa-shimāl
ᶜAla ṭifl ᶜandī yilāghīnī
29 Jātnī-l-layālī sōda wa-shummāl
Qādir yā rabbī anta tuᶜṭīnī

Unlike the other two poets, Jābir makes his invocation more than a token offering, spoken as a formulaic line. God, the Prophet, the collectivity of the Arab Nation, the praising poet, and the listening audience (who together are part of the Nation—"we") are mentioned in order. This mention is not coincidental, but expresses at once the historical framework within which the events will be revealed and the poet's tone, his attitude toward both his subject and his audience. His elevated diction, with the case endings and vocalization of High Classical Arabic, linguistically separates him from his listener; it raises his voice to partake of that heard daily throughout the Muslim world, through the centuries, calling the Word of God from the minaret. The poet thus links himself to the listener through the sacred words, the sacred language intoned to the community at large to which both poet and audience lend their ears and presumably submit. His authority firmly established, Jābir then calls for his listener to bend to, to lean to, to heed (*iṣghā*) his words.

Like Sayyid and Fārūq, Jābir almost immediately brings a character on the scene to introduce the emotional dilemma of the story. Rizq's lines make up part of the invocation poem as he laments his fate and complains to God what a disappointment (cheat) it is to have no son and heir. Jābir's music, thought, and verse highlight and detail Rizq's pain and humiliation, the immediate impetus for the story action, while introducing what will be major themes of the epic tale. When the character Rizq speaks directly to the audience, the diction level becomes that of colloquial Egyptian. The lamentation molecularly builds the basic idea of the story to come: Rizq's lack of a child. The introduction also presents the story's major premises in commonplaces of Egyptian folk wisdom concerning the vagaries of fate, happiness and hardship, and man's relationship to his God. The rabāba and voice musically anticipate thematic elements and underscore certain notions and words. Lines 14–18, for example, all deal in some way with the no-win, zero-sum game of fate, an important idea that will run throughout the story. The poet signals the importance of this attitude as he twice repeats line 14, "We were on high, but our time laid us low," embellishing the verse with the syllables "aaahhaa, aaahaa" (colloquial Egyptian for "alas"), sung in between. The poem is monorhymed in [ān], the end-rhyme of the b-hemistich made more salient by the frequent first hemistich end-word terminating in [nā]. The ornamental syllables echo the assonance of these end-rhymes. The breathy nasality of the rhymes lends a painful, lamenting, sobbing tonality to the passage.

With line 16, the music of the rabāb changes. A strong, insistently stressed beat resounds. The verse line "If the days of happiness and joy would return" is repeated as the instrument strikes twelve stressed notes between the repeated lines. This instrumentalization not only serves to reinforce the wish; it also serves to anticipate a change that is about to occur in the verse form and mode of narration. The rabāb maintains the new musical beat through line 36 and the end of the monorhymed poem. Eight beats of the rabāb then signal the transition from qaṣīda to seven lines of rhymed prose. The prose, like that of Fārūq and Sayyid, recapitulates the reason for the hero's misery in a declamatory style, accompanied by the sustaining note of the rabāba. Then the instrument again picks up the pulse and tune introduced at the end of the qaṣīda and the poet begins to sing the murabbaʿāt, or quatrains, that will provide the main verse form for the long narrative to come. As the story develops, the poet will interrupt the quatrain form and its musical rhythm only to highlight certain scenes and feelings. Khaḍrā, the mother of the black baby who will be the future hero of the Banī Hilāl, for example, defends her honor in a dignified qaṣīda, rhymed in *lām* (11. 918–928), when she stands accused by Rizq and the tribe of bearing a child sired by a black slave. Jābir uses the qaṣīda form often to open continuing sessions of the sīra with an invocation to God and with a lyrical recapitulation of the emotional situation pertinent to the current action.

Jābir's poetic narrative of the birth of the black hero, Abū Zayd, consistently works at several levels as song, story, and rhyme. The listener continues with the poet to comprehend at once (1) the linear sequence of what happens next, as the paratactically built lines add together the molecules of the story; (2) the logical typology, the paradigm left in the mind by the poetry; and (3) the mold cast by the music. Jābir interweaves the three levels fully to produce an entertaining and meaningful re-creation of the epic tale transmitted through some 800 or 900 years to explain how the Arab tribes living in southern Egypt today came to be there, how the various tribes and clans to which North African Arabs trace their ancestry once formed part of the great, federated tribe of the Banī Hilāl, and how the black hero Abū Zayd led the Bedouin tribe out of the desert famine to the green pastures of the West.

Jābir always steps back from the scene of action and, in the voice of the wise old sage, comments in proverbial tones on the situation he has just dramatized. His narration is generally distant compared to al-Sayyid al-Ḍūwī's informal, close-to-the-action presentation in colloquial Arabic. Jābir's language is mixed. Sometimes he speaks in the prophetic, sacred diction of God in the Koran, and at others, in the profane discourse of everyday men in the marketplace. Such "Middle Arabic"[5] serves the tone of Jābir the Sage well as he comes close to both the drama and the listener only to distance himself to preach a lesson about the present in the past to his beloved children gathered round him.

## NARRATIVE STYLE AND LOGIC

Jābir's style is much more overtly argumentative than Sayyid's matter-of-fact, deductive exposition of the story action. Jābir's logic generally proceeds inductively. He presents a scene, then draws a conclusion and a moral from it. For example:

> Eighty knights obeyed him [Rizq]
> They said: let's visit the tomb of Tuhāmī
> The money was paid to them
> He's a good man, he has pride.
>
> He inspected the whole thing
> Al-Tubbaʿī son of Nāyil
> And he did the deed in its place
> And he dressed the men of al-Hilāyil
>
> He took them on horses
> Approaching and decided on Hijaz

A Sultan in Saddle, is just One
A man who gives to everyone. (11. 102–113)
For two years she did not conceive

Soon there finished three years
Four, she did not bring forth a child
Five, she has tears glistening
The burdens of trouble are not light
When ten years elapsed
She had not borne children
Neither girls nor boys
This is the judgment God wishes. (11. 312–320)

In the third quatrain cited above, Jābir uses the whole formulaic line "the burdens of trouble are not light" (ḥumūl al-balā mish khafīfa) to draw a conclusion and to cap a quatrain; the formula also serves to generalize and summarize the situation outlined in the preceding three quatrains. To summarize Jābir's paratactic logic in more hypotactic terms: although Rizq is a good man, as demonstrated by his generosity to his tribesmen and his religious acts of charity, his new wife did not conceive for ten years because it was not divinely fated. (She in fact will conceive, but first it will be a daughter; it will be another eleven years before she is to bear a son.) Jābir is carefully establishing that this is God's will as he caps the end of the section with the whole formulaic line "this is the judgment God wishes." It will be an important point in the scenes to come wherein the black son and heir granted through divine powers in answer to a woman's earnest prayers is denied by his father and his tribe.

Sayyid also uses whole formulaic tag lines and descriptive epithets to foreshadow action. Whereas Jābir pronounces epithets and tag lines as his own evaluations of character and action, Sayyid usually places them in the mouths of characters. He rarely speaks them in his own voice. For example, Sayyid focuses his story from the beginning on Khaḍrā and he terms her Khaḍrā al-Sharīfa over and over. The epithet stresses her nobility of birth, her lineage descending from the Prophet. Later, the epithet is put in the mouth of Hamāma, the wife of Ghānim, to describe the girl as Khaḍrā the spoiled (il-ʿaqīqa). The poet thus signals the coming treachery implicit in the jealous epithet. For, in Sayyid's version, it is Ghānim and his wife who cause the scandal over the birth of a black baby and who suggest that Khaḍrā is an adulteress. In the broader epic tale to come for which the "Birth of Abū Zayd" episode provides the background, the audience knows it will be Diyāb's betrayal of Abū Zayd that will bring anarchy to the tribe in North Africa.

Fārūq uses descriptive epithets like Jābir's in a moralistic, judgmental way. There is a difference, however, for Jābir's moralizing is earned. He establishes himself in his narration as a gentle sage, a bearer of the wisdom of the ancestors. Fārūq's narrative is too hurried for the listener to get a real sense of him and his moral perspective. Fārūq must rely on mere repetition and insistence of the descriptive, evaluating tag in order to gain the adherence and comprehension of his audience. Implicit in Fārūq's repetition of the most common whole-line formulas expressing the basic ideas of the epic again and again is an agreement with the audience: you know and I know what this is all about and so I won't spell it all out for you in detail. Fārūq actually says this several times: "And what I've said I won't repeat" (1. 275). But he does repeat, and frequently. And in the very repetitiveness of his poetry, in the very unembellished sameness of his musical motifs, he is counting on the audience's prior comprehension of background detail. He repeats a general refrainlike epithet (Bedouins who eschew blame or a Bedouin whose roots are clean) where the other two poets would be adding detail upon detail to build up the scene, the action, and the motivation of the characters.

## RHYMING AND WORDPLAY

Rhyme very quickly establishes itself to the listener's ear as a salient feature in all three performances. Virtually every line contains end-rhyme, which may be monorhyme or couplet rhymes making up quatrains (*abab*). The end-rhyme signals for the ear the completion of a thought unit, or a poetic line. Musically, as we have heard, the poets couple lines so that the musical phrase coincides with two poetic lines. Rhyme and melody appear to be equally important to the poet's improvised construction of quatrains in performance. Once in the midst of a session, as a new thematic section was beginning, Jābir began to construct his sung line of verse, but immediately aborted it to interject quickly to his accompanist "mā lak?" (what's the matter with you?). Ḥasan had struck up the wrong melodic motif on his rabāb; he had begun the reciting tune instead of the initial tune, so Jābir stopped, signaled to his brother who corrected the instrumental tune immediately, and the pair continued harmoniously. All this happened so quickly in the performance that the audience could barely perceive it. On another occasion, when Jābir was asked what he did when he "forgot" a line or ruined a verse in performance, the poet responded, "I rebuild the rhyme. The last word is what's important."[6] This comment about how he "remembers" the lines in performance is instructive. Jābir's comment along with his jibe at his erroring accompanist suggest that the real improvisatory art is in the rhymes and melodies. Melodic patterns would seem to give stability to the singer's performance, to act as a mold or frame into which to insert the words. The phrase the singers and audience use to describe this is "to mount it on the rabāb" (*yirakkib*). While the melodic formula or the tune gives the performing poet a temporal mold and regularity, rhymes provide the singer with a working conceptual gestalt as well as a mnemonic device.

Fārūq, as we noted, decorates his opening end-rhymes with paronomasia (punning) throughout. The lines all end with variations of the same phonemes: kh/ā/l/ī. Line 1 ends with *khāllīh* (his uncle), line 3 with *akhallīh* (I take him), line 4 with *khallih* (vinegar), line 8 with *khilli* (horses). Lines 5 through 8 play with the sounds /j/ā/h/: *jāhā* (came to her), *jāh* (support, noun), *jāh* (to support him, verb). This punning on rhyme words is actually atypical of Fārūq's poetry, for once he begins the quatrains that narrate the bulk of his episode he seems lucky always to find simple rhymes. Listening to Jābir and Sayyid, one hears the quatrains rhyming *abab,* but the ear quickly recognizes also that at least one set of the crossed rhymes features paronomasia. Egyptian folk poets call this feature *zahr* (flower), the more literary Arabic terms being *jinās* (punning), or *tawriya* (double entendre). The folk term, as Cachia points out, makes an analogy with a flower. The art of explaining the hidden meaning in *zahr* is *tazhīr,* on the analogy with the opening of a flower. Poets aim for lots of flowers (zahr, puns) in their rhymes. They derogatorily call quatrains constructed with mere rhymes and no rhyme-puns *tastīf* or stacking.[7]

The audience thus expects the skillful murabbaᶜ builder to

pun his rhymes. Jābir's first quatrain, for example, plays with the rhyme words:

> I became old and my back was *bent* [wi-ḥanēt]
> From God we get our desires [al-maṣāliḥ]
> I cried for my troubles and *moaned* [wi-ḥannēt]
> In my house there's no *fine* boy [fāliḥ].
>
> Balaghanī-l-kibar yā ḍahrī wi-hanēt
> Mini-ḷḷāh tiqḍā-l-maṣāliḥ
> Bakēt ʿalā-l-balāwī wa-ḥannēt
> Fī bētī mā fīsh ṭifli fāliḥ

In the interest of "floristry,"[8] the last word of the line often departs from normal language, either classical or vernacular. The poet may add meaningless rhyme syllables:

> I look with my eyes
> I look with my eyes right and *left* [wa-shimāl]
> For a boy to have to entertain me
> Night came to me black, and *disaster* [wa-shummāl]
> You are the Almighty, O Lord, and can give to me.
> Quatrain 2
>
> Balūj bi-ʿēnī
> Balūj bi-ʿēnī yamīn wa-shimāl
> ʿAlā ṭifl ʿandī yilāghīnī
> Jātnī-l-layālī sōda wa-shummāl
> Qādir yā rabbī 'anta tuʿṭīnī

The poet often contorts normal pronunciation, distorts word forms, or creates new words whose meaning is understood from the context:

> "Leave your affairs to God on *High* [mutaʿāl]
> In the mountains walk and in the *country* [shī rīf]
> If you want to have *children* [ʿiyāl]
> Marry a virgin *noble*woman [sharīfa]."
> Quatrain 4

Amrak li-rabbī-l-mutaʿāl
Fī-jbāl imshī wi-shī rīf
In kān murādak itkhallif ʿiyāl
Tazawwaj bi-ʿadhrā sharīf(ah)

The singer's listeners demonstrate a keen awareness of this wordplay, bursting out with "Allāh" or other complimentary expressions to express approval of particularly clever jinās. The complex richness of the rhyme's acoustics, combined with the turns of meaning, calls the listener's attention to the final word of each line. Musical lines are binary; the musical line thus coincides with the poetic couplet. Inasmuch as the second and fourth lines often feature paronomasia, rather than simple rhyme or simple semantic repetition, the end of the musical phrase coincides with the semantically stressed wordplay. The concluding instrumentalization picks up and draws out, and echoes, the verbal jinās. The singer typically uses vocal elongations, vocalizing, and mellismas to stress semantically loaded syllables containing multiple meaning. Such vocal ornamentation combines with the play on homonymy in the voiced words to echo sound and thereby reinforce meaning.

Jābir, for example, often stresses the puns with vocal ornamentation that the rabāb duplicates and carries into the vocal silences between lines of verse, while the singer takes a breath. The instrument thus extends the rhyme word into vocal silences, making it echo in the hearer's mind. While the listener semantically assimilates what he has heard in the line just recited, the rabāb's ornamental extension of the rhyme word echoes the sung vocalization of the rhyme syllable and causes it to remain in the listener's mind. All this happens in the vocal silences between lines of sung poetry before the poet goes on to the next poetic line of narrative and to the new piece of information to be communicated.

The homonymic homophony I am describing from the oral performance is much easier to *hear* than to understand in a linear, written account. The process of the performed communication is nonlinear and nonanalytical; it is experientially perceived. A written analytical account such as I am attempting in these pages removes much of the living fun of the actual event being transacted between the poet and his patrons. The interested reader may obtain samples of performances which various Cairo music companies have recently recorded. Abnoudy has also recently made an edited version of Jābir's "Birth of Abū Zayd" (under analysis here in its full text) widely available.[9] In the meantime, let me give more specific examples of the oral word and music play and the way in which it works conceptually to create a kind of musical metaphor. It is important to understand the technique, for Jābir's and Sayyid's very art resides in an echoing concatenation of sound and meaning which superimposes images conceptually to create metaphor musically rather than syntactically. The technique of constructing meaning is, I grant, complexly obscure; and it is intended to be so, for, as I shall suggest in chapters 6 and 7, the shāʿir's performance, like his style, represents a masked aggression on the part of the contained in-group of the poet and his public against the powers that oppress them.

The rhymes interacting with the rabāb serve to link ideas and to foreground and background information.[10] For example, Jābir presents in the third, fourth, and fifth quatrains of his narrative exposition (which continue the passage above) the crying, childless hero Rizq after he has heard a voice calling him to find a noble virgin and to marry in Mecca the High. The mixed feelings of the hero fill in the background of the scene as Rizq goes home from the scene of divine revelation:

(3) He heard a call from God
O brother, everyone has his happiness
O, Rizq, listen to God
Marry in Mecca al-Saʿīda.
(4) Leave your affairs to God on High
In the mountains walk and in the countryside [shī rīf]
If you want to have children
Marry a noble virgin [sharīfa]
(5) He heard this and the heart of the boy rejoiced
He heard this and the heart of the boy rejoiced
[il-fatā-nsarr]
Afterward his tears were flowing [damʿ nāzil]
He turned his horse home to go [ṣār]
The hero returned to his house [ʿal-manāzil].

(3) Simaʿ nidā min qibali-ḷḷāh
Yā-khī kulli man hū saʿīd

Yā Rizq(i) iṣghā ʿala-ḷḷāh
Tazawwaj fī Makkah-s-saʿīd(ah)
(4) Amrak li-rabbī-l-mutaʿāl
Fi-jbāl imshī wi-shī rīf
In kān murādak itkhallif ʿiyāl
Tazawwaj bi-ʿadhrā sharīf(ah)
(5) Simaʿ dōlah galb il-fatā-nsarr
Baʿd mā kān luh damʿ nāzil
ʿAdal muhurtuh lil-balad ṣār
Rajaʿ il-baṭal ʿal-manāzil

The rhyme words of the passage all recall each other acoustically, as rhymes of course always do, and they connect ideas. Rizq arrives at his house. The very words "to his house," *ʿal-manāzil,* echo two lines later the flowing tears, *damʿ nāzil.* Thus we perceive the man arrive at his tent, astride his horse; in the rhyme echo we still hear his tears flowing down.

The next quatrain (no. 6) reiterates the feeling, as "crying with his tears becoming sadness," Rizq enters the tent of Sirḥān to tell the sad story. At this point in the tale, the rhyme-puns redouble for the next eight quatrains. That is, every rhyme word plays with the sound and meaning of every other one since both the *a* and *b* rhymes feature jinās:

(6) "He was crying and the tears *became sadness* [ṣār ḥann]
He was crying and the tears *became sadness*
On the earth his tears were an *irrigation* [riwāya]
He approached the tent of *Sirḥān*
And he explained to him the *story* [riwāya]."

Why is the hero crying after God has seemingly solved his problem? God has informed him that a noble virgin awaits him in Mecca, that he only need go to Mecca to have a child. The contradiction is stressed by antithetical repetitions—first the poet repeats twice the seemingly appropriate response of happiness at God's solution to the problem (in quatrain 5: "the heart of the lad rejoiced); there follow seven lines full of sadness and tears. In the contradiction, the poet signals to his listener a double meaning that anticipates metaphorically through a kind of "pun logic" what will happen in the linear progress of the story. In the above passage, sadness and the name of King Sirḥān are conceptually linked by their paronomastic echo of each other; and the story (riwāya) itself, in the associative language of the rhymes, is an irrigation of tears (riwāya). The rhyme-puns thus offer the attentive, intelligent listener the gist of the story, condensed, far in advance of the surface sequence of the narrative events. Jābir's conceptual superimposition of images, as I have maintained, creates not syntactic, but musical, metaphor. Jakobson defines poetry itself as this kind of stressed projection of the paradigmatic axis of language onto the syntagmatic.[11] We need not, however, stray so far afield for a metacommentary, for Jābir himself comments on the mellifluous quality of the meaning in his song: he calls his narrative "a flow of words like dissolved honey."

The simile suggests that the poet is fully aware of how deeply he has colored his narrative message with significant connotation. Indeed, Jābir can never resist explicitly telling this to his *ḥabā'ib* (loved ones), as he calls his audience. He teases with lines like:

> Look and see the story (or the simile, comparison) (l. 1125)
> Look and see the meaning. (l. 559)
>
> Unḍur wa-shūf il-hikāya
> Unḍur wa-shūf il-maʿānī

Such verses occur at particularly symbolic junctures in the story. Or again, he might say:

> Heed the words of my poetry and odes
> Heed the words of my poetry, if you're smart (l. 4080)
>
> Iṣghā kalām shiʿrī wa-aqṣāyid
> Iṣghā li-ashʿārī izā kunt shāṭir

or

> Be attentive to the story/purpose/rhyme [riwāya]
>
> Khud bālak min-ir-riwāya

I purposely give a multiple translation for the rhyme word, *riwāya*. Given the curious plurality of meaning in the rhyme words of this tale because of the many deformations, neologisms, and puns, I hear a triple level of meaning. The poet is signaling that a dream episode is not to be taken only literally; he is also telling us that his story, his rhyming technique with all its embellishment, has a purpose. The audience is explicitly admonished, indeed challenged, to hear the various levels of the story being performed. The "smart" listener who heeds well the verses will hear the story symbolically and metaphorically anticipated in the rhymes. Even the not-so-smart listener will have the major ideas of the story superimposed, one on the other, reinforced by the music and the echoing, adumbrating rhyme word.

## MUSICAL METAPHOR

One of the ideas crucial to the story of the birth of Abū Zayd is the imputation that his mother Khaḍrā is guilty of adultery and fornication with a black slave, after she delivers her black baby—a child conceived following her wish for a son like the blackbird she saw vanquish a whole flock of other colored birds near the lake of ritual purification. Very early in his narration, by the twelfth quatrain, Jābir centers the attention of his listener on this theme:

> He listened, the Prince. Praise be the *Beautiful One*
> [al-Zayn].
> He took the word of the king as a trust
> This Arab is pure of lies and *embellishment/adultery*
> [al-Zayn].
> The words of the Arabs have their place. (ll. 90–94)

> Simaᶜ il-amīr ṣallū ᶜalā-z-zēn
> Akhad kalām il-malik siqa fi makānuh
> Rājil khālī min il-kizb wa-z-zēn
> Kalām il-ᶜArab luh makānuh

Egyptian aficionados of the Banī Hilāl saga informed me, as we listened to the singer toying with the word *zayn*, that what the poet really meant was *zinā*, that is, "fornication" or "adultery," not "embellishment" or "beautiful," as I had heard it. I was listening only on the surface level of the story. The meaning insisted on by my fellow listeners becomes more clear in the context al-Sayyid al-Ḍūwī gives to the formula. He uses this same *jinās,* but puts it in the mouth of Khaḍrā defending herself after she has been accused of fornicating with a black slave:

For these, O, Rizq, pray for the *Beautiful One* [al-Zayn]
O, Prince, O, Delight of my eyes
I am free from lies and embellishment/adultery [al-Zayn]
Forbidden is dirt from my clothing.

O, Rizq, who harmed you
O, master of the Clean Turban
At least let your talk be modest, O, Prince
I am one of the lineage of Ṭāhā, a noble woman.

When this talk was said
By the life of the Lord of Creation
You are a leader and a companion of power
O, Rizq, be polite, be the way you were raised.

By the life of the Prophet so *Beautiful* [al-Zayn]
This I am reading, the letters of the alphabet
And I am free from lies and *adultery/embellishment* [al-Zayn]
A lasting fact, look at my blankets.

Sayyid stresses the jinās by repeating it two quatrains later, juxtaposing it with Khaḍrā's protestation that her bloodstained bed covers will prove her innocence. Sayyid's version of the tale thus concentrates the audience's attention on Khaḍrā's point of view. Jābir focuses instead on Rizq's feelings of betrayal, and the formulaic jinās expresses Rizq's character as an honorable man. The meaning of the rhyme word will be transformed when Jābir uses it later in much the same context as Sayyid employed it above. Here, describing Rizq's moral character, the figurative rhyming anticipates ironically what is to come in the course of the linear action of the story.

The Egyptian audience, at least the smart listener in it (as later both Jābir in his song and listening Egyptian friends and neighbors pointed out to me), hears the story and appreciates it on two levels: the sequential, logical level of expository, story narrative and the figurative, nonlinear, poetic level of deeper meaning. The Egyptian listener brings with him to the audition of a performance of the sīra a firm knowledge of the story and of its formulaic locutions, its typical metaphors and figures as used by poets in previous tellings of the old tale.

Good poets working within the tradition are aware of their public's prior knowledge of the song and they play off the prior meanings embedded in formulaic locutions. One such formula in particular is the play on the word *zayn,* which is used in religious formulary to describe the Prophet, but which also means sham, embellishment, or ornamentation designed to conceal the truth, and also sounds suspiciously like a word referring to illicit sexual intercourse. Thus when that particular jinās occurs in a context such as Jābir first uses it near the beginning of his story of the birth of Abū Zayd, it has echoes. Although in the local context it means simply that Rizq is a man who does not tell lies or make false embellishments, in the larger context of the audience's knowledge of how they have heard the word *zayn* used in past songs and how they know it will eventually be used in the present singing of the story, the wordplay serves to prefigure the story to come.[12] It reminds the audience of what the story is really all about by the kind of echoing back to previous contexts and echoing forth into the context that Jābir will establish as he sings his version. This echoing paronomasia is what I term "musical metaphor."

Jābir's art is sure. It rests in his firm mastery of the formulaic conventions of the story, music, and poetry; it rests for him, as well as for his audience, on previous contexts, previous tellings and hearings of the sīra. His originality lies primarily in the voice he gives to the conventional elements, marked in his ornamental style and in the moral quality and philosophic vision he gives to his re-creation of the ancient song. For Jābir has a great vision of the tale. In the first twenty lines of this song,[13] which will run to some ninety hours before he finishes it, Jābir tells his jinās-sensitive audience what that vision is. As the character Rizq Ibn Nāyil begins his lamentation on the vagaries of fate, Jābir sets forth an implicit thesis in the wordplay of the first ten lines. The thesis, which will run throughout the long sīra, resides in a transformation of the word "cheat"/*khawwān,* which recurs four times within the six lines:

> "I trusted you, Fate, and you cheated me [rajᶜata khuntanī]." (l. 13)
> And I never expected you to be cheating [khawwān] (l. 14)
> "Why do you cheat me, O Fate, breaking my bones? [bitkhūnnī lēh]." (l. 15)
> The deceived's nature is cheating [khawwān]." (l. 18)

Four lines later the same sound configuration based on kh/w/n occurs again. In line 22, however, the word is *ikhwān* or brothers. Khawwān, meaning deceitful, or cheating, reverberates in the ear and mind as the poet pronounces ikhwān, brothers, through his clever musical creation of metaphor. The paronomasia thus sets forth the notion that is central to *Sīrat Banī Hilāl:* the betrayal of brothers is the greatest pain and the downfall of all. The epic will go on to chronicle the migration of the tribe to Tunisia under Abū Zayd's leadership, and its eventual breakdown and dissolution because of intertribal quarrels between brothers and cousins.

## POETIC COMPETENCE

The mark of the good poet, then, is just this kind of musically figural control of story and context. Tradition has it that a shāᶜir must be able to recite the *Hilāliyya* for ninety-nine successive nights, from dusk until dawn; otherwise he will not be considered a "poet."[14] This is a very stringent test. Even Jābir could not have met it; but Jābir offered his audience something else, what Geertz might term "deep wordplay."[15] A superb poet working within an extremely developed and sophisticated oral tradition, Jābir plays off the fact that his audience knows any given episode of *Sīrat Banī Hilāl* as well as he does. He also counts on the fact that his audience's ear is as sensitive and acutely tuned to jinās, to hidden meaning and multiple meaning, as his own tongue is adroit at fashioning it. Jābir constantly scores important meaning and helps his audience understand the significance of the sīra of their ancestors' migration to Egypt and North Africa. Jābir, of course, cannot resist directly moralizing and preaching and asking his listener, "Did you get it?" Al-Ḍūwī scores his singing of the song just as adroitly, but he always leaves the metaphor implicit. He never preaches. He lets the poetry and story stand for themselves. He is considered a better musician and possibly a cleverer builder of quatrains than Jābir. But Jābir, from all accounts, tells the fullest, most interestingly detailed story.

Fārūq, by contrast, offers no real understanding or interpretation of the story to his audience beyond his repeated truisms, spoken as a refrain, that life is hard. Almost immediately after the first session of Fārūq's performance, fellow listeners (doorkeepers, former Egyptian village men) told me, "He's OK, but not great," and, as Abnoudy puts it, "The rabāba doesn't lie." Fārūq's fragmented, abrupt music at the very beginning of his performance signaled to his Egyptian listeners that he would not be able to take them very far into the sīra or explain it well to them. The rapid music and condensed story suggest also a memorized song that the singer was eager to sing out just as fast as possible lest he forget the next line.[16]

The sīra audience is demanding and knowledgeable. They not only hear, they listen for, jinās, and take pleasure in it as much as in the music and story. Fārūq and Jābir contracted with their audiences to treat ornamentation very differently from the onset of their songs. Fārūq's opening jinās on *jāh* (came to her, support) and khāllīh (uncle, keep him, vinegar, horse) have no deeper significance. Jābir's wordplay, however, toys with the listener, teaches him, and delights his ears with its resounding music. The meaning of a pun like *ikhwān/khawwān,* or the play on the sacred and profane in *zayn—zinā,* sounds through Jābir's long version of *Sīrat Banī Hilāl* and through Upper Egyptian culture.

# PART III
# Upper Egypt Interprets Itself

# 6
# PUNNING AS UNDERSTANDING

The poetic world of the *Hilāliyya* is the world of the Bedouin tribe complete with all its antagonisms, its blood feuds, its honor code, its elaborate Chinese-box morality of social obligation and respect. It is primarily a drama of honor and shame. Fārūq tells us this in a striking formulaic refrain:

> Bedouins God made respectable.
> Bedouins respecting others' opinions.
> Bedouins eschewing all blame.

The poets themselves state and restate their subject matter and intentions in a few formulaic lines. They will recite the sīra from the Arabs of old, and they will tell about Zughba and Hilāyil, Bedouins eschewing all blame. Jābir and Sayyid reveal the drama of Bedouin blame and shame in its subtler complications to show, through a configuration of puns, metonymy, and disjunctive logic, the deep meaning hidden within the traditional story. In its narration of the conception and birth of the tribal heroes, "Mīlād Abū Zayd" provides a myth of origins. It accounts for the origins of strife in the community.

The poets, as we have heard in our close listening to them, spell out the kind of understanding they expect from their listeners, the kind of comprehension that leads to meaning. All three tell us in a common formulaic locution to hear the story and understand it, as well as to heed it and understand it. In the way they each vary the formula, Jābir and Sayyid elaborate the kind of comprehension they seek from listeners. Sayyid tells us "ismaʿ niẓām al-ḥikāya" (listen to the order of the tale). *Niẓām* means structure, order, composition, organization, or method. The closely related *naẓm* likewise means system, order, but it also means poetry, verse, or string of pearls; as a grammatical-rhetorical term, it means rhythm. A further derivation from the triconsonantal root is *manẓūma* or didactic verse, that is, verse with meaning and intent to teach.

Jābir clarifies how the poetry teaches, if we have listened intently to his variations of the formula. He says "ismaᶜ kalāmī wa-ifhamuh" (hear my words and understand them) and also "Iṣghā kalām shiᶜrī wa-aqṣāyid" (heed the words of my poem and odes). The rhyme word may mean odes, but like Sayyid's *niẓām* it also connotes intention or purpose. In yet other variations on the phrase, which we noted in our listening analysis above, the esteemed shāᶜir cautions his smart listener to pay attention to the riwāya, which polyvalently denotes at once story, purpose, rhyme; he warns us to look and see the *maᶜná*. This rhyme word translates as meaning or sense. It is used in Arab rhetorical terminology to refer to content, as opposed to form; it can also stand for allegory or figurative expression. An unmetrical poem with end-rhyme is termed *muᶜanná,* whereas *maᶜnawī* suggests the ideal or spiritual versus the material. By his punning logic, Jābir suggests that the intended meaning, the spirit, of the story is in the rhymes. The rhymes, which are the basis of the shāᶜir's prosodic system, contain, as we have learned, puns. Punning, then, with its multiform multiplicity of meaning, is understanding. Meaning is buried in the rhyme puns and in the story. The story and the rhyme puns are designed to teach; in other words, the story, through its style and composition, will teach the sharp listener a way of understanding or a mode of perceiving.

The listener may of course hear only the surface narrative of event, as Jābir teases his audience they may, and not really understand. Jābir and Sayyid caution the listener to take particular note of certain junctures in the tale. Both agree one of these is the scene of the birds at the lake, the scene where Abū Zayd and the other future heroes of the tribe are conceived. Another is Khaḍrā's accusation and defense, and yet another the scene in which ᶜAṭwān attempts to rape the outcast woman. Following the advice of the poets, I propose to look closely at these scenes and consider them within the rhetorical structure and meaning given them by the poets.

Let us begin in the middle of things with Khaḍrā's accusation and defense. Sayyid frames the scene with the admonition "listen to the composition of the story"; he sings it once before the public revelation of the child's color and again as Rizq enters Khaḍrā's tent to confront her. When Rizq's black newborn son is brought before the tribal leaders assembled to name him, Ghānim's wife calls attention to the fact that something is out of place, the order of things has been violated. She asks Rizq what slave gave the new baby his black color:

> Is it true that kings give birth to slaves?
> O, Master of the Clean Turban.
> By God, it's a scandal and a shame made public!
> Look in the breast pocket of Sharīfa!

The whole tribal leadership then asks, "Since when did kings bear slaves?" The tribal voice of scandal is raised and the tribe, collectively outraged, calls out to exile Khaḍrā. Rizq becomes upset at the talk and leaves his cousin Sirḥān's dīwān to rush home to Khaḍrā al-Sharīfa to confront her:

> Hearing the talk increased his distress
> The man with the clean honor (shawl?)
> (*abū al-ʿurūḍ al-naẓīfa*)
> He left the dīwān of his cousin
> And rushed home to Sharīfa.
>
> Ibn Nāyil entered the house inside.
> By the life of our Lord the Creator
> He was a prince, a leader, a brave man.
> Listen to the order of the story!
>
> She received him saying to him good morning, O Dandy
> I suppose the nights hurt you [i.e., you are feeling bad].
> O, did your enemies give you a bitter drink?
> This return is not our habit.
>
> I see you, Rizq, changing your blood [i.e., angry],
> The man with the shawl tilting to the summit.
> Did any of your cousins make you angry?
> Zughba or Hilāyil?

He said: my anger is because of you,
You mother of earrings!
I don't need males or females (children).
It was never my hope, Sharīfa.

Was it fair, Khaḍrā, to beget me a black slave [*ʿabd*]?
So listen, I want to tell you—
People's lives are not in their own hands.
Now—leave, go to your father's house!

When did a king have a *slave child* [*ʿabdān*],
O mother of earrings and bracelets?
By God, it's a scandal and a shame *made public* [*Faḍīḥa wa-ʿār bān*]
When was it a hope, Sharīfa? what hope is there?

Khaḍrā answers Rizq's and the tribe's accusations.

For these, Rizq, pray on *al-Zayn* (the Beauteous One).
O prince, delight of my eye,
I'm free of lies and adultery.
Dirt is forbidden from touching my clothes.

Who harmed you, Rizq?
You, master of the clean turban!
At least be modest in your talk, my prince!
I'm a descendant of Ṭāhā, a *Sharīfa*.

Since when was this kind of talk allowed to be said?
By the life of our Lord the Creator,
You are a leader and a powerful man.
O, Rizq, be well brought up!

By the life of the prophet so Beauteous [*zayn*],
Here I am reading the letters of the alphabet
And I'm free from lies and adultery!
A lasting fact—look at my covers!

He said to her, "leave our land,
"You with your light clothes!

"For this is a black slave, not our son.
"This was not my hope for us, Sharīfa."

The terms of the argument between Rizq and Khaḍrā are clear. The tribe and Rizq believe they have been dishonored by Khaḍrā's acts. Rizq aligns himself with the tribe against his wife and repeats the words of accusation which the wife of Ghānim had leveled earlier. The repeated line contains a pun central to the poet's interpretation of the scene (ll. 1–4 and 29–33 as numbered above). A pun and an interpretation reside in the word(s) *ʿār bān*. On a literal level, the words signify "shame appeared." *ʿĀr*, according to Zeid,[1] refers to an act by an individual which reflects on the honor of the entire group. He distinguished *ʿār* (shame, disgrace) from the less serious *ʿayb*, a kind of shame or blame that reflects only on an individual. A slight variation on the sound configuration, *ʿurbān*, however, means Arabs, Bedouins, or the derogatory A-rabs. Sayyid thus echoes the word *Bedouins* in the phrase "shame appeared"; *ʿār bān*, with paranomastic efficiency, calls to mind the Bedouin tribesmen and their strict moral economy of checks and balances, honor and shame. The historic Hilālī tribe, whose deeds the shāʿir recounts to his twentieth-century audience, were a Bedouin tribe. Within the Bedouin honor code the greatest dishonor of all is a violation of sexual honor by transgressing the private sanctity of the wife in her relationship to her husband. The term for this, according to Zeid, is *ʿirḍ;* in Upper Egyptian, *ʿarḍ* (pl. *ʿurūḍ*). The epithet normally attributed to Rizq incorporates this concept of family generative honor; poets call him periphrastically "The man with clean honor" (Abū-l-ʿurūḍ in-naẓifa[2] or alternatively, il-uṣūl in-naẓīfa). The circumlocution substitutes a certain notion of honor for Rizq's name and for the man himself. The man's private relationship with his wife thus can either accrue honor or dishonor to him. This relationship of individuals subsumed in the concept of ʿirḍ embodies the honor of the family and the tribe with contractual force. To violate it, to go outside the marriage contract, is a serious breach of the greater social contract. To breed a child and heir of a noble family with a black slave is an even more outrageous flaunting of the moral order, for it defies economic and class hierarchies of kings and servants, free person and slave. The scandal that erupts is this.

The poet plays with the words for shame and scandal to

attune the listener's ear to an important convergence of meaning. He uses the word *faḍīḥa* for scandal or public disgrace pleonastically with *ʿār bān. Faḍīḥa* connotes public disclosure or uncovering of faults, exposure of something shameful. The triliteral root can mean to uncover, to expose, to disgrace, as well as to ravish, to violate, or to rape. The sexual transformation of meaning is pertinent. The very next line spoken is a direct sexual innuendo: Ghānim's wife says, "Look in the breast pocket of Honor (Sharīfa)." Sharīfa, the attribute for Khaḍrā, is a metonym that substitutes Khaḍrā's noble ancestry as a member of the Prophet Muḥammad's lineage for her name. Sharīf is a title given the Prophet's descendants. It means noble, highborn, honored. The word *ʿibb* (breast pocket) almost certainly carries a double meaning, connoting also *ʿayb,* blame, shame, defect. The line in question thus could also be heard as "look to the shamefulness of Sharīfa." Her imputed shame is inside, within her clothing, in her breast pocket—a rather obvious displacement upward and outward.

In her response to the scandalous allegation, Khaḍrā invokes the name of the Holy Prophet and maintains she is free from lies and adultery, that dirt is forbidden from her clothes. The outward represents the inward. The woman's clothes stand metonymically for her honor, and dirt for fault or dishonor. The word *muḥarram* (forbidden) is loaded with significant connotations as that which is inviolably sacrosanct. Khaḍrā thus advises Rizq to be more modest and respectful in the way he talks to her; she cautions him to be mindful of his upbringing, literally, to protect his good breeding. He should know better than to heed dirty talk. The word *al-rabāya* (breeding, upbringing) end-rhymes with *al-barāya,* God's creatures. The rhyme serves musically and conceptually to link God with Khaḍrā's breeding. This wordplay reinforces the play on *zayn* (the Beautiful One/adultery), which was pointed out to me by Egyptians as a particularly significant jinās and which Khaḍrā reiterates twice in her four-quatrain-long defense. The terms of her defense insist on her own education and breeding as a descendant of Ṭāhā the Prophet and as a literate person. The English double entendre of breeding is appropriate and similar to the Arabic word in its range of connotation. Khaḍrā points to her "covers" (*ghaṭā*), her bed blankets or perhaps her veiled hair and body. Her covers are testimony to her innocence. They are outward manifestations of her personal purity and integrity, as well as the external proof of the innocence of her "breeding."

Jābir uses this same metonym in the scene where Khaḍrā conceives Abū Zayd, the night after her wish on the birds:

> He took his entry into her in relaxation, at ease.
> The free one, blameless are her covers [ghaṭāhā].
> And the musk and perfume rose in the air
> And she prayed hard to the Prophet Ṭāhā

Jābir links Khaḍrā's "covers" to the religious context by means of double end-rhymes; in rhyming ghaṭāhā (her covers) with Ṭāhā, the name of the Prophet taken from the opening letter of a chapter of the Koran, the poet again connects Khaḍrā's good "breeding" or sexual probity in reproductive matters with her holy ancestry. The conceptual link between the sexual and the religious contexts, between the seeming profanation of values and the known sacred, serves in the narrative of Sayyid and Jābir as a major argumentative move. This fusion of contexts implicit in the jinās and rhymes are crucial to the intention and meaning of the tradition. This figurative lineage of ideas offers clues as to the meaning of events by a kind of dissociative logic that distances the listener from certain characters and their moral dilemmas while attaching sympathy to the moral stances of others. Two sets of values conflict with each other: the tribal hierarchy of propertied men sees events one way; a woman still weak and bleeding from childbirth, a newborn babe with his innate goodness as a descendant of the Prophet's line, and a slave family know the facts to be otherwise. The age-old philosophical pairs of seeming and being then set up the disjunctive line of reasoning that offers the listener a greater perspective by which to understand the story.[3]

The group, the tribal collectivity, provides constant monitor to the outward actions, behavior, and general demeanor of individuals. The shāʿir's disjunctive moral logic pits the individual against the group, the self against the other, the in-group against the out-group, the inside against the outside. In the eyes of the tribe, Khaḍrā becomes utterly reprehensible, the more so because of her high birth and lineage. To quote Zeid once more on Bedouin ethics, the higher the status of the kin group in the community, the more rigorous and binding are the obligations and responsibilities imposed.[4] Khaḍrā has seemingly violated the status hierarchy by lowering herself to sleep with a slave. But as the tale will tell and as poet and audience already know, right and honor and truth are on Khaḍrā's side. Hints of this appear whenever fate intervenes. In the lottery to divide Rizq and Khaḍrā's joint property, for example, the divine messenger-agent Quṭb casts the die and Khaḍrā wins the greater part of the herds. The word used for livestock is *māl;* the same word means money and property. A slight sound variation means hope or desires (*āmāl*); in addition, master, often a reference to God, is expressed *māl.* The audience has already heard how Rizq's high status in the tribe depends on his wealth in cattle and camels to bequeath a son. His hope(s) (āmāl) for a son he says is his wealth (māl); he is worthless without an heir to inherit his wealth. The very first scene of Jābir's version stressed this ethic as the opening dilemma; I cite a translated excerpt replete with jinās and internal as well as end-rhyme play on *māl* (property, livestock), *āmāl* (hopes), children (*ʿiyāl*), worry (i.e., his mind bent down, *māl*), camels (*jimāl*), illness for me (ʿayā lī), I have not (mā lī):

> One day he was inspecting the *property* [al-māl]
> given him by God the Creator
> He saw the *property,* he was worried and upset [ʿaqlu . . .
> māl]
> He saw so much, it was endless
> He found property [māl] left and right [shimāl]
> horses and camels [jimāl]
> He said O property [māl], after me who will inherit you?
> Ah, woe is my lack of children [yā mā lī] [ʿiyālī]

In a society which measures status and worth by wealth in cattle and camel herds, Khaḍrā's winning all the livestock by an act of fate is very significant. Indeed, she has taken all Rizq's wealth along with his hopes. In the eyes of the tribe, he is worthless, deceived by his noble wife and robbed of all his hopes; rhyming and assonance paranomastically echo this concept in *māl/āmāl,* for *āmāl* (hopes) contains and subsumes *māl.*

The moral logic and terms of the story become more clearly

spelled out in Abū Zayd's first heroic act—killing his teacher. How is killing your Koranic school teacher a heroic act, it might well be asked. Let us listen to the poet's rendition of the scene. Sayyid presents Khaḍrā seeking out her protector, Fāḍil, chief of the Zaḥlān, to ask that he educate her son. She tells him, "This is no joke/ but a fire burning in my gut/ I need a teacher for my son/ to teach him the alphabet." Sayyid's account of how little Abū Zayd already knows B when the teacher says A, and D when he says C is very close to Fārūq's fairly brief telling of the same scene. The teacher begins on the second day to insult the child. He calls him a black, purchased slave. The third day he hits him with his stick and calls him "son of the stranger," a crow, and wonders that a slave should aspire to learning. The little boy goes home to his slave-nurse, Saʿīda, and his mother. He tells the two women about the teacher's insults. Khaḍrā advises him to behave himself and be polite. Saʿīda, however, is enraged at the hurtful lies and counsels revenge: "Whoever hurts us, we'll hurt back/ they can't say we are strangers." The boy returns to school the next day carrying a lance, and when the teacher continues his name-calling, this time calling the lad "ill-bred," a slave, and the black son of a stranger, the "far-reading one" whose face "cuts the liver" (makes me puke), this time Abū Zayd strikes back with his lance.

Jābir Abū Ḥusayn's version of the hero's encounter with schooling is about five or six times as long as either Sayyid's or Fārūq's. When Abū Zayd is six, his stepfather decides it is time to teach the boy to read the Koran. Jābir stipulates that Abū Zayd was being raised alongside the sultan's kids and educated along with them, but that he was the only one who was "strong." The teacher, however, found him dull, until one day when Abū Zayd sat listlessly, he addressed him and said "Say Alif." Abū Zayd responded "tabarrak" (be blessed). The muʿallim asked: "Who taught you that? It's from the second part of the Koran." Abū Zayd responded, "Ever since my childhood I was educated/ the Lord of Creation gave to me." The teacher decides to test the lad further and quizzes him in riddles. The poet Jābir sets his scene off from the usual narrative quatrain format by casting it in a more stately qaṣīda form. In the monorhymed dialogue, Abū Zayd answers a long series of mysteries pertaining to abstruse religious doctrine, known only to learned shaykhs. I translate a sample of the riddling exchange:

I ask you about One that cannot be paired
I ask you about two that have no third
Tell me what this means, O Son of the Chieftains
Tell me about three that have no fourth
(etc., through Ten)
The black boy answered him and said to him
Heed the meaning of my speech, O, Clever One
The One that has no Other is my God above all capable of all tenderness
Two that have no third are the night and the day
About the three, my dear, I'll inform you
Thrice divorced cannot the same man marry a fourth time.
(etc. through Ten)
That is your answer, Teacher
It's easy for me to understand the first symbols of the Book.

In Jābir's interpretation of this scene, it is absolutely clear that the boy's learning is truly phenomenal and that it can only derive from God the Most Generous One. The teacher embraces the gifted little boy who soon becomes the teacher's pet. Jealousy on the part of the other noble children at school then leads to name-calling and fights. The boys ambush Abū Zayd on the way home from school and call him the crowface son of a stranger. He tells them to stop, for they are not strangers but cousins. King Fāḍil's son answers that they are not cousins, but, instead, Abū Zayd is an intruder, the son of a slave and a whore, a stranger who will soon swim in his own blood. The language of invective here is very strong: *yā sharmūṭa* (a slut, more specifically, a rag into which to ejaculate), *ibn al-radiyya* (son of the base one). The enraged Abū Zayd attacks Gorda, Fāḍil's son, and almost kills him. Gorda then goes home and tells his indignant mother what the riffraff son of a purchased woman had done to him. By showing this point of view, Jābir stresses the overweening of a stranger who has dared to try to kill the son of the tribe's leader. The boy's teacher thus turns on him when he arrives in school the next day and takes up the insults and abuse.

Jābir's version makes very clear Abū Zayd's motivation in killing his teacher. Abū Zayd has been wronged. The Koranic teacher, who should have been better aware of the black boy's extraordinary gifts and innate knowledge than anyone else, deserves to die. All three poets agree that Abū Zayd's literacy and precocious learning come from God and from his breeding. And yet it is his breeding that is in question. His ancestry, his color, his status as a guest taking refuge, his mother's honor—all these are imputed and insulted.

By calling him a stranger and an intruder, as well as a black bastard, the schoolboys have pointed out Abū Zayd's rather tenuous position in the community. Their father Fāḍil, the head of the household (*bayt*) as well as chief of the larger tribal kin group, owes Khaḍrā and her son protection. This obligation derives both from the right of refuge and from the right of neighbors to claim hospitality. *Sharaf* (honor) accrues to the kin group which shelters strangers and defends the weak, the poor, and the outcast against the strong and powerful. Concomitantly, shame befalls the individual and his group who denies the needy or gainsays the guest. The context of the particular situation determines whether any given action may be honorable or shameful.[5] To tolerate an overweening guest brings sublime honor and implies a high degree of self-control on the part of the host. It involves, in the phrase of an Egyptian anthropologist, "swallowing" outrage and hostility.[6] Sayyid echoes the Egyptian anthropologist's metaphor, virtually saying the same thing in his use of wordplay on Abū Zayd's name. After the child-hero has killed his teacher, the teacher's brother, who must secure vengeance to acquit family honor and set the blood balance right, twice says, "Food sticks in my gut." Two-time repetition in oral narrative serves, of course, to emphasize a point, to make sure the audience hears the line. The word for food is *zād,* a punning etymological allusion to Abū Zayd, whose name means father of provision/food/increase. Sayyid is aware of the connotations of Abū Zayd's name; for Sayyid gives the boy his name when a passerby says "Al-khayr ḥa-yizīd" (goodness/wealth will increase), and the mother decides to call her child Abū Zayd. The poet uses the play on *Zayd* as the foundation of several quatrains' rhymes. In fact, the very first two lines of Sayyid's rendition play on the name of Abū Zayd's father, Rizq (see p. 93–95 above for the transcribed text). "Rizq" too refers to nourishment, subsistence, livelihood, or sustenance, in terms of a blessing from God, as in "our daily bread."

Fāḍil's name, like the name of virtually every other character in the *Hilāliyya* cast, involves an etymological play on meanings.

Fāḍil is the man who gives Khaḍrā refuge. The name itself means outstanding, excellent, distinguished, learned, and cultured as well as abundance or excess; variations on the root can expand its meaning to grace, favor, gift, kindness, merit, benefit. Sayyid plays with these meanings. In the scene where Khaḍrā meets Fāḍil at the outskirts of his lands, for example, Sayyid calls the outcast woman "*sharīfa bint al-afāḍil*" (the noble daughter of good family). He rhymes this epithet with Fāḍil's name.

As the two names Zayd and Fāḍil suggest, a narrow boundary exists between excess and merit. The line is slim too between good and bad, between honor and shame. Right depends on the context and the point of view. The little intruder, from one point of view, is an outrage. Killing one's Koranic schoolteacher simply will not do, and the law of blood vengeance is in effect. The matter can only be settled in bloodshed, and the teacher's brother must fight Abū Zayd to right the wrong done his family in the murder of one of them. The teacher's brother, now an adult man, a "right-wing government minister" in Sayyid's version, thus combats a seven-year-old black child. The child wins the combat and avenges his name and his mother's honor. Two systems of morality are in conflict. The Bedouin tribal ethic demands that the family protect the stranger and succor the weak. The jealous schoolboys and the schoolmaster violate this ethic with their insults to Abū Zayd and his mother. But the black child does try them severely, he does exceed the limits. By any standard of reason, a seven-year-old bastard should be illiterate; it is an outrage to reason and to the order of things that he is not.

Every action must be viewed in its larger context as a reaction to some previous act, as redress to set the moral balance right. This is the balancing logic of the large-scale chiastic structure rabāb poets use to construct the Hilālī tale. (See chap. 4 for a diagram of the chiastic, ring patterning of the tale.) The oral poetic patterning device, chiasmus, reflects the moral balancing logic of the Bedouin ethical code and behavior patterns. It is part and parcel of the shāʿir's dissociative argument and style of reasoning. Abū Zayd's knowledge of the alphabet and his heroism in killing his teacher can only be understood segmentally and paratactically in the terms established in the chiastically paired parts of the story. While Jābir explains in more linear detail that the boy's learning has divine antecedents, Fārūq's and Sayyid's listeners must almost totally fill in this information either from their own knowledge of past auditions of the story or infer it from other segments of the narration in progress.

Jābir tells us this over and over in his formulaic lines that signal the smart listener to heed the passage. In the segmental mode of composition that the tradition and its poets use, the part contains the whole, the episode the larger sīra, and the most minute level of composition, the rhyme, incorporates the story. As the riwāya pun suggested, the rhyme and the story have an intended purpose and meaning. This larger meaning can be learned or inferred by the smart listener from the smaller part. Jābir frames the scene in which the women wish on the birds: he states explicitly both before and after the scene, "Look and see the meaning." The scene takes on an ominous portentous quality, for it allegorically represents all the intertribal strife and competition that will cause the eventual downfall of the tribe. The end is foretold in the beginning. The conception contains the kernel, the seed of dissension crucial to both this episode ("Mīlād Abū Zayd") and the *Hilāliyya* in its entire three cycles. The Hilālī heroes' fate and their respective standing in the tribal hierarchy is acted out by the fighting birds of different color. Each colored bird stands for one of the future heroes. Diyāb's mother wishes on the treacherous red bird, for example, and Diyāb will be known in his adult adventures as Diyāb al-Aḥmar (the Red). Jābir's Khaḍrā appears fully aware of the import of her wish; she utters *zaghārīṭ* (ululations) and proclaims, "Even if you were pitch black, I'd wish for you/ let them blame me/ I am afraid to wish on you/ O, family of the Prophets, help me/ I am not counting on the opinion of this one or that one/ My God, I am afraid they will blame me/ Rather I leave it entrusted to my Lord/ my happiness is in submission." The woman wishes and asks God to give her a clever lad who will live long after Rizq to execute all his affairs. Jābir comments on the scene, calling Khaḍrā a free one for whom God opened the doors of heaven to grant her *duʿā'*, which means prayer, but also connotes curse.[7]

The pun contains the truth, for Khaḍrā's ardent prayer contains her curse. She has bred her little black son in a contract with God. She conceives from Rizq that very night. The tribe, however, judges on face value when the child is born black. Surface appearances testify to her immorality and questionable "breeding." Jābir shows the whispers spreading through the assembly of tribal leaders as the black child is carried around by Rizq's slave, who has been commanded to present the baby for naming and for reception into the community of men. In his flexible manipulation of oral narrative style, Jābir zeroes in on two gossips, Ghānim and the judge, Fāyid. Ghānim notes the baby's color when the slave carries him around the dīwān at the end of seven days' feasting to celebrate Rizq's prosperity and happiness—an heir has been born from a high lineage, his mares have foaled, and his slave has produced a son. Jābir specifies all this wealth at the end of Session II, but he has also warned us in the prologue that one cannot ride on high for long, time subdues, the strong become weak, the noble humiliated, laughter becomes tears (see chap. 5, pp. 98–101, above, for the complete text of this passage).

Fate intervenes in the form of a jealous brother at the beginning of Session III. When Rizq's brother ʿAsqal sees the newborn's color, he swipes at him with his sword. Rizq doesn't understand how his son insulted the uncle and asks, "Why do you hurt my newborn/ I am so happy, God has given to me/ It's a trust, so what's wrong with you?/ My mind has gone out of balance [i.e., I can't cope with this]." ʿAsqal responds, "Where is your son, you madman?/ We live and see wonders!/ Now you've brought dirt to our town!/ She preferred the son of a foreign slave to you!"

The scandal spreads. Only Sirḥān stands up for Khaḍrā, as "this woman who knows God and who is related to the Beloved Prophet." Sirḥān explains the scandalmongering as the jealousy of a brother whose greed would have him the only heir to all Rizq's wealth. Rizq ignores the good counsel, calls it enemies' talk. He, like the tribal collectivity, misconceives the truth. He tells Khaḍrā in very angry, very graphic dirty words what she has done to him. She has made him a laughingstock, shamed him publicly, made the private public, and bared that which should be covered.

Fearing scandal and the shame it engenders, Rizq and all the Hilālī respect loose talk over truth. In this, they profane truly sacred values and insult the honor of women (*ʿarḍ in-niswān,* in the words of the poet). No longer willing to protect her, they cast her out, bleeding from childbirth. The true harem—the inner sanctum of the family, the center of the household and all honor—is thus violated and exposed to outside dangers. The most sacred has been profaned, the inside has been turned outside; that which should be covered, uncovered and disclosed. Sayyid expresses this same reversal of the inside and the outside through a series of metonymies. In his allusively poetic style, which contrasts with Jābir's more detailed, linear, descriptive style, he uses periphrasis frequently, substituting circumlocutions for a noun not named. This kind of heroic-epithet formation (or kennings as they are termed in the Anglo-Saxon oral epic tradition) operates as a kind of portmanteau device whose substitutions, suggestive associations, and implied comparisons are complex. Clothing, for example, in Sayyid's version, takes on particular symbolic prominence.[8] The poet opens his tale with a clothing epithet; in the second quatrain Rizq is called "a man with light clothes" (i.e., he's noble in that he can wear light, white clothes and not get dirty). The third and fourth quatrains focus on the scene of Rizq dressing for a Ramaḍān feast in King Sirḥān's tent (see pp. 93–95, above, for the Arabic text and translation). Rizq is again referred to metonymically as "the man with the shawl tilting to the summits."

Although Sayyid uses metonymic naming such as this frequently, in the scene of Khaḍrā's defense, which we have studied closely above, its frequency increases significantly. Throughout the scene in which Khaḍrā is being cast out of the tribe, references to clothing and coverings appear, standing for the inner state or quality. Ten such metonymic substitutions can be heard in only thirteen quatrains of Khaḍrā's accusation. Such repetition reinforces the basic question of whether or not Khaḍrā's bed covers were turned back illicitly. Some of Rizq's epithets, for example, become ironically invoked. In a sarcastic use of the periphrasis normally used to praise him, Rizq's fellow tribesmen refer to him in the new context as the "man with clean roots/honor/shawl"; the cuckolded man is addressed as "O, Master of the Clean Turban." The poet substitutes interchangeably in the formulaic pattern of the line the words turban (*ʿamāma*), or honor (*uṣūl*), roots ʿurūḍ). Outer apparel thus reflects the inner moral state, which is connected with one's origins, and through which one gains public face and status. Rizq castigates Khaḍrā, calls her "O, Mother of Earring and Jewelry." Khaḍrā's outer, bodily adornment, depending on the context in which the periphrasis is used, can either praise her beautiful femininity or blame it as a tawdry lure. The poet has described Khaḍrā before her name was besmirched as one for whom "dirt doesn't touch her clothes," and whose skirt is never dusty, that is, she is a noble lady of good reputation; Khaḍrā herself takes up these descriptive periphrases in her own defense when her husband accuses her. The series of metonyms culminates in Rizq's banishment of Khaḍrā, wherein he calls her "The one with light clothes," that is, they come off easily.

Jābir emphasizes this dialectic of the inside and the outside more explicitly than Sayyid in a number of ways. After Khaḍrā and her black servant depart, they pass through uninhabited mountains until they arrive at the outskirts of the Banī ʿUqayl. From the no-man's-land between the tribal encampments, Khaḍrā writes a letter to Ghānim, the troublemaking gossip. Her insults to him call attention to the basic issue; she tells him he doesn't know the *ḥalāl* from the *ḥarām* (the licit from the illicit). She prays to God that Ghānim's harem (*ḥarīm*) will be exposed and ridiculed; in short, that what he holds most sacred and inviolable be violated just as his talk has violated Khaḍrā.

The very next episode of the tale illustrates by example what Khaḍrā means in her contrast of the ḥalāl and the ḥarām. Jābir emphasizes the coming scene by breaking the flow of the music and the sung quatrains; he calls particular attention to the episode's levels of meaning by singing in introductory quatrains, "Look and see the ḥikāya!" The ḥikāya, like the story of the Birds at the Lake, is doubly meaningful. It serves to predict the next larger episode of the *Hilāliyya* after "Mīlād Abū Zayd," which is the encounter of the Hilālīs with the enemy ʿUqaylī tribe, who will kill off the fathers of Abū Zayd's generation and whom the audience know to be the true outsiders. More important, however, the episode also serves as symbolic comment on what Khaḍrā's own tribe has done to her.

Let us summarize the scene Jābir asks us to look at. The drama takes place in the borderlands, between the abodes of the Hilāl and Zaḥlān. This no-man's-land is the domain of ʿAṭwān the outlaw.[9] It is the precinct of the outcast and the tribeless. Khaḍrā arrives and settles down for the night amid her herds with her slaves and the newborn babies. As they sleep, ʿAṭwān and his men raid their cattle. Sharīfa (as Jābir calls her, reminding us of her family's genealogy originating with the Prophet) goes forward in all politeness (*adab*) to meet the rustlers and to claim the rights of guests and women to security. She points out in parallel quatrains that it is a shame (ʿayb and ʿār) to harm guests; their protection is a sacred trust (*amāna*). As the woman kneels before the raider, her veil falls to uncover her beauty. Jābir inquires rhetorically to the audience at this juncture, "Who is going to protect her but God?" The pathos of the scene increases as ʿAṭwān pulls her to the ground to rape her, even as she pleads that she gave birth less than seven days earlier and is still bleeding. Bared, defenseless, she cries, "I am a woman alone without a man." She tears at her clothes in grief and cries to the Highest, saying, "Your wish is my command, O, Lord and Creator!"

At this point a new character enters to voice a new ethic—the voice of Muslim measure and balance. Sulaymān, ʿAṭwān's cousin, stops the rape in progress as he yells, "Aren't we all Muslims? You son of a bitch, you ill-bred brat! I swear I'll kill you! don't touch that woman!" He defends Sharīfa with his sword and then turns to cover her nakedness, to put her veil in place. Sanity is restored, the boundaries reasserted. The ḥalāl and the ḥarām (licit and illicit) are very clear. In the paratactic, building style of oral poetry, the scene juxtaposed beside Khaḍrā's abstract formulation of the problem of the ḥarām versus the ḥalāl can be understood as an elaboration of that problem. Sulaymān defends Khaḍrā's honor against rape, the first genuine sexual attack on her integrity. All the violence done her up to this point is just dirty talk—talk that obscures reality, strips the modest woman bare with words while covering up her true virtue. Sulaymān covers her up again. He recalls the Muslim honor code and thus reinforces the religious and sacred connotation that surrounded Khaḍrā in the first scenes of the story as she entered her marriage contract.

Here we are with Khaḍrā and her supposed illegitimate son outside the boundaries of civilized humanity when she is attacked by an outlaw. Certain words are never directly spoken by the poet, but the range of connotations he controls within the tale appear to point to them. When Khaḍrā says, "You can't tell the ḥalāl from the ḥarām," while holding her presumed illegitimate son, her assertion brings certain unspoken words to mind. *Ibn ḥalāl* means legitimate son. *Ibn ḥarām* is the Egyptian word for bastard, but it is a term rarely spoken aloud because it is so strong. The first form of the verb *ḥaram* can mean to disinherit. Khaḍrā and her *ibn ḥarām* are in *arḍ al-ḥarām* (no-man's-land). Khaḍrā, as we know from the elaborate detail of Rizq's pilgrimage to Mecca, is the daughter of the Sharīf of Mecca who is the guardian of the sacred sanctuaries of Islam, called al-Ḥarām.

In the disjunctive logic of the shāʿir, which works out of the paratactic segments of his oral style, we recall that Jābir overtly termed Rizq's trip to Mecca to seek Khaḍrā's marriage a pilgrimage. The entire journey was cast in ritualistic terms, the vocabulary partaking of the religious lexicon, as Rizq visited *al-Bayt al-Ḥarām* dressed in ritual garb and drank from the holy well of Zamzam. The poet stresses Khaḍrā's noble ancestry. The marriage contracted in Medina and the House of the Prophet is conceived of as a union of groups, of families. The religious, sacred overtones of the marital and sexual union culminate as the hero claims his wife:

> He entered into her, the lad, carefully
> Praise be the Prophet, a crown for us
> and sadness and annoyance went away
> And the whole city rejoiced.

The group thus sanctions the contract between individuals as the marriage sanctified in the sacred precincts of Islam is consummated. All is in harmonious balance. And then God again directly intervenes in the course of human affairs to arrange Abū Zayd's conception. When the tribe misconceives things and banishes Khaḍrā with her black gift from God, the divinely consecrated marriage contract is dissolved. Nine times Jābir repeats the quatrain with the pun on *zayn* (The Beautiful One, lies, embellishment, adultery) when Khaḍrā is accused. ʿAsqal uses the wordplay to insinuate that she who claims to be related to al-Zayn (the Beautiful Prophet) is really more associated with zayn (zinā), that is, lies, embellishments, and adultery. Khaḍrā takes recourse to the same zahr (wordplay) to defend herself, but reverses the meaning: what looks like zayn (zinā) is really descended from al-Zayn (The Beautiful One, goodness, and prophetic beauty). Who is right and who is wrong, the tribe or Khaḍrā? The lexical ambiguity of the pun stresses the moral ambiguity of the situation.

The near-rape, however, removes all the moral ambiguity. In the drama enacted, Jābir passes audience identification to Khaḍrā in her pathetic plight in outlaw country and thereby passes audience adherence to her moral point of view. He invites the listener to judge actions, to evaluate the ethical system of the community. The moral logic of his dissociative argument splits the tribal value code and thereby provides distance and perspective on it for his listeners and implicitly criticizes it. When the tribal ethic becomes a profanation of sacred Muslim values, when its network of mutual obligation, its code of checks and balances on behavior both within the in-group and without it, its hierarchy of the insider and the outsider,—when this elaborate moral scale sways too far in any one direction so that true justice is miscarried in the interest of apparent honor,—then the tribal honor code is all wrong. It violates the overriding principle of Muslim measure and balance (*mīzān,* in the words of the poet). True honor, in the terms in which Jābir and Sayyid put the tradition, resides in upholding the Prophet's message of modesty, measure, and charity toward one's brother—the Muslim ideal of trust, peace, and security (*amān*) in which the powerful and strong protect the weak and needy. The shāʿir's disjunctive logic points out an incompatibility in tribal reasoning. Jābir particularly shows how petty tribal gossip—talk that judges by apparent truth instead of real truth—leads to disaster and real dishonor.

The dichotomies established by the philosophical pairs of the real versus the apparent truth serve as redefinitions. Literacy becomes more than knowing the ABCs. True literacy is religious understanding. True nobility of ancestry likewise takes on a holy connotation in the terms of the shāʿir. Property and wealth (the outward attributes of power, prestige, and high status) can fluctuate. The tribal ethic, in its focus on the more superficial aspect of values, which misses their true essence, is thus counterposed to true Muslim ethics.

The poet's pun logic provides a particularly appropriate vehicle by which at once to express and interpret moral ambiguities or hidden, taboo meaning. Punning, paronomasia, and such associated wordplay have a particular status and capacity in the Arabic language. A glance at any Arabic dictionary demonstrates a marked peculiarity of the language—many words can also mean their opposite; the homonym is an antonym.[10] This feature of the language expands the potentiality for punning, indeed invites it. Where dichotomous, antithetical meanings are not already denoted by a given word, the flexible triconsonantal root system of the language in its various forms has a plasticity of meaning. The pun exploits the possibilities of the triconsonantal pattern to the full. Multiple meanings emanate from the root paradigm, and disjunctive meanings are potential in any one word. The pun calls forth a range of indeterminate connotation potential within the sound configuration of three consonants.[11]

The fine craftsmen among the Hilālī poets, of whom Jābir and Sayyid are representative, are expert punsters. They use punning as a basic argumentative and structural device. Indeed, the good artist within the tradition builds the very meaning network out of puns. He uses them to interpret meaning and to teach his listeners a way of understanding the tradition. Puns, moreover, can have crucial salience in a shāʿir's oral performance, as we have seen, because of their coincidence with end-rhyme. The musical convention of rabāb accompaniment further accentuates their force and argumentative potential. As a figure of significant phonetic repetition, the pun links disparate and often contradictory contexts through its lexical ambiguity. It thereby works in a semimetaphoric way to expand and produce a new total context.[12] Its semantic-associative-dissociative process, however, connects ideas on a nonlinear, nonsyntactic level much the way music does—creating what I have called musical metaphor.

Just as some poets, like Fārūq, miss the obvious punning potential of key passages,[13] so listeners need not understand the puns. They may only hear repetition. Should they listen in this way, they will only hear a story of old, a romance of the Bedouin invaders which rouses little and makes no comment on the present. The poets' comments to "heed the tale," to "look and see" the meaning or the rhyme or tale, can be understood as mere pointers to the next episode (which they are), or even as mere filler tag lines to fill out the rhyme and construct the quatrain in the fast-moving experience of oral composition (which they also are). The case is not so simple with good, intelligent poets, for the rousing good story contains an invitation to identify with the action, to view it and the characters symbolically. In this invitation, the poet volunteers to interpret not only the traditional tale, he also offers a guide to understanding traditional society.

The insistent, repeated play on *zayn,* for example, as we have seen, contains hidden, various levels of meaning. It can be heard as a systematic key to the whole story of the birth of Abū Zayd.

The pun implicitly compares the religious and the erotic realms. Khaḍrā claims to be descended from al-Zayn (The Beautiful One) and thus free from zayn (lies and adultery, fornication and false embellishment). Sayyid's metonymies, calling her "the Mother of Earrings and Jewelry," suggest by extension that her bodily adornments are lures. Her personal physical beauty is also called zayn. The pun sets up a double-edged metaphor, for the same attribute may refer to her noble lineage as a descendant of the Prophet Muḥammad.

The pun thus establishes a comparison between the sacred precinct and the sexual. The linking context is lineage or ancestry as conceived within a nation founded by a religious leader. The individual's relationship to his group—both the immediate family group beginning with husband and wife and the larger group of clan and village—is structured by his direct links, on the basis of blood, back to the founder of the Nation of Islam. Sexual generativity, then, in the terms of the pun analogy, continues the divine nation and larger group. Socially sanctioned coitus between contracted man and wife, which produces an heir, guarantees both symbolically and practically the continuance of the Prophetic life. Its obverse, adulterous fornication, threatens the status quo, it threatens the community in its common past and present as well as its communal future. In short, it threatens the tribal genealogy that refers to both the past and present simultaneously.[14]

The shāʿir's art is basically metonymic, and the metonym of the outside standing for the inside provides all the poets of the tradition with a basic integrative rhetorical device for the larger sīra as a whole as well as its basic concept. Outside penetration of any sort threatens the stability of the community. Rhythmically, the story progresses through alternation of internal and external threats. In the latter part of *al-Hilāliyya,* conflict with the enemy tribe generally represents the outside threat to the kin group. However, the opening episode, the myth of the birth of the hero, is the myth of the origins of strife *within* the community. As such, the erotic-sexual metaphor takes precedence over the combat myth basic to later episodes and to epic tales in general. The child (*khalīfa,* offspring) of the Hilāl, their future legendary leader, is cast out of his own tribe, to be taken inside the harem (protected household) of the Zaḥlān, the enemy group. He rises, through a series of confrontations and duels stemming from his quarrel with his teacher, to become the strongman of the Zaḥlān. When the Hilālī refuse to pay the taxes they owe the Zaḥlān, Abū Zayd al-Hilālī is sent against them, against his father in man-to-man combat to settle the dispute. Abū Zayd thus merges the two groups once he is recognized as the legitimate son of the Hilāl. The boundaries of the inside and the outside of the two groups expand and collapse as the family reconciliation mirrors the merger of groups into one large united community. This merger of the in-group and the out-group recurs over and over in the spiraling cycles that comprise the *Hilāliyya,* the greater, total tale that exists only in the heads of the tradition's adherents (poets and patrons alike) and that is metonymically implicit in each episode. Ḥandal of the ʿUqaylī, in the very next larger episode after the birth tale, will kill off the older Hilālī generation. Abū Zayd will seek blood vengeance and at the same time find his bride, ʿAliyya al-ʿUqayliyya, from among the enemy, thus merging once more the protected inside of opposing groups—the nuclear family. In the third and final large cycle of episodes, the *Taghrība* (Westward Migration), the tribe will disintegrate, the heroes die as the inside divides against itself in the tension between the heroes of Hilāl and Ghānim, Abū Zayd and Diyāb ibn Ghānim. As the conception scene at the Lake of the Birds predicts, the black bird and red bird set upon each other to sow the seeds of dissension and dissolution and discontinuity of the united kin groups. Khaḍrā's curse on Ghānim, whose vicious talk began the cycles of disruption and displacement when Khaḍrā was banished from the tribe, will be fulfilled.

Certainly, the birth tale can be heard as a tale of oedipal conflict with a strong mother-son incest component. It lends itself easily to a reading on the universal level as a myth of the primal horde killing off the father and absconding with the mother—or, at least, as a tale of all this narrowly averted. Perhaps such a universal psychological constellation of meaning is implicit in the tale. The range of meaning and connotation intended by the poets, however, can be implied through their interpretive style; for the shāʿir's style leads the attentive listener inside the story into the deeper meaning of the tradition through the seemingly surface embellishments of music, rhyme, puns, and metonymy. The pleasure that the listeners take in wordplay and in an artistic execution of a well-known episode from the saga not only leads him to comprehend the meaning of al-sīra but also teaches him a mode of perceiving his daily life and history, his pattern of experience through time.

The pun logic and spiraling metonymies of the shāʿir's composition represent a compendium of Egyptian peasant life as it is lived and a kaleidoscope of interrelatedness in which poetic discourse and life lived converge as parts of a greater mosaic. The poets guide the listener to understand the story segmentally and disjunctively in symbolic terms. The "Birth of Abū Zayd," as we have seen, explains the origins of strife in the fictive community that makes up the *Hilāliyya*. Perhaps more important, however, the story provides a myth of the origins of conflict within the present-day community of listeners and poets. The central meaning good poets give the myth of the birth of the hero in its Upper Egyptian reindividuation is not the universal human developmental issue of father-son conflict, nor is it the mother-son incest that the "family romance" universally implies.[15] The genuine taboo and problem buried figuratively in the tale is the cultural ambivalence surrounding the inside and the outside, the question of personal and social boundaries.

The discursive context of the narrative event has the male shāʿir interpreting a tale of conception, pregnancy, and birth to an audience that is normally and traditionally all male in a sexually dichotomized society. The shāʿir takes the men of his audience inside the tribe's harem to glimpse a series of events normally protected from the male view. Hamed Ammar, in his psychosocial documentation of growing up in an Egyptian village, says that pregnancy and birth are so much within the female purview that it is a taboo subject for men.[16] A man must even avoid mentioning his wife's pregnancy. He also notes that great emotional tension surrounds pregnancy and childbirth. In a community where money and children are cited as the main joys of this life granted by the Koran, birth is God's creation.[17] The desire for children is intense, and sexual intercourse with one's mate to produce heirs is considered a good religious deed (*ḥasana*).[18] Many rituals and social obligations surround the highly charged event. Women engage in "many and multifarious ritualistic devices" to induce pregnancy, including ritual pilgrimages, like Khaḍrā's, to specially endowed sites, saints' shrines, lakes, or the Nile. After the birth, mother and child must be secluded for forty days. While the child is seen to be protected during this period by angelic forces, the mother is viewed as too vulnerable even to cook, wash, or say her prayers. A rigid system of food, confinement, and other taboos protects the mother from the evil eye and potential future sterility. She covers herself and the child when visitors come to the house and pretends to be suffering from pain. Visitors guard against praising the child too overtly except in safeguarding religious formulas. The child's sex is usually kept secret at first, only to be declared openly later when the child is named in a public ceremony of reception into the family and neighborhood at seven days.[19] For the first forty days, the child should be shielded from "blacks or any other foreigners or strangers whose origin is not known."[20]

In the "Birth of Abū Zayd," the shāʿir focuses attention on the tribal women performing ritual fertility ablutions at the Lake of the Birds. Male poet and male audience thus penetrate the secret female conception rites. The nine months are carefully cataloged by all three poets. The shāʿir shows the men of the tribe gathering amid great feasting and abundance to receive and name the child. What has been kept secret, however, is not his sex, but his race. Normal birth rites are violated when Rizq approaches Khaḍrā and banishes her from her rightful prophylactic seclusion; he turns her out, bleeding from childbirth, child in arms, to face all the dangers implicit in the outside world. This is the sin. This is the ultimate shame, the taboo violated.

Two puns (*aḍdād,* words which mean their opposite)[21] summarize the nexus of meaning implicit in the violation: ḥarām and ʿabd. We have already seen the argumentative function in Jābir's narrative of the concept of ḥarām. We have examined the way in which it disjunctively and inferentially links narrative facts and segments, connecting Khaḍrā and her son with the sacred, most protected precincts of Islam (al-Bayt al-Ḥarām) as well as with the inner sanctum of the individual household (the bayt and its ḥarīm). The three consonants ḥ/r/m contain an ambivalence of denotation, for they can refer to both the sacred and forbidden. *Ḥaram* and *ḥarām* both mean forbidden, prohibited, unlawful, sin; they also mean sacred, sacrosanct as well as accused. *Ḥarāmī* refers to a thief; *ḥirm* means anathema, excommunication; *ḥirmān* disinheritance, deprivation. Ḥarīm is the harem, the women's apartments in the household, the family; it also may mean wife or lady; *ḥurma* means woman or old woman, and is used to refer to a man's wife—*ḥurmituh,* his "old lady." *Iḥtirām,* from the eighth form of the verb, means respect or veneration. *Iḥrām* is the state of ritual purity a pilgrim to Mecca enters as well as the garment he wears. Ibn ḥarām, as we have seen, is a bastard son, also a scoundrel; whereas al-Ḥaram refers to Mecca, and *al-Ḥaramayn* to Mecca and Medina. In its doubling of veneration and horror, the word incorporates the very essence of taboo.[22]

Like the Zayn pun, the word's ambiguity links the erotic and the religious realms; the profane contracts of men are implicit with their bonds to the divine and vice versa. Khaḍrā makes the distinction between the ḥalāl and the ḥarām overtly. *Ḥalāl* refers to that which is legal, lawful in a contractually binding way. Looking back at the story in the legalistic terms Khaḍrā set up, we can understand the woman to be entering a contract with Rizq (marriage) and a contract with God (the answer to her prayers, a son granted). Neither of these does she break. Rizq entered a contract with Khaḍrā, while in a ritual state of purity in the sacred shrines of Islam, to sire a son and heir. He renounced it, broke the marriage contract, and disinherited his descendant (khalīfa). In so doing, Rizq ignored the divine provision, violated the ḥarām and the ḥarīm, all the while spouting humble formulas about the Lord as the ultimate provider. Public shame before the gossiping men of the tribe became his motivation. The shāʿir's rendition of the birth of the hero then can be seen as a drama of sharaf (male honor), which is a public matter of bravery, loyalty, and property, versus ʿirḍ (female honor), which is a more private question of sexual chastity and modesty.[23] Talk made the private public and cast the inside outside, excluded the secluded and thus made true morality immorality and profaned the sacred.

Understood in the punning mode of the shāʿir's argument, the tale becomes a fertility myth. In both the shāʿir's discourse and Egyptian peasant culture, the word is a living presence with the power to persuade men as well as angels or demons. Ammar comments on the prophylactic power of names given newborn babies, the awareness everyone has of the meaning behind names. The poets too are aware of the etymological efficacy of names, using them as mnemonic organizational devices as well as interpretive tools. Sayyid and Jābir both play with the naming of Abū Zayd, the former with the pun on food, provision, and increase implicit in the name; the latter with the quasi-mystical, religious epithets of Barakāt (Blessings) and Salāma (Blameless) attached to the newborn. In Jābir's version, the holy man, divine agent Quṭb, presides over the naming of the new baby. In casting out Khaḍrā (whose name means verdant greenness) and Abū Zayd (father of provision), Rizq and the Hilālī tribe invited sterility and doom. For they cast out the heir, the khalīfa, the descendant and offspring, who in genealogical terms embodies both the past and future. They have earned their fate. And in rejecting their link with their past,—the khalīfa, they are doomed to repetition, to unending journey, to upheaval, to cycles of famine and war. In violating the seclusion taboos surrounding the birth process, they have engendered movement, change, and violence. They now must conquer al-Khaḍrā, the promised green land of Tūnis, the elusive fertile female. They must avenge the father who cast her out. The woman—suspect, full of mystery and potential danger in her reproductive capabilities—serves as the mediator between men and God, between man and his fate, between mankind and his history, a genealogy that embodies the past and future in the present new generation of offspring. Further fictive generations are doomed to repeat the cycle over and over again in attempting to right the balance. The violation of the taboo at the same time generates the spiraling metonymies and cyclical rings of the discourse. The Egyptian audience through one generation after the other will hear the *Hilāliyya* over and over again, almost compulsively. For it offers clues as to who they are and where they have come from and why things are as they are.

The traditional tale suggests the answer in the slave motif. "Mīlād Abū Zayd" combines two common motifs that provide the initial episode of an inordinate number of Arab and Egyptian folktales: lack of a child[24] and the erotic triangle of a cuckolded husband and a copulating wife and black slave.[25] The missing child in this tale turns out to be a Negro. Khaḍrā is accused of sleeping with a black Sudanese slave. In Jābir's version of Khaḍrā's seeming transgression, Rizq goes over in explicit detail the scene he imagines of Khaḍrā's most private parts bared for a "black slave," a "foreign intruder," the "son of a black stranger." Fārūq has Rizq ask, "What slave hugged and kissed you?" He goes on to assert, "She gave her love to slaves, and her passion to inferior ones." Khaḍrā has violated the hierarchy of the high and mighty versus the lowly and inferior; she has violated the norms that interdict intercourse between different social groups. She has permitted inside the harem one who by definition should always be an outsider. She appears to have violated the laws of tribal exclusion and inclusion. Fārūq's version of Khaḍrā's defense clarifies her identification with slaves. In exile, about to be attacked by unscrupulous outlaws against whom her slave will defend her, Fārūq's Khaḍrā writes a letter not to Ghānim but to Rizq. In it, she expresses her bewilderment that he should insult both her and his slaves; I translate:

> She wrote in a letter and she said a mawwāl
> While tears down her cheek were flowing.
> What is disappointing you, Pasha Hilāl?
> What is the anxiety, Ibn Nāyil?
>
> From your house you cast me
> And tears wet my palms.
> Along with your slaves, you insulted me.
> And it is God who rewards and satisfies.

Her son Abū Zayd is called a slave. Khaḍrā's loyal household includes a family of slaves. Abū Zayd's lifelong companion and shadow is Abū Ghomṣān, the black slave child conceived at the Lake of Fertility and born in the general wealth of reproductivity which visits the tribe nine months later to end seven years' sterility. The slave child receives his name, Abū Ghomṣān (= Abū Qumṣān or father of shirts), according to Jābir's narration of the story, in a naming ceremony in no-man's-land, at the crossroads between tribal encampments. Khaḍrā, her servant woman, and the divine agent Quṭb al-Rijāl, continue the interrupted naming ceremony and name the slave baby in honor of the shirt Quṭb throws over the child to protect him when he is dropped on the ground. Abū Zayd likewise will wear the belt of Quṭb all his life as a protective device.

The word used repeatedly to refer to Abū Zayd and the slaves is *ʿabd.* Around the slave motif coalesces a plurality of meaning significant to the nexus of the tale. In its disjunctive denotation, the word *ʿabd* functions like *ḥarām* to combine both a pun and the philosophical pairs out of which the shāʿir constructs his dissociative argument. The word contains the same ambiguous moral ramifications implicit in the Zayn pun. ʿ*Abd* may refer to a Negro slave or it may refer to a servant of God, or even simply to humanity or all mankind. The pun implicit in the levels of meaning quite efficiently reduces any social hierarchy or any concept of insider and outsider. The apparent lowly slave, the foreign black outsider to the tribe, is also a servant of God and part of the human race. Abū Zayd incarnates this relationship—the apparent black bastard outcast from his family and tribe to become a stranger and guest taking refuge. As the listener identifies first with Abū Zayd's mother, then with the black hero himself, he becomes him. Abū Zayd is all of us. He is the Upper Egyptian peasant listener, the historic bedouin tribesman invading the Nile valley, the dark-skinned gypsy rabāb poet singing the *Hilāliyya,* and the American critic come to record the epic. All boundaries, all categories of inside and outside; included, secluded, and excluded; foreign and familiar dissolve in the identification with the hero.

# 7

# AL-SĪRA, THE BIOGRAPHY OF THE EGYPTIAN PEASANT

The dialectic of the inside and the outside pervades the shāʿir's discourse as an integrative and interpretive figure. In its transformations of the boundaries between the included and the excluded, the foreign and the familiar, the shameful and the blameworthy, the honorable and dishonorable, free and slave, the permitted and the forbidden, the sacred and the taboo, the repetitive figure plays itself out as a highly charged symbol that extends into the very core of Egyptian peasant society. The objectification and reification of the metaphor of the inside and the outside appears to be systematic throughout the culture—a symbolic complex expressive of a deeply felt cultural reality extending into everyday attitudes, values, ways of perceiving. It finds expression in the boundaries of vertical and horizontal social structure, family structure, and personal and group psychology as well. It integrates and informs rituals, social beliefs, patterns of social togetherness and avoidance, unity and separation—in short, the patterns of social differentiation and discrimination. The shāʿir's performance of *al-Hilāliyya* before his peasant audience itself dramatizes and provides a ritual reenactment of the moral and social dilemma central to both the collective text and the collectivity, the community itself.[1]

The Hilālī poet sings what is perceived to be the history of the Egyptian peasantry. Poor people, who work at back-breaking labor for very little gain, have somehow managed to keep the poet in business for centuries; they pay his professional fees to hear him sing the song of the nomad tribe which invaded their homeland some 800 years ago. The Egyptian peasant audience, from all accounts, identifies the Hilālī legend as the true story of who they are and where they came from. The word for the genre, *al-sīra,* in fact means biography, life, or way. *Sīrat Banī Hilāl* or the *Hilāliyya* might best be translated as "The Ways of the Hilāl," for this English rendition conveys, as the folk term does, at once biography, going, and journey, as well as manner and customs. Popularly, the *Hilāliyya* is known as either *al-sīra* or *al-kitāb* (the book). The term "sīra" immediately also brings to mind another text of great cultural significance in Arabo-Muslim society: *Sīrat al-Nabī,* the Biography of the Prophet Muḥammad, a fixed text from the high, classical-language written tradition. *Al-Kitāb* (The Book) of course is the Koran, the sacred text of the community of Islam, which is memorized and recited by the faithful. Up until about twenty years ago, the primary means of instruction in Upper Egyptian villages was provided by the Koranic schools and the shāʿir and maddāḥs' transmissions of oral history. Traditionally, the first crop went to pay the barber, the Koran chanter, the Imam, and the poet.[2]

In his short book and his 1976–1977 series of newspaper essays,[3] in which he describes the place of al-sīra in the Upper Egyptian community, Abnoudy makes explicit the association of the poet with religious authority. He compares the poet to the Imam in the mosque reciting the Koran. He sees the relationship between the shāʿir and the fellah (peasant farmer) in an extended metaphor as "an integral part of the Ṣaʿīdī landscape, extending from one side of the country to the other, from antiquity down into the present and on into the future—like the waterwheel that irrigates the Nile valley fields and like the Imam who recites the Koran in the Mosque." According to Abnoudy, the poet gives voice to the song hidden deep within the heart of the Egyptian peasant, to his innermost turmoil and pain under the yoke of physical labor endured daily.[4]

The Hilālī poet thus has a privileged community status. Abnoudy stipulates that the role of the poet is deeply revered and respected in the oral, folk culture. The poet has a mission and a profession: to become a poet, a man must learn *Sīrat Banī Hilāl.* To be called a poet, he must combine intelligence with knowledge of public taste; he must live the life of the people and share their daily existence. He also needs to have a fine voice and a capacity to assimilate the oral tradition and to re-create it as he has inherited its themes, ideas, forms, melodies, and rhythms. The poet must prove to his audience that he possesses the *Hilāliyya* and knows it better than any other poet.[5]

Another Egyptian commentator reveals in yet another way how passionate was the involvement of the excitable audiences he observed in the 1930s:

> When the *Hilāliyya* is recited you will find the audience's zeal for listening changed into a dreadful sort of partisanship. The brothers of yesterday degenerate into the enemies of today. One group will fanatically take the side of the Banī Hilāl. Another will take the side of the Zanātī. Some want the poet to recite one episode, others another. The rāwī responds only to those who give liberally. If the balance sways in favor of one group, then the rāwī will recall what the majority wishes. . . . He will recall wondrous things and marvelous events and decorate the events so as to weave for the hero a garment that will stir the hearts of his followers with wonder and burn the breast of his opponents with envy.[6]

Overt audience antagonisms such as al-Zayyāt mentions still predominate sīra performances in Upper Egyptian villages today. The poet and his village patron, in fact, engage each other directly in exchanging insults. Poets very directly castigate the fellahin, on whom they are dependent to sell their verse wares. The most esteemed poet, indeed, appears to be the one who knows how to carry on a dialogue with his listeners and pile insult on insult in witty wordplay.[7]

The strife surrounding a performance, the animated audience identification with the sides of the fictive conflict, is accounted for by al-Zayyāt in terms of latent tribalism. According to him, the sīra stoked up old tribal animosities and buried resentments. Abnoudy,[8] in his very recent report of the tradition, and Mukhlis,[9] in his work in the early 1960s, both point to the connection of the *Hilāliyya* tradition with folk history and tribal genealogy. Abnoudy particularly sees the sīra as the justification of Upper Egyptian class hierarchies based on ancestry.

Whatever the reason, the *Hilāliyya* rouses its listeners and has maintained an audience 800 years after the events it celebrates. Two biographies of Upper Egyptian villagers, side-by-side with

Ammar's documentation of growing up in an Egyptian village, offer provocative evidence as to why the Hilālī Bedouin drama of honor and shame still maintains an audience of passionate adherents. The case histories of Shaḥḥāt and Jābir Abū Ḥusayn, a member of the audience and a poet, particularly illuminate the nature of the identification both the poet and his public bear for this oral poetic history.

In his biography of an Egyptian peasant farmer, *Shaḥḥāt,* Critchfield gives particularly interesting testimony to a spontaneous performance of the Hilālī hero's birth story at a party in the village of Berat, near Luxor.[10] Critchfield's description of the shāʿir's performance before a real audience (rather than one assembled at a researcher's behest in the interests of recording the epic) shows how immediate is the appeal of the sīra and how direct may be the identification of the hearer with the story.

The occasion for the party to which a "very old and very famous poet" has been invited is a celebration for a young man's recovery from an illness into which he fell after his family forbade him to marry a gypsy girl from the Jamāsah tribe dwelling on the outskirts of the village. The tale sways the young man literally and metaphorically, physically and morally, as it symbolically embodies all his concerns. Critchfield describes the youth's passionate identification with the rabāb poet's mythic discourse during seven nights of a week-long performance. The past conveyed musically to this audience in the village of Berat literally sways the hearer: bodies incline and tremble, voices breathe "Allah!" between lines of poetry. With closed eyes, the hearers lick their lips, swallow, and bodily incorporate the ebb and flow of the poetry.[11]

A hot-tempered, romantically impulsive young man with Semitic features and the Arab's lanky, lean frame, Shaḥḥāt descends from a paternal great-grandfather who belonged to an Arab nomad tribe like the Banī Hilāl. His mother tells a story about his own birth which is not unlike Abū Zayd's. Her personal memorate of the pilgrimage she made to an ancient temple's pool of ritual ablution to pray for a strong son after many years of barrenness and miscarriages reverberates with the same intimations of taboo and transgression that echo through the conception of Abū Zayd as told by the Hilālī poets. The mother explains her son's hot-blooded temperament not in terms of his Arab genealogy, but in terms of divine retribution for her own blasphemous polytheism and infidelity to Islam. For, after her eight-year-old and nine-year-old sons died and then two more male babies died at birth, in desperation she prayed to Ammon-Ra, an ancient Pharaonic god, to give her a strong son who would survive to manhood. She made a pilgrimage to the ancient temple adjacent to the village, circumambulated its pool seven times in good Islamic ritual style, and drank from its black depths. In a gesture of repentance for her heresy, she named her baby Muḥammad in honor of the Prophet and henceforth became known herself as Umm Muḥammad (Mother of Muḥammad). Lest the evil eye take notice of the boy, however, she nicknamed him Shaḥḥāt (Beggar).[12]

One can imagine the immediacy of Shaḥḥāt's identification with Abū Zayd's conception and birth. The parallel between the tale Shaḥḥāt's mother tells of his conception after a ritual prayer offering and the story of Abū Zayd's conception at the Lake of the Birds is remarkable. Such a coincidence of story pattern with patterns of life experience makes for a highly charged symbol.[13] The *sīra* not only accounts for Shaḥḥāt's Bedouin origins, it offers a verbal, ritual dramatization of his own life, both in literal terms and in figural, emotional terms.

Shaḥḥāt's Arab ancestry is common among Upper Egyptians. Although many people of Berat descend from pure Pharaonic stock, Arab blood is frequent from the intermarriage of fellahs with the Bedouin tribesmen. Shaḥḥāt's village views the Bedouins as "fierce, wild horsemen who lived on the sands and rocks far east of the Nile." Shaḥḥāt's paternal great-grandfather, for example, came to Berat after a bloody battle with his tribe. He brought with him a string of camels that he traded for land. He settled in the town, married one of its daughters, and in his prosperity bought ten acres.[14] Under Islamic inheritance laws, Shaḥḥāt's father inherited one of the original ten acres, and with the death of their father, Shaḥḥāt and his five siblings inherited a divided interest in that single acre. Islamic inheritance is such that a single cow or water buffalo may have as many as twenty-five or thirty owners. Bitter disputes between close relatives over property and rights of ownership are common. Frequent litigations arise over little more than a few feet of land or a fraction of an interest in a waterwheel or plowshare. One of Ammar's informants confided, "In these days more often than not heirs insist on dividing land, and this occasions the hottest disputes between brothers and sisters and relatives. Lawsuits over land have cost the people the land itself. . . . Our life is mostly spent in settling my right and your right—hakki, hakkak [*ḥaqqī, ḥaqqak*]."[15]

The view of the Egyptian fellah embroiled in incessant quarrels, mutually distrusting and hostile, is nothing new. A perplexing seventeenth-century Egyptian text, *Hazz al-Quḥūf* (The Shaking of Skullcaps) by Yūsuf al-Shirbīnī, taken up after the 1952 revolution by leftist and populist commentators, cites the extreme materialism of the fellah. Shirbīnī, himself a former country boy who went to Cairo and al-Azhar to become a religious shaykh, viciously mocks the rural people with whom he grew up in a satirical tract directed at an audience of townsmen. He describes Egyptian farmers as so crassly materialistic that concerns about livestock and canal dredging override religious duty and kinship bonds; there is so little trust between them that amān (the pledge of security for refugees) is not kept, few intimate friendships exist, hospitality is deficient; they are exploitative and fond of power to the extent of respecting the oppressor and if not oppressed, oppressing others. An eighteenth-century writer similarly chronicled the fellah's great misfortunes, mentioning their black faces, poverty, hard work, fights with governors and tax collectors, and frequent internecine wars.[16]

The fellahin have until only recently (1952) been seen as "passive," unresisting, and even stupid. As Ammar tells us, they have submitted to a multitude of social orders, only rarely taking part in any resistance, leaving the battles to the military and ruling classes: "to them, a military defeat meant the ousting of one ruling power by another."[17] It is the rulers who have engaged the main interest of historians, even though, as Ammar asserts, it is "the habits and traditions of the common folk that have, in fact, been the ultimate determining forces." Hussein sees the Egyptian masses as victimized and oppressed both externally by foreign powers and internally by a "savage bureaucracy."[18] The rural Egyptian village has long united against the outside, against any central authority, be it local urban bureaucracy or foreign invader reaping the profits of the fields in one way or another; it has historically turned inward onto itself and, as Ayrout puts it, against itself.[19] It is a world structured vertically in terms of class, status, and power hierarchies, both within and without, and horizontally in terms of oppositions.

Vertically, property, wealth, personal power, and education provide an individual and his family with respect. To have status is to have land. A proverb indicates that the lowest on the hierarchy are the donkey, the dog, the Negro, and the man without land.[20] Within this ethic, children are deemed an absolute value. Ammar's informant ʿAlī remarked on the tragedy of having land but no sons.[21] Shaḥḥāt's mother, the shrewdly realistic Umm Muḥammad, was more explicit in her statement of values: "Marriage means you are establishing a household. You must become a real man who looks to the needs of the house and the land, a man who fathers many children and raises them. It means to prosper and lead a decent life so that everyone must respect you."[22] Critchfield describes this peasant village woman's hard-earned knowledge that freedom and dignity depend on observing the time-honored codes. She sees people as being kept in place more by Islamic law and peer pressure than by their own virtue. To her, family, property, and social position are everything. Ammar's study verifies her assertion of the village ethical code. Prestige and status in the village of Silwa also depend above all on one's claim as an heir to land. "To have origin in the village is to have land," Ammar maintains; "if you have no kirat (land measure) handed over to you from your ancestors then you are not a full member of your clan." Ammar quotes two variations on a child's bouncing-ball rhyme which encapsulate a typical view of property: "My mother gave me a chicken, the chicken bought me a goose, the goose bought me a small goat, the goat bought me a sheep, the sheep bought me a small donkey, the donkey bought me a cow, the cow bought me a kirat (1/24 of a feddan); the second version concludes differently as the cow buys a bride and the bride brings the child a bridegroom (a son).[23] Like Umm Muḥammad's formulation, the children's rhyme in its two versions equates property, growing prosperity, marriage, and offspring in the form of an heir (khalīfa).

Age, sex, and family lineage are less manipulable status indexes than land and property. As a Muslim community, and a relatively homogeneous society in which relationships are personal, controls familial, and sanctions sacred,[24] social behavior and mutual obligations are built on the family relationship pattern with regard to age, sex, and status. The outside world is dangerous and the family the source of all support and nurturance, though in matters of property, even it can turn against the individual as rampant individualism reigns. Marriage with cousins thus is preferred. Social acts and value judgments fall into two main categories, according to Ammar, the ḥarām and the ḥalāl, the forbidden and the permitted. Both words have distinctively religious connotation. Great respect is accorded the "ashrāf," the plural of sharīf, a concept we saw in the *Hilāliyya*. These people have the most distinguished genealogy as descendants of the Prophet of Islam and as such earn great status and rank in the community in view of their greater chance of salvation.[25] The sacred pervades daily life. The vertical hierarchy extends to the supernatural realm. Formulaic locutions on the omnipotence of God and Fate abound, pious locutions of submission to Destiny and the Will of God. Outwardly, Ammar recounts, no dichotomization of rich and poor exists. All live in an apparent egalitarianism of dress and demeanor in a Muslim brotherhood united by the commonality of Believers.[26]

In actual fact, however, daily life is one of constant confrontation and struggle, and horizontally, the society is structured along oppositional lines. Critchfield comments on how relatives and neighbors in Berat gathered to hear the old storyteller as if thirty years of feuding among blood relatives was of little account.[27] Both before and after the Hilālī poet arrived in Berat, Shaḥḥāt, his mother, his uncle, their cousins, and neighbors spent their days haggling and quarreling, contending over this or that, striving for dominance. In a world where upward mobility is potential and status in the village hierarchy can change according to fluctuations in material wealth, much jostling for property occurs and much enmity arises out of jealousy upon seeing close relatives or neighbors prosper. Shaḥḥāt's mother, for example, came from a very poor family who could not offer a dowry on her marriage. She expressed constant animosity toward her husband's family members who had somehow mysteriously become rich, one rising from fishmonger to innkeeper. She also resented Fārūq, her husband's drinking buddy and former serf who sharecropped her husband's government-deeded land. Fārūq had prospered through contracts to sharecrop for several landowners. He soon accumulated so many fields to work and manage that he could in turn subcontract them to others and spend his hours in leisure.[28]

Foster offers an explanation for such strife and resentment as

Critchfield observed and Ammar chronicles.[29] He describes the basic premise of peasant societies the world over as one of an "image of limited good"—a zero-sum game wherein there exists only so much bounty and any change in material wealth upsets the balance. In the narrow green belt of the Nile valley this perception is more than an image. It is a geographical and nutritional reality. As Ammar asserts, the land for generations has provided the tangible bulwark against starvation and insecurity.[30] The green river belt delimits fertile life from the sterile desert only a short distance beyond; this world indeed has limited good—both geographically and agriculturally. Land is a very restricted resource. It is divided up and parceled out according to strict inheritance rules. Consequently, when one person gets more of the land, or the goat's milk, or the wheat millet for bread, it means someone gets less. Within this geographic and economic reality, Umm Muḥammad's suspicious rancor is not without reason and represents an entire cultural and social ethos.

The suspicious oppositionalism of the Egyptian peasant farmer-laborer, which has so plagued his upper-class distanced critics from Shirbīnī onward, can certainly be explained in economic terms. Ammar offers a more complex analysis of the peasant agonisms he grew up around in his compassionate psychoanalytic, anthropological study of the community of Silwa, in the southernmost province of Egypt, a "typical" Egyptian village. Ammar explains the uneasiness and tension in interpersonal relationships that extend into the village social structure itself as specific emotional adjustments to the harsh realities of economic life, to historical forces of oppression, and to child-rearing practices. The peasant's only sense of security, Ammar maintains, resides precisely in his insecurity; insecurity is what he knows and understands because he has always lived it and adjusted his practices, beliefs, and ideas in relationship to it. The family guards its private affairs with great caution, for fear others may gloat at their expense or find some way of attacking their moral integrity. An almost morbid fear of shame exists. Villagers describe each other mutually as greedy, envious, and malicious; they put it in the following terms: "People would distribute your property while you are alive" (p. 230). Danger is potentially everywhere outside the family, in everyone and everything.[31]

Within the family, mother and children have a close, intimate relationship marked by a great deal of sibling rivalry and jostling for the mother's attention. The bond between mother and oldest son is particularly passionate. Father and mother have a quite formal, distanced, legal relationship. The child's relationship with his father is similarly formal and distant. Both solidarity and friction are cultural expectations among siblings and Ammar sees this as reflecting itself in the village structure as well as in the structural relations with the world outside the village and with other villages. Another Egyptian writer, the folklorist El-Shamy, comments that many of the folktales and practices of the folk culture reflect a widespread conflict between matrilineal versus patrilineal affiliations.[32] Sibling relationships remain intense and often provide friction in families and give the family group a certain instability.

Ammar explains that much of the conflict seen in daily life, the rancorous lawsuits over land, the other quarrels that can be pursued with seemingly endless effort and expense, all these derive from status anxieties and social rivalries combined with what this Egyptian scholar terms a "weak ego structure."[33] Ammar goes on to explain that one of the "important psychological mechanisms in the personality is the power of fate." He describes fate in the psychoanalytic terms of Kardiner[34] as a projective mechanism that shifts personal responsibility to others or onto supernatural forces. It is a cultural mode of displacing dependency onto parent surrogates and thus escaping blame and punishment. Like El-Shamy,[35] Ammar correlates the concept of fate with the presence of very little anxiety about sickness and other misfortunes. Ammar sees such a projective mechanism as arising out of conditions of a closed economy together with a stifling weight of social and parental pressures.[36]

The personality structure as well as the social structure and cultural ethos thus partakes of the "paranoid" end of the "depressive-paranoid existential continuum" identified by psychoanalysts and applied at the cultural level by anthropologists.[37] The paranoid constellation involves essentially what El-Shamy and Ammar have outlined as the Egyptian peasant personality and social structure: an inability to refer responsibility to the self, an incapacity to feel ambivalent about oneself, and a need for recognition; projection thus becomes a major part of the ego defense system. All feelings are projected outward to others, to objects. The world thus becomes fraught with danger. The individual is perceived as inadequate and powerless. This sense of powerlessness may be inherent in any hierarchically ordered society, and, indeed, derive from it.[38] The self is determined by what we can control; what we cannot control is the world. Boundaries between the self and other thus are those of control and countercontrol. What cannot be controlled is experienced as an outside force, as something alien, as an opposition.[39]

This results in the Egyptian village community in strict boundaries of insider and outsider, self and other, in-group and out-group, the community versus enemies or strangers, which exist both within the village and without. Contesting siblings or other family members unite against the outside neighborhood or greater extended family group, neighborhoods and clans against groups they define as somehow culturally "other" or "outside." Ambivalence denied within the individual is projected outward into a highly dichotomized world of male and female, landed and unlanded, privileged and unprivileged, up and down; a world of exclusion, inclusion, and seclusion. The insufficiency of the individual is only counterposed by the overweening individual who feels freed from responsibility.[40] And in everyday face-to-face interaction, striving, competitive individualism runs rampant. Shared responsibility and brotherhood is the ideal.[41] Kinship, friendship, and shared living bind people together in a web of reciprocal obligation and, according to Ammar and El-Shamy, maintain social equilibrium through an elaborate system of social behavior which counterbalances the competitive tendencies in the community. Fate, in this view, shunts directly overt hostility and shifts responsibility from those who actually have power or advantage to place it on a kind of mechanistic concept of human destiny. Ammar quotes Kardiner as saying that the chief function of a belief in fate is to compel the individual to accept his role in life and not bother those who exploit him.[42] Any outbreak of violence likewise can be blamed on fate. Magic and other manipulation may avail, but it also may not; both the individual and the group are controlled by forces beyond.

Ammar attributes much of the overt aggression prevalent in the Egyptian peasant community in part to "bottling up personal, spontaneous feeling, or at least to the very limited scope for its outlet or for its direct expression as action."[43] Abnoudy similarly describes the isolation of the individual who is doubly dominated by the group will and by back-breaking toil. In Abnoudy's lyric account of the relationship between the peasant and the poet, the shāʿir gives voice to the song within the workingman. Epic song in Egypt, according to this man who has earned much respect as the spokesman of the folk, gives rise to a voice of protest which the individual, fettered by work and the false dignity imposed on him in the factitious solidarity of the group, cannot utter. Song enables the individual to break the chains forged by his links of obligation to ancestors and contemporaries. Epic song especially liberates the individual and expresses the pain he cannot himself articulate. As Abnoudy puts it:

> The professional poet breaks the barriers of convention and group taboos and interdictions. The plaint that arises is clear, freed of all fetters and beautiful. It is no longer perceived as an undignified weakness of a person. The poet sings of woman, poverty, pain, sexuality, drunkenness, freedom, and the exploitation of man by man. The audience approve of him and express their admiration directly. The poet helps them to become frank and sincere, to appear under their true face and to not fear to be as they are in face of the group.[44]

Shaḥḥāt's case is illustrative of the relationship between the poet and his public. The young man's case history illuminates the cathartic function of al-sīra in a rigidly stratified community where the full force of group pressures and sacred sanctions come to bear on nonconforming individuals. The Berat audience put aside thirty years of incessant quarreling among blood relatives to sit together and hear the shāʿir recount how the seeds of strife were sown in a Bedouin Arab tribe long ago. As we mentioned, the party at which the poet performed for a whole week was given to celebrate Shaḥḥāt's recovery from the illness that struck him like a frenzy of possession after his family closed in on him and would not permit him to cross over village social boundaries to marry his beloved Suniya.[45] Within the strict village hierarchy based on ancestry and property, Shaḥḥāt could not marry the winsome girl who grew up beside him. She belonged to a Jamāsah family, the traditional water carriers and milk sellers, "latecomers" to the village. Suniya's family's group was despised as virtual outcasts, presumably for engaging in a low trade, selling substances that by traditional values should not be sold at all. The Jamāsah[46] in folk history are said to have come late 1300 years ago to a gathering called by the Prophet Muḥammad. They henceforth came to be shunned by good Muslims. One man in Shaḥḥāt's village defied convention and married a Jamāsah. Although he was a village official and a descendant of the man for whom the town was named, his family now lives on the edge of the desert far away from all neighbors, ostracized by fellah and Jamāsah alike.

The social stratification within the peasant village is hierarchical and rigidly enforced in spite of the seeming egalitarianism of everyday encounters.[47] While Shaḥḥāt's Bedouin blood could be tolerated, an easy explanation for his impetuous nature, his marriage with a pariah could not. The Jamāsah are one of the numerous groups living in Egypt who are vaguely termed "gypsies" (ḥalabī or *ghagar*).[48] These groups include the Nawār, the Ḥalab, the Bahlawān, and the Jamāsah.[49] All are disdained for their trades, feared to be robbers and kidnappers. They are considered to be Muslims only by convenience, and therefore somehow different, somehow "other," from outside the local, host population.

The Nawār, for example, came from Kurdistan through Syria. The Bani Nūr, as they are called, settled in Syria, Iraq, Kuwait, and the Sudan. In Egypt, they settled down in Simbillawen (al-Manṣūrah), Fayyūm, Farshūt, Bardir, and Luxor (Qinā) to live at the desert limits, just beyond the inhabited village areas. On the boundaries between the traditional domain of the nomadic Bedouin population of Egypt and the settled fellah-farmer, they learned musical instruments, song, and dance, and came to earn their living as artists. The story of how they came to a life of wandering, exile, and perpetual pariahship resembles in many details the history of the Banī Hilāl's wanderings as a virtual outlaw tribe after attacking the Prophet in Mecca and Medina. The eponymous ancestor of the Nawār, Ḥāmid Abū al-Nūr (Father of Light) was accused of stealing the golden lamp of the sacred shrine in Mecca; his tribe and all his lineage were banished and henceforth doomed to wandering and perpetual insecurity as outcasts from the Community of Islam.[50]

Today many of these people are professional entertainers, dancers, jugglers, and musicians. The professional musicians of Egypt work in itinerant groups and travel throughout the country to earn their living. Entire families, as we have seen in the cases of Shamandī and Fārūq, devote themselves to the musical trade, forming bands of performers. Today the Hilālī epic is performed almost exclusively by such gypsy musicians. Not all members of a family troupe are poets. Only certain of them, those with good memories and a keen artistic sensibility, learn the epic art through oral tradition from the older generation of poet-musicians. The Nawārī gypsy, Yūsuf Māzin, whom I quoted above at length, gave an oral history of the tradition to Canova,[51] in which he described the gypsy-poet-musicians. He mentioned several rabāb poets well known throughout Egypt as professional artists (*fannān*), including Shamandī (of chap. 3), Muḥammad, the sons of Tawfīq and Qināwī, who are from the Matāqīl, a group of Sudanese gypsies who were formerly slaves. Among the Maṣālīb, a group of wandering musician-vendors, he mentioned Sayyid and ʿUthmān. These are some of the best known and most widely respected poets, but there are many others who earn their living as beggars. Certain villages have entire streets on which poets and musicians live. These poets are like Fārūq whom my Cairo household staff found wandering in the streets. They also travel about on trains, often selling baskets along with their poetry and songs.[52] Living in the periphery of the community, suspected as beggars and vagrant outsiders, these poet-musicians-vendors are at the bottom of the social scale.[53]

Perhaps it is contradictory, as Canova claims, that the poets who sing the myths of origin that chronicle the Arab heroes are not considered to be of Arab origin.[54] The anomaly, however, contains its own explanation. It points to the paradoxes of Egyptian life, the tensions inherent in such a highly socially and sexually differentiated community. The anomaly of the outsider, the outcast, the racially despised gypsy as the bearer of the communal history provides its own metasocial commentary, one that is implicit in the oral poetic tradition known as *al-Hilāliyya*. For the *Hilāliyya* in many ways is primarily a critique of social differentiation and the whole business of ranking people hierarchically and then organizing collective life around that fixed ranking.[55] The hierarchies or differentiations the sīra concerns itself with seem to be primarily those of race, sex, and property. The poets' puns and metonymies—formulas of attribution, the stock epithets of the epic poet's trade—all point to the tyranny of the dichotomy between the inside and the outside, the individual and the group, male and female, free and slave, the pure and the impure, the sacred and the profane, the taboo and the violation.

The sīra offers, as I have maintained, an explanation for all the conflict, quarreling, and open aggression present in rural Upper Egyptian society. Daily acts of eating, siring children, social intercourse with fellow men, sexual intercourse with one's wife—all these quotidian acts take on a magic emanence in the sīra, taking on the ritualized quality fixed in words. If we can believe Douglas's[56] analysis, exaggerated seclusion and avoidance rituals (such as those surrounding menstruation, conception, and birth in Ammar's account of Silwan life) develop around sexual relationships in social structures that rest on grave paradox. Notions of sexual pollution are likely to flourish when the overtly espoused principle of male dominance is confounded in some way and contradicted by other principles of behavior. If men define their status and prestige in the community in terms of rights over women, then in Douglas's view, the whole society is founded on a contradiction.

Rizq and his tribe do define honor in terms of controlling one's harem and maintaining its purity and thus racial purity. Khaḍrā's imputed adultery shames Rizq before the collectivity. He in turn blames Khaḍrā for being impure, a "dirty rag of a slut," who defiled the lineage by breaking caste and contaminating the tribe's honorable blood with the blood of a lowly stranger, a black slave. The status hierarchy makes male power dependent on property, inheritance, and family, and on having strong sons and pure daughters. The very signs of male superiority and dominance, however, indicate male vulnerability. The fertile female is a prized possession like hardy livestock (in the Bedouin ethic of the sīra), fertile land (in the ethic of the fellah audience), or a labor force of children and slaves to work the fields. As the mediator in all this, as the outward sign of status, lineage, and good(s), the female regenerative powers become a potential danger. The power of the female is the threshold to all power. And sex is consequently allotted a disruptive role in the social system.[57]

Certainly the Arab and Egyptian story tradition assigns a disruptive role to female sexuality. Myriad tales begin, as we have already noted, with the motif of sexual infidelity, often with a black slave, or with some problem of potency, sterility, or childlessness.[58] This alterity and potential disruptiveness of woman, at one level (perhaps the deepest, most buried one), is the myth of the origins of strife in the Upper Egyptian community. The whole truth, however, is not so reductive. The female/male dichotomization extends as a metaphor for the entire hierarchy of differentiation which exists at every level of Egyptian existence—political, economic, geographic, social, racial, legal, and religious.

The greater cultural anomaly resides in the politics of conquest and outside dominance which has existed for centuries in Egypt, coexisting with the inward-turned peasant populace at once indifferent to the outside and hostile to interfering central authority.[59] The historic anomalies begin with the ambivalent relationship of Arab Bedouin immigrant and native fellah farmer. Most of the nomad tribes of Egypt were latecomers, like the Hilālī and the Nawār, who came as refugees not to sack the palaces but to inhabit the hovels, to quote Polk,[60] and to live in continual conflict with the farmers. In the popular imagination, however, they were often confused with the Islamic conquerors of earlier centuries who brought the fellah his religious credo. Thus, a complicated picture of identification with the aggressor emerges. The life-styles of the fellah and Bedouin naturally conflicted; Bedouins constantly raided and overran the settled fellah's lands and property. Their relationship is complexly ambivalent, for settled fellah frequently claim descent from Arab tribal genealogy like the Hilālī.

Part of the appeal of the Hilālī legend and myth of origins may be found in the fellah's relationship with the conquering Arabs; it is a complicated relationship based on ancient racial rivalries and naturally competitive ways of life, a history of murderous raids, bitter feuds, and mutual animosity. Yet the romance of the conquering Arab plays heavily in the fellah's imagination and his self-definition. For as A. M. Ammar points out in the *People of Sharqiyya*[61] and H. Ammar reinforces in *Growing Up in an Egyptian Village,* the fellahin take great pride in describing themselves as "descendants of Arab stock related to the Prophet." A. M. Ammar accounts for this identification of the conquered fellah with the Muslim Arab invaders on two grounds, one pragmatic and the other romantic. He points out that, historically, lack of a strong government effectively gave power over to the nomads. Ruthless raids by the Bedouins on villages and fields during the "dark years of the Middle Ages" had the fellah at the mercy of the tribesmen. Consequently, people of purely indigenous origins frequently purchased tribal identity, thus forging links with the Arabs which were helpful on two fronts: an Arab genealogy offered protection from the Bedouin marauders who would not attack their own people, and it offered exemption from military service, a genuine calamity in the view of the ethnocentric fellah. Less pragmatically, too, the fellah desired to be a member of a noble race of gallant warriors with a stern ethical code, honorable, proud, powerful men all.

This complex identification with the invading Bedouin gives the *Hilāliyya* its subject matter and its power. The gypsy rabāb poet sings to the fellah audience the history of his Bedouin "ancestors." The rhetorical dynamic of the discursive situation is potent. The bawwāb ʿAlī, we will recall, reminisced about "sitting around outdoors on benches" in his village listening to the shāʿir, seated on the doorstep of a house, singing this history and genealogy. The rhetorical community such as ʿAlī described and Shaḥḥāt participated in invests the shāʿir with a great deal of authority, as they assent to listen to his reinterpretation of the *Hilāliyya.* The poet is the medium who guides the fellah into the Bedouin world of the past, who lets the male world of discourse symbolically penetrate the ritualistic mysteries of regeneration, and who conveys the vibrant Word of the common past to the present generation of listeners. The poet at the same time penetrates another world, for his performance transgresses and breaks down real social boundaries. Traditionally, the usual stage for a performance has been (as ʿAlī describes it) the stoop or threshold step of a café or a private house, the *ʿataba.*[62]

The poet, in a real-world extension of the poetic figure of the inside and the outside, sits on the threshold, at the boundary of the inside of the house and the outside. He turns inward onto himself in the effort of concentration needed to recall and improvise the *Hilāliyya* before his audience. His eyes often close, his body sways with the music. His humming rabāb, his voice lifted in song, his poetic diction—all these distance the poet from his audience. They make him one with the Tradition, the Voice of the collective text he conveys, bringing them word of their illustrious ancestors. The poet is apart, on the ʿataba, both literally and figuratively; he is on the threshold between mantic possession by the tradition and conscious design in an improvisatory performance.[63] Yet he is one with the audience, all attention focuses on him, and his listeners adhere and assent to his reinterpretation of an episode from *al-Hilāliyya*.

In a curious concatenation of meaning, the word for threshold is *ʿataba;* it means simply entryway or doorstep, but it also can mean in its verbal transformations crossing a threshold, trespassing, and by metaphoric extension, the root also denotes crossing over boundaries of blame; the verb *ʿatab* means to blame or to scold, to censure. And if my semiotic zeal does not carry me into the sin of *annominatio,*[64] the word is, furthermore, the term poets use for the opening three lines of the murabbaʿ, the threshold lines that provide an entryway and buildup to the fourth line, the *ṭāqiyya*. The latter means literally skullcap; in poetic terminology, it figurally represents the high point of the quatrain. These terms for the poetic format of narration, the murabbaʿ, provide, as we shall see in the course of this chapter, a gloss on the discursive situation. The quatrain first builds a threshold, a doorstep, through which the poet crosses the boundaries of blame to censure the listening community clad in gallābiyya and skullcap; the point of the ʿataba (the first three lines or the scolding) thus is in the ṭāqiyya (the last line or the skullcap).[65]

The *Hilāliyya* does indeed appear to penetrate the listeners' skullcaps and to transport the participants in its re-creation—poets and audience alike. As the flow of verse streams[66] from the poet's lips, the Word has visceral vibrancy. It literally sways the hearer; as I have said, bodies incline to the rabāb, voices breathe "Allah!" between lines of verse, and listeners lick their lips, swallow, and almost bodily incorporate the poetry. During a coffee break of a performance I recorded in 1978, the itinerant poet-musician Fārūq made a provocative comment about his own identification with the Hilālī tradition and its hero, and, possibly also, about his relationship with the tradition, with "the myth thinking itself"[67] in him, taking him beyond ordinary discourse: "When I sing Abū Zayd, I feel another man." In his performance, he is in fact "another man." For Fārūq is a gypsy, like the overwhelming majority of Hilālī professional poets today. After the performance, wherein the poet with his rabāb takes center stage to praise and blame, he will leave, go home to the village periphery, to the outskirts of town where his family lives, alongside the other marginal peoples and tradesmen. The gypsy poet is an outcast, defined as an outsider in the strict hierarchy of social differentiations and status discriminations that permeate Egyptian society. The gypsy shāʿir, in his performance of a collective text that expresses the deeply felt "history" of the fellahin, is himself an anomaly, much in the way that the black slave, the Hilālī heir Abū Zayd, is an anomaly with which his tribe must reckon.

The community, as we have seen, traditionally has invested the gypsy shāʿir with a great deal of authority. As the fellahin come to listen to the shāʿir's performance of the *Hilāliyya* once more, they assent to his authority and to the interpretation of events he offers. They give prior assent to his mediation of their experience both as individuals and as a group. The gypsy shāʿir, in his performance of a collective text expressive of communal values and a cultural ethos, is, as I have suggested, like the anomalous Abū Zayd. The gypsy poet's performance brings the community together rhetorically for the moment: the alienated boy-lover like Shaḥḥāt, the forbidding father, fighting brothers and uncles, feuding neighbors, can all put the strife aside for the moment to join in hearing the *Hilāliyya,* the epic of the outcast, wandering outlaw tribe. The performance itself thus becomes an institutionalization of an anomaly, expressive of the paradoxes of daily life.

The rhetorical transaction harks back to the past, to past renditions of the sīra by other poets to other audiences in other times—the ancestors of the present poet and audience. The rhetorical community of adherents reflects the ideal community of the Islamic nation as it embraces the whole community and preaches the anomalous lesson about fear of others, about racial and sexual power hierarchies. Sitting on the raised ʿataba with his listeners around him, the poet implicitly censures the agonistically divisive society of which poet and audience are all part. His discourse, while perhaps solving nothing, ventilates and illuminates everything. The shāʿir is the sole individual in the community authorized to express the inexpressible, to utter the unutterable, and to vocalize the rancor of the individual transgressed by the all-enclosing, all-encompassing concentric circles of oppression, repression, and obligation.[68]

The poet gives meaning and interprets experience through his manipulation of the formulaic figures of speech of his oral mode. The good poet knows how to draw out and stress the contradictions and anomalies present in experience and in the traditional story matter. His punning logic creates meaning through its perception of disparity; paradoxical conflicting meanings contained within the pun give new significance to old facts. Therein lies an interpretation of Egyptian society from the point of view of the disinherited, the dispossessed, and the politically disaffected. The intimate outsider to the community, the gypsy shāʿir, offers the fellah audience no filopious history, but rather a subversive genealogy replete with the paradoxes of Egyptian society.[69]

Yūsuf Māzin[70] tells the story of another poet, who is not a gypsy by birth but a fellah, an insider cast outside. Jābir's life story is one made out of these same social paradoxes and anomalies that the *Hilāliyya* ritually exposes. Jābir, who was known as the premier "Shāʿir al-ʿArab" (Poet of the Arabs) until his death in September 1981, was not a gypsy entertainer, but came from peasant origins. Māzin tells the story of how Jābir learned poetry because he married a Maṣluba, a girl from the gypsy tribe of wandering musicians from which al-Sayyid al-ʿḌūwī also comes. Jābir's family disowned him; his brother, a teacher, sees the poet as a family disgrace. Jābir then too is an outcast who learned the itinerant musician's craft and trade to earn a living for his family. He became the best singer of the *Hilāliyya* in all of Egypt in that he was noted for knowing the story best. His interpretation of the old tale is a very moral one. It emphasizes the ups and downs of the village status hierarchy, the limitations of a zero-sum society wherein one brother turns against another. Jābir sings his version of the epic with a particular poignancy and truth that has earned it great esteem, for his *Sīrat Banī Hilāl* truly is the "sīra"—that is, in the root meaning of the word *sīra,* the "biography" of the Egyptian peasant.

# 8

# THE GYPSY ON THE DOORSTEP: A DIRTY STORY OR A SUBVERSIVE GENEALOGY?

Viewed from within its traditional community of adherents and from within the texts its performances generate, the Hilālī tradition, as we have seen, encompasses and dramatizes collective identity of the Egyptian peasant community in all its contradictory essence; the poet is the medium who utters the unutterable, speaks the unspeakable, and expresses the inexpressible in full face of the traditional community. The contradictions and anomalies inherent in the discursive situation of gypsy poet conveying the biography of the fellah do not stop with the gypsy at the threshold blaming his turbaned listeners; rather, they extend beyond to the literate world of the urban bourgeoisie dressed in Western garb and to the worlds of outside influence, prestige, and power, both foreign and domestic.

Belief in a heroic age can be an engaging fantasy with which to identify from an Orientalist's armchair, but, as Bowra tells us, at close quarters it may well be extremely unsettling. The gypsy on the doorstep has some disturbing things to recount. His tale of continual strife and violent upheaval, of famine, migration, and war engendering war is not pretty romance of yesteryear's adversity overcome. Rather it is oral tradition argumentation that partakes in deep-seated cultural struggles. The rhetorical scene wherein the shāʿir tells his tale of the origins of strife in the community itself represents a scene of strife and communal division.

In the seventeenth century, Yūsuf al-Shirbīnī viciously lampooned the Hilālī poet and his fellah audience in a colloquial-language parody of al-sīra.[1] A Ṣaʿīdī himself, Shirbīnī pursued one of the sole paths of upward mobility then available to rural village boys through the religious hierarchy of the *ᶜulamā'*. His attack on the Nile valley dirt farmer, whose dusty roots he shared and whose dung-encrusted clothes he disdained, was directed at a literate, urban audience. Shirbīnī used the poetic formulas and rhythms of the shāᶜir's oral verse to write a mock epic lament wherein "Abū Shādūf" bemoans his fate. He accompanied this "text" with a mock scholarly commentary in the literary idiom. The purpose of the ironic piece is to deride the despised, dirty class of agricultural workers and village dwellers, whose ranks Shirbīnī only narrowly escaped.[2] His hyperbolic mockery of the language and locutions of *Sīrat Banī Hilāl* in *Hazz al-Quḥūf* (The Shaking of Skullcaps) stands as a testament to the enduring quality of the "cultural war" surrounding the shāᶜir's discourse.

While a performance uplifts both its gypsy poet and its peasant audience, the privileged, literate stratum of Egyptian society counterphobically looks down on it with loathing and fear. The powerful have often feared al-sīra to the point of denying it or suppressing it. ᶜAbd al-Laṭīf, writing in 1946, comments on the nefarious influence of *Sīrat Banī Hilāl* on its Egyptian audience.[3] According to this Egytian writer, the story inspired Bedouin and other provincial people to imitate the "stealing and killing ways" of Hilālī heroes. Al-Zayyāt in *Fī Uṣūl al-Adab* also documents the unruliness of Egyptian audiences who listened to the rāwī recite the Banī Hilāl epic.[4] He asserts that the words of the shāᶜir influenced men's ears, causing old tribal alliances and animosities among members of the audience to flare up. Al-Zayyāt and other Egyptian commentators tell us that arguments and fights would frequently break out within the ranks of the *Hilāliyya* audience as the poet's recital fired passions in favor of one contending hero over another. Hostile government and religious authorities cited the unruliness of the "mob" making up the poet's public as the reason for interdictions. Officials have often banned sīra recitation through the ages;[5] its performances have been cited as sowing discord and rebellion.

In the larger Egyptian society, the *Hilāliyya* is viewed as low class, beneath contempt, as disruptive "illiterature." Mūsá Sulaymān, writing in 1950, reflected the stance of the typical Arab man of letters in his scorn for the sīra's "coarse vulgarities"; Sulaymān, cited at the beginning of this study, sees the sīra as "ignorant of authorship, anonymous, wretched in language and style, a register of the conditions of the vulgar, deprived of color and literary splendor."[6] The Egyptian critic Ghālī Shukrī, in 1970, in a book on what he calls "resistance literature," explains such negative judgments on the part of both aesthetes and officialdom as the result of aristocratic social and cultural pretensions, as a "reactionary position assumed by generations of 'professors' of the official literature, who in every age preached that the unique adab is the philology and literature preserved in the museums—all the rest is contaminated by Satan and his vulgar followers."[7]

Al-sīra is somehow a "dirty story," one best kept separate from what are perceived as the more positive aspects of the culture. Clearly, it is not a part of "high" Egyptian culture or Arabic letters. It is illiterature. It belongs to the illiterates. It belongs to the 85 percent or so of the Egyptian population which cannot read and write; that is, in the broader sense, the serving class off of which a small ruling sector has traditionally fed. If my rhetoric discomforts, I apologize, but the metaphors are not mine. They are the poets' and tradition's. Their political ramifications are indeed discomfiting.

Not for naught does the biography of the Egyptian peasant (al-sīra) begin with the telling of a dirty story. In the sīra, Ghānim tells a "dirty story" about Khaḍrā, the mother of a great tribal leader; he "soils" Khaḍrā's skirt and Rizq's turban, as the poets put it. The greater plot development of the sīra's episodes resides in the working out of that dirty story; that is to say, the tale narrates the conflict that arises between the progeny of Ghānim and Rizq (Diyāb and Abū Zayd), and the disruption caused by retribution against the family of Ghānim who told the dirty story that besmirched Khaḍrā and begot the tale. That dirty story becomes aired and ritually reenacted in the gypsy's rhetorical confrontation with the larger society.

The shāʿir makes his traditional argument in no grossly overt way. He does not overtly criticize the status quo or cast aspersions on the power hierarchy; rather, his preachments and lessons are implicit. They suggest themselves analogously with the disjunctive moral lesson taught in al-sīra. The gypsy poet guides his listeners to understanding current history and events, current political and economic realities, as well as the more recent past, in terms of the analogies the Hilāliyya provides in its puns and chiastic structures.

The key puns the gypsy poet ties his tale around provide a frame of reference within which to understand not only the life and times of the Banī Hilāl and the social tensions within the Upper Egyptian peasant village community but, more significantly, the history of modern Egypt. Through the masked aggression of the poet's pun analogies, the fellah can hear an interpretation of life, just as the foreign critic or the upper-class power elite might also, should they listen, should they dare to penetrate the boundaries of veiled meaning.

I have called the poet's punning, and the disjunctively comprehended meaning of things he teaches, masked aggression. For if the ramifications of his symbol are carried to their logical conclusion, the whole structure of Egyptian life and history are encompassed and potentially criticized. In the transpositions of the sīra wherein the stranger and outsider are taken into the bosom of the group, where the mother and child are cast out of their rightful group only to be harbored by a foreign group, where the black slave becomes the ultimate free man and champion of individual energy as the charismatic group leader whose name will be remembered through the ages—these transpositions provide a paradigm for a larger understanding.

We have seen Shaḥḥāt listening to the poet's discourse. The symbolic transformations of the inside and the outside contained in the gypsy's tale give meaning to the transpositions Shaḥḥāt himself experiences as the family turns on him to join the voice of collective wisdom forbidding him, and as his inner fears and resentments at having his romantic hopes for a life of self-expression quashed by social expectations and obligations are expressed in terms of evil spirits which afflict him with illness, and later, in Critchfield's account, as Shaḥḥāt's own mother becomes his litigious enemy in a clash between her brother and son over a piece of property. Family conflicts become intrapsychic conflicts, and vice versa; the family clashes internally yet closes against the outside neighborhood and village; villagers antagonize endlessly, but join together against outside authority; the fellah ostracizes the gypsy, but is dependent on him to make symbolic sense of his existence; the Bedouin invader raids the settled farming villages, yet the fellahin identify the invading Arab tribesmen as their brothers in the community of Islam and claim a common genealogy back to the Prophetic antecedents of the Nation. The identity of the conflicting village groups of Bedouin, fellah, and gypsy merges and the boundaries collapse in the *Hilāliyya* recital. While the rhetorical ritual of sīra recitation breaks down social boundaries in the village community and brings people together to appreciate a truth that overrides their daily antagonisms and binds them together, other status categories do not dissolve so easily. The people who gather together to hear the gypsy's tale and who are bound together in their identification with the plight of the outcast black hero are the dispossessed and the disinherited, the politically disaffected masses of impoverished Egypt.

The contained in-group of the shāʿir and his village audience share a truth, a perception of history that is at odds with official Arab-Muslim history. The poet's puns disguise meaning in such a way that only the initiated aficionado of the tradition can hear the several levels of meaning intended. The out-group looks on the rhetorical scene with contempt and incomprehension. Today, that out-group is made up of literate urban bureaucrats clad in Western clothing. As Cachia indicates, "nothing concerning popular literature comes closer to being definable than the kind of audience it attracts: villagers of any status, but also town people who have had either a traditional type of education, or very little formal education at all; the hallmark of the overwhelming majority of them is the wearing of the gallābiyya."[8] Clothing, education, and other less immediately definable factors, such as attitude, then separate the two worlds.

The shunning and avoidance of the sīra tradition by literate classes (to the point of official suppression in less tolerant ages than the postrevolutionary climate of Egypt since 1952) is perhaps with good reason: the *Hilāliyya* expresses the latent hostility of the Egyptian peasant to social cleavages based on education and literacy. It perceives the hypocrisy inherent in cultural dichotomizations. The hero's first heroic deed is to kill his teacher who is trying to teach him the alphabet. As a symbolic statement, this act of heroism has particular potency in a society dichotomized into literate ruling elite versus mass traditional oral culture. Illiteracy in Egypt today is general and widespread. Even in the wake of massive government efforts since 1952 to provide schools, the percentage of literacy has in fact decreased over the past decade in terms of actual numbers of the population who can read and write.[9] Through the centuries since the advent of Islam, the traditional Koranic school (kuttāb) has taught the Egyptian peasant his letters. Traditional literacy in the peasant society has been defined as learning to "read" the Koran. The kuttāb's method of teaching stresses rote memorization and recitation, probably honing oral memory better than teaching flexible reading skills.[10] This school is the one familiar to the *Hilāliyya* poet's audience, most of whom cannot read at all or are marginally literate.

Schooling in *al-Hilāliyya* is approached with great ambivalence. In the three versions of "Mīlād Abū Zayd" to which we have listened attentively, Khaḍrā wants her boy to learn to read and write as part of his education as a proper, well-behaved Muslim descended from the Prophet's line. Thus, at age seven, little Abū Zayd goes to the kuttāb and encounters the religious establishment in the person of the schoolmaster. Jābir and Sayyid, as we have understood them in their versions, redefine "literacy" in religious terms. True literacy is a divine endowment of the black slave child-hero. The Koran teacher, called the *muʿallim* or *faqīh* in the sīra, represents the religious hierarchy at the village level. (Al-Sayyid al-Ḍūwī overtly lumps the religious establishment with the political as he terms the teacher's brother "a right-wing government minister.") This respected personage, the Koran schoolteacher, is revealed as a liar and a hypocrite. In calling Abū Zayd a black bastard and his mother a slut, the teacher aligns himself with the erring tribal patriarchy who falsely accuse the Prophet's kin. In this, the official representative misrepresents the true spirit of Islam.

Herein lies the key perception of the *Hilāliyya*. In his puns and chiastic patterns, the shāʿir consistently points up the anomalies of collective experience. His version of history is at odds with official histories of the high tradition of Scriptural Islam. Contradictions inherent in Muslim law and Muslim experience are perceived in the sīra as the hypocrisy of the powers-that-be. The Koranic teacher and his right-wing government minister brother, as representatives of literate officialdom, the religious hierarchy of the ʿulamā', and central governmental authority, converge against Abū Zayd and his mother. The patriarchy of tribal leadership, village religious order, and the national government ignores a prior bond with God in its rejection of a woman's word of honor, in its mistreatment of a black child and a black slave. The patriarchy ignores true learning and genuine knowledge. It flouts the true status hierarchy that is based on nobility of lineage with direct links to God through the Prophetic nation of the Muslim Community (Umma). Muḥammad forged the coalition that was Islam out of discontent with tribal hierarchies based on birth. His original mission appealed to the unaffiliated and the discontented of Arabia. Himself of "low" birth and occupation (a cameleer and merchant), the Prophet launched a campaign against genealogical aristocracies. His new coalition abolished the old, tribal hierarchical order and substituted the concept of the Umma. With his creation of this concept, Muḥammad effected the transfer of believers' allegiances from kin group to the Umma, an ideological group based on religious belief. Ideally, the Muslim submits to the authority of the egalitarian brotherhood of fellow Muslims bound by their belief in one God and his Prophet's mission.[11]

Al-sīra contains and explains contradictions inherent in the society founded on the ideal of the Umma. Islamic society, while espousing an ideal of commonality and unity, was based on a strict dichotomy of the outsider (easterner) coming into a western territory to conquer and settle it, and assimilate it to its ways; the "willing submission" (*Islām*) to outside rule, the willing "resignation" to central authority that was the Islamic conquests paradoxically implied an exploitation by that outside rule. The native Egyptian population thus has experienced a history of boundary transgression of one sort or another, foreign occupation, domination, and absorption, exploitation, and expropriation of the limited wealth and food source. *Sīrat Banī Hilāl* reflects and incorporates this history into a verbal fabric, a mythic history bound together in the rhymes of oral poetic memory. It symbolically expresses the animosity felt and the humiliation endured.

Shaḥḥāt's village of Berat appears on the Egyptian landscape as all-consuming, its villagers preoccupied with their own and each other's business to the point of ignoring the outside world.[12] Central government authority is accounted by all chroniclers of the Egyptian fellah as an uncomprehending, hostile force—outsiders come to tax, to impress labor, to conscript into military service, or to redistribute property.[13] Historically, the central authority has been an outside one. Egypt has been ruled, since the decline of the Pharaohs, by outside occupation forces—at first by Persians, Greeks, and Romans; then by the Arab invaders who gave them their major religion, language, and customs; most recently, by

European colonizers; and finally today, by what one Egyptian nationalist terms a "savage bureaucracy of the bourgeoisie."[14] Between the seventh century and the thirteenth century, the force of the Islamic incursions was strong enough to Arabicize and Islamicize quite thoroughly most of the Egyptian fellahin. Successive Islamic caliphates established military rule by foreign occupation forces, frequently redistributing lands and taxing agricultural produce to the point of confiscating most of it. Poverty, misery, and hard work as virtual serfs became the fate of the fellah under Mamluk and Ottoman rule (Mamluk rule 1250–1517; Ottoman, 1517–1901).

The Egyptian sīra concerns internal and external conflict, the problem of different groups living together in the restricted agricultural space of the Nile valley. Ideally, collective wisdom preaches that all should live together in a unified brotherhood that takes in and shelters the stranger under the mutual tent of the "willing act of submission" that is the peace and unity of Islam. Arab-Muslim identity, however, involves certain anomalies and paradoxes that reside in both familial and political institutions. The early (seventh-century) invasions of Egypt and North Africa by Islamic military forces brought about a cataclysmic change in the identity of area inhabitants. Identification with the aggressor was such that within several hundred years the mass of the population had adopted the language and customs and religion of the conquerors.[15] New ways, new conventions coexisted with the ongoing sameness of the natural cycles of agricultural seasonal production. The occupation brought with it also a new elite, a military ruling force that would exploit the fellah and look down on him as a slave toiling endlessly. Al-sīra concerns the loss of power inherent in such boundary transgression as the Islamic coalition of identities entailed. It perceives the problems inherent in identification with an appealing and powerful aggressor from outside who absorbs and assimilates the inside of the group, merging its identity with its own. The *Hilāliyya* teaches in its disjunctive analogies that strife derives from social differentiation and social boundaries that are contradictory to the principles of the Islamic brotherhood (even though they exist and the Islamic state power hierarchy was founded on them).

Pipes and Mernissi show this same contradiction at work in Arabo-Muslim institutions (albeit in different and separate contexts). Pipes, in his book on military slavery under Islamicate rule, postulates that the ideal of the Umma created a practical problem of leadership and authority. The Caliphate was supposed to be the tangible expression of loyalty to the Umma, symbolic of the power and unity of the Umma. In reality, as the Islamic nation expanded beyond the confines of Arabia, the size and diversity of the Umma made unity difficult. In their loyalty to the notion of a great universal collective brotherhood that was the Umma, the people by and large turned away from the actual rulers. The local representative of the Caliphate was seen as transitory, local, arbitrary rule and the ruling structure as strikingly isolated from people's lives.[16]

Mernissi maintains in her book on the Muslim-Arab family that there exists a basic cleavage between the Islamic ideal of the Umma and the reality of the world of family relationships and sexual power differentials. She sees a conflict between the kernel of the Muslim message—which is a democratic glorification of the human individual, regardless of sex, race, or status—and the everyday antagonistic model of family sexual organization, which is based on inequality, segregation, separation, division, subordination, authority, mistrust. The ideals of the Umma of course are the opposite of what Mernissi terms the conflictive relationship of the family.[17]

The disjunctures Mernissi and Pipes perceive in Arabo-Muslim institutions bear striking resemblance to the anomalies in the shāʿir's discourse. The Egyptian *Hilāliyya* particularly explicates the moral and emotional ramifications of the conflict from the folk point of view. That the hero's first heroic act is to kill his teacher who is instructing him in the alphabet is particularly charged.

The *Hilāliyya* in its first episode of the "Birth of the Hero" comments, as we have seen, on cultural dichotomization into high and low on the basis of literacy. Questions of learning and literacy and religiosity and authority are treated directly in the teacher-killing motif as part of the origins of strife within the community. The sīra tradition exposes a deep, societal cleavage in pitting the black slave child against the Koranic schoolteacher. The lesson implicit indicates the rift between "high" and "low," learned and popular, written and oral, officialdom and folk culture. The sīra too perceives the historic anomalies of the Islamic Caliphate. While preaching all-embracing unity and common humanity, the Caliphate not only established a military garrison state in Egypt which expropriated land ownership and food through exhorbitant taxation, it also brought with it an elegant court society, complete with its own tradition of language and letters. The "true," "pure" language of the Koran, and the Arabian peninsula, before the Islamic expansions to new regions, was the linguistic vehicle of literate high culture. *Fuṣḥá* (pure) Arabic was distinguished from the bastardized, unintelligible Arabic of the common people, *ʿāmmiyya*. This Islamic elite society of refined court letters, restricted to the circles of the urban ruling class and religious authority, was cut off from the masses of people.[18]

The slave motif also takes on particular potency to the Egyptian audience in its anomalously ambivalent perception of their history and experience. The slave motif and an allied motif (horse-getting) may be direct reflection in the sīra of history under Mamluk rule.[19] The slave/free man antithesis of the sīra no doubt arises from the humiliation experienced by a people bound to the land who experienced usurpation of that land and its wealth at the hands of a slave dynasty which ruled Egypt as a haughty aristocracy for some 600 years, only to be routed at the beginning of the nineteenth century by the equally tyrannical rule of Muḥammad ʿAlī. Imported, foreign slaves desported themselves as landed nobility even to the point of prohibiting native Egyptians from riding a horse.[20] Horse riding, as indicative of freedom and nobility of ancestry, appears in the *Hilāliyya* as a fully developed motif. In the three versions of the one episode of the *Hilāliyya* which we examined previously, this motif appears; Fārūq, for example, mentions in his first few introductory lines that Abū Zayd will ride a horse as soon as he is old enough; the poet also develops the horse-getting motif later in the narration of the episode.

Although the slave motif provides a basic, key point of symbolic reference in the versions heard today, since the hero Abū Zayd is a black man, nineteenth-century manuscripts and printed editions, probably based on eighteenth- and nineteenth-century oral versions, appear to develop the slave motif at even greater length and detail. The early nineteenth-century version of the Birth of Abū Zayd on which Lane based his translated excerpt in *Manners and Customs*,[21] for example, elaborates on Abū Zayd's position as a slave in his early years as a refugee in the Zaḥlān tribe and reveals his true nobility only in his confrontation as a slave on the battlefield with his father.

The occupation of Egypt by the Mamluks has been called one of the strangest and most remarkable institutions in premodern Egypt.[22] From the upper end of the social spectrum, a military elite of white slaves ruled for over 600 years; even after their power was broken by Muḥammad ʿAlī in 1811, many white slaves continued to be imported to hold high positions in the army and bureaucracy. At the lower end of the power spectrum, until the end of the nineteenth century when slavery was abolished, many black slaves were imported to do domestic work. The tight Islamic family system incorporated these black slaves into the family structure and granted them many privileges of kinship.[23] Abnoudy, commenting on the state of the slaves in the sīra, mentions the close, "shadowlike" quality of the relationship between slave and master.[24] The experience of slavery at either end of the hierarchy thus has been anomalous, with foreign slave rule at the upper end and black domestics as family intimates at the other end. Abū Zayd in many ways incarnates this historic anomaly, epitomizing the great black military leader risen up from the domestic realms by virtue of his innate superior qualities.

The history of land tenure in Egypt too makes the issue of slavery an ambiguous one. The fellahin were virtual serfs for many centuries as land ownership fluctuated between state and private property, and one regime liquidated the administrative systems of another. Baer documents these changes, showing that although during the nineteenth century some of the land gradually became registered in the names of the fellah who tilled it, most often it was lost again because of tax burdens, the corvée for public works, conscription into the army, loss to creditors, or through recurring droughts, floods, or plagues of one kind or another. By the end of the nineteenth century, according to Baer's figures,[25] landless peasants made up from one-tenth to one-fifth of the population. Today the Egyptian population increases at more than a million per year. Food shortages are rampant. Egypt imports more than 40 percent of its food. It is a time of social upheaval and displacement. Over the centuries of foreign occupation and exploitation of the farm worker, political regimes have varied, the power structure changed, but the life of the peasant farmer remained unchanging:

a cycle of dependence on the seasonal flooding of the Nile. This too is changed now, and with it the rhythm of everyday life.

The government, anxious to feed its burgeoning population, has built dams to irrigate the valley and make it less dependent for crops on the yearly flood cycle of the Nile. The Upper Aswan Dam, completed in 1971, stopped the yearly flood on which the agricultural cycles had been dependent for centuries. Instead of one crop per year, the newly irrigated fields, fertilized now with chemical fertilizers in place of water buffalo dung, can produce two to three crops a year. The effect of the dam in fact has been to give the farm worker an excruciating work schedule throughout the year, to increase the salinity of the soil and thereby reduce crop yield, to cause soil erosion and spread the parasite-caused disease, bilharzia, that cripples and kills the Egyptian peasant.[26]

Increased mechanization, dam building, and the burgeoning population growth of this century have swelled the class of workers with no fixed occupation to overwhelming numbers today. These displaced people migrate to towns and cities in search of work. They are servants, willing to serve in virtually any trade for a pittance. These uprooted masses from the countryside and towns constitute a vast reservoir of labor power forced, as Hussein puts it, "by misery to submit to the worst possible working conditions," and exploitation by the bourgeoisie. Hussein puts the number of *tarāḥīl* (migrant rural laborers) at three-fourths of the rural population. Perhaps one-sixth of the peasant population owns a few qīrāṭ (= kirat, 1⁄24 of an acre). Together these two groups make up the mass of the Egyptian population. Two-thirds of them are unemployed or "victimized by the most brutal pressures at the hands of employers."[27] In the words of this Egyptian Nationalist and Communist:

> Their miserable existence would be considered unbearable by the poorest members of the bourgeoisie; it has driven them to the cities, where they constitute an urban disinherited mass deprived of material resources and access to regular work, and where they experience essentially the same conditions of insecurity and instability that drove them from the countryside. They are not integrated into urban life—two thirds of them are unemployed—but here their situation is somewhat better than in the countryside since the city offers more oppor-

> tunities, more marginal employment. The work they do requires no training; they hire themselves out for the lowliest jobs to any employer; they are waiters in small cafés or do odd jobs in barber shops and small stores; they are temporary laborers in capitalist enterprises (especially in construction), itinerant peddlers, servants, and caretakers; . . . Altogether they constitute more than half of the urban population. Their class position is comparable to that of the rural proletarianized masses to whom they are tied by kinship or feelings of solidarity, or with whom they share a common region of origin. (*Class Conflict in Egypt,* p. 38)

These are the dispossessed and dispersed, the majority of the people of Egypt. They are also the audience of the *Hilāliyya* poet, the ever-increasing numbers of "outcasts," strangers, and marginal people. The gypsy entertainer is not the only itinerant worker. He is joined today by a vast company of uprooted, displaced workers.

Urbanization has steadily increased from the end of the nineteenth century until the present as landless peasants swell the class of workers and people with no fixed occupation. Hussein calls this the legacy of European capitalism and comments on the isolation of individuals, family groups, and clans dispersed to create "a disorganized mass whose uncertain and shifting mode of existence is not conducive to unity."[28]

The disruption, fragmentation, and dispersal of the collectivity that historians trace through the nineteenth and twentieth centuries in Egypt becomes in the *Hilāliyya* a leitmotiv, a refrain. Jābir decries this lack of unity and the passing of an integrated world in which a man knew who he was and which group he belonged to by virtue of his birth. His antitheses of high and low, his proverbial comments on the perfidy of enemies who laugh when you cry, lament the passing of a more stable world. Fārūq stresses the changes in the formulaic refrain that Bedouins used to eschew blame: they were a respecting people (i.e., they knew their place).

To know one's place today is more difficult. The government's solution to peasant problems, to the displacement of a vast, hungry, and ever-growing population, seems to be irrigation, mechanization, foreign trade, education, literacy, and birth control.[29] Official government policies are usually based on achievement-oriented values that are often in direct conflict with peasant values and commonplaces of opinion. Birth, for example, as the sīra demonstrates, is an absolute good in the peasant society of Egypt. High mortality rates make each child precious.[30] In a traditionally agricultural society, children endow parents with status, heirs, manpower, and leisure.[31] Massive government efforts to provide public education in the Ṣaʿīd since 1952, such as birth control measures, have proved largely futile. Literacy and education offer the displaced peasant multitudes the opportunity to take their place in the urban bureaucracies. Leaving the village, however, has always been seen as the worst possible fate, whether for military service or to seek work.[32]

The gypsy shāʿir offers today's audience consolation for their woes through symbolic identification with a hero and heroic tribe who have endured the agonies of famine, migration, war, internal dissension, and political and social discrimination. We have heard him also offering his listeners a masked critique of the world they live in, indirectly confronting them with their own failings while allowing them to ventilate felt hostility toward their oppressors. In the mouths of the poets studied in this work, the basic perception of the Hilālī tradition appears to be a paradoxical statement of the hypocrisy inherent in cultural dichotomizations and discriminations.

All do not consistently lament the passing of old ways, however. Fārūq, for example, seems more tolerant of changing social values. Less suspicious of learning and change than Sayyid or Jābir, Fārūq, in his version, comments directly on literacy as achievement. He suggests in fact that literacy may well equal happiness, security, and respectability. In an exchange between Khaḍrā and Abū Zayd's stepfather, the man says he will send the boy to school and "he will finish his studies and open a clinic/ science and reading will protect him/ he will be happy and he will have a diploma." Fāḍil's hopes for Abū Zayd's pedagogic career and his ambitions that he "open a clinic" (i.e., become a doctor) surely cannot materialize. As narrative detail, this ambition conflicts with the linear development of the traditional tale, for Abū Zayd must, by mythic necessity, grow up to lead his people to North Africa. Within the traditional narrative story line, the hope is absurd. It can only be understood in the context of the individual poet inserting a notion of his own which is extraneous to the Hilālī tradition. It inserts a new and very real ethic of achievement and

1. Fārūq ᶜAbd al-ᶜAzīz with rababa at the home of Abnoudy

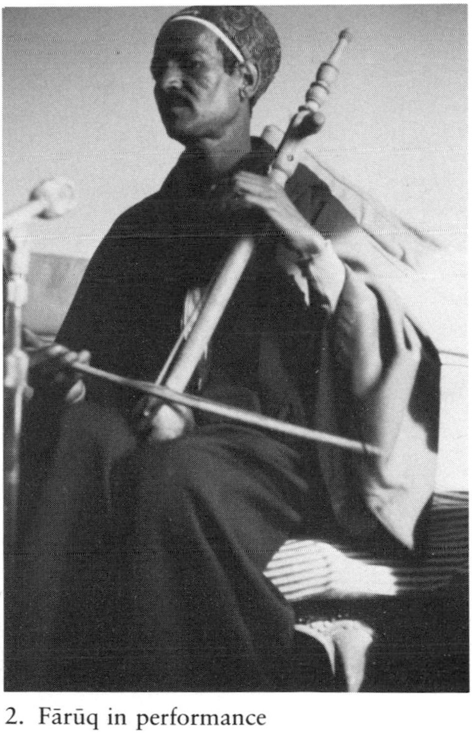

2. Fārūq in performance

3. Fārūq in performance (2)

4. ʿAlī pointing out Fārūq's "Ayat" during a performance

5. ʿAlī listening to Fārūq

6. Abnoudy listening to Fārūq

7. ʿAbd al-Raḥmān al-Abnoudy

8. Shamandī in performance

9. Shamandī in performance (2)

10. Jābir Abū Ḥusayn (*photo by Atiyat Abnoudy*)

11. Jābir Abū Ḥusayn with accompanist (*photo by Giovanni Canova*)

12. Tunisian reverse glass painting of Zāziyya
(*property of Micheline Galley, photo by Galley by permission*)

13. Tunisian pulp print of Abū Zayd's encounter with the enemy

14. Tunisian pulp print of ʿAntara

15. Tunisian pulp print of Abū Zayd rendered by a second artist

16. Tunisian pulp print of ᶜAntara rendered by second artist

17. Dhiyāb spears the Zanātī Khalīfa in the eye. Tunisian folk print.

18. Tunisian reverse glass painting of Abū Zayd vs. the enemy. (*Property of Bridget Connelly, photo by Henry Massie*)

upward mobility into the sīra. Fārūq's own sons, he testifies, attend school. The poet Fārūq thus speaks here in his own voice, letting newer values coexist with the traditional ones embedded in the inherited formulaic language and story structure of the poet's artistic medium. The gypsy poet along with his fellah audience today can hope that education will make their sons doctors, lawyers, and part of the literate establishment. Fārūq typically inserts randomly into his narration contemporary values which sometimes seriously conflict with the dissociative logic of the whole story.

Side-by-side with such random interpretations that probably have a fairly wide audience appeal as wish-fulfillment fantasies, Fārūq uses an even more overtly explicit dichotomy of experience and ethical conflict than the other two poets. His split of nomad versus urban, Bedouin versus sedentary, echoes as a refrain. Fārūq fails to hear the conflict between the story of Abū Zayd killing a hypocritical religious teacher and the wish that Abū Zayd grow up to be a literate, prestigious doctor. The narrative detail has purely local relevance as an association Fārūq brings to the notion of education. The Bedouin–urban split, however, echoes through his rendition of the episode as a memorized formulaic locution—almost in the way Lévi-Strauss describes a myth as "thinking itself" in a man. The tradition in Fārūq's head runs off in one direction telling the story as it must be told, while his more conscious, intentional mind as a living, performing musician-poet inserts detail from daily life. He never really manages to integrate the two.

Fārūq, who was named for the ex-king Fārūq, takes the political bite out of the sīra and makes it less subversive in its message—more a romance of the days of yore for its own sake. He does not comprehend[33] the deep meaning structure of the traditional tale sufficiently to offer a coherent interpretation of it through narrative detail or, as we heard earlier, through the decorative details of figures of speech. With the two poets who comprehend the sīra in its full depth of intention and meaning as a collective text, narrative detail and decorative embellishments (such as rhymes, figures of speech, music) quite consistently coalesce the greater narrative intention. In short, the part contains the whole, the episode reflects the entirety. It serves metonymically to bring to mind the whole Hilālī story latent in the minds of the audience.

It also serves to invite analogies between the Hilālī story-history and the current social and political story.

That story is, as I maintained at the outset of this chapter, a "dirty" one, one somehow best kept separate from the "purer" aspects of the culture. We have seen how *Sīrat Banī Hilāl,* in one of the Egyptian audience's favorite episodes, "The Birth of Abū Zayd," provides its listeners with a rather subversive genealogy, in which the erotic sphere converts metonymically to integrate a whole larger sphere of social disequilibrium, disruption, and dominance wherein self-definition and group identity arise out of oppositionalism, through discrimination between self and other. In its disjunctive style, the sīra points out the limitations of the logical model of opposition, for such differentiation leads to class and status hierarchies that are contradictory to the original principles of the culture—namely, the brotherhood of all men as servants of God. Such ambiguity and ambivalence are hard to tolerate. And, as Douglas has taught us, anomaly leads to anxiety, which leads to suppression and/or avoidance, politically and culturally, no less than personally. Indeed, the rhetorical scene of the *Hilāliyya* performance puts the culture's "dirty story" on display.

For the epideictic event that is a shāʿir's performance displays things with which everyone in the society is uncomfortable—issues (like those of the sīra) of purity and impurity, honesty and dishonesty, the ideal and the real. Suppressed and avoided by the politically and economically dominant sectors of society, the recitation of the sīra represents the institutionalization of an anomaly. The ritual performance integrates one sector of Egyptian society while another looks on at the scene with loathing and disdain. The ritual rhetorical enactment of the gypsy shāʿir on the fellah's doorstep brings into the open cultural anxieties about status and power. For the poet and his audience, the performance manifests both a boundary transgression and dissolution; in so doing, it coalesces a greater truth through the veiled aggression of its rhetorical style. For the bourgeois bureaucrat or the political official, however, the sīra has historically been a source of fear. The ritual of recitation airs differences, puts them out in the open on the threshold between the factions of a dichotomized society. It displays a dirty story about a bastard in a bastardized language. That display expresses cultural ambivalence and conflict, the denial of which has given over to the strict dichotomies that make up Muslim Arab society: male/female, inside/outside, in-group/out-group, ethnically dominant/foreigners, Muslim/stranger, the economically stable/the poor, free/slave. Mernissi categorizes the Muslim community into two subuniverses,[34] which are strikingly similar to al-sīra in their perception:

| | |
|---|---|
| Umma | family |
| religion | sexuality |
| power | impotence |
| male | female |
| equality | inequality |
| reciprocity | lack of reciprocity |
| aggregation | segregation |
| unity, communion | separation, division |
| brotherhood, love | subordination, authority |
| trust | mistrust |

Ambivalence denied and conflict suppressed result in rigidity, socially and politically no less than personally; it results in strict categories of the good and the bad, the ideal and the base, the sublime and the grotesque, the high and the low, the in and the out, the black and the white, the pure and the contaminated. It can be expressed as a kind of one-sidedness of the morally righteous individual or the high, religious culture; in Arabic aesthetics, it finds expression as a denial of the vernacular and the exclusive embrace of the high, written canon of Arabic letters. This tradition denies fiction as lies and sees representation beyond certain circumscribed patterns as dangerous heresy in its competition with the divine, with the official revealed truth of the Nation. In short, it has resulted in a strict split (a defensive "splitting" to use the psychoanalytic term) between Scriptural Culture and Folk Culture, between Classical letters and Oral Traditional Culture.[35] This of course is the split embodied between Abū Zayd and his Koranic schoolteacher. It is the pattern of differentiation the sīra performance puts on display.

To air these differences, to reveal these patterns of conflict and incompatibility between the real and the ideal in the society is to threaten the boundaries of discrimination, and thereby the boundaries of power. The danger in the sīra, then, has historically been the risk of boundary transgression and the inherent loss of power such transgression implies.[36] The perception the *Hilāliyya* purveys is dangerous. It makes public the limitations of the rigid categories on which the social order is founded. It thus threatens the set order of things, the economic and political status quo. It becomes consequently "dirt," or somehow "taboo." Appropriately, its active bearers, the gypsy shuʿarā' professional musicians, are in the normal course of daily life a despised caste who live at the community periphery. The sīra performance in its rhetorical integration of the agonistically divided village community thus represents an institutionalized way of dealing with anomaly—what Douglas calls a collective text.[37] The semiotic event of the shāʿir on the peasant's threshold singing his sīra offers its own interpretation,[38] and through its self-reflecting semiosis, Egypt interprets itself. The ritual of sīra performance rhetorically reconstructs the community; it inversely and subversely reenacts the form of social relations, gives them visible expression and thereby enables people to know their own society.

The quest for purity—whether it be purity of race, language, or artistic form and idiom—is the enemy of change. It represents an attempt to force experience into logical categories of noncontradiction; such a stance forces its holder into contradictions and dichotomizations.[39] Denial and suppression of the sīra and other vernacular folk traditions thus has had serious implications for the study of Arabic letters and culture, because the whole of the Arabic imagination cannot be comprehended without the fellah and the gypsy shāʿir. The two play off each other and off the rejecting outside world as a whole culture complete with all its ambivalence and ambiguities and paradoxes.

Today a broader audience of Egyptians has opened up to the shāʿir's message. The voice of Cairo intellectuals increasingly defends the popular tradition and looks on the scene of the shāʿir entertaining his folk audience not only with a new tolerance but often with genuine empathy and identification. Abnoudy, who has informed much of the present work, as an "ideal audience" member[40] and aficionado of the tradition, himself represents this new kind of audience. In his radio commentary and in his newspaper articles on the *Hilāliyya,* Abnoudy presents Abū Zayd and the Hilālī in conflict with their enemies not as relics of the past, but as a living presence, as a living genealogy. Abū Zayd, he says, is the "missing hero" in Egypt, the leader who never emerged to coalesce the people. His own identification with the sīra and its heroes is impassioned, his plea on their behalf convincing, his comprehension of their message sublime. A boy from the south, Abnoudy was born in 1938. He reached adolescence with the Revolution. His own revolution—his break with his father and with the high culture split off from the common man—came a few years later. Abnoudy's case offers an interesting departure from the centuries of educated people's view of the folk culture, which Shirbīnī's lampoon of the *Hilāliyya* exemplifies. For rather than deny and disparage his rural origins in his writings, as the seventeenth-century village boy[41] gone to Cairo did, Abnoudy embraces as his own the vernacular poetic tradition along with its whole culture. Abnoudy has become one of Egypt's most famous and most beloved poets.[42] His poetry, however, is written in the colloquial tongue; its vocabulary and cadences echo those of the shāʿir in a lovingly affectionate way, very unlike Shirbīnī's vicious parodic adaptation of the shāʿir's mode. Abnoudy's denial, rejection, and disdain is reserved for the ossified, aristocratic poetic tradition of the "high" language of Classical Arabic poetry in which his own father composed verses. His father, as we noted above (chap. 2), was an Azhar-educated shaykh who wrote village marriage contracts. Abnoudy has chosen to identify rather with the peasant and with the peasant poet. As lyricist to ʿAbd al-Ḥalīm Ḥāfiẓ and other renowned Egyptian singers, Abnoudy has a wide audience, a mass appeal that extends from the shāʿir's audience and beyond it to the bourgeois city population and the world of Marxist intellectuals alike. In 1975 and 1978 he had two series of daily radio programs in which he presented *Sīrat Banī Hilāl* and several rabāb poets.[43]

Like the gypsy shāʿir, Abnoudy is a bridge between cultures, a mediator who presents people with themselves and with their whole history. This is part of his symbolic appeal and his persuasive force. Abnoudy makes radio and recording stars of the gypsy poets or the outcasts like Jābir Abū Ḥusayn. The outcast gypsy poet who paradoxically bears the history of a group who despises him potentially reaches not only the fellah's doorstep; now, thanks first to Abnoudy's radio show and then to his cassette recordings, the shāʿir can reach every home with a radio turned on at 10:00

P.M. or anyone who walks past a café in the popular quarter of Cairo at that time or rides in a cab, or whoever buys the cassettes. Abnoudy is reaching all levels of classes in his diffusion of the *Hilāliyya.* He is creating symbolically a new audience for the shāʿir's anomalous social and political message. Workers and displaced peasants, village men of all classes flock to Abnoudy, send representatives to him and to the radio station to acclaim the Hilālī program. People rally to Abnoudy as a popular songwriter and poet who has a history of being jailed for speaking out against the political regime. He is a dramatic personage. And he is a preacher and a teacher, just as a good folk poet like Jābir is. Abnoudy interprets the poet on his radio shows and cassettes for the intellectual and bourgeois audience who are also his admirers. As the lyricist to ʿAbd al-Ḥalīm Ḥāfiẓ, Shādiyya, Fā'iza, and other such famous singers, TV, and nightclub personalities, and as a publicly performing poet himself, Abnoudy has access to another more bourgeois audience; this elite middle class is the very audience which historically has perhaps most vehemently turned its back on the sīra tradition as beneath contempt. Often its members seem either ignorant of the tradition or to have forgotten the existence of the shāʿir in their rigid morality and their parvenu's embrace of urban ways. Abnoudy today, however, as part of the intracultural dialogue he is creating, brings these people back to the sīra and to the truth about themselves.

I have called Abnoudy the poets' premier patron and "ideal audience." I intend by this appellation to separate him from the patrons who comprise the poets' "real" audience—men, like ʿAlī the bawwāb, who have not moved to Cairo, but remain back in the villages in a more geographically and morally contained group. The rhetorician Chaim Perelman conveniently distinguishes the real audience of the speaker from his wider, more universal one. The "real" audience represents the more local, specific, "target" audience which is bound in time and space and which the poet normally addresses directly in the face-to-face performance dynamic. Perelman uses the term "universal" audience, in place of the more Kantian term "ideal audience" I have employed, to refer to the broader audience of posterity which transcends specific, local time and space to comprehend the more universal appeal in the speaker's message.[44]

Abnoudy, once part of the "real audience" as a teenage boy

back in his southern village of Abnoud, thus has become the poets' "ideal audience" in his presentation and translation of the poets' message to a broader audience both in Egypt and abroad. How this patron-poet will change and reinvent the tradition as it exists in the years to come remains to be seen. The tradition, as the Egyptian folklorist ʿAbd al-Ḥamīd Hawwās put it in his Hammamet lecture, is evolving from orally performed narrative event and lyric folksong or folk ballad adaptations to Abnoudy. Already, Abnoudy's serious intent to record the "whole" epic from beginning to end puts the tradition in new terms. Never before have single poets like Jābir been asked to sing the whole epic. Local, spontaneous, "real" performances have always been (and I suspect further research in southern villages will demonstrate, remain) like the one Critchfield documents; that is, partial tellings of the tale through an episode geared to a particular group of patrons, over a week- or month-long party to celebrate a particular event. Particularism then appears to mark the "real" tradition today. In the nineteenth century, one might speculate, although we have no genuine evidence, the café poets may have strung out long narrations over a year. We do know, however, that these poets specialized in telling only particular episodes of the tale. None attempted to tell the "whole" "Book" as authentic "history." Abnoudy's quest (and that of the researchers who flock after him to this rich field) to record the whole in a fixed text is not new, for the eighteenth- and nineteenth-century folk redactors attempted the same in their manuscripts and "yellow book" editions (which we shall discuss later in developing a theory of sīra transmission).

Whatever Abnoudy's potential influence on the tradition's future development, he has himself become a transmitter and poet of the *Hilāliyya*—the "ideal" patron and the literate poet-transmitter who fixes the tradition for a wider posterity. He reaches and teaches a new, broader audience. His lesson is one of self-pride, his mission educational. He is a folk intellectual, a peasant boy who made a choice to embrace the folk, vernacular culture of the common man he grew up alongside.

Since 1952, the shāʿir's anomalous vision has found a new audience in men like Abnoudy. Other postrevolutionary critics and historians, with a new ideology and historiography that officially embraces the peasant as a heroic figure,[45] are keenly aware of the poet's metalepsis of the inside and the outside as a dialectic that symbolizes a problem that pervades the whole society. The shāʿir's tale, and the anomalies of experience and social identity it contains, offers a corroborating parallel with the postrevolutionary intellectual's view of the folk culture as resisting outside authority, always at odds with the dominant power. The Hilālī metaphor works for a new generation of intellectuals with a changed and changing perspective.[46] It works as an integrative interpretation of power politics in Ottoman and Mamluk society. It also works to interpret the rift between levels of society and culture—the differentiating power of literacy and possession.

Shukrī, for example, sees the sīra as a sort of historical romance, an epic of resistance which expresses the lot of the Arab people against either a foreign power or internal despotism. More specifically, Rushdī Ṣāliḥ shows how *Sīrat Banī Hilāl* too can take a direct voice of political diatribe. He reports a passage of versions of the *Hilāliyya* spread throughout the area of al-Minya in which the revolt of ʿUrābī Pasha (1881–82) is directly referred to as the Hilālī heroes and their enemies assume the character of political personages of the era.[47] Shukrī convincingly argues that it is this very spirit of rebellion in popular narratives that causes official disdain and ignorance.[48] Maḥmūd Dhihnī and Fārūq Khurshīd are two other Egyptian intellectuals who have embraced the formerly disdained sīra. Khurshīd, like Shukrī, counterposes the siyar with "official literature" (adab); for him, the siyar represent the real life of the Arab people, while adab remains a limited, aristocratic, and intellectual mannerism.[49] Dhihnī challenges the notion that the novel is purely a borrowed form in contemporary Arab letters; he shows its indigenous roots in the sīra tradition. Yūnis, in his pioneering 1956 work on Arab folklore, comprehends the living oral versions of *al-Hilāliyya* in very much their own argumentative terms; he sees them as satisfying a popular need for some kind of psychological equilibrium between what is and what ought to be.[50]

Such defenses of al-sīra appear very true. They also seem very abstractly intellectual and distanced from the real-life performance. The folk poet needs his village patrons and the antagonism they provide him in the living performance. Indeed, Cairene poets and other poets taken out of their home context may not perform with the same vivacity and maliciousness of intent as their village brethren. The "foreign" audience of a studio recording may in fact account for "bad" performances such as the ones I received from

Shamandī. Shamandī and Fārūq both commented on how difficult it was to sing without an audience. Even for studio performances to record the sīra, Abnoudy provided an audience for the poet and made a little party of the event. The performances I recorded were better with Abnoudy present, since the poets were animated by his presence and sought to please such a demanding patron who could potentially make them stars. Abnoudy himself, while listening to a poet, often interjected comments, insulted the poets, and drove them to what he conceived to be a "better" performance and rendition of the story, a more "authentic history." Further field research in indigenous contexts is surely in order; it will, I suspect, verify that this insulting, participatory exchange is paramount in the village performance and indeed is the essence of the poets' meaning and intention.

How much "studio performances" take out of the live, spontaneous performance may be vast. Much of the ritually hostile interaction of poet and patron the field-worker may observe may well have vanished in the researcher's commissioned performance, out of its true context, away from its real audience. The ritual ventilation of hostilities which the sīra performance represents may be the tradition's greater cultural intention and meaningful significance, for the experience of the sīra and the transaction involved in its performance partakes of deeply significant oral, traditional argumentation about deep cultural anxieties. With the gypsy on the doorstep, the fellah audience openly confronts these fears; with Abnoudy on the radio, the intelligentsia and the bourgeoisie must also confront themselves vis-à-vis the culture they view as somehow "other."

PART IV

# Sīra and Epic and the Oral Way of Knowing

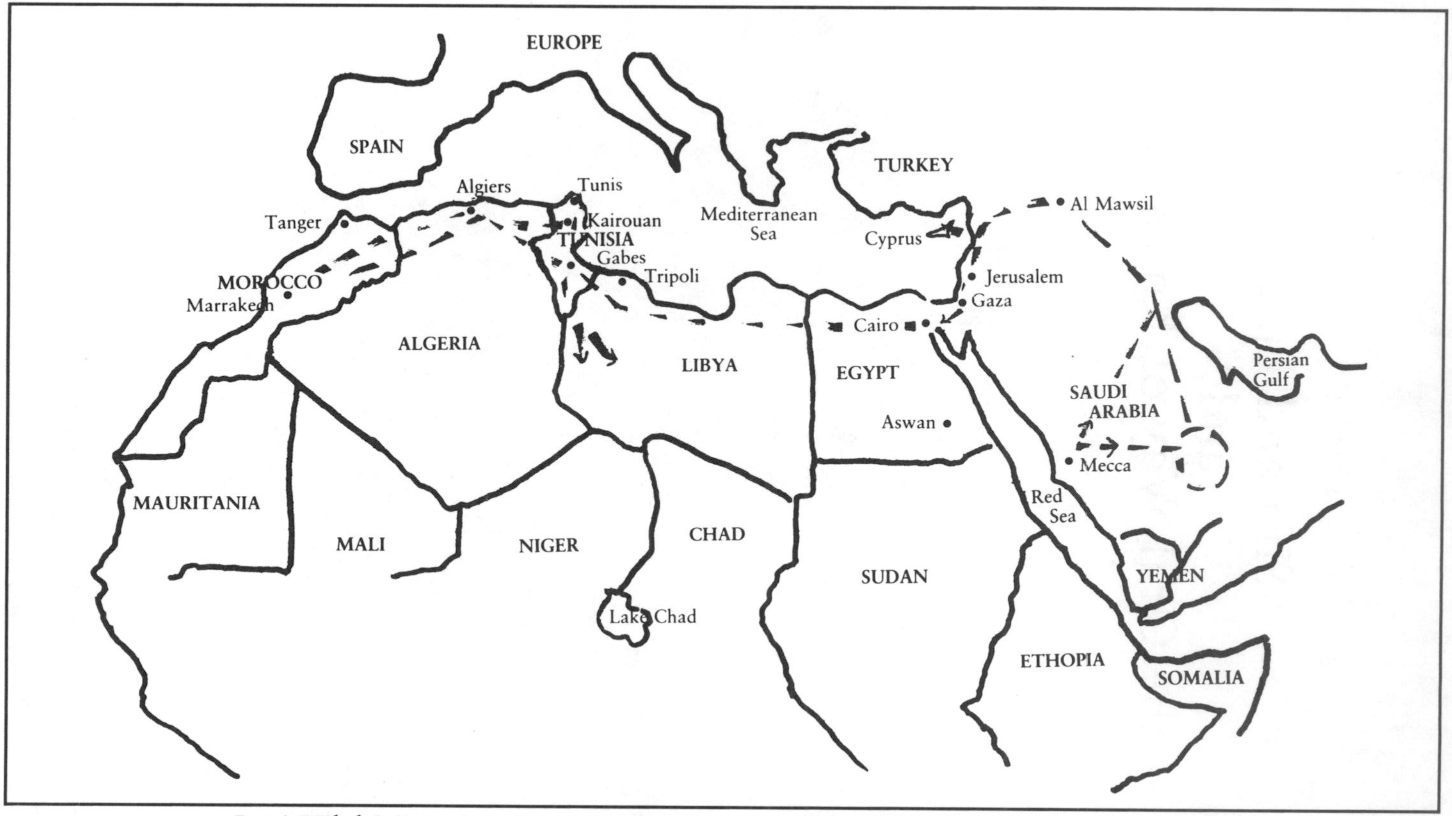


Beni Hilal Migration Route ( ) (adapted from Pantucek, pp. 44–46)

# 9
# TRANSFORMATIONS OF *SĪRAT BANĪ HILĀL* IN AFRICA

"Every country has its sīra. Our sīra here is Arabic. It has collected books since the days of the Pharaohs. Our Baḥrī (Deltan) sīra is not like the Ṣaʿīdī (Upper Egyptian) sīra." These are the words of the Egyptian rabāb poet Shamandī.[1] And although *Sīrat Banī Hilāl* may not be as ancient as this performer suggests, it has survived for the telling some 800 years after the events it celebrates, while similar heroic narratives have perished. It continues to be relevant to the moral and psychological concerns of the people making up the Egyptian oral folk culture. It also has remained relevant to the ethos of people spread all along the migration route of the Hilālī tribe. For wherever the tribe traveled and settled, there also spread its word; and the traditional story matter has wide dissemination throughout Arabic-speaking countries.

Art, as Geertz tells us, is a local matter.[2] And the Hilālī narrators in the different areas where the legendary tale appears rework the traditional nucleus matter to suit local realities and audiences. Persuasive communication for the collective text of oral cultures, perhaps even more so than in the more individual texts of literate cultures, rests on a sense of shared experience and history. It also rests on shared categories and paradigms for organizing experience, on a shared perception of the world, a shared criterion for evaluation and judgment, and the shared sense of identity which stems from this; it depends too on shared expectations as to story-telling decorum and subject. In the various places where the *Hilāliyya* is heard, narrators shape and reshape it to suit local audience values, attitudes, and predispositions; they reshape it to adapt to regional major premises about what is true and tailor it to local generic expectations, story-telling decorum, and attitudes toward story and history. The social status of the narrator also varies and serves to indicate the relative status of the tradition in the community. In Algeria in the 1960s, audience and Hilālī tale-spinners alike in the community of Bônois thought the "Story of Diyāb," which they told in informal family story sessions as "exotic," came from elsewhere.[3] In the Bornu Province in the 1930s, an Iesiyé Arab muᶜallim (teacher) who told four ḥikāyas viewed them as history, as a genuine genealogical account of how the Arabs came to far western Africa.[4] Sudanese narrators too categorize the Hilālī tales as qiṣṣa or ḥikāya, both of which synonymously mean nonfiction stories. Some tribes of Kordofan consider themselves the descendants of Abū Zayd and tell Hilālī tales to explain how they came to Africa.[5] In rural southern Tunisia today, Hilālī legends are told informally in the everyday prose-speech of "talk" by amateur raconteurs as men gather together to relax in the back of a shop or garage and tell tales their fathers and grandfathers told them.[6] In the days of the French Protectorate, Tunisian professional artists (painters, musicians, storytellers called *fḍāwīn* (sg. fḍāwī) elaborated the heroic tradition, which played a complex role in the folk arts and imagination.

Hilālī stories, poems, and songs have oral currency throughout North Africa, wherever the historic tribe has an impact of one sort or another—in Tunisia, in the Lake Chad area, in the Sudan, in Libya, and in Algeria. Prose tales also can be heard today in Jordan and in various Palestinian refugee camps.[7] These versions, wherever they are told, may be one of two things: either condensations of the "entire" Hilālī tale or elaborations of certain episodes. The former include highly synoptic accounts of the cycles that make up the Egyptian tale: (1) the birth of the hero and the experience of the tribe in Nejd, their early migrations in search of green pastures; (2) the *Riyāda,* or the scouting expedition undertaken by Abū Zayd and his three nephews to Tūnis the Green; (3) the Taghrība, or the immigration of the greater tribe to Tūnis, their encounter and eventual defeat of the Zanātī Khalīfa after many adventures along the route via Iraq and Ethiopia, Syria, and Gaza, warring against Jews and Christians, converting certain heroes to their cause; (4) the Seven Thrones, or the dissension caused by the irrational power lust of Diyāb the Herdsman; and (5) the War of the Orphans against Diyāb's power hold and the dispersion of the tribe.[8] In the various areas where the *Hilāliyya* is recited, different episodes and different heroes emerge from the long tale as significant in the local oicotype by virtue of their frequency of telling; narrators in the diverse areas foreground varying concerns and motif sequences.

The "Birth of Abū Zayd" in its Egyptian versions performed by a caste of gypsy singers highlights social differentiation, race, and inheritance as crucial issues. Lack of a child and the negritude of the child born are consequently stressed, along with the baseness of his mother and the vileness of the black slave. As a myth of origins of strife in the community and as an explanation for the conflict that will break apart the Hilālī brethren in the latter part of the tale, the Egyptian versions stress the perfidy of Ghānim's dirty story about Khaḍrā the Pure Lady of the Prophet's lineage (al-Sharīfa). The black racial motif disappears altogether in the Shuwa version of the stories of Abū Zayd al-Hilālī collected by J. R. Patterson in the 1920s in the Bornu district near Lake Chad. Audience members and the storyteller are all black. Recounted by an Iesiye Arab teacher, race and social differentiation are not the issues in this far western version of the Hilālī tale; nor are the problems of cuckoldry, infidelity, inheritance, and honor central. Rather the Nigerian tribal patriarchy fears the newborn babe's colossal strength (e.g., at seven days the baby Abū Zayd grasps his father's finger so tightly the man cannot break loose); the tribesmen fear that the child will grow up to be a cannibal and devour his father and all the tribe. The men of the tribe thus flee and leave the boy to grow up alone with his mother and their slaves.

In the Tunisian *Hilāliyya,* too, status differences and race anxieties are peripheral issues, replaced by the larger anxieties about food and survival. For example, Ḥājj ʿAbd al-Salām al-Muhadhdhabī,[9] the Tunisian rāwī whom Baker recorded in 1972 in southern Tunisia, does not really develop the blackness of the child. He tells his audience that the infertile Khaḍrā who could not give birth to a son strolled one day in a garden where she saw a flock of sparrows. A great, black raven terrorized them and would only let the little birds eat one grain at a time. Khaḍrā makes her ablutions and prays to the Lord, beseeching him to grant her a son like the raven, even one as black as the bird, even one who will terrorize mounted knights. The narrator goes on to mention that the child is indeed born black and that the tribe laughs when presented with the new baby. The narrator's discretion and delicacy as to why Rizq and the Hilālī tribe banished the baby and his mother is such that Baker feels impelled to add a footnote explaining that Rizq's fury and the tribe's laughter can be accounted for by the fact that the rāwī does not feel impelled to mention what his listeners already know, namely, that the child is so black they can only assume Rizq's wife has been unfaithful with a black slave.[10] Perhaps the narrator's reticence is because he is a religious man, a seventy-three-year-old who has made the pilgrimmage to Mecca and therefore has a certain holiness; Ḥājj ʿAbd al-Salām was also a village Koranic schoolteacher before his retirement.[11] Several factors then may account for the good shaykh's modesty in his narration of the birth of Abū Zayd, including the fact that the primary audience was a woman researcher.

Another Tunisian version develops the black slave motif a bit more specifically. In the 1927 version of the *Hilāliyya* collected by Guiga "from the mouth of an old Tripolitanian man" on the Tunisian-Libyan border, the birth of Abū Zayd is condensed into perhaps three or four minutes of narration.[12] Al-Amīr Rizq is absent from the tribe, fighting at the head of the Hilālī armies against the Syrians on behalf of the Sharīf of Mecca, his father-in-law. His wife who has given birth only to a daughter meanwhile decides to offer a plate of couscous to the birds of the sky in the hope they will intercede and God will give her a male child. A black crow eats the couscous as the woman prays to God (who saves beasts from certain death by making rain fall) to give her a boy in the image of the black crow, a lad whose saber will make enemy blood flow. "The daughter of the Sharīf of Mecca," as this narrator calls her instead of Khaḍrā, gives birth to a child "black as night" but with the physiognomy of a white child.[13] The narrator exclaims to the audience, "God preserve us! what will al-Amīr Rizq say when he hears that a bastard has been born in his house!" The angry Rizq sends word for Khaḍrā to be sent into exile and her dowry returned.

Significantly, neither of these Tunisian rāwīs develops the scene of the wish very fully. In the Egyptian versions, we saw the many colored birds fighting among each other for dominance, with the green, white, and red birds defeated by the black bird.

These birds significantly represented the various Hilālī heroes, the red bird particularly being Diyāb al-Aḥmar (the Red), the son of Ghānim whose gossip defiled Khaḍrā, the hero who will be the head herdsman of the Hilālī tribe in their journey westward. The Egyptian shuʿarā' deem it important in their version of the birth tale to foreshadow the strife to come and to point the finger at the family of Diyāb b. Ghānim as the troublemakers. Tunisian rāwīs and North African narrators in general develop the last cycles (the intertribal conflict over power in the Maghrib) and thus make Diyāb the central hero of their tales. They consequently do not blame the family of Ghānim for disseminating conflict within the clan.

Tunisian rāwīs indicate that Diyāb originated from a different tribe and thus had different loyalties. They give this genealogical difference as the reason the Hilālīs all "hated Diyāb."[14] Whereas the Hilālī heroes in the Egyptian shāʿir's performed versions of the "Birth of Abū Zayd" were all born to the same greater tribe and conceived during a particularly significant ritual pilgrimage to the Lake of the Birds, Tunisian narrators account for the heroes' origins separately and give fully developed birth tales for the characters they consider to be the major personages of the drama, called in the local dialect: Bū Zīd (= Abū Zayd), Dhiyāb (= Diyāb), and Zāziya (= Jāziya).

In their work on heroic literature, the Chadwicks[15] claim that the birth and childhood of the hero is not really essential to the heroic tale itself. They instead prefer to view such tales as products of a "later" phase in the development of the legend, a phase associated with the accumulation of "myth" around the person of the hero. Or as medieval French scholars put it for the case of the chansons de geste, in the process of epic cyclicalization, sons engender fathers.[16] Whether this is true or not, the myth of the birth of the hero abounds today as a fully developed cycle of the sīra in Egypt and elsewhere. As such, it acts as a kind of backdrop to the major conflict of the sīra; it explains the origins of the epic heroes, the origins of their conflicts, their familial and tribal affiliations. The retelling of this birth cycle reveals a concern with origins on the part of both singer and audience. It sets up the terms through which the migratory saga should be understood; it also explicates the origins of the heroic dilemma and the meaning of the heroic life in terms of present-day experience. As a "later" accretion to the traditional hero tale, it most closely adheres to a present point of view and to the present storyteller's narrative etiology.

According to Okpewho, the birth and ongoing life cycle taking the hero to his death finds particular currency in African epic. Versions of the *Hilāliyya* from the Sudan and the Lake Chad area particularly stress the story as the life cycle of an individual, thus adhering to an African epic pattern.[17] The individual hero (Abū Zayd) further becomes in the Lake Chad oicotype of the *Hilāliyya* a twin hero (with Diyāb) in congruence with local West African tale patterns.[18]

Dhiyāb,[19] who is the central hero of the Tuniso-Libyan oicotype, has his own birth tale, as does Jāziya, the sister of King Ḥasan of the Hilālī, who in her transformation to the Tunisian Zāziya gains a central role. Dhiyāb, as Baker summarizes the Tunisian tale from her recording of diverse rāwīs,[20] is born when his mother, the second wife of Ghānim of the Zughba, is left behind in the desert by the departing tribe. Wolves gather around the helpless woman and her newborn who are left alone in the desert. Meanwhile Ghānim notes that his wife is missing. He extracts a confession from his jealous first wife that she tricked the pregnant woman into staying behind. Ghānim finds the weakened woman fighting off wolves with a tree branch as she lies with her babe. They name the boy Dhiyāb, because he was nearly eaten by wolves (*dhi'āb* in Tunisian dialect is wolf; *dhīb* refers to jackals). Dhiyāb's name etymology thus is his genealogy: his name glosses both his past (i.e., his birth) and his future as the ultimately ambivalent Hilālī hero—the sulking herdsman whom Egyptian poets of the East blame for the dissolution of tribal unity and the dispersion of Arab power.

Tunisian, Algerian, and Libyan versions of the Hilālī saga highlight Dhiyāb as the main hero alongside Jāziya, or Zāziya or al-Jāz, who has a lesser role in the Egyptian shāʿir's cast of characters. The Tunisian Zāziya was born, according to Baker's rāwī Naṣr b. ʿAbd Allāh,[21] from the marriage of the Hilālī Prince Sirḥān with the daughter of a jinn (genie, devil). The story goes thus: A hungry dog approached Sirḥān for food and even though rations were short, the prince treated the dog as a "guest." The dog then led Prince Sirḥān to a woman and a girl child in an underground cave, whereupon the dog turned into none less than the King of the Jinn. Sirḥān marries the jinn's daughter. Their issue is Zāziya, princess of the Hilālī.

The Tunisian oicotype foregrounds Zāziya as an all-powerful generating force, the protector of the tribe who bears children and grinds grain like all the tribal women, but who also girds herself for battle to do man-to-man combat; she also sacrifices herself for tribal survival by marrying a loathsome enemy and bearing him children in exchange for grain and pasture.[22] Guiga's Tripolitanian narrator tells us that Zāziya shares the command of the tribe with her brother Ḥasan b. Sirḥān and his wife Shīḥā, who is also Bū Zīd's sister.[23] What appears to take the foreground in the Tripolitanian narrator's rendition of the greater Hilālī tale is the power potential in the male-female interaction. He revolves each short episode in his *Hilāliyya* around female power, female judgment of tribal heroes, or a central interaction with a female character.

The Tunisian rāwī ʿAbd al-Salām has a similar narrative structure. He himself tells us twice, at the opening of narrative sessions, what his concept of an episode is or what a tale (qiṣṣa) contains:

> That's one tale
> They have forty tales about eloping with women:
> Your son elopes with the king of Libya's daughter
> So Libya and Tunisia go to war
> My son elopes with the daughter of the king of Algeria
> They all go to war, and go out after each other
> Finally they eat each other up.[24]

Or again at the opening of his rendition of the Birth of Bū Zayd, ʿAbd al-Salām repeats virtually the same thing to introduce the new tale and close off the one he has just told:

> After that, now they have other adventures
> about elopements with women
> and about how Bū Zayd's mother married his father
> and how he happened to be raised an orphan
> And how—a tremendously long adventure.
> Another raid
> This—was the end of their westward migration
> Until they began to eat at each other

Another raid—
They call it the raid for Khaḍrā, Bū Zīd's mother.[25]

Just as Ḥājj ʿAbd al-Salām tells his audience, each episode or tale revolves around women and war, and each episode is conceived of as an adventure contained within a greater cycle of adventures. ʿAbd al-Salām explicitly links war with erotic attachment and the power of the female in his introductory announcement of his subject to his assembled audience:

What was the reason that brought them to the
    land of Tunisia
How they got together
And how they sent the scouting expedition
and how they undertook the scouting
and how Bū Zīd fought
and how they took the prisoners
and how Khalīfa Zanātī's daughter fell in love with
    Mirʿī
and how the najʿa [tribe] went traveling
and how—at the end—
the old witch (the old sabbath woman) sowed discord
    among them
and they squabbled with one another.[26]

The source of the discord to come is a woman, the Tunisian narrator tells us directly; he also stresses this interpretation both in the thematic structuring of events in the tales and in the greater mythic destiny he assigns to things. That is, a story line for each segment of the *Hilāliyya* features a girl from one group falling in love with a lad from another, or girls are demanded as payment for food, fodder, and grazing grounds for the flocks and the tribe. Tunisian rāwīs repeat this basic narrative situation over and over as a basic motif around which the tale (or adventure as the rāwī calls it) revolves. The greater mythic or abstract explanation ʿAbd al-Salām gives for the source of discord is the Old Sabbath Woman, the hag who embodies all evil.

The power of woman serves as an explanation for all problems as well as their salvation and solution. As one Baker rāwī puts it in a riddling sequence between Bū Zīd and his son contained in the episode of the Birth of Ṣabr b. Bū Zīd:

> What puts out the blazing fire, O Ṣabr my son?
> —The flood waters put it out, father mine.
> What can overcome the flood waters, O Ṣabr my son?
> —The heights and the peaks, father mine.
> What can overcome the heights and the peaks, O Ṣabr my son?
> —The swift horse, father mine.
> And who can overcome the swift horse, O Ṣabr my son?
> —The strong man, father mine.
> And who can overcome the strong man, O Ṣabr my son?
> —The woman and her wiles, father mine.
> And who can overcome the woman and her wiles, O Ṣabr my son?
> —Only the tomb and the grave, father mine.[27]

The riddle contains a falsity and a paradox in terms of the Maghribī *Hilāliyya*'s basic terms. The woman can of course overcome the tomb and the grave, for in her reproductive capacity lies the survival of the group. The Hilālī woman, as epitomized in Jāziya/Zāziya, offers herself as the sacrifice for group survival again and again. And virtually every Maghribī episode centers around three basic motifs: (1) the female (bride-getting), (2) feeding (food-getting), and (3) the fighting such quests for fertile life engender.[28]

Baker describes the flexible, segmental structure of the Tunisian *rāwī*'s tale.[29] While the notion of westward migration integrates a fluid flexible story matter that makes up the *Hilāliyya* in Tunisian popular imagination, each episode concentrates on a single crisis or event. A sequence of unitary episodes makes up a fluid whole, a sort of arabesque presented as a series of rapidly changing scenes. Baker mentions that each of the "independent but complementary units" of the rāwī's tale has its own internal order, but she does not go on to delineate what that order is beyond a certain "thematic" "unifying matrix," namely, westward migration and the "heroic" quest for group survival. Chronological order of the complementary fragments or episodes making up the rāwī's tale, Baker tells us, is of little import. I should like to suggest, however, that what matters is the internal order of episodes. Baker quite astutely compares the rāwī's narrative style to the "kuttāb pupil repeating a series of undifferentiated items without exercising critical judgment"; but I should like to call attention to the argumentative effect of this very kind of repetition as a rhetorical device, and also to the importance of the beginning and end as a framing device in such an "undifferentiated" and flexible medium. Viewed thus, such undifferentiated items become their own kind of critical judgment by virtue of the selective choice the rāwī exercises in his juxtaposition of narrative segments.

If the source of the tribe's trouble is not a woman, then it is food, water, and grazing rights. Of the thirty-three Tunisian episodes Baker summarizes from the narratives of sixty rāwīs she recorded, all but perhaps four center around a struggle over either a food/water source of some kind or a conflict over a bride. Baker[30] found in her collecting that the most frequently told tale among nonlettered narrators was the Marriage of Zāziya to the enemy ruler Sharīf b. Hāshim in exchange for grain and grazing rights, a story that in its 1970s Tunisian version retains all the basic elements of the version recorded by Ibn Khaldūn[31] some six centuries ago. It also parallels the version Bel collected in Algeria at the turn of the century. Its story is this: The Hilālī arrive in Tūnis to buy wheat, or in search of pasturelands, after a great God-given drought; they bargain with the ruler of Tūnis, the Sharīf b. Hāshim and agree to give him Jāziya/Zāziya in exchange for the food and pasturage. She marries him and has two children before her tribe can follow the rains to freer green pasture. When the tribe is about to depart, Jāzya engages the Sharīf in a chesslike game (kharaba),[32] agreeing with him that the loser will strip naked for the winner. She loses, but her hair covers her entire body and saves her modesty. The Sharīf loses the next round; his ugly body covered with sores embarrasses him so that he agrees to whatever Jāziya wishes. She convinces him to follow her tribe south. Further tricks ensue and she escapes to her tribe. The enraged Sharīf returns home to gather his army and sets out to confront the Hilālī troops, but cannot avail and is vanquished.[33]

The trickery and eroticism that distinguish the Sharīf b. Hāshim episode appear to characterize generally Tunisian Hilālī tales. The basic plot of the story of Jāziya against B. Hāshim is that of a great number of Tunisio-Libyan folktales based on the Hilālī legend. The basic pattern of tales in the Baker collection goes thus from initial to closing sequence: the initial situation is almost always a lack and an ensuing arrival in a place held by enemy forces; the arrival constitutes a boundary transgression that entails a conflict over (a) water and pasture, (b) food or food source, (c) a horse, or (d) a woman. This initial motifeme sequence can be resolved by direct combat (resulting in either victory or defeat for the Hilālī) or by means of bargaining followed by trickery. The latter can either vanquish the foes or delay direct hostile confrontation in combat. If the source of conflict is pasture, the seeming resolution involves the sacrifice of a Hilālī woman in marriage to the enemy. This, however, usually leads to a trick, an escape, a pursuit, combat between major oppositional forces, and defeat for the enemy.[34]

The opposition met by the nomadic desert tribe in its quest for food, water, pasture, and fertile life sustenances makes up the core of the *Hilāliyya* as interpreted by African narrators. Narrators foreground this encounter with the political powers ruling the lands through which the tribe migrates in the way they order story motifs. Significantly, arrival is the initial situation of many Hilālī episodes. As a story element, it involves geographic boundary transgression and it prepares for the next probable motif, which is conflict and opposition. The ways in which African and North African versions of the *Hilāliyya* resolve this dilemma of boundary transgression reflect a basic concern in the society surrounding the tale-tellers and their audiences.

Tunisian folk paintings and prints give visual expression to the initial situation conflicts perceived in the Tunisian oral tales. Reverse glass paintings that date from the era of the French Protectorate depict the nomad confronting the urban power as he arrives in his domain. Again and again the same scene (with different heroes and different enemies) appears: the hero astride his charger, lance in hand, strikes down the enemy townsman, cutting through his helmet, unraveling his chain-mail links one by one in a pool of blood on the ground. Behind him the woman appears borne on a camel litter, while the city walls and a green oasis appear opposite the enemy. The hero confronting the enemy takes up the center of the picture, protecting the woman secluded in her *jaḥfa* (= howda or camel-borne litter) while the enemy defends his city's gardens against the mounted desert marauder with his hungry herds of camels and sheep (see pls. 12–18).

Reverse glass paintings of heroic story matter flourished in Sfax in the early part of the century, during the French Protectorate, when the painter's workshop formed a sort of artisan's headquarters where folk poets, musicians, and storytellers (fḍāwī) congregated.[35] The workers in the visual medium painted stories, or rather popular history, at the behest of patrons who commissioned a reverse glass painting to decorate a bed's headboard, a woodwork shelf for a clock or gun rack, or a woodwork cupboard. Many versions of the same painting exist since the basic scene would be modeled to fit different mountings. Galley and Ayoub[36] have suggested that one such painting functions as a protective emblem of fertility. In their analysis of an image of Jāziya depicted in a Tunisian reverse glass painting, they demonstrate, with parallels from the story tradition circulating in the Maghrib, how Jāziya is viewed as a guarantor of group survival, as a procurer of food, and as a model of group values in her sacrifice of herself in marriage to the citified enemy ruler in exchange for food for her tribe and their ever-present hungry herds. Blessed with stunning beauty, lush hair, and eternal youth, she is the emblem of sexuality, fecundity, and marriage. And as her name's etymology implies, she ever represents the recompense her tribe must offer in exchange for fertile land and water: *Jāziya,* the feminine active participle of the root j/z/y, expresses the idea of recompense, reward, compensation. I have suggested elsewhere that Jāziya's name may also take on connotations through punning associations with the similar sounding roots j/a/z from which derive the ideas of traveling, crossing, and prize; and j/u/z, which forms the notion of marriage and coupling. I might add the suggestion that Jāziya's name is also a pun on *jizya,* the land tax or head tax non-Muslim subjects paid Muslim sovereigns.[37] Zāziya thus rewards the Hilālī as their protective barter against starvation. Her birth tale repeats itself endlessly as Jāziya, the jinn's granddaughter, repays the Hilālī for the food they offered her grandfather and in return for which he gave them his daughter in marriage (see pl. 12).

The artist "presents" Jāziya/Zaziya in the portrait just the way Tunisians present the traditional bride mounted on a sort of stage and framed in her bridal array and elaborate eye makeup. The Hilālī heroine is portrayed not in Bedouin garb as one might expect, but in more contemporary bridal dress; she wears the bride's crown. Her upraised hands hold a bouquet of five flowers in the right and a bird in the left. Zāziya fixes the viewer with a direct stare from large eyes and pointed pupils that seem to pierce the onlooker. In their analysis of the picture's motif of the five flowers, Galley and Ayoub document the potent significance of the number five in Tunisian folk beliefs. They recall that the Hand of Fāṭima hangs on the doors of homes to avert the evil eye, and that the outstretched hand is a gesture that wards off the same. They fail to mention the probable fact that the flowers in themselves may represent verdant life and growth—the flowering of life as it were. The bird motif is similarly shown in Tunisian culture to be a prophylactic good luck omen. In the case of Zāziyya, the bird more specifically may represent her tribe about to depart, for several oral versions tell how the tribe alerts Zāziyya to their imminent departure south after the rains by releasing messenger pigeons.[38] The sacrificed bride thus receives the signal she can rejoin her rightful tribe and husband (Dhiyāb in some versions).

The portrait normally would have hung in the nuptial chamber bedroom of a traditional home. Galley and Ayoub mention the fact that such portraits were commissioned on the occasion of weddings to celebrate the marriage and to decorate the bridal chambers. These reverse glass paintings were viewed as good luck omens. The authors conclude that the cultural intention of Zāziya's portrait was to safeguard the bridal couple and to ensure fertility. To extend Galley and Ayoub's conclusions a bit further, the portrait thus becomes in its cultural uses and intentions an iconographic depiction of the etymology of Jāziya's name.

During my research in Tunisia in 1973–1974, I saw similar paintings in the private boudoir of the eighty-year-old (or thereabouts) grandmother of my friends in Nabeul.[39] This grandmother's reverse glass paintings depicted the Hilālī heroes slicing down the enemy before the city gates. Hung alongside the heroic depictions were reverse glass painted calligraphies of "Allāh," God's name, and various propitiatory invocations taken from the Koran. When I inquired, I was told these paintings were all simply "porte-bonheurs" to decorate the room, which the old lady had possessed since she was a bride. She believed they brought "baraka" to the room. Given their place of prominence in the traditional bedroom, it appears that the intention traditional Tunisian culture assigns paintings of the Hilālī heroes and heroines in their quest for Tūnis the Green (al-khaḍrāʾ) is emblematic of fertility and fruitful marriage.

The tradition of reverse glass painting in Sfax artisans' workshops ended,[40] only to be replaced by print-media versions of the Hilālī heroes. Just before World War II, witnesses tell me, fḍāwīs sold cheap prints of the heroic paintings in the marketplaces.[41] Plates 13–17 reduplicate the cheap, comic-book quality prints I found in the souks in Nabeul. Storytellers, according to the various vendors I spoke with, evidently used to lay these prints out on the ground in front of them while narrating the episode illustrated. Like reverse glass paintings, of which they appear to be copies, the pulp paper prints come in many versions of the same scene. The prints, as the paintings, represent visual, spatial translation of the storyteller's oral-aural temporal medium of words.

The artist's stylized technique of composition is formulaic, very similar to the traditional story-telling technique. While the Hilālī narrator juxtaposes narrative segments in a paratactic adding style that does not know the hypotaxis and subordination of written style, the glass painter employs a medium that knows no perspective, nor lights or shadows. All highlighting is by disposition and color. In its colorful dualistic disposition of motifs, the painted history serves to interpret the fḍāwī's tale and to draw out its basic terms.

A reverse glass painting of Abū Zayd (with Nāʿisa his bride and his retainer-slave) against al-Harrās[42] which I purchased from a Tūnis antique dealer in 1978 poses the situation more clearly as one of entry and boundary transgression. The Bedouin horseman with his retinue of slave and camel-borne lady are only entering the scene; half of them still cannot be seen and are lost in the picture frame. The Bedouins appear as intruders thrusting onto the scene, penetrating the center to strike down the urban knight holding the center and inside of the picture. The potential sources of the conflict—the lady and the settled area's green garden-city—frame the two combatants. This visual abstraction of the storyteller's message makes its antitheses and the dialectic of the image particularly clear:

nomad vs. urbanite
periphery vs. center
outsider vs. insider
desert vs. sown
death vs. life
killing vs. fertile propagation

---

female = power (food holding, city, greenness, garden, herds, wealth)

The woman serves as the barter, the go-between. In Lévi-Straussian terms,[43] one might say the woman mediates between the desired goals of the group and its opposition; she serves as recompense for the grain, pasture, and water the encroaching Hilālī tribe needs to survive (see pl. 18).

Given that the Hilālī narrators used printed versions of paintings like mine to illustrate their tales in marketplace performances and given the place of prominence assigned the reverse glass paintings in the heart of the traditional home, it may not be rash to assume that what the paintings depict summarizes and glosses the essence of the narrative versions. Tunisian renditions of the *Hilāliyya,* as other North African versions, are tales of symbolic boundary transgression, incorporation, and assimilation, and the consequent confusion of identities such transgression entails. This applies to both the group and the individual level of experience, for the tales in their Tunisian oicotype are primarily stories about African Arab identity. North Africans witnessed successive migrations of Arabs coming from the outside to settle down and live among them, to intermarry and introduce them to Islam, to teach them the sacred tongue of Arabic, and generally to incorporate their identity in theirs. The encounter of the hungry nomadic Hilālī in quest of a home with the sedentary agricultural power (which the paintings and tales represent) is indeed the genealogy of the North African Arab. The paintings and the stories repeat certain motifs: (1) arrival in a place, (2) confrontation ensuing from the boundary transgression, and (3) the sacrifice of a nubile, marriageable female in recompense for that encroachment. In the repetition of these three motifs, the tradition and its artists foreground a conflict surrounding penetration, incorporation, and assimilation, and a conflict surrounding marriage as a mediator between social groups.

Many tales, as I have outlined, repeatedly recount the sacrifice of the woman for food, grain, or pasturage. Other tales demonstrate over and over the disruptive power of female sexuality and desire. The rāwī Ḥājj ʿAbd al-Salām, for example, in his long narration of the *Hilāliyya* from scouting expeditions of Abū Zayd and his nephews (al-Riyāda) through to the death of Abū Zayd, Ḥasan, and Jāziya at the hands of Dhiyāb, to the flight of Dhiyāb's descendants to Fez and their subsequent return to conquer Tūnis, says that the cause of all the strife among the Hilālī heroes was a woman: "The Old Sabbath Woman sowed discord." That woman was Saʿda, the daughter of the Zanātī Khalīfa, over whom Abū Zayd, Ḥasan, and Dhiyāb fought. With the Hilālīs capturing the Berber Zanātī girl, the balance of power has shifted and the nomad tribe has gained control of fertile green Tūnis. Dhiyāb will strike down the Zanātī Khalīfa in a battle commemorated in frequent stories and in a very famous, much-seen reverse glass painting (see pl. 17).

In the picture Dhiyāb holds the side of the green city, while the enemy is on the desert periphery; the two horsemen face each other and Dhiyāb spears Abū Saʿda al-Zanātī Khalīfa (the father of Saʿda, as the written legend on the painting indicates) in the eyeball—or more specifically, in a version Baker collected, in the "eye of the stirrup."[44] The downward displacement of the trope thus renders the Berber ruler lifeless, impotent. His daughter will bear children for the Hilālī tribe as one of their wives just as Jāziya bore the Zanātī's children in her sacrificial marriage contract with him to feed her tribe. The powerful woman in the *Hilāliyya* represents the group's regenerative powers. To sacrifice Jāziya to the Berber king of Tūnis, or to sacrifice any female of one group to another tribe, is to violate the sanctity of the group. To let the enemy penetrate one's woman is to penetrate the entry point of the group,[45] and to merge the progeny of Hilāl and Hāshim or Easterner and Westerner; it dissolves the differentiation between nomadic Eastern invader and sedentary native inhabitant of the Maghrib. Penetration of the female by a foreign group means penetration of the group and the dissolution of group boundaries. As such, it threatens ethnic and racial identity;[46] it threatens the genealogy.

The Sudanese folklorist Hurreiz[47] gives a somewhat similar interpretation to Hilālī legends, which he says are told in the Sudan as the history of the Muslim Arab settlement of Africa. As such, they reflect the dilemma of African-Arab identity. Among tribes anxious to emphasize their Arab ancestry, the tales often stress the relationship between an Arab refugee and an African chief who offers him hospital asylum; Hurreiz mentions that many narrators assign the collapse of dynasties in Arabia as the impulse for Arabs migrating in search of an African homeland. The Sudanese folklorist gives a translated text of the legend which begins with the birth of Abū Zayd and ends with the killing of Diyāb, who appears as a scourge of which the country is well rid.[48] The Hilālī legends are part of a broader spectrum of legends about Muslim ancestors who arrive from the outside to live with the African natives, intermarry with them, and introduce them to Islam. These legends are "common among the Abdallah, the Nuba, and the Fur of the Sudan as well as in Mali and among the Hausa of Nigeria."[49] Hurreiz also describes Sudanese traditions that attempt to identify the tribe ethnically with both Africa and Arabia through an African maternal ancestor and an Arab paternal ancestor. The legends, Hurreiz maintains, reflect a Sudanese dilemma. They try to solve this dilemma by a synthesis of Sudanese genealogy which traces their origins to both races and both cultures. The Sudanese stories of Abū Zayd al-Hilālī, in Hurreiz's interpretation of them, are an example of Sudanese narrators' unconscious attempt to identify themselves and their audience with Africa through the character of Abū Zayd, who is noted for his blackness. Hurreiz sees a special significance in the Sudanese oicotype of the Hilālī legend. The black Sudanese Arabic-speaking audience identifies with Abū Zayd's suffering, for their predicament in the context of the Arab world is analogous. In Hurreiz's summary of the legend:

> Abū Zeid, unlike the rest of his people, the Arabs of Banī Hilāl, was born black, and as a consequence he and his mother suffered. He was forced to grow up away from his father and the land of his paternal ancestors, and yet he came to be more valiant and worthy than others who did not have his blackness and who did not suffer because of their color.[50]

Other tales popular in Arabized parts of the Sudan similarly exploit color and ethnicity: the romances of ʿAntar and Sayf ibn Ziyazan (Dhī Yazan, in Egypt) celebrate a black hero who is born in Africa or whose mother or father is African. "Through these folktales," in the words of the Sudanese scholar," a Sudanese who identifies with the hero tries to assert his blackness and his Africanism in the non-black Arab context in which he finds himself."[51] The Sudanese folktale in general then reflects the process of acculturation and accommodation of different groups living together in North Africa and the Sudan.

This concern with group identity and tribal allegiance appears central to the African *Hilāliyya* in its multiplicity of forms. Versions I have studied from Tunisia, Algeria, and Bornu do deal with assimilation, or, as Hurreiz put it for the Sudan, they "spell out clearly the nature of the process of acculturation resulting from the interplay, compromise and accommodation of two different cultures."[52] But what they spell out even more clearly is the ambivalence that surrounds any process of assimilation which involves identification with an invader. Narrators of Tunisian and Nigerian tales particularly emphasize the fears and anxieties at stake. They revolve their tales most centrally and crucially around food anxieties about deprivation and starvation, around fears about power and the nature of leadership, fears about the male-female power dynamic. The overriding anxiety, however, I would submit, is fear of penetration and incorporation. This is the conflict that generates the narratives and gives them continued significance to narrators and audiences alike in the areas where they are heard and told.

Ḥājj ʿAbd al-Salām says explicitly that incorporation is the issue. With famine as the initial situation, this rāwī makes hunger the consuming motivation of his interpretations of the saga. He begins and ends his long tale with the same rhetorical figure of speech in which he says that the conflicting parties will "eat each other up." He repeats this five times at openings and closings and in the middle at the story's turning point. I have cited the first two instances of this figure of speech—at the beginning of the Ḥājj's Taghrība and at the opening of his version of the birth tale—in their context on page 000 above. A third instance comes at the end of the Taghrība after The Old Sabbath Woman has sowed discord and dissension among the Hilālī heroes, after Dhiyāb has murdered Ḥasan, Abū Zayd, and Zāziya; and after the orphans of the murdered heroes have ambushed and killed Dhiyāb; and after Dhiyāb's wife escapes with his infant son to Fez, where the boy grows up to succeed to the throne of his adopted father, the sultan of Morocco:

> Time passed
> Dhiyāb's people were being unjustly treated
> By the son of Bū Zayd and the son of the Sultan Ḥasan.
> They suffered injustice.
> As before, they transmitted
> A complaint to the son of Dhiyāb
> who assembled his soldiers
> And came to Tūnis.
> When he reached Tūnis
> at first he drew his sword
> He said: "In the name of Allah—Allah is great"
> And advanced to meet them
> Whomever he struck he cut off his head
> "Hold the sword!"
> He said: "By Allah, I will not hold the sword from you!"
> Finally—Ayya—
> The government went to the son of Dhiyāb and the son of Ḥasan
> Ah—Iyh! That's right! to the son of Dhiyāb
> And those others were removed
> And the Hilālīs stayed "eating" each other.
> Now the Hilālīs were:
> Drīd—Drīd was the clan of Zāziya
> And Jlāṣ, the clan of Dhiyāb
> And the rest were diverse [groups].
> This is their story about the Taghrība [westward migration].[53]

In terms of the comparison collapsed in the figure of speech, intertribal fighting, strife, and killing are equivalent to gobbling each other up, to consuming each other. The trope substitutes for an outward-going aggressive act its opposite—an in-taking, inward-directed act; that is, the narrator substitutes eating for fighting. Ḥājj ʿAbd al-Salām's repeated figure makes aggressive action into more pacifistic action; it transforms and subverts negative, destructive, hostile force into positive, constructive, life-giving energy. The reversal perhaps represents a denial of aggression.

By placing this figure of speech at the beginning and end of his narrative, the rāwī has stressed it. As an opening statement, the figure functions as an organizing contract with the listener. It focuses his attention on what will be significant in the narrative to come, it summarizes what is to come. It also helps the rāwī gather his thoughts. As a closing statement, the trope summarizes and concludes the story just heard, it serves as a reminder and fulfillment of the opening promise. It reinforces the opening interpretation of the gist of the story while leaving the comparison of strife to incorporation fresh in the mind of the listening audience. The rāwī also employs the metonym in the very middle or the turning point of his narration of the Taghrība, saying:

> Hostility was established between them
> On account of Khalīfa Zanātī's daughter.
> Khalīfa Zanātī's maternal aunt heard of it.
> She who was called Old Sabbath Woman of the West
> said: "Here come camels moseying along and grazing
> The Hilālīs we'll set on each other, soon they will eat
> each other."[54]

And again at the climax of his version of Bū Zayd's birth and encounter with his father, Ḥājj ʿAbd al-Salām repeats the metonym of "eating each other up." As the two conflicting tribes of Zaḥlān and Hilāl, represented by son and father, are about to meet, the rāwī narrates:

> They set out.
> They were going on and on.
> Now as you would see in our present time
> Whoever owns land stays on it
> "Don't get on my land!"
> That najʿa [clan] with its (. . .)
> Came to eat the najʿa which was on its way
> They came all panicked
> "Don't camp there! Don't cross over there!"
> They fell upon one another
> Peace be upon you![55]

After the rāwī's apology ("Peace be upon you!") to his audience for such hostile expressions, the hyperbole of the figure of speech becomes even more exaggerated. When Rizq, Bū Zayd's father, wounds the boy's adopted father, the boy announces he will present his stepfather with "the liver of him who wounded you for you to eat."[56] And again two times he repeats the threat "And I will roast his liver for you to eat."[57]

This is of course traditional "war rhetoric" whose hyperbole dates back in the Arab oral culture to at least the Battles of the Prophet when Hind Bint ʿUtbá "ate" the liver of the foe who had killed her brothers, husband, and father.[58] I would argue that this is not "mere rhetoric" and that under the rhetorical turn of phrase lies a greater vision and a larger truth. In the metonymic turn of phrase, the antecedent (what happens, i.e., fighting, killing) is replaced. The replacement (eating) is likewise a substitution of the specific for the general; that is, a substitution of "eating" for the more abstract notion of political incorporation.[59] I do not make this connection haphazardly, for the Tunisian rāwī makes many overt analogies and specifically connects group conflict over land and boundaries with incorporation. In the passage cited above, for example, the rāwī compares the story situation to present realities. He has mentioned earlier that the situation is like the one between the Banū Yazīd or the Hammāma. Baker explains in her notes that the Mhādhba have frequently been the unwilling victims caught between two neighboring rival tribes, the Banī Zīd (al-Ḥāmma of Gabes in southern Tunisia) and the Hammāma of the Gafsa region. The rāwī, ʿAbd al-Salām b. ʿUmar b. Kāmil al-Muhadhdhabī, is from the Mhādhba group. He and his audience, as Baker notes,[60] experience particular satisfaction whenever they see the tables turned against a stronger tribe in favor of a weaker tribe, its erstwhile victim. The rāwī continually interprets story events in this manner, offering his audience analogies from present-day experience and political realities.

Abderrahman Ayoub, the Tunisian Hilālī scholar, sees substitutions and analogies such as the Baker rāwī inserts in his narration of the *Hilāliyya* as the very life source of the epic. The Hilālī audience, as Ayoub defines it, is formed through its identification with the Hilālī as an "exploited mass," which is distinguished by its opposition to the exploiting powers. In their identification with the Hilālī, audience members ("exploited masses" in

Ayoub's Marxist-structuralist terms) reject all power that dominates them. He sees the narrative basis of *Sīrat Banī Hilāl* as the permanent struggle in which nomads engage against urban power centers and he traces the actual and potential transformations of this "thematic axis": nomad versus townsman becomes peasant versus bourgeoisie, working masses versus exploiting power, colonized versus colonizer, dominated mass versus dominating power. According to Ayoub, these potential substitutions vivify the corpus, giving it life without which it would be in a state of mummification, existing only in libraries in manuscript form, instead of living in the imagination of one generation after the other in oral lore in the areas where the historic Hilālī tribe traveled.[61]

The significance of the Hilālī saga recounted in Baker's recording session in the far south of Tunisia was not lost on rāwī and audience. The collector, too, comments on the "inferior economic and political position of the South in relation to the rest of Tunisia, and probably Tunisia as a small nation in relation to her stronger neighbors."[62] The Tunisian storyteller normally relates his prose tales informally in the company of men gathered together to relax in the back of a shop. The sixty narrators Baker recorded in 1972 were for the most part retired farmers, farm laborers, seasonal workers. Many had worked as migrant laborers in France, others had served in the army as part of the French forces.

The pleasure ʿAbd al-Salām's audience took in the underdog reversing the order of things is a key to their continuing identification with the story as an active part of their oral lore. Trickery is a major heroic and narrative strategy that also pleases the Tunisian audience; it operates, Baker points out in her conclusion, as a primary narrative device in the Tunisian *Hilāliyya*. The audience, according to the folklorist Webber, is one which avoids overt confrontation and direct disputation.[63] In Tunisian, unlike Egyptian, culture confrontation is avoided, and thus much interaction proceeds by indirection. One must understand subtle interactions, intentions, and meanings. The tale-telling ritual in Tunisia is concomitantly informal. The rāwī and his audience sit around together in the back of private garages or stores, often on the floor on mats. The rāwī uses normal speech, undistanced from his audience by musical instrumentation and song vocalizings. The Egyptian poet performs, as we have seen, out in the open, seated on a little stage often out-of-doors at the entrance of a house or café. His is a public, as opposed to a private, event. The shāʿir's puns, which are anticipated and appreciated by his audience, also represent more directly open interpretations and confrontations than the rāwī's buried metaphor. The Tunisian audience must absorb the rāwī's interpretation through a dead metaphor or a buried symbol to learn the message of his metonymically expressed fear of confrontation and subsequent incorporation.

Where and how the narrator assigns the blame for the roots of the problems the Hilālī heroes have with each other and with their opponents is a variable from one area where the legend is told to another. This assignment of blame is crucial to the local comprehension, interpretation, and appreciation of the epic tale of migration and resettlement. The Egyptian shāʿir, as we have discussed at length, blames Ghānim and his progeny (the family of Diyāb). Blame squarely rests with a person and his issue who can be held directly responsible and eventually confronted for all the trouble. The Tunisian rāwī, however, defuses the hostility inherent in assigning blame to an individual. He makes the source of the conflict more indirect, less able to be confronted openly or resolved, for the source is the mythological, cosmological force of The Old Sabbath Woman.

The North African audience identifies with Diyāb in his role as the outsider somehow at odds with the brethren in the Hilālī confederation of tribes, and also in his role as the one who routs the bastions of power. Diyāb's most frequent epithet as used by North African narrators is al-Aḥmar, the Red. Contrasted with Abū Zayd's Tunisian epithet of al-Adraʿ, the Piebald (i.e., black on the outside of his clothes, white on the inside), Diyāb's epithet may well refer to the color of the Berber race. An Algerian song, collected by Bel at the turn of the century, more explicitly links Diyāb with the Berber tribes and brings up Berber identification as a significant element. I should like to discuss this Algerian version later in another context, however, and for the moment continue with our close attention to ʿAbd al-Salām's Tunisian Taghrība.

What is also notable about the conclusion of both Ḥājj ʿAbd al-Salām's long tales, the "Taghrība" and the "Birth of Abū Zayd" (or the "Raid for Khaḍrā" as the rāwī himself calls it), is Dhiyāb's prominence. The Ḥājj ends both stories with the family of Ghānim. The episodes Baker recorded from various other rāwīs also culminates with the spearing of the Zanātī Khalīfa by Dhiyāb. Ḥājj ʿAbd al-Salām's intention in concluding his story with Dhiyāb seems to be genealogical. He traces the roots of present-day inhabitants of Tunisia to the clans of Zāziya/Jāziya and Dhiyāb. This link, in fact, represents the narrator's final words on the subject of the Westward Migration of the Banī Hilāl.

Dhiyāb, who was born on the periphery of the tribe, among the wolves as his birth tale and name etymology inform us, serves as the herdsman for the migrating tribe. Compared to Bū Zayd's status as a warrior knight (*fāris*), Dhiyāb's position as the head herdsman has lower status. In the council of tribal leaders in Ḥājj ʿAbd al-Salām's version, Dhiyāb is always absent—as an outsider to the central clan leadership.[64] It is Dhiyāb who not only vanquishes the Berber ruler of Tūnis with a spear to his eye[65] and kills Saʿda, the war booty, but also infamously slices the Hilālī ruler Sultan Ḥasan from ear to ear,[66] then bludgeons Bū Zayd with an iron club,[67] and kicks Zāziya to death.[68] Dhiyāb, the wolf-jackal, fulfills his etymology in his narrative destiny. Like the wolf who lurks on the outside borders of civilization,[69] he springs unsuspected to devour all who oppose him. The rāwī makes the interpretation explicit in two similar dreams had by Maghribī rulers, Ḥāsis of Algeria and the Khalīfa Zanātī of Tūnis:

"O, our brother, I had a dream
that the enemy came like the locusts that fly and creep
But that at their head was a cavalier with a name
    similar to a wolf
Approximately resembling it
His name is not exactly Dhib
But something close to it"
(They didn't know of Dhiyāb)
"But he and I met in a duel in the battlefield
I was like—
He was like a wolf
And I just like a sheep.
My heart just quakes from that dream."[70]

Dhiyāb the Wolf does indeed "eat up" foe and kin alike in the terms of the metonym the rāwī uses to integrate figurally what he conceives as the major themes of the saga—the quest for food, the fighting it engenders, and the fear of incorporation that migratory boundary violations unleash.

What keeps the hungry Hilālī hordes still on the march in the imaginations of southern Tunisian peasants and, I would submit, African Arabs in general, is the symbolic thrust of the *Hilāliyya* as a saga of boundary transgression and power relationships—whether they be political, economic, social, geographic (north-south, east-west), familial, or sexual. For the fear of penetration and incorporation subsumed in ʿAbd al-Salām's metonymy extends as an organizing metaphor to virtually every level of reality both within the text he narrates and without it in Arab-African history and experience. Its ramifications are personal and political confusion of identity. In the text under consideration, for example, identity confusion is a major theme and operates at several levels. After Dhiyāb renders the external enemy, the Berber Zanātī Khalīfa, impotent, the Hilālī contingent incorporates Berber territories and women as their own; then, with the foreign enemy vanquished (assimilated?), the Hilālī heroes begin to oppose each other in countless civil and personal struggles. They merge the opponent, as it were, into their own identity and internalize the conflicts that seem implicit in the power gained by acquiring agricultural land-wealth. Hilālī narrators all use disguise and trickery and ensuing identification as a typical motifeme sequence. With the conquest of the Maghrib, the narrative sequence becomes one trick or disguise after another in a rhythm of identity concealment and revelation. Male-female identity confusion emerges as the central, larger motif.

Three times a male becomes a female or a female a male in the culminating episodes of the Seven Thrones and War of the Orphans cycle in the narration of ʿAbd al-Salām. Once Dhiyāb dreams he is dancing in women's clothes. The dream's interpretation and narrative fulfillment indicate that the necklace and *khulkhāl* (silver anklets Tunisian Bedouin women wear) symbolize that Dhiyāb will wear chains and be bound.[71] The dream anticipates the riddling trick Ḥasan plays on Dhiyāb when he comes to celebrate the wedding of his niece and Ḥasan's daughter. The riddle ends with Dhiyāb in handcuffs and thrown in prison after his men are hanged.[72] A second time, in the very next narrative sequence, Bū Zayd's wife, who has returned to Nejd miffed over an insult from Zāziya, is about to marry a suitor. Bū Zayd, on the advice of an old woman, substitutes the boy who accompanies him on his return trip to Nejd for the bride. An old man advises the puzzled groom how he can distinguish a man from a woman in a bloody scarf test: dirty a woman with a bloody scarf and she will become afraid and surrender; spatter a man with blood and he will redouble his opposing thrust and strike harder.[73]

The third time this motif appears, a woman becomes a man and the scene is the battlefield rather than a wedding feast. Zāziya, who fled with the orphans of Bū Zayd and Ḥasan after Dhiyāb's perfidious murder of the two leaders so that he can rule alone, has become a judge in the realm of al-Andalus which is ruled by a Jew. The narrator begins at this juncture to refer to Zāziya in the masculine form and, as Baker points out, this is not inadvertent, for the rāwī will do so consistently when she plays an aggressive leadership role.[74] Zāziya later dons men's clothes. Dressed as a knight,[75] she meets old Dhiyāb's troups who are carrying parasols! She meets Dhiyāb, who is now the ninety-five-year-old sultan of all the Maghrib, and fights him bravely. He asks whose son is this brave boy and the woman reveals her identity, only to be kicked to death by the man who killed her brothers, and who has been her husband.

Three-time repetition of this series of male-female identity reversals and revelations serves to highlight it as a major narrative concern, albeit a subliminal one. Concealment leading to revelation becomes the basic narrative pattern and in its specific manifestation suggests a hidden, underlying discomfort with the relationship between the sexes—perhaps a discomfort with marriage and the penetration of boundaries, both personal and group, that coupling implies. For in the incorporation of identities that patrilineal marriage and sexual union inheres, prior loyalties to siblings and clan and the prior family group are violated. The woman in a patrilineal marriage, as part of two groups, is ever the outsider in her husband's family, to which she gives progeny and issue. The Tunisian Dhiyāb openly "eats up" his women—Saʿda the Berber girl and Zāziya, the jinn's granddaughter who becomes the incarnation of Hilālī honor, wisdom, and reproductivity. The logical outcome of this dilemma perceived in the southern Tunisian *Hilāliyya* is, if not sterility and doom for the group, at least ongoing tension and dissension.

Fear of exogamous marriage (outside the group), if not fear

of marriage per se, is clearly the issue in Hurreiz's Sudanese text. The Manasir narrator Tam Zein features a scene wherein Abū Zayd says that since the journey west can be tolerated only by Hilālī women who are tough enough to take it, anyone married to a woman not of the Hilālī tribe must divorce her. Diyāb disguises his foreign wife and when she gets hungry along the road, she cannibalizes him, eating a piece of the flesh of his thigh. When his leg putrifies and the tribe senses the bad smell, Diyāb divorces the outsider and sends her back to her people.[76]

A Nigerian interpretation of *Sīrat Banī Hilāl* similarly focuses on the group's fear of cannibalism, of the group being devoured by its leader. Puns on the nature of the leader abound as the narrator senses and plays with the doubling and ambivalence contained in the names of the heroes. Abū Zayd and Ḍiyāb (as he is called in Shuwa Arabic with a velarized ḍ) complement each other as supportive friends and twin heroes. Abū Zayd in a pun on his name, which means "father of provision" or of "increase," is the "moon of food [honey]"; he is also a destructive raven to the sultans, as he himself boasts; he is "Abū Zayd of those who err—Abū Zayd the left-handed—who is like a tornado showing the way to men." Ḍiyāb, in contrast, in puns on the local Shuwa dialect etymology of his name, is like a "wasting disease," sweet as butter, fresh milk, and prime meat, like a snake with a bite of live coals. While Abū Zayd's name and epithets stand for increase, growth, provision, and augmentation, Ḍiyāb's suggest the opposite. In the Bornu dialect of the narrator, Ḍiyāb's name and his punning epithet, Ḍiyāb Ḍīb, refers not to the wolf, but to a "wasting disease." The name derives in the local dialect from either ḍ/w/b (to wear out, to wear off) or more likely dh/a/b (to dissolve, vanish, waste away). The Bornu dialect, according to Lethem,[77] distinguishes little between the sounds [ḍ], [dh], and [d]. This gives rise to another series of puns on the nature of the leader, who may *dalla* (lead) or he may *ḍalla* (mislead, err). Abū Zayd, the Iesiye Arab, provides his own destruction as he destroys the female symbol of life, the crow's nest. He dies of thirst while the necrophagous vultures flocking around his corpse die of fright, and the people, unable to experience happiness without their "father of increase," their "leader-misleader," drown themselves in the river and leave only forty remaining in the group.[78]

Whether heard among hungry berry hunters in the lower

Lake Chad region, whose ancestors were pushed ever farther south and west,[79] or among Tunisian farm workers in the dispossessed south (the region whence that country's many food riots today stem), or among Sudanese tribesmen, the African *Hilāliyya* chronicles the settlement of Africa by the Arabs. It is a folk history of the Arab conquests, which follows "history" only in its larger outlines, but sketches a detailed portrait of the psychology of assimilation of identities, the ambivalence and fear, the traumas still fresh in Arab-African identity. Hilālī narrators are aware of this. They find their genealogies, as we have seen repeatedly, in the etymologies of the Hilālī story/history. They adapt it to present realities and point out its analogies with current experience. One Algerian *ṭālib*'s (teacher) reinterpretation of the Sharīf Bin Hashimī episode is particularly telling as an example of the ends to which Hilālī narrators put their subject matter.[80]

The seventy-nine-line poem composed in monorhymed couplets in Algerian dialect with certain Berber characteristics is a version of the episode where Jazya [*sic*] tricks Sharif Ben Hashem [*sic*]. The narrator who dictated the poem to Bel was a ṭālib from the Beni Chougran tribe named Si Bou Chentouf (Bel's spellings). Like the Tunisian rāwīs, he focuses his narrative around the figure of Diyāb. He opens his song differently, however—with a fictive speaker lamenting his plight because his beloved has departed for the south leaving him sad and alone. The speaker compares himself to Diyāb the Hilālī after the scission that separated the tribe,[81] then goes on in his extended simile to narrate the arrival of the Hilālīs in Tūnis to buy wheat after seven years of drought and famine and the bargain they arrange with Ben Hashem. The quirk in this version of the episode is Diyāb. The Hilālī, on making their contract of Jazya in exchange for food, fear Diyāb's anger, and must reckon with the absent herdsman before closing the deal. They send their most beautiful girls to intercede with Diyāb and to gain his permission to sacrifice Jazya for the tribe. Diyāb demands 1,000 head of sheep, 2,000 girls, and 2,000 warriors, which he takes and goes into the night to the desert to form his own tribe (11. 19–20). After Jazya (= Jāziya) tricks the Sharīf in order to depart with her tribe (this follows the Tunisian story I have already summarized), her sedentary husband follows after her with a force of warriors (11. 60). The foiled husband recaptures Jazya and taunts her that Diyāb is powerless against him. Diyāb, who has been away on a hunt for his favorite game bird, returns with his army. Diyāb confronts Ben Hashem and routs his army. The defeated man is overcome with sadness, he cannot eat, Tūnis girls have no appeal for him. His longing for Jazya kills him. The speaker concludes his song with the couplets:

How sad this tale. At least the Banī Hilāl
ended up by getting their beauty back. O, you, Object
of my sadness!

What calamities the Beni Hashem underwent! What bitterness
they experienced! The fractions of the tribe scattered
to the East and the West, while some stayed.

One part of them set itself up in the region of Fez.
As for me I long for the people of my tribe and its
valiant warriors.

How can I not cry at this separation.[82]

The speaker ends his plaint by identifying with the Berber contingent, the Beni Hashem, and laments the dispersion of their tribe—rather than the tribes of Hilāl and Ghānim. The speaker's identification with the Hilālī's enemies changes the whole point of view of the story and markedly affects its intention and meaning. It makes it less a celebration of the victory of the Hilālī than a recollection of the defeat of their opponents. It also makes it less a glorification of the Arabs at the expense of the local Berber people and more a lamentation on the loss of a united people, a cry of despair over the whole struggle caused by the arrival of the Hilālī and the ensuing conflict over fertile land, food, and the childbearing woman.

Bel, the collector of the poem, mentioned that he searched a long time for Hilālī legends in Algeria, but that hardly anyone even knew the names of the heroes of the tales. He finally found the old ṭālib, who was willing to dictate the words.[83] It is curious to note in this respect the manner in which the narrator Si Bou Chentouf shifted the narrative intention and point of view by surrounding the Hilālī episode with a frame that set up a fictive speaker who turns out in the end to be one of the Beni Hashem, the native Maghribī tribe which the Hilālī displaced. The ironies implicit in the discursive situation of the French colonial invader collecting this particular version of the Hilālī legend are vast. One wonders if the talented and clever folk poet might have been pulling Bel's leg and concealing a hostile message to his scholarly scribe audience. Bel missed the ironies and published the poem for the delectation of his French scholarly audience as an example of romantic legendary lore of "nos sujets Algériens" who are like "tous les gens d'esprit simple, fort amateurs de contes merveilleux, de récits fantastiques, de légendes extraordinaires."[84] He comments on the corruption of history in this popular story and quotes Ibn Khaldūn's version of "what really happened."

While Bel, in his desire for linguistic and "historical" integrity in his interpretation of the text he collected, missed the point of the story, another French colonial observer in Algeria around the same time did not. Desparmet recognized the outright xenophobia of the siyar he heard declaimed by maddāḥs from street corners, at markets, or in cafés, at private home parties, circumcisions, and harvest festivals.[85]

During the French conquest and occupation of Algeria, the siyar flourished. At the turn of the century, the Algerian popular poet chanted verse narratives celebrating Islamic military victories (called "ghazawāt," raids, a word also used by the Tunisian rāwīs today). The function of these epic songs, according to audience testimony collected by Desparmet, was to "refresh our hearts and to solace our bitterness." Desparmet quotes one man as saying "in our time life has nothing good in it except in the world of imagination and dream." The *ghazawāt* (raid poems) thus served, according to Desparmet, to maintain a "sacred hatred of the infidel French invader and to nurture an inner resistance to the influence of the invaders." The maddāḥ's epics celebrated uniquely the military glory of Islam, exploits of the companions of the Prophet, the great ancestors, and the world conquerors; they praised past heroism and contrasted it with the cowardice of the present generation. The Algerian singers proposed the early heroes as models for their contemporaries in a society depressed by conquest. Epic themes of past Islamic victories provided a balm to wounded self-esteem and calmed the humiliation and inferiority felt daily before the occupying forces. Desparmet argues that the epics were the fruit of outright xenophobia. He suggests that the epics made superficially Arabicized Berbers identify with the Islamic Nation group just as the French foreign presence threatened to stifle it. The maddāḥ's songs thus served to foster Islamic national consciousness and to unify the various indigenous Maghribī groups under the aegis of Islam against Christian-French crusader invaders and occupiers.

Whether or not epic serves such specific propagandistic and nationalistic intentions as Desparmet asserts, the *Hilāliyya,* wherever it has flourished, certainly does appear to express the tensions inherent in the history of successive invasion and foreign occupation which Egypt, the Maghrib, and the Sudan have experienced in some 1,300 years of modern history. The various times and places *Sīrat Banī Hilāl* has thrived as a vital oral poetic tradition and genealogy seems to verify Chadwick and Bowra's notion that epic flourishes in times of foreign occupation[86] as well as Desparmet's thesis that the basic thrust of Arab epic, and I would hazard all epic, is xenophobic.

Whatever the Algerian rāwī Si Bou Chentouf's intentions vis-à-vis his foreign-colonizer audience may have been, what he foregrounded in his rendition of the famous poem was the dialectic of identification and identity. His fictive speaker shifts his identification from Diyāb at odds with his tribe to Sharīf Ben Hashem defeated by the invading Arabs. With such an opening and closing frame, the Algerian poet-transmitter effectively made the Hilālī legend into an explanation of how his own tribe came to inhabit Algeria after the fall of Tūnis to the invading Arabs. He thus explains who he is and who his people are, and how things came to be as they are.

The concealed message to the French occupier which I suggested potentially exists in the text Bel collected in Algeria reappears again and again in the Hilālī matter. Ayoub refers to this "double articulation of the message"[87] as a base ingredient in the Hilālī epic tradition through its many cultural transmissions and transformations. Tunisian rāwīs themselves specifically point out in the story of Dhiyāb versus the suitors of Zāziya the importance of understanding hidden meaning. When she invited seven suitors to her tent for a meal, Zāziya gave them, along with their food, a series of three riddles or tests. Dhiyāb alone knew that when Zāziya said "seven come in, but leave 14 behind," she meant "leave your shoes at the door"; Dhiyāb alone plunged his arms deep into the couscous while the others mocked him and ate politely on the surface; he alone found the dates and silver crescent (hilāl) Zāziya had hidden in the plate of food; and Dhiyāb alone, even though he was much shorter than the others, knew how to reach the dates hung at the top of a greased tent pole by cutting them down with the sword while the others grappled and slid. He knew all this because he was the "most intelligent of all and understood the meaning of things."[88]

Progression from concealment to revelation provides the basic narrative movements of the *Hilāliyya*. This same rhythm becomes the basis for knowing and understanding. The puns, double entendres, riddles, tricks, disguises, and dreams in which the rāwī's very style abounds all progress from concealment to revelation, from confusion to understanding. Wordplays (like Ḥājj ʿAbd al-Salām's integrating figure of speech that reverses aggressive outgoing action, fighting and killing, into passive self-oriented action, eating) and identity reversals conceal a hidden interpretation for the listener to perceive or not. The listener who models himself on Dhiyāb in the story cited above and who learns from the repeated stylistic devices and repeated narrative elements that signal hidden or symbolic meaning will see through the *Hilāliyya* narration in any of its multiple episodes and cultural transformations to a greater knowledge of history and experience as taught by the story.

As a sīra, and, as such, the autobiography of the ways of its tellers and audiences, *Sīrat Banī Hilāl* is a saga of identity. That identity is one forged out of the coalition of peoples that make up "Muslim Arabs," an identity forged out of ambivalence, conflict, and oppositionalism; one based on unity in multiplicity. In the moral of the *Hilāliyya* in Africa, the group consumes itself once the outside enemy is vanquished. The rhetorical scene, ever more present today, of the foreign or educated-class outsider collecting the sīra from a rāwī or shāʿir is not without its ironies. For the rhetorical transaction through which the oral performance takes written shape recapitulates and acts out the dynamic of human interaction the sīra makes manifest in its many faces and forms: self-definition becomes counterdefinition in this continuing saga on the xenophobia of identity, and, conversely, penetration equals incorporation.

# 10

# ETYMOLOGY AS GENEALOGY: ON GENERATION(S) AND TRANSMISSION(S)

*Sīrat Banī Hilāl* is a saga of identity and, as such, a saga of alterity. As a sīra, it represents the autobiography of the ways of its tellers and audiences. The *Hilāliyya* makes manifest in its several versions a basic dynamic of human interaction: the fact of life that what we define ourselves against is crucial to our self-concept. In our foes, as in our nightmares, we know ourselves. This differentiation is the essence of the conflict epic and the combat myth[1] which lies at the roots of the Arabic folk genre al-sīra, a genre primarily and ultimately concerned with identity. In the listener's and poet's identification with the tradition, both transmitter and receiver find themselves, understand their own and their group's identity. The folk genre provides, in its several forms and faces through different times and places, and, I would generalize, in its various heroic subjects, a conundrum of Muslim identity. For, as the Egyptian *Hilāliyya* taught us in its punning antonymy of homonyms and its spiraling metonymy of the inside and the outside, self-definition for both the group and the individual is counterdefinition and identity is essentially a xenophobic process. Contradictorily, however, as Tunisian, Sudanese, and Algerian versions of the saga teach us, boundary penetration leads to recognition of the other and leads to incorporation and assimilation.

The fear of strangers and fear of the out-group, anxiety about the unknown, is very real in the oral traditional cultures which maintain and generate the sīra tradition. Their history, as we have seen, is one of invasion and boundary transgression, conquest, and penetration by one foreign political power after another. The Maghrib, no less than Egypt, experienced a tumultuous history of racial and cultural contact and a political history of successive rule by outsiders. The hardy, indigenous Tunisian Berbers, like the native Egyptian fellahin, participated in (and survived) a series of short-lived reigns by foreign rulers—Carthaginians, Romans, Arabs, Spaniards, Turks, French—one after the other.[2]

The sīra, as a genre, incorporates this history and the identity that emerges from it, one forged out of the coalition of peoples which make up present-day "Muslim Arabs," out of ambivalence, conflict, and oppositionalism; an identity based, contradictorily, on unity in multiplicity. The lessons taught in the *Hilāliyya* are congruent with contemporary social theorists' notions of identity. Barth and Spicer[3] separately generalize that the identity and experience of groups who persistently perceive themselves as separate from the larger culture or the official culture is during times of political repression most often stored in symbolic form. When overt opposition is futile (during times of military defeats, foreign occupation, colonization, or other culturally repressive regimes), cultural identity is "intensely maintained through moral and language participation rather than political action." In the case of such dominated peoples as the Egyptian fellahin, open rebellion and revolts have been only occasional, and resistance to outside, central authority passively aggressive.[4] Such repressed groups maintain themselves through their perception of the moral world, which is at odds with the dominant one.

Middle Eastern and African Arab-Muslim society has been characterized as intensely oppositional and intensely xenophobic. Mernissi[5] has said specifically of modern Arab-Muslim societies that one of their most meaningful features is their ethnocentricity, expressed politically in extreme nationalism and psychologically in passionate xenophobia. Despite the ideal of group solidarity, internal divisiveness appears to dissolve only in the face of outside aggression. In colonial settings, such as African Arab society and Egyptian society have been until only fairly recently, different histories and cultures come together and perforce accommodate to each other. Barth tells us, "all act to maintain social differentiation, to maintain dichotomies and differences."[6] To maintain ethnic identity and racial distinctions, the population becomes categorized into "exclusive and imperative status categories," with separate standards applied to each group. In such colonial situations, people avoid what Barth calls "status situations discrepant with one's own." All work to maintain boundaries, and the boundaries most vigorously upheld are those by which the majority population excludes pariah groups (viz., the case of the Egyptian "gypsies"). The insider is identified on the basis of shared criteria for evaluation and judgment. Others are strangers who do not share similar understandings.

A network of social obligation and duty thus defines the in-group. That inside is potentially infinitely expandable in an oral traditional society, however, which values face-to-face contact and context so very highly. Self-knowledge and self-definition, too, are group and context oriented, dependent on relationships. Friends are those with whom one has shared something or with whom one has broken bread. El-Shamy, the Egyptian folklorist, notes the solidarity of the group as a major feature of Egyptian social organization. He comments that incorporation of the unknown stranger into the group is a major phenomenon that is only counterposed by an equally strong impulse to exclusion. El-Shamy remarks, in an article on Egyptian folk therapeutic practices (among which he includes epic narration in performances), that shared responsibility is promoted by both the ideal and the real cultures, by both classical and folk doctrines. He maintains that this concept indeed constitutes a basic factor of social organization and social group formation—both enduring community groups and spontaneous, temporary groups. He cites the strength of such notions as the "nation of Believers" (the Umma), the idea of coming from the same locality, and religious proverbs that endorse group unity and responsibility. El-Shamy mentions the manner in which "simple instantaneous companionship and the sharing of bread and salt will impose responsibilities of friendship which are intrinsically binding."[7]

But, as Mernissi has reminded us, group identity and self-definition come also through opposition. Spicer puts it thus: "the oppositional process produces intense collective consciousness and high internal solidarity."[8] He sees the boundaries between the group and others as a specialized vocabulary of identity. Groups maintain their integrity and "purity" by means of the agonistic concept of the inside and the outside. On the individual level, which the group experience recapitulates, contemporary ethnopsychiatrists also discuss identity in terms of boundaries between self and other. Self is determined, according to Weidman,[9] by what we can control; what we cannot control is experienced as something alien, as an opposition. In an inherently hierarchical society where dominance and submission enter into every relationship, the individual is seen as powerless, acted on by a potentially destructive environment. Fatalism, group responsibility, and the essentially projective, "paranoid" personality thus evolves as a coping mechanism. Face-to-face context and relationships are preferred for their certainty. Much literature suggests this is the predominant pattern of identity and worldview for the migrant or for colonized people, for each has experienced loss of control and loss of power in their political incorporation by a foreign power.[10]

Bowra's work on heroic epic underscores this same mind-set that derives out of perceived powerlessness as the generating force behind epic narrative. In the politically or spiritually restricted world that an oral traditional culture often represents, the bard turns his nonliterate public's attention to another time in their history, to what is termed a "heroic age" of turbulent political changes, war, and open conflict and direct confrontation. In his essay on the Heroic Age,[11] Bowra identifies certain types of political and psychological changes (all of which the Arab-Muslim countries of Africa have witnessed) which promote identification with a Heroic Age: (1) conquest, (2) migration and resettlement, and (3) the disintegration of a seemingly solid political system or the overthrow of a priestly caste. Bowra sees epic narrative, along with the concept of a Heroic Age on which epic is based, as arising not so much out of the character of the bygone age itself as from the view posterity takes of it and the psychological factors that shape it:

> When heroic legend takes up the past, . . . it sees it as in some sense akin to the present, but more vivid and more dramatic. . . . The power of a belief in a heroic age may be seen from the indirect but undeniable influence which it has on men and events, even when it has become a distant memory. This is not merely because it provides thrilling stories which are absorbed in childhood and remain with a man through his life; it is rather that the notion of it is so vivid and so firm that the imagination instinctively feeds on it and is unconsciously moved by its spirit and its example. Just as the belief in it is commonly formed after some defeat or disaster, so the

> memory of it may be stronger among people who suffer from a sense of deprivation or inferiority or servitude. To them it brings confidence and hope. They feel that, if they have been free and brave in the past, freedom may be won by bravery in the future. . . . The belief in a heroic age has its engaging side if it is not too near to us, but at close quarters it can indeed be disturbing and formidable.[12]

Sir Cecil Maurice's evolutionist perspective on epic literature and the heroic age associated with it views both from a "civilized" retrospective. That is, he sees the heroic outlook as "a stage in the development of human society" which is essentially liberating in its function of "freeing mankind from primitive prohibitions and deterrents," discrediting superstition, and generally "honoring man over magic or gods or other oppressive agents."[13] Other writers who have taken up the subject of the hero, including Otto Rank, Lord Raglan, and the Chadwicks, share a similar evolutionist point of view that is somewhat disturbing in its ethnocentricity and its superior stance toward the oral cultures. Perhaps a less invidious organismic model of development and growth would be one derived from current developmental psychology. For the sīra no less than other great epics lays bare human patterns of growth; it elucidates and illustrates universal human development. The cycles of *Sīrat Banī Hilāl*, for example, repeat the life cycle of the heroes. The sīra is a family saga of birth, growth, generational conflicts, political conflicts, old age, death, and the succession of a new generation. The sīra provides a true biography of the hero(es); and in the tale's rhythm of concealment and revelation, it symbolically communicates an autobiography of the fictive group and the identifying group of listeners.

The *Hilāliyya* in many ways chronicles normal human developmental patterns, as Massie, a developmental psychiatrist, has pointed out.[14] Its structural patterns, based on arrivals/departures or separations and adventures followed by returns and reunions, parallel not only the pattern universally identified as the epic or heroic pattern but also, and perhaps more important for the significance of the epic genre generally, it parallels the child's process of identity formation in a pattern of separation and individuation from the mother—what Mahler calls "the separation-individuation process."[15] This pattern is made particularly explicit in the framework around which the Iesiye Arab storyteller weaves his tale: in a cyclical mode of composition, the tale is made up of thirteen departure-adventure-return journeys. The first two adventures of the boy-hero, his initiation adventures as it were, are in fact journeys away from his mother to meet the directions (North and South) and to meet, in victory counterbalanced by defeat, the double-edged lesson of life to come.[16] All the Hilālī storytellers work within this same larger story pattern that has as its root a basic human emotional process. In its reindividuation of the process of maturation, the sīra (or heroic epic in general) reinvents and interprets the life cycle of the individual and thereby gains its ongoing appeal as a source of universal identification and a chronicle of human identity. The splitting, too, by which sīra and epic polarize the world into good and bad, right and wrong, hunger and plenty, nomad and settled, rural and urban, male world and female world, is a universal normal developmental pattern in the child, a stage through which we all must pass to grow into full, mature human beings. Representation of the world as highly dichotomized is generically typical of epic, for epic knowledge is somehow agonistic, much like the two-year-old child discovering and testing the limits of his own individuality. Boundaries, preoccupations with arrivals and departures, predominate in the genre as they do in the early life separation anxiety we all experience in our first sorties into self-discovery. The sīra rhythm alternates victory and defeat; victory is always attenuated by defeat, unity attenuated by internal divisiveness, and one cycle of upheaval and conflict settled only momentarily before the stasis of peace hurtles again into conflict and upset. In this rhythm it parallels the child's rhythms of annihilations and resurrections, rather than cause and effect.[17] The epic hero and the *sīra* hero represent the brave child in us all, the adventurer who re-creates the world anew in his journey-quest.

On the level of the group experience, too, the hero of epic and sīra recapitulates individual human experience. In the rhetorical transaction whereby people gather together to tell and to hear their story/history, conflicts are made manifest. The etiology and genealogy of the present situation is exposed and laid open for the ears to hear, if they will, often in the connotative etymologies of words and names. This level of the human processes of interaction are less explicit, less on the surface of the narrative. They reside not so much in the linear morphological structure of the tale as in its textural elements. They reside in the interpretation and reindividuation specific cultures give to the traditional inherited story line. Herein lies the narrator's individuality and craft—in the way he focuses the story point of view and interprets the basic conflict and anxiety that generate the story in both the reality of daily life and the fiction he re-creates.

We heard the way in which the Egyptian gypsy shāʿir blamed his peasant audience for their faults, confronting them openly by his very presence on their doorstep. We also heard the Tunisian rāwī narrating his tale of the ancestors in quite a different rhetorical dynamic. In the Tunisian south, a culture which has been described as avoiding overt confrontation, the narrator sat informally among his listeners and used the language of daily talk to tell the tale. His stance toward his audience was not confrontational or castigating, rather it was one of authority and wisdom. The best rāwī, among a sampling of sixty amateur tale-tellers, was a retired schoolteacher, a local voice of authority and respect, a man quite unlike the Egyptian gypsy entertainer in his social status. The cultural intention of each performance tradition, both the professional and the amateur, appears to be to defuse anxiety by naming it. The specific processes of accomplishing this, however, vary greatly. The Tunisian rāwī blames all the anxieties on the anonymous force of The Old Sabbath Woman; the Egyptian shāʿir, as part of an openly confrontational society, more specifically blames human agents, not excluding his audience, for creating the conflict and the seeds of dissension in social differentiation and status hierarchies. In both oral cultures, to name the anxiety—to name the ancestry, genealogy, and etymology of the conflict—is to know it. The shāʿir and rāwī, through their interaction with their listeners, create and re-create the common memory of the past that is the sīra recitation. In the contract effected between teller and listener, the community agrees to an interpretation of their common past and their immediate present.

Memory is in many respects what we agree on about the past by virtue of our own retellings of it. By recounting past events we re-create the past in the present for present purposes. The bard generating and transmitting oral traditional histories like the sīra especially does this, for oral epic tradition is by nature homeostatic; it lives in a present that sloughs off irrelevant memories.

The present conditions the past, and oral traditions reflect not so much idle curiosity about the past, according to Ong, as a reflection of present cultural values.[18] Ayoub's research in Libya and Jordan has brought to light two striking instances of this phenomenon in the case of the Hilālī tradition. He shows how the Libyan, Jordanian, and Palestinian storyteller each recasts the *Hilāliyya* in terms of the present cultural situation and how each uses the past to commemorate and protest the present through his "double articulation of the message," which casts the present in the past. Palestinian versions, for example, state explicitly in their openings that "Sīrat Bū Zayd belonged to the past, but today we have our own siyar." Bū Zayd the Palestinian is a *fidā'ī,* a freedom fighter, who travels a Palestinian itinerary and carries modern weapons. Diyāb the Libyan likewise is a figure of the present day and has direct parallels with two contemporary political figures: ʿUmar al-Mukhtār (the primary leader of the Italo-Libyan war at the beginning of the century) and the present leader of Libya, Col. Muʿammar al-Qadhdhāfī. Older storytellers assimilate Diyāb's exploits with the former, while younger narrators identify the hero with Qadhdhāfī.[19]

Knowledge, then, is present experience. But the present is ever conditioned by the mold of the past and current events are recounted and perceived in terms of story patterns. The present is filtered through the past, and the past has relevancy only in terms of present experience. Gizellis[20] has shown the case of modern Greek balladeers who recount current events in the highly formulaic mode of perception which filters historic events through known, set phraseology (formulas in Parry-Lord parlance) and themes. The schema or mold of the traditional story formula thus influences historical event and how it is viewed. The traditional audience understands present experience in terms of past tellings of other events recounted in the story tradition. It sorts and organizes new information through the known, "inscribing" it in presupposed patterns of thought and cultural major premises.

Lord also asserts that "history is truth eternally re-created in song, not as a dry record of the past, but as a vital memory of the past as exhortation to present action."[21] Okpewho agrees, and speaks of the "journalistic temper of understanding," stressing the epic vision as the "timeless seen through the eyes of the present."[22] The Egyptian and Tunisian artist and audience of the *Hilāliyya,* no less than the Greek or African, have what Okpewho calls "a very pressing sense of real and concrete presence." Knowledge and knowing in Arab oral culture is always contextual, experiential, and relational; that is, knowing is contingent on immediate experience and relationships with those present. Unlike the knowing of literate societies, it is not linear or progress oriented, nor goal oriented or object oriented. Gilligan, a developmental psychologist and educator, uses this same distinction in discussing what discriminates the female model of psychological development from the male.[23] What the American psychoanalytic field is beginning to differentiate as "female" culture may simply and more broadly be a description of traditional oral cultural values that are oriented toward face-to-face relationships and people and human generativity in a very basic survivalist sense. But I digress.

What one knows in an oral culture is what one can recite, or concomitantly, what one has heard. Knowing and saying, hearing and learning have close links in a culture which sacralizes the Koran as its preeminent text and foundation of learning. Learning in the kuttāb (Koranic school) is first of all rote memorization of the Koran; the word *Qur'ān* indeed means recitation of *The* Word.

One cannot overemphasize the significance and the power of oral recitation in Arabo-Islamic culture. The recitation of the Koran evokes the moment of divine revelation; it exists in eternal time and transcends linear time. Islamic revelation, in Nelson's analysis, "does away with the atomism of tense: there is no past, no present, no future, rather one absolute present. The revelation is the past in that it is the beginning and source of knowledge and action. It is the present in its continuousness, and the future in that it is the complete and final message."[24] Nelson cites a correlation of "non-progressive continuity between the reality of the revelation, the structure of the Koranic text, and the performance structure of its oral rendering. That *tajwīd* evokes the moment of revelation, that the various manifestations of the Qur'an are, at the same time, the whole, reinforce this continuity." Koranic recitation thus re-presents the Ur-rhetorical scene and the Ur-cultural performance event that all other recitations somehow recapitulate.

The believer worships by reciting God's direct speech, which was communicated to his Prophet as "the only miracle in Islam" and transmitted orally before its transcription and collection in written form.[25] What you know, you can recite and perform orally;

knowledge, then, is memory. And talk can be divine, the telling more important than the act, speech of greater consequence than event; for in speaking the experience, the collectivity gives it credence and status.

History (or the agreed on record of past events and experiences) in the Arab oral cultures we have been considering takes shape through the living, musical ritual of poetry performance. And it is in this context that I should like to offer a rhetorical theory of Arab epic transmission with specific reference to *Sīrat Banī Hilāl* in its oral and written versions, but one which I would hypothesize to be true for all of the Arabic folk epics grouped under the general title of al-sīra which come down to us in manuscripts and printed pulp editions. I include *Sīrat ʿAntar, Sīrat Baybars, Sīrat Sayf Ibn Dhī Yazan, Sīrat al-Amīra Dhāt al-Himma,* and just possibly also certain *Tales of the Thousand and One Nights.*

First let us consider the nature of the Arab heroic genre that is designated al-sīra. All the above-mentioned vernacular-language works share the same native category or taxonomic title: al-sīra. This appellation they share too with the sīra of the Prophet Muḥammad compiled by Ibn Isḥāq and Ibn Hishām into a fixed, written text. By virtue of their common generic designation, as one might expect, the works share certain formal features as well as a certain subject matter. They also share, as we have elaborated in chapter 1, a similar ambivalent status in the total community as "illiterature"; that is, these vernacular-language folk narratives are assigned high status as history in the oral culture, but a low status in the literate culture of the same countries. All the siyar mentioned narrate similar events: the travels and quests in the name of Islam by a great hero. That hero is most often black. Sayf ibn Dhī Yazan and ʿAntar, like Abū Zayd, are born black. Both are the sons of black African slave women who later turn out to be the issue of royal African blood. One major sīra hero is not a man at all, but a woman warrior, Dhāt al-Himma, whose name means variously in its transformations of pronunciation, "woman of noble purpose," or "wolf."[26] This amazon leader of the tribe, the daughter of a female jinn, gives birth to a black son who joins her as one of a triad of heroes defending Islam against Christian foreigners. The "romance" spans the first three centuries of Islam and depicts encounters with the Franks, Berbers, but most particularly the Byzantines. *ʿAntar* likewise spans some five hundred years in its narrative. ʿAntar and Sayf both wage wars for Islam anachronistically before the birth of the Prophet. ʿAntar's adventures take him beyond the bounds of Arabia to Spain, Morocco and Egypt, Rome, and Ethiopia, the land of the Negus in whom he discovers his great grandfather. *Sīrat Sayf* celebrates the wars of the Muslim Arabs against the pagan Abyssinians and Negroes. Sayf prepares the way for Islam and Muḥammad in the campaigns he wages for Allah and the Muslim community. Baybars comes to the scene a bit later at the end of Ayyubid times and the beginning of Mamluk rule as the champion of Islam against the Byzantines and Crusaders and the Mongols. The sultan Baybars, who was brought to Egypt as a Mamluk (slave) boy, rules justly, defending the people against degenerate Mamluk soldiers.

A recent study of the *Romance of ʿAntar* by Norris[27] views ʿAntar's adventures as an elaboration of tales of expeditions to secure trade routes. Epics of Sayf and the Banī Hilāl also, in Norris's view, recount Arab expeditions into Africa and describe the Arab-Muslim founders of African kingdoms as civilizing heroes. All three siyar, according to him, reflect in their common concern with the black slave hero a popular comment on a debate that has long divided the lettered of Islam, a debate on how to deal with differences between races and peoples.[28] Norris suggests that the common features in *Sayf, ʿAntar,* and the *Hilāliyya* all stem from "some common pre-Islamic archetype preserved in the oral folklore and ballads of the Arabian nomads and the popular histories of Arabia." The English scholar then traces the combat of color, intermarriage between different realms, and the royal status of women as basic concepts in the "Arabian Romance" and links them with a supremely traumatic event in Arabian history—the long period of Abyssinian domination which culminated in the alleged attack on Mecca by the army of Abraha and his elephant.[29] Popular tales, poems, the sīra of the Prophet, the later romances (as well as, I might add, reverse glass folk paintings) feature this conflict of Arabs and Abyssinians. All present, Norris tells us, the aftermath of the Abyssinian occupation as a war for Islam and Arabia transported to the heart of Africa. Popular memory of this early disaster marked Ethiopians in the Arab imagination as the supreme enemies of Islam in Africa. Hence the combat between black and white in folk epic was to symbolize either ideological and religious conflict or ethnic and religious accord, depending on whether the motive of the story had a relationship with Abraha and the liberation of Yemen or with the Negus and the many cultural and commercial links between the Arabs and Ethiopians. *Sīrat ʿAntar* and *Sīrat Sayf,* according to Norris, explore and exploit this dilemma. Both *Sayf* and *ʿAntar* attempt to transcend and explain the dichotomy between black and white, human and jinn, resolving the dilemma as each sees the other reflected in "some aspect of the hero's personality." The important theme is demonstration of the common ancestry of the warring Arabians and Ethiopians, a unity lost in the remote past.[30]

Although his intent to point out the structural similarity of several siyar effaces any reality of narrator and audience implied in the texts, Norris's study does point to an important generic feature of the various siyar: their concern with the anomalies of Arab-Muslim identity as a basic content. While he speculates that the similarity of the siyar stems from a common pre-Islamic archetype or prototype of the "Arabian Romance," I should like to suggest that it is more useful to think of their similarity as stemming from the common experience of Arab-Muslim identity formation and from their common "language" and formation as part of an orally transmitted folk genre.

Folklore genres, according to Abrahams (extrapolating on the rhetorical theory of Kenneth Burke and the genre theory of Northrup Frye), give names to traditional attitudes and traditional strategies a performer uses in his attempt to affect his audience.[31] Critical consideration of genre looks at traditional forms and conventional contents as well as the patterns of expectation the poet and his public carry into the aesthetic transaction. Analysis of the speaker-audience relationship in the various modes of sīra transmission suggests insights into the rhetorical purposes of the genre within the given culture or group which participates in the transmission of the genre. *Sīrat Banī Hilāl,* I would submit, is typical of the sīra genre as a whole, its advantage for the scholar being that it is still a fluid, living epic in both oral, ceremonial performance and in its written versions. It has somehow resisted the ossification into single-version print to which all the other siyar have succumbed. I suspect that the multiple forms in which the Hilālī matter exists represent a typical model of the transformations through which the legendary matter making up *Sīrat ʿAntar,*

*Sīrat al-Amīra Dhāt al-Himma, Sīrat Sayf,* and so on, also went. Tracing the various transmutations of one such saga may provide suggestive data about how other siyar were transmitted and ended up in the relatively fixed texts of ambivalent status which they represent today. Analysis of the *Hilāliyya* in its various manifestations—oral and written, performed and print, professional and amateur, verse and prose, sung and spoken, manuscript single episode booklets and printed edition multi-episode synopses—may lead the researcher to a more complete understanding of the creative mechanism and genesis of the sīra genre as a whole. Such analysis may also lead to a fuller comprehension of the complex relationship between the oral and the written in Arabic-speaking culture.

All the written texts of the siyar which come down to us share a common format: all are enormously long, multivolume collections of "booklets" strung together chronologically and centering around either one hero or a family of heroes. All are episodic and repetitious; none ever end with the conclusion of an adventure. *Sīrat ʿAntar,* for example, appears in 32 to 45 booklets; *Sīrat al-Amīra Dhāt al-Himma* appears in 55 volumes according to Lane, and in a 1909 edition, in 5,084 pages in 15 volumes;[32] *Sīrat Baybars* appeared in 50 parts in Cairo in 1908–1909, though most manuscripts date from the eighteenth century and one sixteenth-century manuscript is held in the Vatican Library.[33] Available folk editions of the siyar give a much more homogeneous, linear impression of the individual sira than do their manuscript versions, which are much shorter, yet often more fully elaborated with poetry. Publication of *Sīrat Banī Hilāl* has been somewhat more sporadic, never appearing in a compact, neatly numbered multivolume edition, but rather more fluidly in a volume now and then. Its manuscripts are many, scattered in libraries throughout the world.

One cannot know what impelled the compilers of *Sīrat Banī Hilāl* and the various other siyar in the eighteenth and nineteenth centuries to string episode upon episode together in the long "romances" (siyar) they compiled. One wonders under what impetus the siyar were collected into books or dīwāns, by whom, and for what audience. At the present state of research, we can only speculate why some of the first uses of the printing press in Egypt, Lebanon, and Syria were put to printing these folk works.

We know from several early testimonies that the siyar coexisted in both written and oral form from at least the twelfth and thirteenth centuries.[34] For example, the Jewish convert to Islam, Samaw'al b. Yaḥyá al-Maghribī mentions around 1163 the pleasure he took in reading collections of legendary histories like *Dīwān Akhbār ʿAntara* and the *Dīwān Dhī al-Himma wa-al-Baṭṭāl.* Another Maghribī shaykh is reported to have heard the *Sīrat Baṭṭāl* recited in Fatimid Cairo during the time of al-Ḥakīm (996).[35] Given their chronicling of the Jihad, that major event of Arab-Muslim countries which converted masses of people to Islam and to an "Arab" identity, and their celebration of the anomalies of that identity, it is curious to remark that one of the few positive written testimonies to the tradition is given by a literate Jewish convert from the West.[36]

One might speculate that such travelers to the urban centers of Islam, on hearing the siyar recited, might have wished to carry texts of those recitals home. One very beautiful, gold inscribed and decorated Hilālī manuscript was commissioned by the bey of Tūnis in 1763. Since Egyptian dialect features predominate in this manuscript, one might assume that it originated in Egypt, possibly taken down from the dictation of a shāʿir al-rabāba.[37] This remains speculation, for sīra criticism and collection to date unfortunately have obscured rhetorical features of the texts that come down to us. The captious tone of European scholars fretting about the "narrators' unlimited fancy" and egregious distortion of historical "fact" indeed only distorts critical comprehension of the narrators' point of view and uses of the traditional matter related. I cite the story of Bel collecting and commenting on the Algerian narrator's text, which I recounted above, as a case in point. The folk manuscripts and printed editions we possess need to be studied with an eye and an ear honed to the rhetorical dynamic that shaped them—the voices implied in the text, voices of poet, narrator, scribe, and editor. The methodology for decoding these folk editions needs to be sensitive to the potential uses and genesis of the text in their cultures of origin in order to uncover the various layers of transmission compilation and editing which formed the present-day texts and written tradition. The problem of dealing with anonymous texts is great, but not overwhelming, since for the most part the siyar are not structurally anonymous. There is a guiding narrative presence in the rāwī, as well as other indicators of the transmission process and the relationship between the oral and the written within the text which the editorial hand has not altogether suppressed.[38]

Ayoub, for example, in his careful critical reappraisal of the 189 Berlin manuscripts of the Hilālī epic, offers evidence from the colophons attached at the end of several manuscripts which suggests that the manuscripts were directly dictated to a scribe by a poet.[39] Most of these manuscripts (119 of them) date from the years 1844–1845, probably a period of great popularity of the *Hilāliyya;* manuscripts dating from 1846 to 1853 are only reproductions of the contents of the earlier ones. The writing hand varies from one group of manuscripts to the other. The language has Egyptian dialect features and is reproduced in a form of phonological transcription which reflects the pronunciation of spoken words. The names of the scribes are for the most part indicated, often with their place of origin in Egypt; so too are postscript indications of persons who "read and appreciated the contents" of the manuscript, presumably the scribes' patrons. Ayoub proposes two hypotheses: (1) the scribe is transcribing the text from a singer's dictation, or (2) the scribe is copying a text already in circulation to sell to a singer. He conjectures that the manuscripts were "aids to the singer to enrich his narration before an audience." He indicates that it is difficult at this stage of his research to say definitely which is the case. He cites the diverse contents of the manuscripts as leading one to believe that they were an "integral part of the life of the poet-singer" in that they contained a list of the scribe's debts, receipts of payments made to the scribe, a medical prescription for constipation, grocery lists, and so on.[40]

In a very interesting recent paper,[41] Ayoub takes his postulate of an orally dictated text by a singer-reciter (chanteur-conteur) as a given. Describing and analyzing yet another West Berlin Staatsbibliotek Hilālī manuscript acquired by the Prussian Imperial Library in 1910 (this one not listed in Ahlwardt, but in Wagner),[42] Ayoub traces what he supposes to be the genesis of the manuscript based on internal evidence. The title page of this manuscript names it *'Awwal min al-Zīr, min Kutub al-Shaykh ʿAbd Allāh al-Baghdādī;* that is, the first part from the story of Zīr, from the books of Shaykh ʿAbd Allāh al-Baghdādī. The colophon indicates that "this is the first book from *Sīrat Banī Hilāl,* people of war and combat, in the handwriting of Rashīd al-Ḥallāq." Ayoub speculates that al-Baghdādī was an illiterate singer-storyteller who performed various episodes of *Sīrat Banī Hilāl.* This is suggested to him by the great number of manuscripts that bear Baghdādī's name among those listed in the Ahlwardt catalog. The Tunisian scholar further speculates that the fact that Baghdādī could not write led him to have his "transmission" written down by various scribes, the most notable being Rashīd al-Ḥallāq, whose name figures prominently in other Berlin manuscripts. Ayoub states that it is "well known" that singers-reciters commissioned manuscripts of their performed narratives. A famous illiterate performer such as Baghdādī might have his version transcribed for a number of reasons, such as establishing a kind of folk copyright and claim to the "authentic," true version as well as earning money from its sale. The prestige and authority accruing to this written version (by virtue of being written) then might impel a second singer-storyteller to pay to have the first manuscript copied so that he might have a chapbook from which to enrich his own future performances.

The present manuscript, Ayoub suggests, was one copied down from Baghdādī's oral rendition by a scribe-storyteller and then purchased by a second professional singer-storyteller. The second performer would seem to be not a Muslim singer, but a Christian. Ayoub bases this speculation on the fact that a second hand has gone through the manuscript and crossed out all the whole-line religious formulas that normally introduce and close verse-sequences in Hilālī manuscripts and printed editions. Also, certain words are crossed out in yet another hand that appears to be "correcting" the language of the first into more classical vocabulary and morphology. Ayoub suggests that the second hand may well be the turn-of-the century German scholar Martin Hartmann, since the margins also contain German translations, while the first hand erasing the Muslim pious formulations is that of the postulated Christian-Arab singer-reciter.

Ayoub's postulations are provocative and even plausible. I should, however, like to offer yet another hypothesis. Ayoub assumes that the second performer, who purchased the manuscript from an analphabetic bard, is literate, so literate as to be able to comb through the written manuscript editing and amending. While the oral tradition of *Sīrat Banī Hilāl* in nineteenth-century Beirut and Lebanon (for which I can find no testimony) may have been quite different from that of eighteenth- and nineteenth-century Cairo, Lane does indicate that the Abū Zaydiyya, the Hilālī poets performing on Cairo café doorsteps to the tune of the rabāb, used no manuscripts. Other performers, the ʿAntariyya who recited *Sīrat ʿAntar* and *Dhū al-Himma,* however, performed with books in front of them, chanting their contents in a rhythmic mode. Possibly, such a fixed text entered the Lebanese Hilālī tradition very early from oral composer-performers located in Baghdad or Damascus. Another possibility, suggested from other manuscript postscripts listing names of appreciative patrons, is that the patron who commissioned the text was not a performer, but rather an audience member who could read and who enjoyed the verse tales he heard sung in the hashish dens of Ottoman urban centers,[43] and who wanted to have a copy of "the book." The supposed use of manuscript versions of the *Hilāliyya* by performers does not alone account for their fairly wide dissemination, especially since we must assume that the great majority of the bards were nonliterate, just as the gypsy performers in Egypt today cannot read. Neither does it account for the even wider dissemination of lithograph and later printed editions. I would suggest instead that the hand Ayoub finds emending and editing the Baghdādī manuscript of *Zīr* belongs not to a performer, but to the Christian publisher of the first edition of *Sīrat Banī Hilāl* in Lebanon. The corrections and hypercorrections of the manuscript's colloquial language which Ayoub documents in his essay are typical of the so-called Middle Arabic of the many printed editions available of all the various siyar. Beirut editions of the Hilālī saga, such as *Taghrībat Banī Hilāl ilá Bilād al-Gharb* and subsequent Cairo editions by Maktabat al-Jumhūriyya (after 1952) which synopsize the Beirut edition, all omit religious formulas at the beginning and end of verse passages.

Indeed, a great deal has been made recently of these religious opening and closing formulas from the scholarly point of view. The proportion of poetry to verse in the manuscript and printed editions also has become a significant scholarly tool. Petráček, for example, maintains that the relatively high proportion of poetry to prose and the narrative functional utility of the verse in early written editions of the *Hilāliyya* point to the oral genesis of the written versions, as does the use of opening pious formulas.[44] I should like to suggest, however, that something quite different is operative in the printed editions and manuscripts, but before continuing this proposition, I would like to discuss certain folk testimony, both from within the folk editions of the *Hilāliyya* and from contemporary Egyptian and Tunisian opinion, as to the relationship between the oral and the written.

Prefaces to some printed editions of *Sīrat Banī Hilāl* comment on the authorship of the dīwān (collection). A British Museum lithograph edition (ca. 1850) of *al-Riyāda al-Bahiyya* (no. 14570a12/ b31/ b33)[45] cites Najd b. Hishām, the rāwī of the siyar of the Arabs, as the composer or compiler (*mu'allif*). The editor tells us that he has collected into a book "the recollections of the Amīr Abū Zayd which was spread [*shāᶜa*] around in all the villages and valleys and was circulated [*intaqala*] from the East to the West . . . and which delighted all mankind for hearing it, dissipated cares and sadness and gave rest to hearts and bodies." The words he uses (*shāᶜ*a and *intaqala* as well as *dhikr*) suggest oral diffusion; the first referring to what is known as public knowledge, the second term further specifying that which moves about or circulates as a rumor, and the third meaning mention, memory, or recollection, renown. The notion of face-to-face, shared interaction and transmission in speech is implicit in the words used. It is unclear whether the actual writer is Najd b. Hishām or not. I have the impression this is not the case, but instead that a second unnamed person is transcribing the text. While this editor apparently means that he took his text down from the oral version(s?), other editorial voices in prefaces to other printed editions seem to indicate a written source for the text gathered together in the current edition:

> Now then, after I had seen the Sīra of the Hijāzī Arabs, which the Hilālī knights relate, were the best of sayings and the most pure and the most original of themes and the most elegant, I gathered from them this book with sublime lines of poetry and witty curiosities and I named it the Book of *al-Alfāẓ al-Ẓarīfa* in the Journey of the Arabs and the Wars of the Zanātī Khalīfa and I arranged it so its themes and poetry and letters and news would delight thereby every hearer and bend the listener's ear to it.[46]

Even the edition taken from a source the compiler evidently *saw* rather than heard stresses the effect of oral performance of the sīra on listeners' ears rather than readers' eyes.

A Beirut edition of *Qiṣṣat Khaḍrā* (1896, British Museum copy), published by Ibrāhīm b. Yūnis al-Ṣādir, claims the publisher as its collector and compiler. After an eloge to God and the Prophet, the editor says "praise be to the one who gave news of the ancestors as an example to those who came later; let every clever intellect take a warning from hearing it"; then he indicates that Ibrāhīm b. Yūnis al-Ṣādir says that the most elegant of stories and most delightful events and poetry which will delight the reader and move the listener to joy was the story of *al-Khaḍrā Bint al-Amīr Qurḍāb al-Sharīf;* therefore, he "attended to its collection and saw to its nature and set forth what was circulated and famous in the way of news about the harsh memory which was recounted about what happened between Khaḍrā and the Bedouin knights from the generation of the father of knight Prince ʿAntar, Lord of the High, ancient kin to Prince Abū Zayd al-Hilālī." The editor proceeds to ask his reader who possesses learning and culture (adab—i.e., literacy of a higher degree than that implicit in the texts to follow) to disregard what occurs in the way of errors ("for God alone is infallible") and then proceeds to the narration of the tale in verse preceded by the phrase "*qāla al-rāwī.*"

Within *Sīrat Banī Hilāl* manuscripts and printed editions, there occur other references to oral transmission. Written folk editions all feature prominently both the voice of the rāwī speaking the narrative and the figure of the poet. The rhetorical scene of the rabāb poet bearing the saga of the Hilālī migration to an internal fictive audience is frequently recounted. The singing shāʿir appears to recapitulate past events or to warn of what is to come in songs of praise to tribal leaders. Often the black shāʿir al-rabāba is Abū Zayd himself traveling in disguise. He announces the eminent arrival of the Hilālī in foreign domains, as they cross the borders in their encroachments westward. One single-episode version first printed in Cairo in 1881 and reprinted in 1952 by Maktabat al-Jumhūriyya, entitled *Kitāb al-Uns wa-al-Ibtihāj* (The Book of Sociability and Joy), begins with the arrival of a troup of four itinerant praise poets in the encampment of Ḥasan b. Sirḥān. The rabāb poet Jamīl b. Rashīd sings the news of the countryside to the assembled tribe, thereby setting up the tale to come and recapitulating the events that have preceded.

Internal depictions of the singer-poet performing before the assembled cast of fictional characters occur in other epics, like *Beowulf* and the *Odyssey*, as well in what many critics see as a self-reflecting device wherein the singer puts himself and his tale-bearing progenitors into the song as a kind of copyright or claim of authorship. In Egypt today, the identification of the singer with the hero disguised as a rabāb poet is close. Abnoudy, who sees Abū Zayd as the "missing hero" come to rescue the Egyptian people, says the gypsy singer may always potentially be, in the minds of his public, Abū Zayd in disguise.[47] Some Upper Egyptian rabāb poets even look like popular depictions of the Hilālī hero. Shamandī, for example, bears a striking resemblance, with his dark face and sweeping mustachio, to depictions of Abū Zayd in folk editions of the *Hilāliyya* and in reverse glass paintings. (Compare pls. 8, 9, and 17).

The texts of *Sīrat Banī Hilāl* constantly push the reader out to the real-world rhetorical scene of the rāwī narrating the *Hilāliyya* and the shāᶜir al-rabāba singing the folk their story/history in his recapitulation of events just past or about to happen. The attentive reader of Hilālī manuscripts and printed editions can easily discern at least two voices at the openings of the separate "books" or episodes of the long tale. These two voices are the collector, speaking in the first person, and the rāwī, who is referred to in the third person and whose words are quoted as the authority for the narration of the story proper. The editorial voice or the voice of the compiler-redactor-scribe (the mu'allif) repeats on every page of the written versions "Qāla al-rāwī" (the narrator said). In the *maqāmāt* of Badīᶜ al-Zamān and al-Ḥarīrī from the high written tradition of letters (adab), a similar narrative device is used; but the rāwī in these works, as Monroe has demonstrated,[48] is a fictive persona used for ironic purposes. The rāwī mentioned in the *Hilāliyya* and in other siyar is quite unlike the maqāma's parody of the voice. Rather, this rāwī is a real person. The device of writing "Qāla al-rāwī" serves to distance the writer-compiler-redactor voice of the text which comes down to us from the voice of the story narrator proper.

Such repeated textual references to the rāwī along with frequent internal scenes of the shāᶜir al-rabāba singing the Hilālī news have a distinct narrative function and intent in the written folk editions (which I distinguish from compilations and collections by outsiders to the tradition like Bel, Baker, Ayoub, myself). These references to a primary oral rhetorical scene function as a contract with the reader. They remind him again and again, by virtue of their repetitions, what the compiler-collector-scribe (al-mu'allif) expects of his audience. He wants the reader to *hear* and to *remember* in his mind's ear the ceremonial performance of the *Hilāliyya* by a rabāb poet. The mu'allif's rendition of the *Hilāliyya* is but a recollection of a true performance; or, to use the scribe's own words, a dhikr—a mention and a retelling of the sīra which commemorates the ceremonial, ritual telling before the assembled community. The rabāb poet we can hear in oral performance today in Egypt asks his audiences to listen and to hear and to understand his words as a mention commemorating the renown of the ancestors. The redactor of written versions constantly refers to *how* the tale is told because his telling is at a remove from the story-history as it is meant to be experienced in the shared transaction of a communal ceremony celebrating the past in the present. The writer-redactor of folk traditions and manuscripts on which the printed editions are based then appears to be reporting a performance by a rāwī or shāʿir.

The folklorist Hymes has suggested in his seminal article, "Breakthrough into Performance," that scholars must not confuse the difference between the knowledge of *what* a tradition is about and knowledge of *how* it is; that is, the distinction between a narrator's assumption of responsibility for knowledge of the tradition versus assumption of responsibility for performance.[49] The ritual telling of myths may have disappeared in a culture all but in memory. Prose narrators of the Hilālī tradition in Tunisia or the Sudan thus may well be recollecting a remembered ritual telling of the tale in a long past ceremonial performance.

In our observation of the Hilālī matter diffused orally throughout Egypt and North Africa, we noted two different types of performance decorum. The tale may be simply told in prose, informally by amateur tale-tellers to people assembled casually, as in Tunisia, where the rāwī spins the recollected tale to buddies gathered in the back of a store or garage. Or it may be told formally by professional singers of tales (poets) in verse and music to an audience gathered for a special occasion to be celebrated by the singing of the sīra, as in Egypt. The shāʿir al-rabāba narrating the *Hilāliyya* to his fellah audience represents a cultural dialogue that reenacts and dramatizes "hot" issues. In the institutionalization of the cultural anomaly of the outcast gypsy bearing the genealogical history of the Egyptian Muslim peasants, the culture ventilates in ritual performance normally taboo subjects that are difficult to bear.

This ritual performance, this ritual telling and symbolic reenactment of the "genealogy" by professional bearers of the tradition has crucial significance for the culture. This significance is attested by the variety of retellings given the epic material by aficionados or amateurs of the tradition. The Egyptian Oral Literature scholar and archive chief, ʿAbd al-Ḥamīd Hawwās, has documented the various modes of amateur *Hilāliyya* re-creations.[50] Hawwās's taped anthology of "performance case histories" demonstrates five modes of nonprofessional renditions: (1) prose narration of the saga, (2) poetic narration, interspersed with prose, (3) musical narration of the story, (4) work songs, and (5) short balladlike versions (mawwāls). These amateur renditions of the Hilālī theme, which may be done in prose, chant, or lyric song, in solo or choral performance, all represent a kind of recapitulation of the ceremony of ritual performance by the professional bard who is the prime generator of the tradition.

Many prose versions of the *Hilāliyya* may be collected from amateurs of the tradition both in Egypt and in other Arabic-speaking countries. People like ʿAbd al-Salām, an uneducated Upper Egyptian fan of the *Hilāliyya,* will happily narrate the sīra for an interested party. ʿAbd al-Salām's prose version of the "Birth of Abū Zayd," which Abnoudy recorded and lent to me, follows al-Sayyid al-Ḍūwī's version very closely, save that it is more skeletal, less fully developed in its fictive realism. It has the characteristics of a summary of the fuller performed version by the shāʿir which ʿAbd al-Salām has heard and is recounting—much as we summarize a movie we have seen and enjoyed. Some prose versions that can be collected today from oral traditional tales told in the Sudan, in Jordan, in Tunisia, and in Algeria are based on oral versions told by grandfather and father to son. A few rāwīs claim to base their tales on their reading of printed editions of "the book."

At least one of Baker's Tunisian rāwīs, Ḥājj ʿAbd al-Salām, whose prose version we discussed at length (chap. 9), told his tale as he could best recollect it from the written version of the Taghrība he had read. His narration was a report of his experience of the book. Other Baker rāwīs were not as educated as this former Koranic schoolteacher and had learned the story from oral tradition as passed on to them by their fathers and grandfathers. These elders' versions, I should like to suggest, may well have been ultimately based on reports of the narrative as performed ceremonially by a professional bard, a fḍāwī in the Tunisian case. Nafṭī Bū Rakhīṣ, a Baker rāwī, adamantly insisted that the information he transmitted came down "from the mouths of the Hilālīs themselves."[51] Prose versions of the *Hilāliyya* seem for the most part to be recollections or reports by amateur bearers of the tradition of the professional performance tradition.

Baker traces the continual presence of Hilālī printed editions (Kutub ṣafrā' or yellow books, so-called for their cheap paper) brought from Cairo, Beirut, Damascus, and other Middle Eastern urban centers by Tunisian travelers, soldiers, and religious pilgrims. She notes that Tunisian storytellers as well as audience members consider the narrative of a literate storyteller more authentic. There is among storytellers the notion of a "correct" account fixed in the written word. One rāwī, Shaykh Maḥmūd b. Muhadhdhab b. al-Hājj Aḥmad Usbūʿī, considered his tale authentic because he derived it from a book purchased in Libya. Another storyteller almost refused to tell Baker his tale because he did not have the official book version.[52] In an Islamic society such as Tunisia, the written form has great authority and prestige. Reverence for the written word is such among the unlettered that any scrap of paper will be picked up off the street and preserved, tucked into a nook in a wall to protect the words from being trampled underfoot. The written word for the analphabetic Tunisian has scriptural connotations and sacred associations. Any piece of paper might have the name of God or His spoken words on it in the form of a verse of the Koran.[53]

A similar status accrues to the written in Egyptian oral culture. As Ayoub has suggested, the first Hilālī manuscripts may have been drafted from oral dictations by bards who wished to lend their versions the authority and status conferred on written books. Such elevation of The Book in popular esteem serves to confuse for the scholar the oral and the written. Most audience members in Egypt as well as most poets will always maintain that the sīra is a Book. An authentic, true written document is conceived as lying behind the orally performed version. Oral performances are viewed by both poet and listener as recitations of a single authoritative Book. The public hears and views the performance of the *Hilāliyya* by an unschooled poet-musician much as it hears a Koranic recitation by a professional Koran reciter-chanter. The oral and the written in Egyptian Arab oral culture thus become thoroughly fused and confused. At one end of the spectrum is the Koran, originally an orally composed and disseminated work, the direct speech of God as transmitted through the Angel Gabriel, and addressed to the illiterate Prophet Muḥammad, and conveyed orally by Muḥammad to his followers only to be written down in bits and pieces and much later collected and redacted into a fixed text. That fixed text is the Holy Scripture on which Muslim life is based. Its authority is absolute, its poetry sublimely unique in its power to move its listeners. People hear it regularly and bend to its rhythms and rhymes and beauty as they listen to professional recitations of it by Koran chanters, such as Nelson has so well documented recently.[54] People learn the Koranic text, incorporate its poetry and music, its rhythms and phrases into their minds and hearts through such ecstatic listening as a Koranic recitation elicits. Some also memorize it word for word in Koranic school.

The sīra performance, in the folk conception of it, parallels the Koranic text; it represents for them a text that is second only to the sacred scripture of the Holy Koran. It gains authority conceived as a written text, as a recitation of the Book. Memory of the inscribed Word is authority. Learning too is memory; and likewise, knowledge is memory in this oral culture—memory of the set phrases and cadences of the Koran or the narrative tales which convey past wisdom to the present community.

The distinction between oral interpretation of a written text and oral composition does not seem to be important to Arabic folk culture. The important thing is that a text is being passed on by word of mouth. The licenses issued to a teacher to give him the right to teach a given book granted him, in effect, the right to pass the written text on orally. Legally, an oath must be oral speech, spoken, not just written. The culture views oral interpretation and delivery, the oral communication of a fixed text, in the same terms as oral re-creation and improvisational composition of a flexible, fluid text like the Hilālī epic(s) we can hear poets orally composing in performances in Egypt today.

How then to tell the difference between the orally composed narrative and the recitation of a written text in a culture which fuses and confuses the distinction? It is a distinction that, from the scholarly vantage point at least, remains important for understanding the mechanism of the genre called the sīra. The written versions of the siyar, both manuscripts and printed editions, give some, often contradictory, indications.

The word *dhikr,* used so prominently by both oral poets and the redactors of folk editions of the *Hilāliyya,* sums it up: the mention contains the recollection and the memory that give knowledge and renown. That mentioned recollection transmitted and spread in shared oral discourse can become a written record of the oral transaction, just as the speech of God dictated to the Prophet became inscribed in The Book. Classical Arabic written discourse retains in its vivid narrative style the aura of oral speech on the model of the speaking voice contained in the Koran and in the early oral poetry.[55]

Cachia in his essays on the Egyptian mawwāl, a tradition parallel to the sīra poetry, maintains that the interface between the oral and the written is indeed complex. The line of demarcation between elitist and popular literature is not a matter of a simple contrast between the literate and the illiterate, or the urban and the rural.[56] The mawwāl tradition of heroic narrative told entirely in song or verse is an art practiced by gypsy minstrel musicians who travel from one rural festival to another, improvising their songs, but it is also an art men of some education practice with pen in hand.[57] Often the literate composers sell their compositions to singers. Cachia mentions one Azhar-trained writer of folk ballads who delivers an *ijāza* (folk license or diploma) to illiterate singers who orally memorize 200 quires of his work to propagate it in oral performance.[58] Present-day singers still remember with respect one extremely prolific mawwāl writer who died about 1936, an Azharī shaykh, Muṣṭafá Ibrāhīm ʿAgāg. All the literate authors Cachia was able to trace were products of Islamic traditional education like this famous Azharite. Many literate mawwāl makers publish their works in kutub ṣafrā', the cheap, pulp-paper folk editions in which we also find the various siyar published.

The famous colloquial-language poet and songwriter, Abnoudy, whose low opinion of the pulp editions I quoted in chapter 2, sees the compilers of *Sīrat Banī Hilāl* in its folk editions as these Azharites of which Cachia informs us:

> The prestige of the epic is such that the obscure, anonymous writers who haunt the galleries of the Azhar Mosque in Cairo or who frequent the poorest quarters of Beirut, earning their feeble living by publishing multiple editions of the epic that are more or less deformed and truncated, have never dared to come out of their anonymity. Before these needy hacks were born, the peasants inhabiting most of the villages of the Arab east and west were singing the *Hilāliyya* and guarding it jealously just as they guard the land which they inherited from their fathers and just as they guard their families' good names. The lamentable, yellow-paper printed editions of the legend contributed in large part to the disaffection and scorn for the epic found among the younger generation. The illiteracy of the peasants sheltered them from it. Not being able to read these mediocre books, they didn't change these poems that they transmit from one generation to the other over the centuries.[59]

Curiously enough, Abnoudy himself takes part in the fusion of the oral and the written. He stands on the margins of the two worlds of intellectual literati and folk poets, who are in their own way intellectuals within the oral, traditional culture, standing as they do as artists and performers outside it to comment, to interpret, and to criticize. Abnoudy's art is openly and avowedly that of the illiterate popular folk poets. His compositions share the oral bard's language and locutions; he uses their forms, their building style, their puns and verbal dexterity. His work belongs more to the conventions of the professional, itinerant folk entertainers than to those of any written convention.

Abnoudy sees the oral *Hilāliyya* as a permanent dialogue between the poets and the people. Today he has become part of this dialogue. In his radio shows and his cassette recordings of various poets singing the sīra,[60] Abnoudy interprets and mediates the poets' sung words for a wide audience. The long-range intent of this cosmopolitan poet-intellectual and spokesman of the disinherited of Egypt is to create his own *Hilāliyya*. To quote the phrase of some of his family and friends in describing Abnoudy's mission, he will be the "Homer" of the grand epic of the Arabs. He will base his final, written version on the versions of the singers he has recorded.

Abnoudy, as I have mentioned, grew up in the far south in the midst of the flourishing oral culture. He heard the folk poets and as one acutely sensitive to the rhythms and subtleties of language, he absorbed the oral poetics and became a poet himself. As the son of an Azhar-educated shaykh, he was born to a certain level of literate culture and education. The poetry he pens somehow manages to convey the heard voice and musicality of Egyptian folk poetry and song, whereas most written renditions of this colloquial poetry, such as those versions of the mawwāl Cachia mentions and the various printed siyar, all fail to translate the aesthetic heard and appreciated by the Egyptian public ear in performance. An early commentator on folk songs, Ṣafī al-Dīn al-Ḥillī,[61] mentioned the difficulty had by the masters of the literate language in attempting to put such verses into writing:

> These are the arts in which declension is ungrammatical, chaste diction is barbarous, and high flown utterance is weak. . . . Easy-flowing, yet hard to control, accessible [to apprehension] yet beyond the reach [of emulation]. The commoners have long reduced the elite to impotence in them, [their poetic arts], their fluent compositions outstripping the resources of the eloquent. Let the master of [classical] eloquence attempt one of these arts and he finds that he has been deluded; he gulps but can scarcely make himself swallow.

Cachia,[62] whose translation of al-Ḥillī I have followed, shows that eminent, educated men throughout the history of Arabic letters from at least the twelfth century onward, have practiced the nonclassical arts, usually known, however, as wits among the elite rather than men of letters. Although Cachia's argument about the transmission and genesis of the mawwāl appears to be leading to quite a different conclusion from mine, I should like to suggest that a fairly clear picture of the transmission and genesis of the Hilālī tradition, at least, does indeed begin to emerge at the margins of literacy where all the numerous folk siyar exist.

Vernacular-dialect poetry, as al-Ḥillī mordantly pointed out, does not generally translate well onto paper. It is a performance art and a musical art. The art of the rabāb poet who performs the *Hilāliyya* in Egypt today demonstrates the close interrelationship of verse and music, voice and instrument that is living song intended for the ear. Indeed, looking at the transcribed text of any one performance of the rabāb poets, the written product makes little sense. It is, like the manuscript and printed editions of the *Hilāliyya,* so-called defective poetry. The poetic form of these oral texts once written down is often impossible to describe or understand. No principle is apparent apart from the sung performance. For, as Herzog tells us,[63] epic song attains and reveals a structure, which the poem as text does not have, through the musical performance itself and through the disposition of various musical motifs. The music and the poem thus form an integral unit. The text is nothing without the music, which provides the medium in which the text is unfolded and carried along. Melody and text are in a complex association at the moment of execution. Melody becomes such a crucial factor in constructing lines and couplets that, as we will recall, when Jābir's brother struck up the wrong tune at one point in a performance, Jābir stopped the line he had begun building and interjected, "Mā lak?" (What's wrong with you?) The accompanying rabāb player then struck up the correct melodic formula and the poet began his quatrain anew. The poet-musician in performance adjusts his text to the tune, using such devices as contraction, particular accents, addition of syllables, ornamentations, vocalizings, and syllable elongations. When a text and melody are separated, their exact relationship is difficult to rediscover, for it can be best apprehended by the ear.

In the opinion of a man like Abnoudy, the low status of Hilālī pulp editions could possibly derive from the fact that they are orally dictated performances and, quite simply, appear in distorted form when transcribed visually into writing. The book's redactors seem to claim as much in their continual citation of the rāwī and the shāʿir as the source of the articulated words of the text and their apologies to the classically adept for errors. From all accounts by other folk tradition aficionados I talked with in Egypt, however, the yellow books are even worse than this.

The poetry transcribed as the voice of the rāwī or poet in manuscript and printed editions of the *Hilāliyya* is judged "defective" poetry with no discernible metrical principle, no internal beauty and rhythm. Its texture too is inferior, I am told, with few striking metaphors, little wordplay or punning. It is full of tedious antitheses and repetitions in lieu of the layers of multiple significance we heard the oral performer weaving into his rhymes. The belabored rhymes of the qaṣīda-form verse in the folk editions for the most part offer no challenge, no concealed message to unravel. The rhyming in these editions is derogatorily termed tastīf or stacking.[64] Such mere rhyming, as we learned from performance dynamics, is not particularly appreciated by the folk audience.

Fārūq, the poet whose verse we analyzed above, rhymes in this manner. Perhaps then the poets orally dictating the texts on which present-day pulp editions are based were poets like Fārūq who used little complex paronomasia. I have not closely analyzed written folk editions of the *Hilāliyya* from a textural point of view with an eye and an ear honed for end-rhyming paronomasia. Written texts need to be studied for this feature since it seems to be paramount in the oral tradition as an aesthetic index of "good" versus "bad" interpretations. The Berlin manuscripts are probably, as Faiq Mukhlis claims[65] and Ayoub's work verifies, the closest oral tradition of the various editions that circulate. Unlike the printed books one can buy in Cairo, Tūnis, Damascus, for example, the manuscripts have had little obvious "editorial" interference; the hands such as Ayoub observed at work "fixing up" Shaykh al-Baghdādī's copy of *Zīr Salām* at least are visible in the manuscript margins. Texts such as these have not been read with any sensitivity to their potential internal aesthetic intentions. If indeed Abnoudy's assertions about the feebleness of the poetic texture of the yellow books applies to the manuscripts, then we may suppose that these writings do not represent a text orally dictated by a poet-singer to a scribe.

Yet another parameter for judging the "orality" of the folk text remains. And that is application of the Parry-Lord method of formula analysis. Of the editions I subjected to statistical formula analysis,[66] only one was an early lithograph in a written hand, *Kitāb al-Riyāda al-Bāhiyya,* published in 1282 A.H. (ca. 1865) by the Kastaliyya Press in Cairo.

One can hear the voice of the shāʿir al-rabāba through the text, which shares the illiterate performing poet's paratactic adding style, use of parallelism and pleonasm, and many of his fixed phrases and formulas. The mode of the texts, however, represents a much more rigid use of the formulaic medium that one hears in an actual performance-composition by an improvising rabāb poet. The Parry-Lord method of estimating the percentage of repeated phrases or formulas reveals that the lithograph edition I analyzed and the printed editions of Maktabat al-Jumhūriyya have a suspiciously high formula density. The verse can be demonstrated to be about 70 to 80 percent formulaic (i.e., this high percentage of its lines or half-lines are repeated verbatim in the corpus more than once).

The poetry of the folk editions, then, seems not to be a flexible formulaic medium of improvisation, but rather a rigidly repetitive one. The 70 to 80 percent range of formula density represents an exceptionally high number. Duggan's computer-generated concordance of the *Song of Roland* and his comparison of its formula density to that of other epic traditions suggest that other oral poetries contain more like 30 to 40 percent repeated phrases.[67] This leads me to believe that the written folk editions of the *Hilāliyya* which come down to us from the past two centuries are something other than orally transcribed texts from a singer's dictation. These folk redactions probably represent, as rhetorical analysis of their opening speaking situation suggests, a report of an oral performance at several removes from the actual performance itself. Their redactors may well have been, as Abnoudy asserts, Azharites like the ones Cachia interviewed who produce mawwāl texts. I would suggest that these men were not unlike Abnoudy himself, if not in their talents, at least in the fact that they grew up hearing the orally performed *Hilāliyya*. They incorporated its themes and formulas by virtue of hearing them sung orally again and again. At a remove from an actual performance, these hack writers attempted to re-create the experience of the ritual telling. The very language of the texts they produced indicates overly stereotyped verse. Such a superabundance of formulas repeated verbatim makes them rigid clichés. The best example of the clichéd quality of the written verse is in opening religious formulas. These repeat themselves very statically from one edition or from one episode to another. The performing poets studied in this work do not use such cryptic, static one-line opening formulas as the books do. Rather the shāʿirs seem to re-create religious formulary in a much more flexible way in their opening lines. Prophetic invocations may be used to open narrative sessions continuing an evening's performance after a coffee break, the length of continuous telling segments being variable according to several factors (including the length of the cassette or tape the researcher is using). The performer may use prophetic invocations very elaborately as Jābir does, letting them do the work of an organizing contract of narrative expectation, or he may omit them altogether as Fārūq did in one of his performances for my household; he may also offer something in between as Sayyid does.

In contrast, in the written texts, formulas become stereotyped and sterile and static. They bear little resemblance to the flexibility of the living crafted verse. At the hands of the hack writers, the formulaic medium becomes rigid, hackneyed clichés quite unlike the flexible gestalt of the singer composing verse on a melodic-rhythmic line marked off by the rabāb. The oral poet's memorable cadences are all lost in this translation into script. In this condemnation of the redactor's craft, I do not rule out the possibility of varying talents and skills as a vernacular poetic craftsman at work in the manuscripts. Some may rise above these "deformations" of the rabāb poet's art. A question also remains open as to whether or not the tradition may simply have changed over the years since the manuscripts were set down. Racy, an ethnomusicologist specializing in Arabic music, tells me that the Egyptian musical milieu is marked by great experimentation and innovation.[68] In Racy's research on the epic tradition, which he reported in a series of lectures given in the summer of 1979 at San Francisco State University, rural epic singers in the Levant form part of a much more conservative tradition. Their performances are always solo and they use monorhyme verse and prose rather than the cross-rhymed quatrain narrative forms employed by present-day Egyptian singers.

Perhaps, at the present state of research, it is premature to state definitively the relationship between nineteenth-century oral performance and the anonymous printed editions. Further investigation of the manuscript tradition and the history of printing popular editions as well as comparative analysis of the texts recorded today from oral performance-composition with early manuscript versions will reveal more detailed information about the history of the creative process and its relationship with transmission. For the moment, however, I should nevertheless like to hypothesize a chain of transmission based on the primacy of the improvising shāʿir whose performance is at once a creation and a transmission.

Certain rabāb poets, like Fārūq, do seem not to be creative, freely improvising artists. In his limited repertoire of one fairly set

6,000-line version of "Mīlād Abu Zayd" and one other episode he knows less well (i.e., narrates less fluidly and coherently) of Abū Zayd in Ethiopia, both of which he performed for me twice over a month's interval, Fārūq seems to perform a memorized text. He evidently learned it orally from his father. In subsequent repeated performances, unlike Jābir's re-recording of a given episode, Fārūq repeated virtually the same text verbatim. He seems not to create fluently in performance-composition, but rather to recite over and over a fairly fixed text. In such performances as his, the oral compositional-transmission process is virtually dead. A fixed text entering an oral epic tradition, Lord has reiterated,[69] sounds the death knell of the living tradition. One might assume this is what happened to *Sīrat ʿAntar, Sīrat al-Amīra Dhāt al-Himma, Sīrat Sayf,* and *Sīrat Baybars* in Egyptian oral tradition. By the time Lane described these story-performance traditions in the early nineteenth century, books had entered into the recitation decorum. *ʿAntar* and *Delhemma* performers "read" from books. *Baybars* and *Sayf* reciters used no book, but neither did they use a musical instrument—another significant marker, according to Lord, that a tradition is on the wane as a living entity. These prose tales seem to have been like the Tunisian rāwīs' prose rendition of the *Hilāliyya,* only occasionally interspersed with verse.

A rather complex picture of the relationship between the oral and the written (as well as between the oral and the oral, the written and the written) in the transmission of siyar thus begins to emerge. In the case of the *Hilāliyya,* which is the most approachable of the siyar in that it still exists as a fluid tradition, I would hypothesize the chain of transmission that I have charted here (table 2). This theory of transmission is a rhetorical one that takes into account at every juncture the dialogic dynamic between poet and audience.

The Hilālī migrations began in times of great tumult and social ferment, of racial and cultural contact following the Islamic conquests and conversions. Their peregrinations, which continued over at least two centuries, coincided with the beginnings of the Turkish encroachment and the establishment of Mamluk rule. Tribal poets, such as those Ibn Khaldūn recorded in the fourteenth century, sang songs and ballads of the exploits of Hilālī heroes. The Hilālī legend, as Schliefer asserts in his often-quoted *Encyclopaedia* article on the sīra,[70] was thus carried with the traveling

TABLE 2

## A RHETORICAL MODEL OF SĪRAT BANĪ HILĀL'S TRANSMISSION AND NARRATIVE LINEAGE

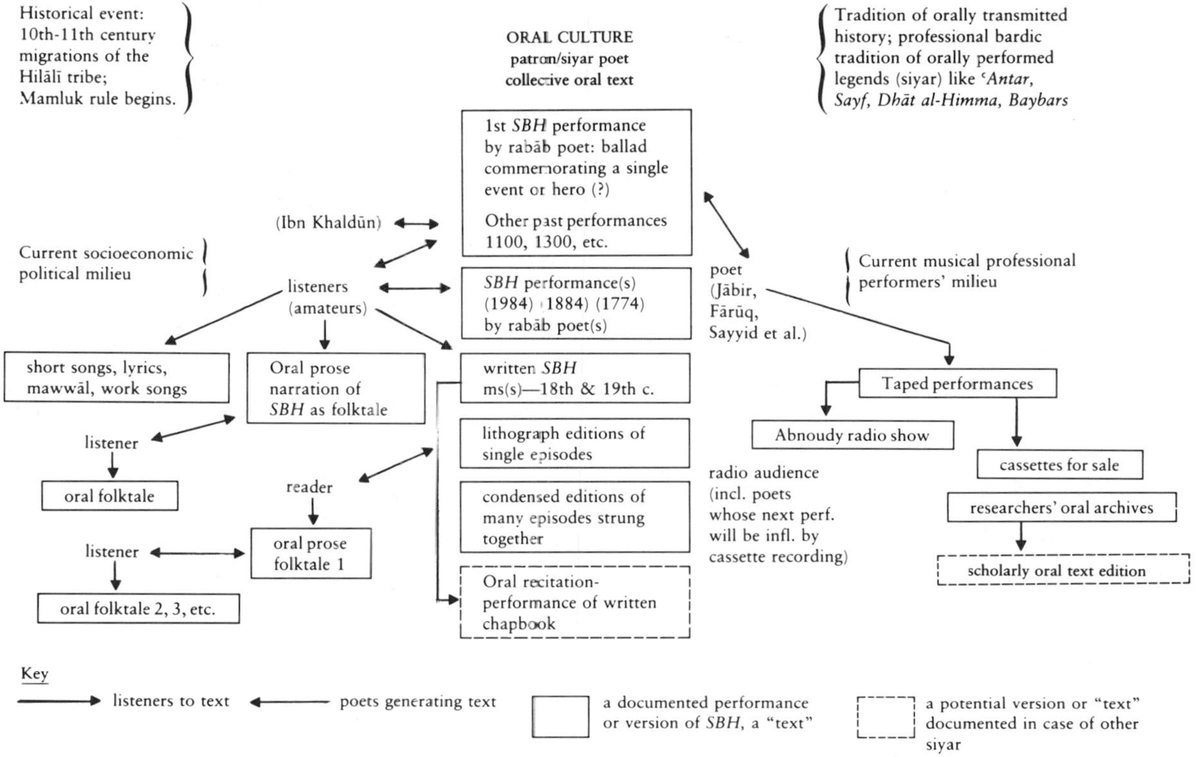

tribe and disseminated as history throughout a broad geographic area. This is probably true, but, in itself, is too simple to be the entire case. The whole story of the epic transmission must be much more complex.

Evidence suggests that there coexisted with tribal poetic history, such as the poems Ibn Khaldūn took down, an urban center coffeehouse custom of public recital of other histories associated with the Islamic conquests and the coming of the Arabs. In the milieux of such professional musicians and entertainers no doubt were poets who transmitted *Sīrat ʿAntar* and *Sīrat Dhāt al-Himma,* and the like. The Hilālī matter was taken up by these entertainers to be performed ritually in cafés and homes, at parties and festivals. In Egypt today, the performing rabāb poet who continues this tradition learned his art by a musical improvisation technique, probably very much in the way Parry and Lord describe the Muslim bardic tradition that exists in Yugoslavia. Whether there may be any relationship between the two traditions, with their common link in the Turkish aşık's art,[71] has yet to be explored by scholars of oral poetry. Any possible genetic connection between the two traditions aside, the process of transmission and composition in performance appears to be much as Lord, following Parry, has so thoroughly described it. Any given poet in any given performance has learned his art and craft from hearing and absorbing past performances, often playing, as the Egyptian rabāb artist Shamandī did as a little boy, the drone accompaniment to the main singer's narrative. To each present performance, the singer brings memories of past performances he has heard and in which he has participated either actively as a performer or passively as a listener.

The poet's public also enters into the transmission process, both in its role as the paying patrons who assent to hear the tales once more and in a more active role of re-creating the sīra in amateur versions. We have evidence from the case of the Syrian tradition of coffeehouse sīra recitation that the patrons often wanted concrete memorials of the story sung. As a commemoration of a particularly pleasing performance, patrons in Damascus commissioned glass paintings.[72] I would suggest also that the poet's patrons (perhaps like the bey of Tunis) often wanted written mementos of the wonderful tale they heard performed. Therefore, either (1) traditionally educated men of marginal literacy wrote down reports of the rāwī's narrative songs from their memories of performance in chapbook manuscripts, or (2) singers dictated the texts to scribes and sold the product to (a) audience members, or more doubtfully (b) to other singers. Less literate audience members commemorate the ritual telling in amateur entertainment for their own daily amusement in lyrics or choral work songs. They also tell prose tales (ḥikāyāt) based on the professional performance they have heard. These amateur reports of the ritual telling, which are in the form of lyrics or prose folktales, then form their own chain of oral transmission as in the Tunisian case.

The bookish tradition originated I suspect from the fairly hackneyed account professional scribblers ("wāḥid Azharī," to quote Abnoudy's phrase) gave of the verses they recalled from rabāb poet(s) performance(s). The "Book" manuscript of a given performed episode was copied by others wishing the text, and published first in its integrity in lithograph editions. Subsequent printed editions frequently lumped several single episodes together; they often abbreviated and condensed the original manuscript by omitting verse lines and summarizing them in prose. One can follow this process particularly in editions of *al-Riyāda al-Bahiyya*.[73]

"The Book" thus eventually came into wide dissemination in its yellow pulp editions. Travelers from other parts of the Arabic-speaking world where the Hilālī tradition had once, perhaps, flourished orally, like Tunisia up until before the war, purchased the Book. Men like Baker's rāwī ʿAbd al-Salām from southern Tunisia traveling to the eastern Arab urban centers with the French army[74] brought the written sources home with them and based subsequent oral tales on the written version, which itself was an account of an oral version. Local publishing houses, like Tūnis' Bāb Manār, sometimes would also publish their own yellow books, like the copy of *Zīr Salām* I bought in 1972 in the souks of Tūnis and Nabeul. The texts were thus available to the single literate man of Tunisian villages, the man who, on reading books, would often recount his readings to an audience of nonreaders, who in turn would tell and retell the tale thus heard from the book.[75] The orally recounted memory of the book thus, for all intents and purposes, becomes the book; it also becomes the book's "fame."

Yet another chain of transmission has begun in the past decade. This time, however, the text is perhaps even more fixed and less fluid than that disseminated by the eighteenth- and nineteenth-century Cairene hack writer. Beginning around 1970, sound recordings of oral performances by rabāb poets singing the *Hilāliyya* began to appear on the market. Over the past decade cassette recorders have become fairly widely available to the general public. The Cairo recording company Nefertiti has been putting out cassettes of Hilālī episodes by some of the better singers since about 1973. Abnoudy's radio shows, first broadcast around that time, have served to make "stars" out of certain performers. Radio listeners often recorded their own cassette copies from the radio transmission and circulated these copies privately. The effect of Abnoudy's shows seems to have been to create a wider demand both for cassettes and for ritual performances at parties like the one Critchfield reports in *Shahhāt* (dating from about this same time).

The radio shows and cassette industry also can be observed to be influencing the performance tradition. Professional singers are very savvy about recording. Many will ask the patron how long the cassette plays—30 minutes, 45, or an hour. Perhaps a more important indication of influence, however, is the way in which professional singers use the prerecorded versions. Often one poet will hear a version by a competitor and then incorporate story details, whole quatrains, or striking wordplay or figures of speech. Fārūq, for example, when I recorded him in 1978, could be heard to incorporate a quatrain of Jābir's which Abnoudy selected to play as the theme song for his nightly radio show. Other incorporations by other singers will no doubt prove to be more or less inventive and creative. It remains to be seen whether the influence of cassette recordings on a large scale will continue to revitalize the tradition as Abnoudy claims his radio show has done or whether it will be a nefarious entry of the concept of a fixed text into the living, fluid tradition. An epic tradition, of course, remains living only by virtue of its fluidity and multiplicity as a dynamic, creative dialogue.

Abnoudy just issued in 1983 a series of six cassettes featuring the ultimate "star," Jābir Abū Ḥusayn. How will such a readily available oral fixed text affect the performance tradition? Will this version come to be the only version tolerated by the public? Will other rabāb poets, as they can so easily do, memorize it in its entirety? How much memorization of fixed text from a cassette takes place today? These seem to be vital questions for the field-workers in Egypt today.

The *Hilāliyya* has resisted ossification for a very long time. Its very multiplicity and fluidity make it difficult for the researcher to grasp and comprehend. New data, new versions, are constantly being gathered. A flurry of collection is being undertaken in Egypt at present. Abnoudy has generated great excitement about the tradition for intellectuals and scholars as well as poets and their public via his radio and newspaper commentaries as well as his varied lectures abroad. He is a man with a multiple audience, the folk listen to him and so do left-wing as well as establishment intellectuals and scholars. He has worked collaboratively with Canova, Ayoub, and myself as well as other foreign Hilālī scholars who seek to find and understand the Arab epic tradition. ʿAbd al-Ḥamīd Hawwās too is prominent in directing scholarly collecting endeavors. Two American doctoral candidates, Slyomovics and Reynolds, have been extensively collecting the *Hilāliyya* under his direction. Reynolds's work is being conducted in a southern village renowned for its many resident poets. Slyomovics has recorded a fine poet named ʿAwaḍ Allāh in a forty-hour version of the sīra (which I hope will soon be available in a thoroughly documented linguistic edition). Abnoudy, of course, claims the longest version by a single poet in the ninety-hour *Hilāliyya* of Jābir, the acclaimed shāʿir al-ʿArab (poet of the Arabs).

The zeal of collectors to record the "longest" single version seems reminiscent of nineteenth-century compilers in their endeavor to string all the episodes of the *Hilāliyya* together into one long book—an effort that in fact had fruition for the *ʿAntar* epic. This quest for a long epic in the style of the Greek songs reminds one that the collection and criticism of any epic today appears to take place in the shadow of Homer. Despite the Egyptian folk tradition that the shāʿir should be able to recite for ninety-nine nights, I wonder if it is not misguided to seek pure length, for the shāʿir's oral art is a metonymic one. On every level, the part contains the whole and stands for it. All good poets know this and use their narration of any one episode, as fitted into a given time frame dependent on the performance parameters, to interpret the meaning and significance of the whole sīra. Indeed, the Egyptian public measures the successful performance of the *Hilāliyya* by this standard, evaluating different poets by their figural interpretive technique.

We heard the close rapport of the poet and his public in Egyptian performances of the *Hilāliyya*. Audience members murmured their appreciation in oaths in praise of God and the poet. They echoed in approving mutters the performer's rhyme words. This sensitivity to the poet's "musical metaphor" bound listener with the creating poet in their mutual participation in rhyme-play.

The word for the narrator of the tradition reflects this tight relationship and transaction: Rāwī means transmitter or narrator, but in its root derivations it connotes a much more specific notion of narration and transmission, for the word derives from the root RWY which also means to twist ropes, to bind fast, to tie up. The word for rhyme letters (*rawī*) and for narrator (*rāwī*) thus implies binding words together, twisting or weaving them like ropes to bind oral memory safely with truth.[76] A passage in the Koran (113,4) glosses this concept of the Arabic oral culture and shows a *kāhina* (priestess, sorceress, poet) spitting on knots to cast her spell of words. The word for poet (shāʿir) implies that the poet-narrator knows by superior intuition; he feels and perceives and senses things in their true essence from an immediate sensual apprehension of experience. He is thus a medium between events experienced and the collective memory of it bound in the rhymes of poetry. The poet is, in a more direct translation of the Arabic word, the kenner.

The contemporary Egyptian poet's "ken" is an anomalous perception of history endured, a knowledge that is aware of the ironies involved in the dichotomies and differences lived daily. That ken is carried in the poet's rhyme puns, which provide the basic perceptual gestalt of the tradition. For in the *Hilāliyya*'s art and craft, rhyme puns provide the poet not just with a flexible formulaic gestalt around which to build quatrains and through which to gloss the significance of the sung story; the poet's punning rhymes also provide the basis of aesthetic appreciation for the audience. Perhaps even more significant, this same paronomastic device operates as a key conceptual basis for transmission and generation of the story.

We saw the etymological efficacy of words on Shaḥḥāt and the Berat audience as the Egyptian shāʿir unraveled his rhymes. In our close listening with an Egyptian audience to performances as well as in our analysis of several contemporary Tunisian texts collected from live performance, we discovered the extraordinary sensitivity of the Arabic-speaking folk audience and oral culture to etymologies and the hidden power of word connotation as well as their taste for reaching into the depths of the offering to discover hidden symbols. Like the Tunisian Dhiyāb plunging his arms into the couscous to find the gold and silver crescent (hilāl) Zāziya has buried there, the audience must reach beneath the surface of the story to find the hidden symbols. Meaning unfolds from the context and from past contexts like a flower. The Hilālī narrator—wherever he is found, in whatever form his tale—offers riddles, puns, rhymes, and other masked figures for the unraveling.

The *Hilāliyya* represents, even in all its multiplicity and fluidity, in all its local variations and interpretations, a collective text of fairly universal appeal spread widely over an Arabicized folk culture. Through all its many cultural transformations, it retains its identity as *Sīrat Banī Hilāl* certainly through its story content based on tribal migrations and their concomitant boundary transgression and conflict. This basic story content reveals a morphology that Ayoub[77] claims is the index of any given episode of the *Hilāliyya:* Departure and/or Arrival, Opposition, Contract (marriage), Dream, Trick (by oppressed side), Confrontation, Victory (by oppressed side), Return or Departure. This is the logic of the narrative, to borrow Bremond's phrase.[78] This linear frame of story progression implicit in each episodic cycle is not the whole story, however; such a morphology might apply to many different story traditions.

What makes the *Hilāliyya* the *Hilāliyya,* what preserves and conserves it in the memory of both its narrators and its audience is something else. This something else is a nonlinear, frequently counterlogical textural feature, for the *Hilāliyya* in all its many transformations retains its identity and its place as a source of identification for its audiences through: (1) its name puns, and (2) the anomalous, disjunctive perception that these puns convey. Just as the spiraling metonymies of the inside and the outside (which the Egyptian shāʿir's rhyme puns set up) function to please and teasingly teach the deep meaning of the sīra by projecting the paradigmatic axis onto the syntagmatic, so punning also works to transmit the *Hilāliyya*'s poetic perception of Arab history.

We have noted in the course of our analyses of various episodes and versions of the saga the narrators' awareness and use of name etymologies. Characters' names reflect their etiology and provide glosses on their function in the narrative; that is, names literally and etymologically signal what characters do in the story and what they stand for. In the poetic logic of the story, genealogy is etymology and etymology is genealogy—at least the genealogy of the story. Its roots, its generating force, its meaning and continuity are found in the etymological derivations of character names. This stylistic device thus has a basic disseminating function: it serves to "memorize" the role of the character in the narrative. The Arabic word for "memorize" is *ḥafiẓa;* to guard, preserve, to protect, to heed, to store, to retain in mind is more precisely the Arabic concept of memorization and memory, and perhaps learning and knowledge. Name etymologies thus preserve the tale's mythic bare bones. In many ways, etymological derivations are the essence of knowing the sīra for the shāʿir and perhaps also for the rāwī.

The biography of the Hilālī heroes narrates the story of the origins and succession of the race(s), but the wordplay the heroes' names contain carries the most significant kernel of meaning, the key to the sīra or ways of the Hilāl. Character names and their playful interaction with each other provide key constellations of both meaning and plot. They contain transcultural universals of Arab experience and identity within a stylistic device that different narrators develop to varying extents. Certain narrators are unconscious of these keys, which nevertheless continue to operate formulaically as a kind of gestalt out of which the *Hilāliyya* generates itself. For in the names of characters, the tradition virtually interprets itself. We have examined at length the etymological uses of Jāziya in the North African narrative. Another example might be culled from the Beirut edition of *Taghrībat Banī Hilāl.*

Book XV of this 26-part edition begins the culmination of the long saga. In it, Diyāb spears the Zanātī Khalīfa in the eye and kills him. This event marks the turning point in the conflict which generates the tale; for in Books XV–XXII, the Hilālī heroes gain the upper hand over their Berber enemy only to turn one against the other in civil wars and fratricidal struggles that will destroy the tribe in the end. Diyāb claims all the West for his alone and in his greed for power kills Prince Ḥasan and then Abū Zayd himself. In the last four books of this edition, their orphans wreak vengeance and succeed to the thrones of the West.

While this Beirut edition appears to contain a few salient rhyme puns, the appropriateness of the name of the character who is featured at the beginning of Book XV (and the turning point in the narrative where the threat to the tribe will no longer be from without, but from within) is striking. Book XV features Fitna, the daughter of Qāḍī Budayr. The word *fitna* means chaos, civil war, strife. It also means, in a more primary sense, allurement or political sedition. By metaphorical extension, *fitna* can mean woman—a femme fatale, a devastatingly alluring woman whose beauty will turn a man to chaotic frenzy.[79] The narrator's use of Fitna to open the beginning of the end of the Hilālī saga provides its own gloss, its own suggestive concatenation of meaning, its own "musical metaphor" to the informed reader. Even minor characters like Fitna function as puns in this way, while the names of major characters symbolically subsume the larger themes of the long tale. The play on Abū Zayd as father of provision or food or increase, which both the Egyptian poet al-Sayyid al-Ḍūwī and the Nigerian Iesiye muʿallim work extensively, for example, is a key to this saga of famine and fertility seeking. Abū Zayd's own father's name is Rizq, meaning sustenance and livelihood.

Khaḍrā, his mother, stands for verdant greenness and fertility. This name echoes through the tale, as the Hilālī tribe seeks its lost verdure, for Khaḍrā is also the name of the servant who informs the Zanātī princess about the Hilālī hero with whom she falls in love, and it is the name of Diyāb's mare. The green paradise to which the tribe migrates and over which the Hilālī heroes struggle with each other for control is Tūnis al-Khaḍrā. The name of the tribe itself is Hilāl, the crescent that appears symbolically in the silver tokens worn by Bedouin women and monthly in the form of the new moon. Their westward migration, in the term *taghrība,* connotes a separation or banishment and exile from their native lands to the westward world (al-maghrib) of oddities and strangers and foreigners (*gharīb*) which is also the place of the setting sun (*maghrib* also means sunset), wherein dwell the blacks or crows (*ghurāb*). Diyāb b. Ghānim, the wolf who is the herdsman, is the son of Ghānim whose name means successful and connotes in its root derivations spoils, loot, booty, and sheep, goats, and small cattle as well as herdsman. I could go on at length enumerating name puns of character and place and how they act to gloss the narrative and to coalesce meaning, but those indicated should suffice to suggest the mechanism.[80]

*Sīrat Banī Hilāl* communicates the ways of the Hilālī tribe, and that way is the way of preserving the memory of the past in song; it is the way of poetry, music, and sound play and rhymes, the way of wordplay and hidden intent communicated through ritual entertainment that dramatizes and reenacts symbolically communal relationships and gives voice to the anomalies of collective experience. Bynum has suggested that the transmitting oral poet is in a parasitic relationship with the self-generating tradition.[81] I should like to suggest rather that the poet and tradition form a symbiotic relationship. The living tradition transmitted through the generations indeed gives life as it lives on in performers' performances; the poet's figural interpretation of story and history carries a philosophy that enhances life and makes it bearable. The durable multiplicity of meaning transmitted in the *Hilāliyya* provides, as the nineteenth-century compilers tell us in their introductions to the printed editions, relief and laughter, relaxation and pleasure, edification and enlightenment in the subversive perception and the subversive genealogy it conveys.

The living way (sīra) contains a bite. The oral way of knowing and composing eludes the learned. As al-Ḥillī reminded us long ago and as the Egyptian shāʿir teaches us today, it renders the high and the mighty purveyors of literate discourse impotent. The mawwāl, which shares its stanzaic structure with the oral, the *Hilāliyya,* and the literate genres deriving from the popular genres (the muwashshaḥa and maqāma are the most striking cases in point), have long had a counterculture thrust. Rarely has the voice of the outsider, the stranger, the commoner entered into literate, written Arabic formal discourse. Only in the muwashshaḥa's stanzaic form and its closing *kharja* in the colloquial language of a woman does the voice of the commoner enter the "pure" language of writing;[82] only in the maqāma does the picaresque of story fiction begin to enter Arabic letters. Written versions of the various siyar, the zajal, the kharjas, and the maqāma exist on the cutting edge between the oral folk culture and the literate educated culture of the power elite. In their various ways, all address the ongoing cultural dialogue that Jāḥiẓ articulated in the polite tradition of letters—the dialogue of the relationships of the peoples of Islam, the strangers and clients, the races, the colors, the tongues, the speech, and the poetries.

Although the verse forms and concerns of the shāʿir and the oral folk culture for which he speaks have occasionally slipped over into literate discourse, for the most part the oral art, craft, and aesthetic have escaped the literate Arab elite, represented in the sīra by the obtuse teacher. This is no less true for the foreign scholar and for the learned world of criticism which has invented the concept of "oral literature," a self-evident contradiction in terms, the coiners of which can only be so literate as to fear the potential invidiousness of calling it, perhaps more aptly, "illiterature."

We have seen how the critic of the sīra and the oral poetry collector as well have often misunderstood and obscured the text by their very literate inability to *hear* the artistry and musicality of what is essentially a performance genre. The "romance" of the oral bard and the new powers attributed to him as a virtual mystique by contemporary oral literature scholars is such as to potentially obscure the experience of an oral poetry and an oral culture's performance tradition. If I had discounted "city" poets like Shamandī and the much less famous Fārūq in my quest for a "pure," rural, spontaneous tradition, I would have ignored the way in which Egyptian epic tradition evolves, the way in which fame and a new audience can affect a poet's very performance. I would have ignored much suggestive data as to why a poet may "forget" the tradition, for many of the poets Abnoudy brought to Cairo or recorded in the country have since given up the epic for more lucrative and easier popular tunes and dance ditties. If I had discounted Abnoudy in my pursuit of "pure" oral poetry by illiterate poets in the country, the model of epic transmission which appears on the margins between oral and written cultures would never have emerged. To ignore Abnoudy and his work of propagating the epic would have been to ignore the potential pathway of the oral into the written. Indeed, Homer and Turold may well have been men like Abnoudy, very literate audience members and patrons of the poets who became, in turn, poets in their own right using the oral bard's poetic language as the vehicle for their written versions. Whether this comparative speculation is true or not, I do not know for certain; but certainly, the oral literature scholar must not fear the possibility of investigating the idea in his quest for a "pure" tradition "uncontaminated" by writing. The oral literature scholar's own categorical discriminations can become too rigidly imperative, even though the name of his discipline contains its own gloss.

Perhaps, however, we are wrong in our criticism of the illogicality of the classicists' and comparatists' term "oral literature."[83] For the oxymoron of the term contains a suggestive anomaly for the unraveling. The margins of orality and literacy in Arabo-Muslim culture, as we have learned again and again, are fuzzy. Scholars who separate the oral and the written too rigidly fall prey to the easy, false dichotomizations of our own logical categories. In the case of Arabic oral traditional culture, these scholarly categorizations can obscure the much more important issue: the ongoing Arabo-Muslim cultural polemic that surrounds the proper relationship of lived human orality and human speech discourse to a source of authority in letters.[84] For the relationship of "oral" and "written" is itself part of the cultural polemic that divides the educated elites and the uneducated masses in Arab societies.

Both the literate and the oral worlds have a stake (albeit a very different one) in the relationship of orality to literacy. Oral traditional performed narrative in Egypt today appears as the "scripture" of the oral culture (i.e., the people who make up the vast majority of the population and who do not read or write). Abū Zayd does not need the teacher's alphabet or the high culture's texts. He and his world have their own "letters" and "texts" in their oral traditions and in their innate powers of oral rhyming. They have their oral Koran, their oral poetry and song and music, their oral biographies, their chains of authority and truth which connect them with the memory of their past. Abū Zayd's oral traditional way of narration performs the same kind of function as writing in literate cultures: it preserves in its oral formulas (or "keys" in Arabic) and figures of speech certain truths for the collectivity; it gains a kind of permanence which is like that of written language. It passes on a revived wisdom "inscribed" as a kind of record in the memory of specialized, talented creators (the shāʿir) and transmitters (the rāwī) who at once create, learn, and preserve that record. The ancient Arabs, in fact, called poetry "dīwān al-ʿArab"—the record of the Arabs. In the culture, the shāʿir represents a kind of intuitive, creative, inspired knowledge in performance, while the rāwī, in his repetitions and transmissions, represents the letter (or rhyme) of the tradition.

Within its own culture, then, traditionally performed narrative has the status of writing. And indeed, in the Egyptian case, the authority of oral narrative may be seen to compete with the authority of written texts of the high tradition. In Egypt, as we have learned in this investigation, narrative had traditionally offered the majority of Egyptian nonlettered peasants their own Truth, their own History and Biography in a text that for them parallels the sacred scripture of the Holy Koran.

The early Arab folklorist, collector, and commentator al-Ḥillī (quoted above), paraphrased the difficulty the literate have in conceiving of the oral poet's technique of poesis so well: we gasp but cannot swallow, we grapple but cannot grasp. The Egyptian rabāb poets, too, showed how the literate teacher did not "get" it, how he missed true, innate knowledge. The adīb and oral literature scholar alike have great difficulty grasping and conceiving the world of vernacular rhyme. Yet preliterate children do it so easily. The oral culture, in which the Egyptian shāʿir's performance represents an epitome of speech (along with the orally recited Koran), is a fully adult world founded on an innate human talent of oral-language learning and generating.[85]

Although "oral literature" has proved to be "an identifiable way of using language,"[86] many of the categorical boundaries scholars set up in their efforts to define it break down in face of the Egyptian shāʿir's performance. Scholes and Kellogg,[87] for example, have implied that ironic distance belongs almost exclusively to written discourse and is not part of the oral mode. The truth contained in the Egyptian Abū Zayd epic contains, however, a large irony in its disjunctive perceptions. The poet's use of his listeners' etymological knowledge is not only effective but also efficient (both argumentatively and morally) in the way it points out ironic disparities lived by both poet and patron.

Numerous other scholars who speculate about the relationship of literacy and mind suggest that logic depends on writing, at least for its codification and systematization. As Rader puts it, writing freezes language so that deductive operations can be made. The essayist, she says, is the active reasoner who consciously uses grammatical and lexically complex, explicit language. Rader and others imply, following Goody's early work, that syllogistic reasoning is the cutting edge that discriminates between the oral and the written.[88] I doubt the usefulness of this index, for the shāʿir's disjunctive logic certainly contains three premises causally interconnected, even though most of such poetic argumentation resorts to a certain limited number of major premises. Perelman separates quasi-logical reasoning (i.e., syllogistic reasoning), which works through association, from dissociative reasoning, which works by breaking associative links. Dissociative reasoning in Perelman's treatise is a very difficult mode of argumentation which pertains specifically to written texts; this rhetorical theorist and legal philosopher rules out oral discourse from his data base. Dissociative argumentation, as he describes it, works much in the manner of the shāʿir's logic: it contrasts philosophical pairs of the real and the ideal to derive a new insight.[89]

I have suggested that the "logic" and intentionality of the oral traditional epic performer-composer reside in such manipulation of the tradition's figures of speech and argumentative tropes. The complex ideational and argumentative structure of the pun, of large-scale chiasmus, and other figures of speech that the poet uses all serve to pack ideas into single words, or formulaic phrase units, much in the way written language does. Chaffe[90] maintains that, indeed, traditional, ritual narrative partakes of the more literate and literary mode; he argues that the oral performer-composer is like the writer, detached from his audience rather than directly involved—interacting with them in the way speakers do in ordinary spoken communication.

Chaffe's index of detachment versus involvement is an interesting one, and one that suggested itself in our observation of the Egyptian oral epic poets' performance, where both involvement and detachment are relative. Even with such an active involvement as one finds between poet and patron in Egypt, the performer is in many ways detached both by the necessity of his narrative story line and by the separation his musical mode affords the situation. The performer-composer is detached from his listeners in communication with the tradition that generates his discourse, probably in an "alerted state of consciousness," much in the way Jaynes describes the oral bard. Even the audience involvement is relative, because the listener is pulled into the traditional mode in his ritually agonistic and interactional response to the poet's insults. The performance, as a special event that takes place in a formal ceremonial situation, detaches its participants (both gypsy poet and peasant-farmer patron) from the way they behave toward each other in everyday social intercourse. In their participation in ritualized wordplay, the members of the community override differences, and, as I have suggested, see themselves.[91]

While Chaffe's detachment-involvement scale is useful, perhaps a more significant index of difference between oral reasoning or knowing and the written is one proposed by the sīra tradition itself: linear versus nonlinear or cyclical thought. Just as the poet's metonymies demonstrate a spiraling interconnectedness of the inside and the outside, just as his episodic art permits prior contexts and meanings to penetrate subsequent ones, so too his chiastic structures link narrative events in a kind of paralleling ring-interconnection of prior and subsequent event. The shāʿir's and the oral culture's way of knowing and memory is in the moment, in the transaction of the moment, in the doing, and in the living experience, rather than in any abstraction of the mind into the future or the past. This connectedness of past, present, and future (as Baker, extrapolating from Laroui, astutely points out) is implicit in the Arabic verbal tense, which abolishes and distends time and space into a future anterior; to quote Baker, time and space partake of an intangible flexibility wherein

> infinite space is translated into terms of timelessness. . . . Time seems to extend in all directions like desert horizons, so that events do not take place on a point in linear time but rather within view of any chosen direction. Only if a past event becomes distinguished such that it becomes a landmark in memory does it remain, like a mountain or a campfire showing at night from afar, part of the environment of the present. The actual distance of an event as measured in time or space is difficult to judge with accuracy. Its prominence depends more on the size it may appear to have, as seen in perspective across the wastes and through the clear desert air.[92]

The Hilālī narrators and the oral mind telescope the centuries of Islamic history into an emotionally perceived immediate experience of the immediate past. As Baker demonstrates from the Tunisian case, anything close to the immediate, be it actual fact or intent or desire, is embraced as the "present."[93]

The aḍdād of the Egyptian shāʿir's puns similarly reduce difference in a nonlinear, circularity of meaning. Homonyms become antonyms. A word means what it means, but it also can signify its opposite just as the past signifies the present and the present the past; just as the episode signifies the whole tale, and the shāʿir's oral discourse signifies the "Book," and the book (yellow book) signifies the oral ceremonial event of communal recitation-performance. In a spiraling breakdown of categorical boundaries and their implicit social, political, and perceptual imperatives, the oral (or illiterate) becomes the literate (even the model of all literate discourse, as in the case of the Koran and pre-Islamic oral poetry), and the literate becomes the oral (in the recitation of an orally memorized text).

Tunisian and Egyptian oral cultures thus stress the connectedness of things, the connectedness and relatedness in emotional and psychological terms of the past, present, and future; of the male and the female worlds; of the private and the public; the familiar and the foreign—all of these are what the poet's metonyms view as a dialectic of the outside and the inside. The oral culture perceives of life as a continuum; the child's world and the adult's world are not so vastly separated, nor are the rational and the irrational. Gilligan[94] has recently called this kind of knowing the female way—which is not goal and object oriented, but focused on connectedness and relationships. Certainly in our own culture in the twentieth-century United States this may be true. We frequently contrast the *seeming* openness, freeness, and egalitarianism of relationships between the sexes in our culture with the *seeming* sexual seclusion and discrimination between male and female in Arab culture. I would suggest that the observable difference of customs arises out of the difference in the ways the two cultures deal with sexual ambivalence and the fear men and women have of becoming the other sex and thus losing their own gender identity.[95] What Gilligan suggests as a female moral developmental pattern differentiated from the male model in fact may not be universal, but culture specific. There is a very real divide between male and female in American society which Gilligan has pointed out as the divide between relationships (female) versus goals (male), the concrete (female) versus the abstract (male), the real (female) versus the ideal (male). American culture compensates for this very real moral divide between the sexes through an apparent familiarity of social sexual relations. Middle Eastern oral traditional cultures by and large have no such divide. Rather the whole culture is focused on a moral of relationships and connectedness grounded in present experience. Sexual ambivalence and differentiation thereby become translated and projected into extreme dichotomies of the male universe and the female universe[96] because in fact male and female in Arabo-Muslim societies are so closely identified in the moral, developmental sense.

The sīra as a genre takes up the divides, the rifts and separations, perceived by the folk culture. Preoccupation with male-female power differentials emerges as a major theme. Many of the siyar deal overtly, as does the *Hilāliyya,* with the anomaly of female power versus female powerlessness. The Hilālī heroine Jāziya is not alone to don male battle garb and lead the troops in battle. The princess Dhāt al-Himma has an entire sīra devoted to her Amazonian exploits. The strict categories and sexual dichotomies of Arabo-Muslim society, wherein female seclusion is supposed to be observed or is in fact observed, do not reflect the emotional reality of experience.[97]

Just as the sīra concerns the ways of human maturation and its implicit conflicts, it also concerns the ways of primary mind process. Only in a hyperrational world such as our Western scientizing, literate, scholarly one could such confusion and theorizing as to the nature and processes of oral composition take place.[98] Our attempts to understand the oral culture in the florescence of "oral literature" studies of the past decades bespeak an attempt to understand ourselves—the part denied and suppressed within as an irrational, intuitive child rather than a creative force; the part neglected and disdained without as the "inferior" culture of the folk, or popular culture, or culture of children, women, blacks, and slaves. This other that we seek in the child, the woman, the peasant, and the folk is within all of us—the intuitive creativity and knowledge of the world of Abū Zayd.

This is the message of the sīra. In the Egyptian performance tradition of the *Hilāliyya* this message becomes socially enacted. The reader of this study of the *Hilāliyya* has witnessed the gypsy poet gathering interested parties to hear and understand his saga of Arabo-Muslim identity. We have participated from a distance and attempted to enter inside the rhetorical scene, which dramatizes and reenacts social difference while transcending it. The sīra is about alterity and difference. The subject it treats is coterminous with its ambivalent status in the community, with the performance genre's own "otherness." Embraced by the folk and despised by the learned, the sīra performance discriminates the levels of the community, the contained inside from the outside. Today, as in the past, foreigners come to collect the sīra and write it down. The stranger and foreigner, as literate, female, Christian outsider, comes to the male, Muslim, oral *Hilāliyya* to learn the ways of sīra poetry, and, in a recapitulation of the anomalous message of the medium, becomes part of the rhetorical scene, part of the group of divided brethren. What an outsider can learn in the scholarly endeavor, as Okpewho has pointed out,[99] is always a mass of words, of impressions. Even though the learned outsider often thinks he understands better than the insider, his is always a partial knowledge, one that misses so very much of the full range of the emotional connotation. Perhaps the shāʿir's rabāb teaches the outsider better in its direct power to move and to sway through its musical metaphor. For today the gypsy's audience has expanded beyond the contained in-group of the Upper Egyptian village to include formerly excluded local urban intellectuals as well as foreign scholars from Italy, France, the United States, Saudi Arabia, Tunisia, and the world. To quote Shamandī once more, "from all over they come to the rabāba and bend to it." Such has been our effort: to bend to it, to hear and to understand from the inside while remaining an outsider.

# NOTES

## 1: In Defense of *al-Sīra*

1. Norman T. Burns and Christopher J. Reagan, eds., *Concepts of the Hero in the Middle Ages and the Renaissance,* Papers presented at the Fourth and Fifth Annual Conference of the Center of Medieval and Early Renaissance Studies, State University of New York, Binghamton, May 1970 and May 1971 (Albany: State University of New York Press, 1975), pp. 83–100.

2. Ibid., p. 84. See also R. Nicholson, *A Literary History of the Arabs* (Cambridge: Cambridge University Press, 1962), p. 325.

3. Mūsá Sulaymān, *al-Adab al-Qiṣaṣī ʿinda al-ʿArab* (Beirut, 1956), p. 82. Cf. Giovanni Canova, "Gli Studi sull'epica popolare araba," *Oriente Moderno* (1977), p. 213.

4. Reported in *Tazyīn al-Aswāq* by Dawūd al-Anṭakī (Būlāq, 1279), p. 55. See Canard, on *Dhū'l-Himma, Encyclopaedia of Islam* 2, p. 238, a sīra whose historical period dates from ca. A.D. 863, composed in a spirit of hostility to the Crusaders. On the variety of spellings and genders conventionally used to refer to the title of this epic, see Edward Lane, *Manners and Customs of the Modern Egyptians* (1860; repr. with preface and notes by Stanley Poole [New York: Dutton, 1954]), p. 420.

5. Ṭāhā Ḥusayn, *al-Ayyām* (Cairo, 1929), pp. 21, 83.

6. M. Villoteau, "Etat moderne de l'etat actuel de l'art musical en Egypte," in *Description de l'Egypte,* Vol. XIV (Paris: Imprimerie Panckoucke, 1826), pp. 228–234.

7. A. de Lamartine, *Voyage en Orient* (Brussels, 1835). The Appendix of this work contains a translation of some of the songs of ʿAntar that Lamartine heard during his voyages. See also "ʿAntar," in his *Vie des grands hommes,* vol. I (Paris, 1859), pp. 267–345.

8. Wilfred Scawen Blunt and Anne Blunt, *The Romance of the Stealing of the Mare* (London: Reeves and Trubner, 1892). See the prefatory comments.

9. A. Vaissière, "Cycle héroïque des Ouled-Hilāl," in *Revue africaine* 36 (1892):242–243, 312–324; J. Desparmet, "Les Chansons de geste de 1830 à 1914 dans la Mitidja," in *Revue africaine* 83 (1939):192–226; V. Largeau, *Flore saharienne* (Geneva, 1879); M. L. Guin, *Rouba, légende arabe* (Oran, 1884), 28 pp.

10. Jacques Berque, *Histoire sociale d'un village égyptien* (Paris and The Hague, 1957), pp. 60–67, 12–16.

11. Villoteau, pp. 229, 231–232.

12. Lane, *Manners and Customs of the Modern Egyptians,* chaps. 21–23.

13. ʿAbdel-Meguid, "A Survey of the Terms Used in Arabic for 'Narrative' and 'Story,'" *Islamic Quarterly* I (1954); and "A Survey of Story Literature in Arabic from before Islam to the Middle of the Nineteenth Century," ibid., pp. 104–113.

14. A. Bel, "La Djazya, chanson arabe," *Journal asiatique* XIX, ser. 9 (1902):289–347, XX (1902):169–236; I, ser. 10 (1903):311–366; and J. Desparmet, "Les Chansons de geste de 1830 à 1914 dans la Mitidja," *Revue africaine* 83 (1939):192–226.

15. M. Marzūqī, *al-Shiʿr al-Shaʿbī* (1971); *al-Adab al-Shaʿbī* (1969); M. Masmoudi, *La Peinture sous-verre en Tunisie* (CERES, 1972); "Une Peinture sous-verre à thème héroïque," *Cahiers des arts et traditions populaires,* no. 2 (Tunis, 1968); "Deux autres peintures sous-verre à thème héroïque," ibid., no. 3 (1969).

16. H. R. Palmer, preface, in J. R. Patterson, *The Stories of Abū Zeid the Hilālī in Shuwa Arabic* (London: Kegan, Trench, Trubner, 1930).

17. C. Pellat, "Ḥikāya," in *Encyclopaedia of Islam* 2, p. 372.

18. Russell Davis and Brent Ashebranner, *Ten Thousand Desert Swords* (Boston: Little, Brown, 1960).

19. G. Canova, paper delivered at the Round Table Symposium on the *Hilāliyya,* Hammamet, Tunisia, 1980.

20. Data concerning the fḍāwī in Protectorate Tunisia derives from conversations with M. Marzūqī, M. Masmoudi, and Hashmī Saʿāda. On the fḍāwī today, see Anita Baker, "The Hilālī Saga in the Tunisian South," Ph.D. diss., University of Indiana, 1978.

See a color illustration of a Tunisian folk poet reciting for a family in *National Geographic* (April 1929), p. 415.

21. Canard, "Dhū'l-Himma," in *Encyclopaedia of Islam* 2, p. 238; Ibn al-Nadīm, *Fihrist,* pp. 300ff.

22. G. Levi della Vida, *Elenco dei Manoscritti Arabi Islamici della Biblioteca Vaticana, Studi e Testi* 67, Codici Barberiniani Orientali, no. 15 (The Vatican, 1935), p. 240.

23. I do not use the term Middle Arabic in Blau's historical sense, rather, I use the term in much the manner it appears in Arabic. Salih J. Altoma refers to the "middle language" (al-lugha al-wusṭá) as the term used for a "variety of intermediary Arabic," which is "the result of Classical and colloquial fusion." See *The Problems of Diglossia in Arabic* (Cambridge: Harvard University Press, 1969), p. 4. According to the folklorist Saad Sowayan, *al-lugha bayn al-bayn* refers to the language that is neither *fuṣḥá* (literary) nor *ʿāmmiyya* (colloquial). Blau, too, seemed content to use the term "Middle Arabic" for the language of the written versions of the siyar when he directed my studies in a reading course on that idiom at Berkeley during the late 1960s. On Middle Arabic linguistic features, see Jacob Blau, *The Emergence and Linguistic Background of Judaeo-*

*Arabic: A Study of the Origins of Middle Arabic* (Oxford: Oxford University Press, 1965).

24. Von Grunebaum states quite succinctly the traditional Western view of the Arabic literary aesthetic in "Growth and Structure of Arabic Poetry, A.D. 500–1000," in *The Arab Heritage,* ed. N. A. Faris (Princeton: Princeton University Press, 1944), pp. 121–142. See also H. A. R. Gibb, *Arabic Literature* (Oxford: Oxford University Press, 1968).

25. See Howard Bloch, *Etymologies and Genealogies* (Chicago: University of Chicago Press, 1983).

26. See Eric A. Havelock, *Preface to Plato* (Cambridge: Harvard University Press, 1963).

27. Max Weber, "Religious Rejections of the World and Their Directions," in *Max Weber,* eds. Geerth and Mills; originally "Zwischenbetrachtung," *Gesammelte Aufsaetze zur Religionssoziologie,* vol. I (Nov. 1915), pp. 436–473, in *Archiv.*

28. Ṭāhā Ḥusayn, *Fī al-Adab al-Jāhilī* (Cairo, 1927), see esp. p. 63.

29. See Charles Pellat, *Le Milieu Basrien et la formation de Jahiz* (Paris: Maisonnueve, 1953); Régis Blachère, *Histoire de la littérature arabe* (Paris: Maisonnueve, 1963); Michael N. Zwettler, *The Oral Tradition of Classical Arabic Poetry* (Columbus: The Ohio State University Press, 1978).

30. A. Bausani, "Elementi epici nelle letterature islamiche," in *Atti del convegno: La poesia epica e la sua formazione* (Rome: Accademia dei Lincei, 1970), pp. 759–769; Giovanni Canova, *Egitto: Epica,* record with notes published and produced by *I Suoni, Musica di tradizione orale* (1982), p. 2.

31. Ibn al-Nadīm, cited in Nicholson, *A Literary History,* pp. 457–458. *Fihrist,* p. 304.

32. Ibn Khaldūn, *al-Muqaddima* (Beirut: Dār al-Kitāb al-Lubnānī, 1967), p. 1126; for a translation, see Franz Rosenthal, *The Muqaddimah: An Introduction to History,* 3 vols. (New York: Bollingen, Pantheon Books, 1958), Bk. III, pp. 414–415.

33. G. Canova, "Gli Studi sull'epica popolare araba," *Oriente Moderno* 57, nos. 5–6 (1977):213; Gaston Wiet, *Introduction a la littérature arabe* (Paris, 1966), p. 103; Ghālī Shukrī, *Adab al-Muqāwama* (Cairo, 1970), p. 53; Henri Perès, "Le Roman dans la littérature arabe," *AIEO* XVI (1958):33.

34. Canard, *Encyclopaedia of Islam,* 2, p. 238.

35. Kristina Nelson, "The Art of Reciting the Qur'ān," Ph.D. diss., University of California, 1980, pp. 22–23, 20–28.

36. Michael Meeker has suggested to me that Early Islam (seventh century) proposes a distinctive oral/written canon that places a specific value on the relationship of personal speech and acts to a scriptural code revealed by God. See Meeker's *Literature and Violence in North Arabia* (New York: Cambridge University Press, 1979), in which he argues that a notion of "writing" somewhat reminiscent of the concept of a sacred writing in Islam is to be found in the stories of poems of the "illiterate" Bedouins. For an admirable early elucidation of the relationship of the Qur'ān to Arabic literature and to the history of the

Arabic book, see Johannes Pedersen, *The Arabic Book,* trans. Geoffrey French (Princeton: Princeton University Press, 1984; originally published in Copenhagen, 1946). See also Kristina Nelson's discussion of the Revelation and its inscription on the tablets in heaven, and A. S. Tritton, "The Speech of God," *Studia Islamica* 36 (1972):5–22.

37. James Robson, ed. and trans., *Tracts on Listening to Music* (London: The Royal Asiatic Society, 1938), pp. 1–4.

38. H. G. Farmer, *Music: The Priceless Jewel,* from *Kitāb al-ʿIqd al-Farīd* of Ibn ʿAbd Rabbihi (Bearsden, Scotland: Issued by the author, 1942), pp. 16–17.

39. Ibid.

40. See esp. A. Guillaume, *The Life of Mohammad,* trans. of Ibn Hisham's *al-Sīra al-Nabawiyya.* See also F. Krenrow, "Shāʿir," *Encyclopaedia of Islam* 2, p. 286.

41. Ghālī Shukrī, p. 54. See also A. S. Tritton, "Shayṭān," in *Encyclopaedia of Islam* 2, p. 374; and J. T. Monroe's translation and introduction to *Ibn Shuhaid's Treatise on Familiar Spirits and Demons* (Berkeley, Los Angeles, London: University of California Press, 1971).

42. On diglossia, see Charles A. Ferguson, "Diglossia," *Word* 15 (1959):325–340; and Salih J. Altoma, *The Problem of Diglossia in Arabic: A Comparative Study of Classical and Iraqi Arabic* (Cambridge: Harvard University Press, 1969).

43. S. Sowayan, "Nabati Poetry: the Oral Poetry of Arabia," Ph.D. diss. University of California, 1982, pp. 17–18.

44. Faiq Amin Mukhlis, "Studies and Comparisons of the Cycles of the *Banī Hilāl* Romance" Ph.D. diss., University of London, 1963–1964.

45. Hamed Ammar, *Growing Up in an Egyptian Village* (London: Routledge & Kegan Paul, 1954), pp. 61–62.

46. ʿAbd al-Laṭīf, *Abū Zayd al-Hilālī,* pp. 113–114; al-Zayyāt, *Fī Uṣūl al-'Adab* (Cairo, 1935), pp. 127–129.

47. Pierre Cachia, "Social Values Reflected in Egyptian Popular Ballads," in *Studies in Modern Arabic Literature,* ed. R. C. Ostle (Warminster: Aris & Phillips, 1975), p. 87.

48. See *Journal asiatique,* 1820–1880, for a long series of debates, publication of manuscript translations, etc.

49. Lamartine, "ʿAntar," in *Vie des grands hommes,* vol. I, pp. 267–345.

50. Lamartine, *Voyage en Orient.*

51. Bouchet, *Précis des Littératures Etrangères* (1888); Debrozy and Bachetlet, *Dictionnaire Général des Littératures* (cited by Chauvin); Vapereau, *Dictionnaire Universal de Littérature* (1876).

52. So great was the admiration and enthusiastic reception of the *Arabian Nights* that even today the average Westerner is greatly surprised to discover the disdain Arabs themselves have had for the collection of tales. See C. Knipp's excellent article, "The Arabian Nights in England," *Journal of Arabic Literature* V (1974):44–54.

53. MacDonald, "Ḥikāya," in *EI* 1, pp. 303–305; Pellat, "Ḥikāya," in *EI* 2, pp. 367–372; MacDonald, "Baybars," in *EI* 1, pp. 589–590; Paret, "Baybars," in *EI* 2, pp. 1126–1127; Schliefer, "Hilāl," in *EI* 1, pp. 306–307, and "The Saga of the Banū Hilāl," in *EI* 1, p. 387; V. Chauvin, "Abū Zaid," in *EI* 1, p. 114;

Paret, "Saif Dhī Yazan," pp. 71–73; Heller, "ᶜAntar," in *EI* 1, pp. 445–448, and "ᶜAntar," in *EI* 2, pp. 518–521; Canard, "Dhū'l-Himma," in *EI* 2; ᶜAbdel-Meguid, "A Survey of Story Literature."

54. MacDonald, "Ḥikāya," p. 305.

55. ᶜAbdel-Meguid, "A Survey of Story Literature," p. 110.

56. Paret, "Baybars," p. 1127; "Saif," p. 72.

57. Paret, "Saif," p. 72.

58. Pellat, "Ḥikāya," p. 372.

59. Ibid.

60. See esp., MacDonald, "Baybars."

61. Heller, "ᶜAntar."

62. Pellat, "Ḥikāya."

63. Schliefer, "Banū Hilāl."

64. Heller, "ᶜAntar," pp. 445–448.

65. See the recent book by Harry T. Norris, *The Adventures of ᶜAntar* (London: Aris & Phillips, 1980).

66. Abdallah Laroui, *L'Idéologie arabe contemporaine: essai critique* (Paris: Maspero, 1970), p. 175.

67. ᶜAbd al-Ḥamīd Yūnis, *Difāᶜ ᶜan al-Fulklūr* (Cairo: al-Hay'a al-Miṣriyya al ᶜĀmma lil-Kitāb, 1973).

68. Ghālī Shukrī, p. 54; see Canova, "Gli Studi," p. 213.

69. See Aḥmad Rushdī Ṣāliḥ's *al-Adab al-Shaᶜbī* [Folk Literature] (1954) and his *Funūn al-ᶜArab al-Shaᶜbiyya* [The Art of the Arab Folk] (1956) for a modern, trained folklorist's presentation of the sīra. See Canova, ibid.

70. ᶜAbd al-Ḥamīd Yūnis, *al-Hilāliyya fī al-Tārīkh wa-al-Adab* [The Hilāliyya in History and Literature].

71. G. Canova, "Gli Studi."

72. For a summary of the controversy among historians and a position on it which takes the tribal history into account, see J. Berque, "Du nouveau sur les Banī Hilāl," *Studia Islamica* 36 (1972):99–111. See also Roger Idris, "L'Invasion hilalienne et ses conséquences," *Cahiers de civilisation médiévale* 11, no. 3 (July–Sept. 1968):336–369; J. Poncet, "Le Mythe de la 'catastrophe' hilalienne," *Annales: economies, sociétés, civilisations* 22, no. 5 (Sept.–Oct. 1967):1099–1120; Claude Cahen, "Miscellanea: Quelques mots sur les Hilaliens et le nomadisme," *Journal de l'histoire économique et sociale d'Orient* 11 (March 1968):130–133; J. Poncet, "Polémiques et controverses: Encore à propos des Hilaliens, la 'Mise au point' de R. Idris," *Annales* 23, no. 3 (May–June 1968):660–662. Ibn Khaldūn, *Kitāb Tārīkh al-Duwal al-Islāmiyya bi-al-Maghrib* [Histoire des Berbères], ed. de Slane, t. I (1847), pp. 16ff.; and de Slane translation, t. I (1925), pp. 28ff. (ed. P. Casanova, 4 vols., 1925, 1968–1969[2] [Paris: Geuthner]).

2: *Sīrat Banī Hilāl,* a Decayed Epic?

1. "Contemporary Arab Poetry, Bedouin and Urban," in *The Muqaddimah: An Introduction to History,* trans. Franz Rosenthal, 3 vols. (New York: Bollingen, Pantheon Books, 1958), Bk. III, pp. 414–415.

2. Wilhelm Ahlwardt, *Die Handschriftenverzeichnisse der Königlichen Bibliothek zu Berlin* VIII, Bk. 20 (Berlin, 1896), pp. 155–462. Martin Hartmann gives a complete listing of various catalogs containing references to Banī Hilāl manuscripts (e.g., Bibliotheca Lindesiana, Trubner, Perthes, Brill, Harrassowitz, Hommer, Pertsch, Ellis) in "Die Banī-Hilāl Geschichten," *Zeitschrift für afrikanische und oceanische Sprachen,* IV Jahrgang (Berlin, 1898), pp. 289–315, esp. pp. 289–290.

3. A. Ayoub, "A propos des manuscrits de la geste des Banū Hilāl conservés à Berlin," *Actes du 2e Congrès International d'Études des Cultures de la Méditérannée Occidentale* II (Algiers: SNED, 1978), pp. 347–363.

4. M. Galley, "Manuscrits et documents relatifs à la geste Hilalienne dans les bibliothèques anglaises," *Bulletin de la littérature orale arabo-berbère* 12 (1981), E.R.A. 357-CNRS, pp. 183–192. See esp., A. Mingana, *Catalogue of the Arabic Manuscripts in the John Rylands Library at Manchester* (Manchester: Manchester University Press, 1934), pp. 866ff.; and Charles Rieu, ed., *Supplement to the Catalogue of the Arabic Manuscripts in the British Museum* II (London, 1894), pp. 745–748.

5. See A. Mansūr, *Fihrist Makhṭūṭat al-Maktaba al-Aḥmadiyya bi-Tūnis* (Beirut: Dār al-Fatḥ, 1969), MSS 5012 and 5013. A critical edition and English translation of the Tūnis manuscript is currently being prepared by Ayoub in collaboration with D. Reynolds.

6. See *Fihrist al-Kutub al-ʿarabiyya al-Mawjūda bi-Dār al-Kutub* (Cairo, 1924).

7. ʿAlī Abā Ḥusayn, *Index of Bahrain Manuscripts,* Vol. I (Beirut, 1977), pp. 253–255.

8. London, 1894, pp. 638ff., cited in Hartmann, p. 290; see also Alexander Falton and A. G. Ellis, eds., *Supplement to the Catalogue of Arabic Printed Books in the British Museum* (1926), pp. 420–421.

9. Karl Brockelmann (Leipzig, 1909), p. 74, Buch 3, 2.2; Victor Chauvin (Liège, 1892–1922), pp. 127ff.

10. F. Mukhlis, "Studies and Comparison of the Cycles of the Banī Hilāl Romance," Ph.D diss., University of London, 1964.

11. J. Schliefer, "The Saga of the Banū Hilāl," in *EI* 1, pp. 306–307, and *EI* 2, p. 387; and Hartmann, pp. 289–315.

12. Claude Breteau, Micheline Galley, Arlette Roth, "La Longue marche hilalienne," *Actes du 2e Congrès International d'Études des Cultures de la Méditérranée Occidentale* II (Algiers: SNED, 1978):334–346.

13. Laurent Charles Féraud, *Kitab el-Adouani* (Algiers and Paris, 1868); M. L. Guin, *Rouba, légende arabe* (Oran, 1884), 28 pp.; V. Largeau, *Flore saharienne, histoire et légendes traduites de l'arabe* (1879), pp. 129ff.; M. Rahhal, "A travers les Beni Snassen," *Bulletin de la Société de Géographie d'Oran* IX (1889):5–50; A. Vaissière, "Les Ouled Rechaich," *Revue africaine* (Algiers, 1892), pp. 209–243; H. Stumme, *Tripolitanisch-Tunische Beduinenlieder* (Leipzig, 1894), p. 107; A. Bel, "La Djazya, chanson arabe" *Journal asiatique,* XIX, ser. 9 (1902):289–347, XX (1902):169–236, and I, ser. 10 (1903):311–366; Col. del Lartigue, *Monographie de l'Aurès* (Constantine, 1904), pp. 291–305; Dr. Provotelle, *Etude sur la Tamazirt ou Zenatia de Qalaat es-Sened* (Paris, 1911), pp. 89–95;

V. Loubignac, *Etude sur le dialecte des Zaïan et des Aït Sgougou* (Paris, 1924), pp. 294–297, 346–347; H. Carbou, *L'arabe parlé au Ouadai et à l'est du Tchad* (Paris: Geuthner, 1913); J. R. Patterson and R. G. Butcher, *Stories of Abū Zeid the Hilālī* (London: Kegan, Trench, Trubner and Co., 1930); M. Paollilo, *Contes et légendes de Tunisie* (Paris: Nathan, n.d.); G. Boris, *Documents linguistiques et éthnographiques sur une région du sud tunisien* (Nefzaoua) (Paris: Maisonnueve, 1951); R. Capot-Rey, *Sahara français* (P.U.F., 1953); L. Saada, "Documents sonores tunisiens concernant la geste des Banū Hilāl," *Actes du 2e Congrès International d'Etudes des Cultures de la Méditérranée Occidentale* II (Algiers: SNED, 1978); Anita Baker, *The Hilālī Saga in the Tunisian South* (Ann Arbor: University Microfilms, 1978); A. Ayoub and M. Galley, *Versions hilaliennes de Tunisie* (Paris: Classiques Africaines, 1983). I understand Baker's tapes are available at the Indiana University Folklore Archive. A. Ayoub, "Aspects évolutifs dans les versions hilaliennes de Jordanie," *Cahiers des arts et traditions populaires* (Tunis, in press); "Poème Hilalien de Dyab le Libyen," *Majallat Kulliyyat al-Tarbiyya* (Tripoli, 1979); Giovanni Canova, *Egitto: Epica,* I Suoni, 1982 sound recording.

14. René Basset, "Un épisode d'une chanson de geste arabe," *Bull. de Correspondence Africaine* III, 1885, pp. 136–148.

15. Basset refers to this poem as *Rouba, légende arabe* (Oran), p. 135.

16. Geneva, 1879, pp. 189ff.; as cited by Basset.

17. Basset, "Un épisode," p. 138, fn.

18. Bel, "La Djazya, chanson arabe," in *JA* XIX, ser. 9, pp. 289–314; XX, pp. 169–236; I, ser. 10, pp. 311–366 (1902–1903).

19. A. Vaissière, "Cycle héroïque des Ouled-Hilāl," in *Revue africaine* 36 (1892):242–243, 312–324. See esp. Bel, pp. 289–290.

20. Martin Hartmann, "Die Banī-Hilāl Geschichten," in *Zeitschrift für afrikanische und oceanische Sprachen,* IV Jahrgang (Berlin, 1898), pp. 289–315. See also Hartmann's *Lieder der Libyschen Wüste: Die Quellen und die Texte, nebst einem Exkurse über die bedeutenderen Beduinenstamme des westlichen Unteräegypten.* (Leipzig, 1899).

21. Edition Ibrāhīm Ṣādir at the Maṭbaʿa al-Lubnāniyya, 1872–1887.

22. Hartmann, pp. 289–290.

23. Ibid., pp. 310–312.

24. Karel Petráček, "Die Poesie als Kriterium des arabischen 'Volksromans,'" *Oriens* 23–24 (1970–1971):301–305. Svetozar Pantuček, *Das Epos über den Westzug der Banū Hilāl* (Prague: Academia Publishing House of the Czechoslovak Academy of Sciences, 1970), vol. 27. D. Onaeva, "K Karakteristike Struktury 'Sirat Bani Gilal,'" ["On the Structural Characteristics of Sīrat Banī Hilāl"], in *Voprosy vostochnogo literaturovedeniia i tekstologii, M.* (1975), pp. 3–16.

25. Pantuček, p. 67.

26. J. W. MacKail, *Lectures on Poetry* (London: Longmans, Green & Co., 1911), pp. 123–153.

27. C. M. Bowra, *Heroic Poetry* (London: Macmillan, 1952). On the Hilāliyya, see pp. 35, 49, 59, 101, 144, 194, 195, 201, 202, 274, 275, 493.

28. Wilfred Blunt and Anne Blunt, *The Romance of the Stealing of the Mare* (London: Reeves and Trubner, 1892).

29. Martin Hartmann also wondered where the Blunts obtained their text and he suggests in a footnote to his 1898 article (fn. pp. 289–290) that they translated from a printed edition that was already in the British Museum Oriental collection. Through the number he cites (no. 14570a.6), I was easily able to trace the volume, which turned out to be an 1865 Cairo lithograph edition, entitled *Qiṣṣat Faras al-ᶜUqaylī.* My thanks to the American Philosophical Society for its grant, which enabled me to work in the British Museum, December 1980, following this lead. See my paper, which uses the Arabic text of the Blunt translation, "Sīrat Banī Hilāl and the Oral-Epic Technique of Poesis," *Cahiers des arts et traditions populaires* (Tunis, in press).

30. MacKail, p. 128.

31. H. M. Chadwick and N. K. Chadwick, *The Growth of Literature,* 3 vols. (Cambridge: University Press, 1932–1940), Vol. I; and *The Heroic Age* (Cambridge: University Press, 1912).

32. Milman Parry, *L'Epithète traditionelle dans Homère* (Paris, 1928); "Studies in the Epic Technique of Oral Verse-Making," I. "Homer and Homeric Style," in *Harvard Studies in Classical Philology,* 1930. Id., II., "The Homeric Language as the Language of an Oral Poetry," ibid., 1932. "The Traditional Metaphor in Homer," in *Classical Philology,* 1933. These references are as cited by Bowra.

33. Bowra, pp. 33–34.

34. Bowra, p. 95.

35. For a stylistic analysis of the original Arabic text, see my "Sīrat Banī Hilāl and the Oral-Epic Technique of Poesis," *Cahiers des arts et traditions populaires* (in press).

36. ᶜAbd al-Ḥamīd Yūnis, *al-Hilāliyya fī al-Tā'rīkh wa-l-Adab al-Shaᶜbī* (Cairo: Dār al-Maᶜrifa, 1956; 1968 reprint).

37. Ibid., p. 164.

38. Ibid., p. 148.

39. Karel Petráček, "Die Poesie als Kriterium des arabischen 'Volksromans,'" in *Oriens* 23–24 (1970–1971):301–305.

40. Albert Lord, *The Singer of Tales* (New York: Atheneum, 1965; original edition Harvard University Press, 1960); Milman Parry, *The Making of Homeric Verse: The Collected Papers of Milman Parry,* ed. Adam Parry (Oxford, 1971); Joseph J. Duggan, *The Song of Roland: Formulaic Style and Poetic Craft* (Berkeley, Los Angeles, London: University of California Press, 1973); Duggan, "Formulas in the Couronnement de Louis," *Romania* 87 (1966):315–344; Michael N. Nagler, *Spontaneity and Tradition: A Study in the Oral Art of Homer* (Berkeley, Los Angeles, London: University of California Press, 1974); Jeffrey Opland, "'Scop' and 'Imbongi'—Anglo-Saxon and Bantu Oral Poets," *English Studies in Africa* 14; Edward R. Haymes, *A Bibliography of Studies Relating to Parry's and Lord's Oral Theory* (Cambridge: Harvard University Press, 1973). *New Literary History: Oral Cultures and Oral Performances* (Spring 1977); John Miles Foley, ed., *Oral Traditional Literature; A Festschrift for Albert Bates Lord* (Columbus, Ohio: Slavica Publishers, 1981); John Miles Foley, *Oral Formulaic Theory and Research: An Introduction and Annotated Bibliography* (New York and London: Garland, 1985).

41. British Museum copy, no. 14570.a.6 of the Arabic collection.

42. Michael L. Chyet, a Berkeley graduate student in languages and cultures (folklore) of the Middle East, transliterated the cited passage from the Cairene lithograph; Maurice B. Salib, Visiting Lecturer in Arabic at the University of California, Berkeley, assisted Chyet.

The following transliterations from both the Cairene lithograph edition and the Beirut printed edition are necessarily only approximations of the pronunciation. Inasmuch as the Arabic texts only provide the consonants, not the vowels, it is difficult to know exactly how the eighteenth- or nineteenth-century poets might have articulated the lines. The transliterations are guesses based on contemporary speech.

43. A. Lord, p. 4.

44. Milman Parry, "The Distinctive Character of Enjambement in Homeric Verse," *Transactions of the American Philological Association* 60 (1929):200–220. See also Michael Zwettler on enjambement in pre-Islamic Arab oral poetry in *The Oral Tradition of Classical Arabic Poetry* (Columbus: The Ohio State University Press, 1978), pp. 63–78.

45. For a bibliographic survey of Banī Hilāl scholarship, refer to Giovanni Canova, "Gli studi sull'epica popolare araba," *Oriente Moderno* 57, nos. 5–6 (1977):311–326. See esp. Faiq Mukhlis on the tedium of the Hilāli sīra.

46. Martin Hartmann, "Die Banī-Hilāl Geschichten," *Zeitschrift für afrikanische und oceanische Sprachen,* IV Jahrgang (Berlin, 1898), pp. 289–315.

47. *Singer of Tales,* Pt. II, "The Application."

48. Documentation for these repetitions may be found in detail in my Ph.D. dissertation, "The Oral-Formulaic Tradition of Sīrat Banī Hilāl," University of California, Berkeley, 1974. The following passage was transliterated and translated by Michael L. Chyet. See n. 42 above.

49. Zwettler, pp. 59ff.

50. The limitations of this method of formula analysis are very cogently discussed in J. Duggan's book on the *Roland.* Duggan based his analysis of formulaic repetition on a computer concordance of the entire *Song of Roland* plus several other chansons de geste. As he points out, the percentage figure reached by random sampling of a short passage does not represent the figure arrived at by means of a computer concordance. Indeed, he discovers that only a 400-line sampling of the *Song of Roland* would represent a figure approximating the computer result.

51. P. 47.

52. A. Lord, "Homer as an Oral Poet," *Harvard Studies in Classical Philology* 72 (1868):24.

53. See Quatremère translation and edition, Vol. III, p. 381.

54. See A. Ayoub, "A propos des manuscrits de la geste des Banū Hilāl conservés à Berlin," *Actes du 2[e] Congrès Int. d'Études des Cultures de la Méd. Occid.* II (Algiers: SNED, 1978), pp. 347–363. Ayoub shows that many of the Berlin MSS have colophons attached which indicate that the text was orally dictated by a poet to a scribe for pay. I will discuss this in more detail in chap. 10.

55. Oral communication, Hammamet, Tunisia, June 1980.

56. Oral communication, Cairo, March 13, 1978.

57. L. Saada, "Documents sonores tunisiens concernant la geste des Banū Hilāl," *Actes du 2ᵉ Congrès Int. d'Études des Cultures de la Méd. Occid.* II (Algiers: SNED, 1978), p. 367.

58. See Abnoudy, *La Geste hilalienne,* translated from the Arabic by Tahar Guiga (Cairo: General Egyptian Book Organization, 1978), p. 17.

## 3: The Poets, the People, and the Epic Tradition

1. Howard R. Bloch, *Etymologies and Genealogies* (Chicago: University of Chicago Press, 1983), p. 33. See also Hayden Whyte, *Metahistory: The Historical Imagination in Nineteenth-Century Europe* (Baltimore: John Hopkins University Press, 1973), pp. 31–38.

2. See also Gregory Gizellis, "Historical Event into Song: The Uses of Cultural Perceptual Style," *Folklore* 83 (London, 1972):302–320; E. H. Gombrich, *Art and Illusion* (Princeton: Princeton University Press, 1960).

3. I have borrowed this phrase from Lévi-Strauss via Sabra Webber, "Living Proof: A Structure for Male Storytelling Events in a Tunisian, Mediterranean Town," paper delivered at the Berkeley Symposium on Middle Eastern Oral Narrative, May 1980; to be published in *Edebiyat,* volume devoted to oral literature (in press).

4. See Del Hymes, "Breakthrough into Performance," in *Folklore: Performance and Communication,* ed. Dan Ben Amos and Kenneth S. Goldstein (The Hague, 1975), pp. 11–74.

5. Oral communication, February 16, 1978. The following narrative account of epic performances is based on information given by poets and audience members about themselves and the tradition as we talked during coffee breaks at performance recording-session "parties." Most of my recordings were made at the Cairo home of Kristina Nelson and Humphrey Davies on a Uher 4200 Report Stereo IC reel-to-reel tape recorder, using Scotch 214 long-playing tapes so as to minimize the tape recorder's interference in the length of a given seance.

6. See also Giovanni Canova, *Egitto: Epica,* I Suoni di Musica di Tradizione Orale.

7. Canova, *Egitto,* pp. 9, 22.

8. *Baraka* is grace, "a beneficent force of divine origin which causes superabundance in the physical sphere and prosperity and happiness in the psychic order." G. S. Colin, "Baraka," *EI* 2, p. 1032.

9. Natalie Moyle discusses the Turkish aşhık's story motif of how he learned his art by divine miracle in her paper for the Berkeley Symposium on Oral Narrative in the Middle East (May 2–3, 1982). The Anglo-Saxon poet Caedmon similarly accounts for his skill of improvisation as a gift from God which came in a dream.

10. On the rabāb, see also *EI* 1 article by H. G. Farmer; G. A. Villoteau, *L'Art musical en Egypte* (Paris: Panckoucke, 1824), vol. XIV of *Description de l'Egypte,* pp. 228–232; E. Lane, *Manners and Customs,* pp. 370–371.

11. Canova, *Egitto,* pp. 6, 7.

12. A number of other poets brought to Cairo by Abnoudy for his radio show

have also become nightclub personalities and no longer sing the old narrative poem.

13. G. Canova, "Notizie sui Nawar et sugli altri gruppi zingari presenti in Egitto," *La Bisaccia dello Sheikh* (Venice: Quarterly Journal of the University of Venice, 1981), pp. 71–85.

14. Ibid., pp. 71–80.

15. Ibid., pp. 79–80.

16. See Lane, *Manners and Customs,* pp. 397–431, esp. p. 398.

17. Ibid., p. 400.

18. Richard Critchfield, *Shahhat, an Egyptian,* pp. 51ff.

19. On Cairo population figures and problems, see John Waterbury, *Egypt: Burdens of the Past: Options for the Future* (Bloomington: Indiana University Press, 1978).

20. See Janet L. Abu Lughod, "Urbanization in Egypt: Present Rate and Future Prospects," *Economic Development and Cultural Change,* vol. 13 (1965), pp. 313–343; "Migrant Adjustment to City Life," *American Journal of Sociology* 67 (July 1961):22–32; "Urban-Rural Differences as a Function of Demographic Transition," *American Journal of Sociology* 69 (March 1964):476–490.

21. Oral communication: ʿAbd al-Ḥamīd Hawwās. Dwight Reynolds, a folklore graduate student at the University of Pennsylvania, spent 1982–1984 in Egypt researching the Hilālī tradition.

22. G. Canova, *Egitto,* p. 2.

23. Oral communication, March 31, 1978.

4: Musical Improvisation and the Oral-Formulaic Mode

1. See G. Canova, "Il poeta epico nella tradizione araba," *Quaderni di Studi Arabi* I (Venice, 1983), p. 90. Canova also comments that the poets reject the appellations *muṭrib* (singer) or *qawwāl* (improviser of verses), but like to be compared to the Koran reciter. He quotes Shamandī as saying, "They come to me in lines like in the mosque."

2. Lord Raglan, *The Hero: A Study in Tradition, Myth, and Drama* (London: Methuen and Co., 1936), esp. chaps. 16, 17, and 18 on the hero pattern. On the possibility that Raglan's pattern is purely Mediterranean rather than universal, see Victor Cook, "Lord Raglan's Hero—A Cross Cultural Critique," *The Florida Anthropologist* 18, no. 1 (1965):147–154.

3. Otto Rank, *The Myth of the Birth of the Hero* (New York: Knopf, 1932; Vintage paperback ed. reprint, 1959.

4. Joseph Campbell, *The Hero with a Thousand Faces* (New York: Meridian Books, 1956).

5. Alan Dundes, *The Hero Pattern and the Life of Jesus* (Berkeley: The Center for Hermeneutical Studies, 1976).

6. Albert Lord, *The Singer of Tales* (Cambridge: Harvard University Press, 1960; Atheneum paperback reprint, 1965).

7. Axel Olrik, "The Epic Laws of Folk Narrative," in *The Study of Folklore,* ed. Alan Dundes (New York: Prentice-Hall, 1965); Joseph Campbell, *The Hero*

*with a Thousand Faces;* Michael Nagler, *Spontaneity and Tradition* (Berkeley, Los Angeles, London: University of California Press, 1974); Lord, *Singer of Tales;* Connelly, "The Structure of Four Banī Hilāl Tales," *Journal of Arabic Literature* 4 (1973):18–47.

8. See G. Canova, *Egitto: Epica,* p. 5, for an outline of the usual organization of a performance by the Egyptian poet-musicians he recorded.

9. The following musicological descriptions of the tradition were written in collaboration with Benjamin Brinner. All musical descriptions contained herein are based on observations by Brinner, who worked with me as a research assistant while a doctoral candidate in ethnomusicology at Berkeley. Brinner is himself a rabāb player. See also Ḥabīb Touma's commentary on the music presented in Canova (pp. 9–11) for yet another description by a musicologist.

10. See George Herzog, "Music of Yugoslav Heroic Epic Folk Poetry," *Journal of the International Folk Music Council* 4 (1958):29–34.

11. On the primacy of duple metre in Middle Eastern Islamic sung narrative, see Regula Qureshi, "Listening to Words Through Music: The Sufi Sama'," *Edebiyat* (in press).

12. The reader may find ethnomusicologist Benjamin Brinner's musical transcripts of the three basic melodic motifs, along with the "Abū Zayd" motif, at the end of chap. 4. These transcriptions are intended only to show the relational patterns of musical elements. They do not transcribe precisely the quarter tones. For more exact analysis of several singers, including Jābir and Sayyid, see Ḥabīb Touma in Canova, *Egitto: Epica,* p. 11.

13. A. Lord, *Singer,* p. 54.

14. Milman Parry, "The Distinctive Character of Enjambement in Homeric Verse," *Transactions of the American Philological Association* 60 (1929):200–220. See also M. Zwettler on enjambement in pre-Islamic Arab oral poetry in *The Oral Tradition of Classical Arabic Poetry* (Columbus: The Ohio State University Press, 1978), pp. 63–78.

15. Oral communication, Zamalek, Cairo, March 16, 1978.

16. A. Olrik, "The Epic Laws of Folk Narrative," pp. 133ff.

17. C. M. Bowra, *Heroic Poetry,* pp. 33–34. Bowra uses the Blunt's translation of *Faras Jabir al-ᶜUqayli* (The Stealing of the Mare), to illustrate the two narrative modes of epic discourse: speeches and third person omniscient. On the law of two-to-a-scene, see Olrik, pp. 134–135.

18. G. Canova, oral communication, Hammamet, Tunisia, 1978.

19. For an analysis of the formulaic language in the printed editions of the *Hilāliyya,* see B. Connelly, "Sīrat Banī Hilāl and the Oral-Epic Technique of Poesis," *Cahiers des arts et traditions populaires* (Tunis, in press).

20. Alan Dundes surveys hero-pattern studies in his introduction to Lord Raglan's essay, "The Hero of Tradition," in *The Study of Folklore* (Prentice-Hall, 1965), pp. 142–144.

21. Vladimir Propp, *Morphology of the Folktale* (Bloomington: University of Indiana, 1958).

22. A broken marriage contract with the woman suspected of fornicating with a black slave serves as the initial proposition in other major Arab folktales: e.g., *The Arabian Nights'* frame tale, ʿAntara ibn Shaddād. See especially Ferial

Jabouri Ghazoul, *The Arabian Nights: a Structural Analysis* (Cairo: UNESCO Publication of Cairo by the Associated Institution for the Study of Arab Cultural Values, 1980), pp. 55ff., on the "erotic code."

23. Ayoub has worked out a very detailed structure of the *Banī Hilāl Epic* based on several versions, including the Tūnis manuscript, several Berlin manuscripts, and oral versions collected in Tunisia and Jordan.

24. Gregory Gizellis, "Historical Event into Song: The Uses of Cultural Perceptual Style," *Folklore* 83 (London, 1972):302–320. See also Kenneth Burke, "Lexicon Rhetoricae," in *Counterstatement* (Berkeley and Los Angeles: University of California Press, 1968; first published in 1931), pp. 123–183. Lee Haring applies rhetorical theory of probability to the folktale motifeme sequence in "A Characteristic African Folktale Pattern," in *African Folklore,* ed. Richard M. Dorson (Garden City: Anchor Books, 1972), pp. 173–179.

25. On the concept of "schema" and reindividuation of the form see both Burke, "Lexicon Rhetoricae," and E. H. Gombrich, *Art and Illusion.*

26. Jihad Racy, a Lebanese musician and professor of ethnomusicology at UCLA, in a series of lectures on Arabic music at San Francisco State University during summer 1979, stressed the orchestral and choral quality of the Egyptian musical milieu. He contrasted this group style with the more soloistic performance mode of the Levant. Commenting on the experimental innovative quality of Egyptian popular music as opposed to the more conservative, traditional milieu in the Levant, Racy speculated that the style of performing such folk traditions as the epic had been influenced in Egypt by the professional musician's zeal for experimentation and variety. The reader may refer to Tiberiu Alexandru's essay for similar data on the Egyptian musical scene in *al-Aghānī wa-al-Mūsīqá al-Shaᶜbiyya al-Miṣriyya,* Anthology of Egyptian Popular Music, Sono Cairo EST 52 and EST 53, 1967, texts in French, English, German; 2 records 33/cm with booklet and notes.

27. See M. Villoteau, *L'Art musical en Egypte,* pp. 228–232; and Lane, *Manners and Customs,* chaps. 11–13, pp. 397–431; see also pp. 370–371 in the chapter on Music, for a description of the one-stringed, square poet's viol used by the nineteenth-century Abū Zaydiyya.

28. This two-stringed viol with round sounding box was called a kamanga in the nineteenth century. See Lane, *Manners,* p. 363. See also G. Canova, *Egitto: Epica.* Canova's record presents five poets using varied instrumentalization of the epic. One of his poets accompanies himself of the *duff,* a large drum.

29. See chap. 3, above, for a full description of the rabāb.

30. See also G. Canova, "Notizie sui Nawar."

31. These questions and methods of procedure closely follow those suggested by Leonard Nathan in his paper entitled "Sanskrit Bards and American Translators," delivered at the Ramayana Conference in Berkeley in 1978. The listening methodology of this study also owes a great debt to two years of training in oral-interpretative theory and practice with Robert Beloof; see R. Beloof, *The Performing Voice in Literature* (Boston, 1966). It was, of course, study with ᶜAbd al-Raḥmān al-Abnoudy which enabled me to attempt a "listening analysis" of Egyptian rabāb poets. He and ᶜAṭiyat al-Abnoudy were my teachers as I endeavored to train my ear to hear the Hilālī poet as the Egyptian audience hears

him. Many of the perceptions of this study result from the long hours they spent listening to the poets with this foreigner to Upper Egyptian culture; any of its limitations are my own. The American ethnomusicologist, Kristina Nelson, who also worked with me in Egypt, first made me aware of the role of the music of the rabāb and voice in the total argument of the performance.

32. Howard R. Bloch, *Etymologies and Genealogies: A Literary Anthropology of the French Middle Ages* (Chicago: University of Chicago Press, 1983), pp. 94–95.

## 5: Musical Metaphor and Poetic Competence

1. The texts that appear in this chapter were prepared in collaboration with Abnoudy, Malak Wassef, Aisha Hassan, Aida, ʿAli, Fārūq, Shamandī, and Michael L. Chyet, who fixed the final, formally consistent transliterations and versions with help from Maurice Salib.

2. See S. Gilman on mixed tense in the *Cid: Tiempo y formas verbales en el "Poema del Cid"* (Madrid: Gredos, 1961). The chansons de geste also are marked by this tense mixture. I believe it is a central feature in orally composed and performed literature that serves to connect the present and future with the past which is being recollected in the epic tale. See chapter 10 for an expansion of this. See also Manfred Sandmann, "Narrative Tenses of the Past in the *Cantar de Mio Cid*," *Studies in Romance Philology . . . Presented to John Orr* (Manchester: Manchester University Press, 1953), pp. 258–281. Similar things go on in the Spanish ballad; see Joseph Szertics, *Tiempo y verbo en el romancero viejo*, 2d ed. (Madrid: Gredos, 1974).

Suzanne Fleischman's recent research on medieval discourse suggests that oral communication (both formal, performed narrative and informal talk) necessarily involves tense switching as a technique of subordinating ideas; S. Fleischman, "Tense-Switching as a Subordination Strategy in Medieval Performance Narration," paper delivered to the Modern Language Association, Washington, D.C., December 27, 1984; see Fleischman's "Evaluation in Narrative: The Present Tense in Medieval 'Performed Stories,'" *Yale French Studies*, forthcoming. The interested reader may also refer to Paul J. Hopper, "Aspect and Foregrounding in Discourse," *Syntax and Semantics* 12; *Discourse and Syntax*, ed. Talmy Givon (New York: Academic Press, 1979); Deborah Schiffrin, "Tense and Aspect in Oral Spanish Narrative: Context and Meaning," LG 59 (1983):760–780; Stephen Wallace, "Figure and Ground: The Interrelationships of Linguistic Categories," *Tense-Aspect: Between Semantics and Pragmatics*, ed. Paul J. Hopper (Amsterdam: Benjamins, 1982).

3. Abnoudy recorded this performance and has transcripted much of it in his article in *al-Masā'*, series of ten essays, beginning December 10, 1976, and appearing weekly.

4. This version of the "Birth of Abū Zayd" was generously provided for me by ʿAbd al-Raḥmān al-Abnoudy from Jabir Abū Ḥusayn's singing of *Sīrat Banī Hilāl*, which runs to over ninety hours on tape. It was recorded over a two-and-one-half year period by ʿAbd al-Rahmān and ʿAtiyat al-Abnoudy.

5. I am not using the term "Middle Arabic" to designate any historical, developmental stage of the language, but rather I intend it in the sense of the Arabic phrase to designate a written version of the vernacular tongue which has been "fixed up." Saad Sowayan terms this language "bayn al-bayn." See n. 23, chap. 1, above.

6. Oral communication from Giovanni Canova, conversation with Jābir Abū Ḥusayn. Canova quotes the poet Nādī ʿUthmān on the importance of rhyme. When asked what he does when he forgets a line or ruins it in performance, ʿUthmān responded:

> If I don't remember a line I mount [*arakkib*] another in its place. I must above all respect the rhyme. If I goof a word, I take a different vocabulary and insert it in the verse. The content, the argument is the same, but the words can change. Sometimes a word comes said before another. For example, when I narrate a battle, I say:
>
> Qalūhā homma l-itnēn
> el-itnēn kānū gawāriḥ
> yedabdabū zayy el-qalʿēn
> el-qalʿēn fī l-baḥre māliḥ
>
> (Thus the two knights met/ the two like birds of prey/ circling like ships/ships in the salty sea)
>
> Or I can change it to:
>
> Qalūhā homma l-itnēn
> min fōq ḍuhur el-kh̲ēl
> ḍallamat w beqyet lēl
> w-ʿattamat fī ʿizz en-nahār.
>
> (Thus the two knights met/ on the back of a horse/ It got dark and became night from the raised dust/ it was night in the middle of the day)

"Il poeta epica nella tradizione araba: Note e testimonianze," *Quaderni di Studi Arabi* I (Università degli studi di Venezia, 1983), pp. 102–103. This essay by Canova continues his valuable publications of testimonies about the oral poetic tradition as recorded from interviews with poets and audience members alike.

7. See Pierre Cachia, "The Egyptian Mawwāl: Its Ancestry, its Development and its Present Forms," *Journal of Arabic Literature* 8:77–103. Cachia discusses the elaborate rhyming and compound paronomasia from the point of view of the Egyptian maker of popular verse (esp. pp. 89ff.).

8. Cachia, in his discussion of tazhīr, states that "explanations are seldom needed by the villagers and inhabitants of the more popular quarters in cities who make up the regular audience of the *Mawwāl*-singer; they are on the lookout for the floristry, take great delight in spotting it, and when nonplussed are loath to admit it. But the puns are often so ingenious and complicated, not to say tortuous, that the casual observer may be thrown off the scent altogether, and assume that what he is dealing with is mere repetition." Ibid, pp. 91–92.

9. ʿAbd al-Raḥmān al-Abnoudy, *al-Sīra al-Hilāliyya,* in six cassette recordings (Cairo: Najmat al-ʿAtaba, 1983). Dwight Reynolds has compiled a discography of commercial recordings which have become available in Cairo since 1978.

10. See Fleischman's work (cited above, n. 1), on foregrounding and backgrounding. See also Stephen Wallace, "Figure and Ground." I am suggesting that the punned rhyme also serves to foreground and background information for the ear much in the way that a figural representation does for the eye. See Gombrich, *Art and Illusion,* pp. 39–40ff., 230–232.

11. See Joel Scherzer's provocative essay on puns, "Oh! That's a pun and I didn't mean it!" *Semiotica* 22, nos. 3/4 (1978) in which Scherzer discusses puns in terms of Jakobsonian linguistics and refers the reader to Roman Jakobson, "Closing Statement: Linguistics and Poetics," in *Style and Language,* ed. Thomas A. Sebeok (Cambridge: MIT Press, 1960), pp. 35–37.

12. The pun on *al-zayn* also might cross-referentially recall that the meaning is in the *zayn,* the textural ornamentation and the embellishment; that is, in the "flowers" of the rhymes. The pun on *riwāya* (story, rhyme, intent) cross-references meanings in the same way.

13. For Arabic text and translation, refer to pp. 98–101 above.

14. Cf. Canova, *Egitto: Epica,* pp. 2–3; Abnoudy, *La Geste hilalienne,* pp. 16–17; Lane, *Manners and Customs,* p. 398.

15. See C. Geertz, "Deep Play: Notes on a Balinese Cockfight" in *Interpretation of Culture* (New York: Basic Books, 1973), pp. 412–454.

16. See pp. 255–256 on Fārūq's second virtually identical performance of "The Birth of Abū Zayd" a month later.

6: Punning as Understanding

1. Abou A. M. Zeid, "Honor and Shame Among the Bedouins of Egypt," in *Honor and Shame: The Values of Mediterranean Society,* ed. J. G. Peristiany (Chicago: University of Chicago Press, 1966).

2. *ʿarḍ* is the Egyptian colloquial for honor; *ʿurūḍ* is the plural. One of my consultants on Ṣaʿīdī dialect translated this phrase as "the man with a clean shawl"; I can find no verification of this meaning but the translation is provocative in light of other clothing epithets used to express inner moral state.

3. The reader unfamiliar with the terms I am using (disjunctive reasoning, dissociative logic, philosophical pairs) may refer to Chaim Perelman's extended treatise on argumentation, *The New Rhetoric* (Notre Dame: University of Notre Dame Press, 1969), trans. John Wilkerson and Purcell Weaver; first published by Presses Universitaires de France (1958), as *La Nouvelle Rhétorique,* pp. 185–192, 410–459, 324–325, 475.

4. Zeid, p. 252.

5. Ibid., pp. 246, 254–256.

6. Ibid., p. 255.

7. *Duʿā'* is an invocation, a request; when followed by the preposition li, it

calls down a blessing on someone; when followed by the preposition ʿalá, it calls down a punishment.

8. On the symbolic use of clothing in the Western European ballad, see Edith R. Rogers, *The Perilous Hunt: Symbols in Hispanic and European Balladry* (Lexington: The University Press of Kentucky, 1980), pp. 58–89.

9. See Abnoudy in his *al-Masā'* essay on the borderlands and the outcast.

10. On homonymy as antonymy, see Jacques Berque, *L'Ambivalence dans la culture arabe* (Paris: Editions Anthropos, 1967), esp. pp. 452–453. On the various kinds of Arabic wordplay, see S. A. Bonebakker, *Some Early Definitions of the Tawriya* (The Hague: Mouton, 1966).

11. The disjunctive function of puns in discourse is fully discussed by Joel Scherzer in "Oh! That's a pun and I didn't mean it!" *Semiotica* 22, no. 3/4 (1978). Scherzer discusses puns in terms of Jakobsonian linguistics. I have purposely eschewed such terminology as overly scientismic.

12. See James Brown, "Eight Types of Puns," in *PMLA* 71, no. 1 (Mar. 1956): 14–26.

13. Fārūq misses an obvious opportunity to make a pun on *zayn* several times during his narration of "The Birth of Abū Zayd." This failure to make the expected pun might also, of course, be attributed to the possibility that Fārūq's version belongs to a different school of performers who eschew a somewhat hackneyed figure. To know for certain, scholars need to conduct further field investigation of poets and their affiliations with each other.

14. The link the sīra poets make between the sexual and the sacred can be observed elsewhere in the culture. A traditional Egyptian Islamic marriage ceremony, for example, is marked by elaborate rituals of public communal prayer on the part of the groom and his friends. When the groom first enters his bride's chamber, he unveils her, undresses her, and kneels before her bared prostrate body to face Mecca and prays. He then leaves, to rejoin his companions gathered in the courtyard performing a *dhikr* for an hour or two before returning to his wife. The public, communal religious ritual then subsumes the private encounter on the "night of the entering" or the wedding night. (See Lane, pp. 162–179, esp. pp. 177–178; Burckhardt's *Arabic Proverbs*, p. 117; on *Dhikr*, see El-Shamy, "Mental Health," and Cynthia Nelson, "Self Spirit Possession and World View: An Illustration from Egypt," *Int. Journal of Social Psychology* 13, no. 3 (1971):194–209.

15. See Otto Rank, *The Myth of the Birth of the Hero* (New York: Vintage Books, 1959), ed. Phillip Freund; originally published in German in 1909.

16. Hamed Ammar, *Growing Up in an Egyptian Village* (London: Routledge & Kegan Paul, 1954), pp. 87ff.

17. Ibid., p. 94.

18. Ibid., p. 97.

19. Ibid., pp. 91, 93, 97.

20. Ibid., p. 102.

21. See J. Berque, *L'Ambivalence dans la culture arabe*, for a discussion of the rhetorical figure *aḍdād*.

22. Sigmund Freud, *Totem and Taboo*, and abstracts.

23. On male versus female concepts of honor, see Elizabeth Fernea and Robert Fernea, "A Look Behind the Veil," *Human Nature* (Jan. 1979), pp. 68–77; see esp. p. 75.

24. See the opening of several tales in El-Shamy's *Folktales of Egypt,* for examples of the childlessness motif. Curiously, El-Shamy's motif index does not list lack of a child as a separate motif, although I suspect it is an Arabic folktale motif of very high frequency and significance since it provides the initial dilemma for so many tales.

25. The most conspicuous example of this, of course, is the initial episode of *Arabian Nights.*

## 7: al-Sīra, the Biography of the Egyptian Peasant

1. Richard Critchfield, *Shahhāt, an Egyptian* (Syracuse University Press, 1978). Critchfield gives his account of Upper Egyptian rural village life from the vantage point of one living it and from "deep personal engagement." The following description of a rabāb poet performing in Berat is a précis of Critchfield's colorful, vivid report of the singer and his audience (pp. 48–57). All references to Shaḥḥāt are from Critchfield's book.

2. Henry Habib Ayrout, *The Egyptian Peasant* (Boston: Beacon Press, 1963), p. 134.

3. ʿAbd al-Raḥmān al-Abnoudy, *La Geste hilalienne; El-Masā'* (Dec.–Jan. 1976–1977).

4. Ibid., pp. 9, 10, 11.

5. Ibid., p. 12.

6. A. H. al-Zayyāt, *Fi Uṣūl al-Adab,* pp. 127–129. My translation follows Mukhlis, pp. 127–128.

7. See Giovanni Canova, "Il poeta epico nella tradizione araba: note e testimonianze," *Quaderni di Studi Arabi* I (Università degli Studi di Venezia, 1983), p. 91. Also, oral communication from Abnoudy.

8. Abnoudy, oral communication.

9. F. A. Mukhlis; Mukhlis devotes his opening chapters to North African history and tribal genealogies.

10. See Richard Critchfield's description of an audience listening to the "Birth of Abū Zayd" in his *Shahhat, an Egyptian,* pp. 48–57. For more on the ecstatic identification of listeners with poetry performances, story-telling sessions, and Koranic interpretation, see Hasan El-Shamy, "Mental Health in Traditional Culture: A Study of Preventive and Therapeutic Folk Practices in Egypt," *Catalyst,* no. 6 (Fall 1972):13–28; El-Shamy comments on the "ego-investment" of narrator and listener; see also Kristina Nelson's work on the Koranic *nadwa,* "The Art of Reciting the Qur'an," Ph.D. diss., University of California, Berkeley, 1980.

11. Critchfield, p. 52.

12. Critchfield, pp. 7–9. Hamed Ammar indicates that such prophylaxis in names is common. See *Growing Up in an Egyptian Village,* p. 92. Unattractive

names are viewed as a safeguard, just as attractive names may father a wish and a blessing.

13. Kenneth Burke, "Lexicon Rhetoricae," *Counterstatement* (Berkeley and Los Angeles: University of California Press, 1968), pp. 152–165.

14. Critchfield, xv, xxiii, pp. 5–6.

15. H. Ammar, pp. 23–24.

16. See Gabriel Baer's essay "Shirbīnī's Hazz al-Quḥūf and its Significance," in *Fellah and Townsmen in the Middle East* (London: Frank Cass, 1982), pp. 3–47, esp. pp. 16, 17, 18–22, on ʿUlamā' attitudes and prejudices vis-à-vis the fellah. Shirbīnī's book was first published in Cairo in 1857 as *Hazz al-quḥūf fī sharḥ qaṣīd Abī Shādūf;* Baer's reference edition is by al-Maṭbaʿa al-Maḥmūdiyya (Cairo, n.d.).

17. H. Ammar, pp. 70–71.

18. Mahmoud Hussein, *Class Conflict in Egypt: 1945–1970* (New York: Monthly Review Press, 1973, 1977), trans. Michel and Susanne Chirman, Alfred Ehrenfeld, and Kathy Brown; originally published as *La Lutte de classes en Egypte de 1945 à 1968* (Paris: Librairie François Maspéro, 1969).

19. H. H. Ayrout, *The Egyptian Peasant,* pp. 111–114.

20. G. W. Murray, *Sons of Ishmael,* p. 161.

21. H. Ammar, pp. 20, 21, 22.

22. Critchfield, p. 29.

23. H. Ammar, p. 22.

24. Ibid., p. 71.

25. Ibid., p. 74.

26. Ibid., pp. 23–24.

27. Critchfield, xv, xxiii, pp. 5–6.

28. Ibid., pp. 15–16.

29. George Foster, "Peasant Society and the Image of Limited Good," *American Anthropologist* 27, no. 2 (April 1965):293–315.

30. H. Ammar, p. 21.

31. Ibid., pp. 229, 230.

32. Hasan El-Shamy, "Mental Health in Traditional Culture: A Study of Preventive and Therapeutic Folk Practices in Egypt," *Catalyst,* no. 6 (Fall 1972):12–28, esp. pp. 25ff.

33. H. Ammar, p. 229.

34. A. Kardiner, *The Individual and His Society* (New York: Columbia University Press, 1939).

35. El-Shamy, "Mental Health," pp. 25ff.

36. H. Ammar, p. 231.

37. See esp. Hazel Hitson Weidman, "Cultural Values, Concept of Self, and Projection: The Burmese Case," in *Mental Health Research in Asia and the Pacific,* eds. William Caudill and Tsung-Yi Lin (Honolulu: East-West Center Press, 1969), pp. 259–285; see also D. A. Schwartz, "The Paranoid-Depressive Existential Continuum," *Psychiatric Quarterly* 38:690–706.

38. H. H. Weidman, p. 278.

39. Schwartz, p. 276.

40. See H. El-Shamy on the "inadequacy of the individual" as stemming from a notion of shared responsibility which frees the "ego" from "responsibility for its own errors," in "Mental Health," p. 25.

41. H. Ammar, p. 53; Ammar mentions that there is a deep-seated expectation of brothers' discord in spite of a highly idealized expectation of fraternal solidity (pp. 45, 40). H. El-Shamy, in "Mental Health," also speaks about the ideal and the real culture's promotion of unity (p. 25).

42. Ammar, pp. 231, 229.

43. Ibid., p. 63.

44. Abnoudy, *La Geste hilalienne*, pp. 5–17; see also Jacques Berque's analysis of the cathartic role of epics and ballads in *Histoire sociale d'un village Egyptien*, pp. 12–16.

45. The following account is based on Critchfield, pp. 24–56.

46. See Ammar, p. 19; on the "gypsies" of Egypt, see Giovanni Canova, "Notizie sui Nawar e sugli altri gruppi Zingari presenti in Egitto," in *La Bisaccia dello sheikh* (Venice, 1981), Quarterly Journal of the *Iranist*, University of Venice Seminar, pp. 71–85. Capt. Newbold, "The Gypsies of Egypt," *Journal of the Royal Asiatic Society* 16 (1856):285–312; John Walker, "The Gypsies of Modern Egypt," *Muslim World* 23 (1933):285–289; John Sampson, "The Ghagar of Egypt: A Chapter in the History of Gypsy Migration," *Gypsy Lore Society Journal* 7, ser. 3, no. 2 (1828):78–90; József Vekerdi, "The Gypsy's Role in the Preservation of Non-Gypsy Folklore," *Gypsy Lore Society Journal* 6, ser. 4, no. 2 (May 1976):79–86; A. T. Sinclair, "Gypsy and Oriental Music," *Journal of American Folklore* 20, no. 76 (March 1907):16–32.

47. See H. Ammar, pp. 40ff.

48. G. Canova comments that the local definition of the two terms, *ḥalabī* and *ghagar,* is very imprecise and comprehensive; no distinction is made, for example, between the true gypsies of Aryan origin (like the Hawwārah) and other family groups of more obscure origins (like the ex-slaves, the Matāqīl of Sudanese origin). *Egitto: Epica,* p. 3.

49. See Canova, "Notizie sui Nawar," pp. 73, 74, 79–80.

50. My account of the Nawār experience follows G. Canova's essay and interview with Yūsuf Māzin, "Notizie sui Nawar," p. 75.

51. Ibid., pp. 79–80.

52. Oral communication, Dwight Reynolds.

53. Pierre Cachia gives a similar view of the maddāḥ, the Egyptian ballad singers, in his "Social Values Reflected in Egyptian Popular Ballads," in *Studies in Modern Arabic Literature,* ed. R. C. Ostle (Warminster: Aris & Phillips, Ltd., 1975).

54. G. Canova, *Egitto: Epica,* p. 3.

55. Clifford Geertz articulates this view in "Deep Play: Notes on a Balinese Cockfight." He further elaborates it in "Art as a Cultural System," *Modern Language Notes* 91 (1976):1473–1498. In his view, "art materializes a way of experiencing." He further specifies, "art forms render ordinary everyday experience comprehensible by presenting it in terms of acts and objects which have had their practical consequences removed and been reduced to the level of sheer appearances, where their meaning can be more powerfully articulated and more

exactly perceived. Art provides a metasocial commentary on the whole matter of assorting human beings into fixed hierarchical ranks and then organizing the major part of collective existence around that assortment. Its function is interpretive."

56. Mary Douglas, *Purity and Danger: An Analysis of Concepts of Pollution and Taboo* (New York: Praeger, 1966), esp. chap. 9, "The System at War with Itself," pp. 140–158.

57. Ibid., pp. 149–151.

58. Hasan El-Shamy cites a recurrent tale pattern in which the hero is always the son of a wife who has fallen out of favor with the husband/father in a polygamous, endogamous marriage; "Mental Health in Traditional Culture," p. 16. El-Shamy sees tales as illustrative of the "demographic composition of Egyptian society and the dissociative processes characteristic of interaction among basic groups." He sees tales as symbolic eliminators of the sources of stress aroused by intergroup and intragroup processes. He mentions other recurrent motifs in Egyptian folklore as victory over foreigners, satisfaction of food, status, sex, affiliation, and other wants. See also El-Shamy's translation of "The Story of Seyyid Ahmad el-Badawi with Fatma Bint Birry." *Folklore Forum* X, no. 1 (Spring 1977). The tale chronicles a Muslim hero vanquishing a female opponent in a major epic conflict between male and female regenerative forces. Cachia's article on ballad values outlines similar motifs and struggles. See n. 51, above.

59. On Egyptian villagers' hostility to central, outside authority in all its forms, see Gabriel Baer, *Fellah and Townsman* (London: Frank Cass & Co., Ltd., 1982), and esp. *Studies in the Social History of Modern Egypt* (Chicago: University of Chicago Press, 1969), pp. 94–95, 96, 107, 190–191, 201–202, 209. Henry Habib Ayrout, *The Egyptian Peasant,* pp. 109–110, 112–115. See also, H. Ammar, *Growing Up,* pp. 71, 81.

60. William Polk, "Introduction to Baer," *Studies in the Social History of Modern Egypt,* p. xiii.

61. Abbas M. Ammar, *The People of Sharqiyya,* pp. 12, 13.

62. See Edward Lane's description of a typical nineteenth-century performance, *Manners and Customs,* pp. 397–399.

63. See Julian Jayne's account of the bardic performance as a "left-hemisphere" activity of the bicameral brain in his *The Origins of Consciousness in the Breakdown of the Bicameral Mind* (Boston: Houghton-Mifflin, 1976), pp. 67–83, esp. 361–378.

64. St. Augustine condemns *Annominatio* as a pathetic servitude that places excessive emphasis on words in a text and on hunting down the limits of their etymologies at the expense of understanding the argument. I would suggest that the Arab epic forces the audience to search the limits of etymology to find, as Howard Bloch tells us in the case of the chansons de geste, their genealogy. See Nicholas Mann's criticism of Bloch in "Models of Descent," *Times Literary Supplement* (Mar. 9, 1984), p. 256.

65. See Pierre Cachia, "The Egyptian Mawwāl," *JAL,* p. 95.

66. The metaphor is borrowed from Egyptian comparisons of the flow of poetry to a river or a sea to express both its inundating richness and its vast extent.

67. As Lévi-Strauss would have it.

68. See the Lebanese novelist Etel Adnan's poetic description of what she terms "tribalism" as the origins of conflict in *Sitt Marie Rose* (San Francisco: New Apollo Press, 1982), esp. p. 103.

69. For an illuminating essay on myths of origins among the politically disaffected, see Judith N. Shklar, "Subversive Genealogies," in *Myth, Symbol, and Culture,* ed. Clifford Geertz (New York: Norton, 1971), originally published as winter 1972 issue of *Daedalus.*

70. G. Canova, "Notizie sui Nawar," p. 80.

## 8: The Gypsy on the Doorstep: A Dirty Story or a Subversive Genealogy?

1. Yūsuf al-Shirbīnī, *Hazz al-quḥūf fī sharḥ qaṣīd Abī Shādūf* (Cairo: al-Maktaba al-Maḥmudiyya, n.d.).

2. Gabriel Baer, *Fellah and Townsman in the Middle East* (London: Frank Cass, 1982), chap. 1, "Shirbīnī's Hazz al-Quḥūf and its Significance." pp. 3–47.

3. ʿAbd al-Laṭīf, *Abū Zayd al-Hilālī,* pp. 113–114.

4. Al-Zayyāt, Cairo, 1935, pp. 127–129.

5. See chap. 1.

6. Mūsá Sulaymān, *al-Adab al-qaṣaṣī ʿinda al-ʿarab* (Beirut, 1950; 2d. ed., 1956), p. 82; see Canova, "Gli Studi."

7. Ghālī Shukrī, *Adab al-Muqāwama* (Cairo, 1970), p. 54; see Canova, "Studi . . . ," p. 213; see also chap. 1, above.

8. Cachia thus uses the audience's clothing as a major criterion through which to define "popular literature." See "Social Values Reflected in Egyptian Popular Ballads," in *Studies in Modern Arabic Literature,* ed. R. C. Ostle (Warminster: Aris & Phillips, 1975), p. 87.

9. John Waterbury, *Egypt, Burdens of the Past/Options for the Future* (Bloomington: Indiana University Press, 1978), pp. 46, 79.

10. Dale Eichelman, "The Art of Memory: Islamic Education and Its Social Reproduction," *Comparative Studies in Society and History* 20, no. 4 (1978):485–516.

11. On the concept of the Umma, see Marshall Hodgson, *The Venture of Islam,* Vol. I, pp. 248, 250, 258, 259, 206–211, 345–350; Montgomery Watt, *Muhammad at Medina* (Oxford: The Clarendon Press, 1956), p. 239; Reuben Levy, *The Social Structure of Islam,* chap. 1; Fatima Mernissi, *Beyond the Veil: Male-Female Dynamics in a Modern Muslim Society* (Cambridge: Schenckman, 1975), pp. xiii-xv; Daniel Pipes, *Slave Soldiers and Islam: The Genesis of a Military System* (New Haven: Yale University Press, 1981), pp. 64–69, 109, 167, 179–181.

12. Critchfield, *Shahhat.* For a particularly acute description of Egyptian peasant village life from one who has lived it, see Hamed Ammar's *Growing Up in an Egyptian Village.* Father Henry Habib Ayrout gives an impassioned, sympathetic account of the Egyptian peasant, from which many current clichés about the "peasant mentality" stem; see his *Moeurs et coutumes des fellahs* (Paris: Payot, 1938); English translation by J. A. Williams, *The Egyptian Peasant* (Bos-

ton: Beacon Press, 1963) with a foreword by Chester Bowles and an introduction by Morroe Berger.

13. Jacques Berque, *Histoire sociale d'un village égyptien.* See also H. Ammar, pp. 80–83, on relationship of Silwa with central authority. Many histories of modern Egypt are available to the English reader. For a general history with a nice bibliographic essay encompassing the most prominent research in the area, see P. J. Vatikiotis, *The History of Egypt* (Baltimore: Johns Hopkins University Press, 1980).

14. Mohammed Hussein, *Class Conflict in Egypt: 1945–1970* (New York: Monthly Review Press, 1973); originally published in French as *La Lutte de Classes en Egypte de 1945 à 1968* (Paris: Maspéro, 1969).

15. See Richard Bulliet, *Conversion to Islam in the Medieval Period* (Cambridge: Harvard University Press, 1979).

16. Daniel Pipes, pp. 62ff., 68, 69, 70, 75. See also Patricia Crone, *Slaves on Horses: The Evolution of the Islamic Polity* (New York: Cambridge University Press, 1980). Ira Lapidus and Edmund Burke, III, have criticized both Crone and Pipes for the moralistically judgmental tone of their treatments of Islam. See Ira Lapidus, review of Pipes in *Journal of Interdisciplinary History* 6 (1982):716–718; his review of Crone in *Journal of Interdisciplinary History* 12 (1982):560–563; Edmund Burke, "Talking Sense About Islam," *San Francisco Review of Books,* n.d.

17. Fatima Mernissi, *Beyond the Veil,* pp. 81–82, xvi. Dale Eichelman criticizes Mernissi's analysis as simplistically anhistorical. I would submit that such impassioned and involved studies of society necessarily sweep across history and often annihilate linear history to offer instead a "felt-history" or a poetic history that interprets events, not from any "rational" point of view, but from a passionately involved one. See Eichelman, *The Middle East, An Anthropological Approach* (Englewood Cliffs, N.J.: Prentice-Hall, 1981), p. 151.

Etel Adnan makes a similar argument to Mernissi's and Pipe's in her poetic novel *Sitt Marie Rose* (San Francisco: New Apollo Press, 1983).

18. On the division between vernacular and written language, see Norman A. Stillman and Yedida Stillman, "The Art of a Moroccan Folk Poetess," *Zeitschrift der Deutschen morgenländischen Gesellschaft* 18, no. 1 (1978):65–89; see also, on linguistic registers, Heikki Palva, "The Descriptive Imperative of a Narrative Style in Spoken Arabic," *Folia Orientalia* 18 (1977):5–26.

19. Ghālī Shukrī maintains that the sīra directly reflects popular resistance to Mamluk rule. See his "Buṭūlat al-Muqāwama fī turāthinā al-shaᶜbī," *al-Talīᶜa* (Cairo, Dec. 1967), pp. 102–105, esp. p. 105.

20. Hasan El-Shamy, "The Story of el-Sayyid Ahmad el-Badawi," p. 5.

21. See Edward Lane, pp. 400–406. Lane's translation appears to be based on a British Museum printed edition of *Qiṣṣat Khaḍrā.*

22. William Polk, "Introduction," in G. Baer's *Studies in the Social History of Modern Egypt,* pp. xvii-xviii.

23. See also Pipes, ibid.; Polk, ibid., p. xviii.

24. *Al-Masā'* essay; I am basing my comments on the text of the manuscript for the newspaper series which Abnoudy gave to me.

25. Baer, *Studies,* p. 215.

26. Critchfield, Introduction. El-Shamy, *Folktales of Egypt,* Introduction. On the transformations of Egypt as a result of the Aswan dam, see Alan Richards, *A History of Egyptian Agriculture* (Boulder: Westview Press, 1981).

27. Hussein, pp. 37–38.

28. Ibid., p. 41. Using Mubarak's biographies as his source, Gabriel Baer shows in *Social History* the changes in the nineteenth century under the influence of European liberalism which helped bring about the current disorganization and dispersion of the Egyptian masses, a view that is shared by Mahmoud Hussein. The last two decades of the nineteenth century brought about the destruction of the traditional socioeconomic framework: the dissolution of the tribal and village community, the disappearance of guilds, and the abolition of slavery, which changed the character of the labor force (pp. 228–229). Prior to the nineteenth century and the European incursions, the village community was marked by three fundamental features: (1) periodic redistribution of lands held in common, (2) collective responsibility for public works, and (3) joint liability for taxes. This changed under European occupation with the gradual growth of private land holdings, individualized rather than group tax responsibilities, and transformation of forced labor for public works to an individual rather than a collective obligation. As Polk summarizes the situation in his introduction to Baer, "this constituted a revolution; loss of these elements of community sharing of obligations caused the transformation of the Egyptian village from community to unformed social mass." It also created social mobility in that a man was no longer necessarily born into his occupational group. Many of humble origin became rich landowners, high officials, or wealthy merchants, and even doctors (p. 229; Baer citing Mubarak).

A similar process of social differentiation occurred with the sedentarization of the nomads in nineteenth-century Egypt. Tribal unity was broken up, according to Baer, by granting large tracts of land as private property to tribal shaykhs and making them village government officials. The development of cash crops and the rising prices of agricultural products provided a powerful incentive to the shaykhs to move to towns and live in large mansions and intermarry with the ruling class. Their former tribesmen, meanwhile, became part of the lower classes, lost among the fellahin. Classes and class friction thus evolved in the former egalitarian Bedouin tribal society. The disappearance of the medieval Islamic guilds also marked a change from the former egalitarian ideal reflected in tribal and village society—the egalitarianism that passed as social mobility increased and the status quo became socially changeable (p. 214).

29. See John Waterbury, *Egypt.*

30. Shaḥḥāt's mother, e.g., bore twenty children, only six of whom are living; see Critchfield. One might also note that lack of a child is a very frequent opening motif in Egyptian folktales. See, e.g., El-Shamy's collection, translated in *Folktales of Egypt,* pp. 4, 39; esp. p. 55.

31. See H. Ammar, pp. 93–96.

32. See Critchfield, pp. 48, 79; Janet Abu Lughod reports on migration to villages and shows how village groups are maintained in Cairo habitation patterns of formerly rural people. See her articles, "Urbanization in Egypt: Present Rate

and Future Prospects," *Economic Development and Cultural Change* 13 (1965):313–343; "Migrant Adjustment to City Life," *The American Journal of Sociology* 67 (July 1961):22–32. See also, for a summary analysis and annotated bibliography, J. Waterbury, *Egypt*.

33. Fārūq stated this himself when I recorded him in March 1978, saying that he had not applied himself to learning all the *Hilāliyya* even though his father told him he would one day regret it.

34. Fatima Mernissi, *Beyond the Veil*, p. 82.

35. See Pipes, pp. 60–61, on Islamicate patterns; see also Oleg Grabar, *The Formation of Islamic Art* (New Haven: Yale University Press, 1973); Marshall Hodgson; on Folk Islam versus Scriptural Islam, see Ernest Gellner.

36. See Mary Douglas, p. 161; on boundary maintenance and group differentiation in the colonial setting, see Fredrik Barth, *Ethnic Groups and Boundaries: The Social Organization of Cultural Differences* (Boston: Little, Brown, 1969). See also Edward Spicer, "Persistent Identity Systems," *Science*, no. 1411 (1971):795–800, for a discussion of the oppositional process of identity as "stored" in "shared symbolic systems."

37. Mary Douglas, *Purity and Danger*, p. 38; p. 128, on rituals.

38. Clifford Geertz also maintains that cultures interpret themselves. See "Art as a Cultural System" and "Notes on a Balinese Cockfight"; see also Mary Douglas, p. 128, on rituals as self-knowledge.

39. Mary Douglas, *Purity and Danger*, p. 102.

40. See Chaim Perelman, *The New Rhetoric*, pp. 30–35ff., for a similar concept of audience.

41. See above on Shirbīnī.

42. A few of Abnoudy's publications include:

*al-Arḍ wa-al-ʿIyāl* (Cairo, 1964)
*al-Zaḥma* (Cairo, 1967; 2d ed., 1976)
*ʿUmmāliyāt* (Cairo, 1968)
*Wujūh ʿala al-Shaṭṭ* (Cairo, 1975)
*Ṣamt al Jady* (Cairo, 1975)
*Shay' min wa-ʿan* Sīrat Banī *Hilāl* French trans.,
A. Guiga [O.F.G.L.: Cairo, 1978])
*Ghinā' al-Ghalāba* (Cairo, 1980)
*Ḥurūf al-Kalām* (Cairo, 1981)

43. Abnoudy's radio programs were broadcast on *Idhāʿat al-Shaʿb* (the Popular Station, which broadcasts in the colloquial dialect) in 1975 as a half-hour weekly series of 60 programs and in 1978 as a daily series of 180 shows.

44. Chaim Perelman, *The New Rhetoric*, pp. 31–35. See also Robert Kellogg, "Oral Literature," *New Literary History* 8, no. 3 (1977):57–66. Kellogg discusses his notion of the "ideal" epic vs. the "real" one in terms of synchronic vs. diachronic descriptions.

45. See, e.g., the leftist writer Anwar ʿAbd al-Malik, writing Aug. 28, 1958, in *al-Masā'*, "al Arḍ wa-al-Fallāḥ fī Ta'rīkhinā"; see also the works cited by

Gabriel Baer in *Fellah and Townsman,* pp. 44–45, 26–29. Baer cites the National Charter of 1962, which officially recognized the fellah as engaged in a permanent struggle with foreign oppressors and exploiters, namely, the Turks, Mamluks, and Ottomans (pp. 27–28).

46. As late as 1973, Yūnis felt impelled to write his "Defense of Folklore" (*Difāʿ ʿan al-Fūlklūr* [Cairo-Beirut, 1973]) against the railing miscomprehension of Shawqī Ḍayf, a noted man of letters.

47. Aḥmad Rushdī Ṣāliḥ, *Funūn al-adab al-shaʿbī* (Cairo, 1956, 1971), pp. 75ff.

48. Ghālī Shukrī, *Adab al-muqāwama* (Cairo, 1970), p. 32. See also Canova, "Gli Studi sull'epica popolare araba," p. 216.

49. Fārūq Khurshīd, *Aḍwā' ʿalá al-Siyar al-Shaʿbiyya* (Cairo, 1964), p. 12. See also Canova, p. 216.

50. ʿAbd al-Ḥamīd Yūnis, *al-Hilāliyya,* chap. 4; cf. G. Canova, "Studi sull'epica," p. 215.

9: Transformations of *Sīrat Banī Hilāl* in Africa

1. Oral communication, Cairo, Mar. 4, 1978.

2. Clifford Geertz, "Art as a Cultural System," *Modern Language Notes* 91 (1976):1475–1476.

3. Claude Breteau and Micheline Galley, "Reflexions sur deux versions algériennes de Dyâb le Hilalien," *Actes du Premier Congres d'Études des Cultures Méditérranéenes d'Influence Arabo-berbere* (Malta: 1972), p. 358.

4. J. R. Patterson, *Stories of Abu Zeid the Hilali in Shuwa Arabic* (London: Kegan, Trench, Trubner & Co., 1930). See the introduction by H. R. Palmer.

5. Sayyid Hurreiz, "Afro-Arab Relations in the Sudanese Folktale," in *African Folklore,* ed. Richard M. Dorson (Garden City, N.Y.: Anchor Books, 1972), pp. 159–160; and Sayyid Hurreiz, "Ja'aliyyin Folktales: An Interplay of African, Arabian, and Islamic Elements," Ph.D. diss., Indiana University (Ann Arbor: University Microfilms, 1972), pp. 306–336. Hurreiz indicates that the Sudanese refer to fictitious tales as *ḥujwa* (pl. *ḥuja*). He discusses these categorical distinctions in his dissertation, cited above, pp. 86–91.

6. Anita Baker, "The Hilālī Saga in the Tunisian South," Ph.D. diss., Indiana University (Ann Arbor: University Microfilms, 1978), pp. 17–18.

7. Abderrahman Ayoub has collected such versions in Jordan among Palestinian refugees.

8. Abnoudy, *La Geste hilalienne,* gives a summary of the various parts of the "whole" sīra; my account of the cycles follows Abnoudy.

9. Baker, pp. 360ff., English translation; pp. 561ff., Arabic text.

10. Baker, p. 362.

11. Baker, pp. 146–147.

12. Abderrahman Guiga, *La Geste hilalienne* (Tunis: Société Tunisienne d'Edition et de Diffusion, 1968), p. 8. See pp. 21–22 for the Birth episode.

13. Other Tunisian versions make Abū Zayd piebald—black on his visible

parts and white on the covered. One of the hero's epithets is "Bū Zayd al-Adra<sup>c</sup>, the piebald." See Baker, p. 183.

14. Baker indicates that the rāwīs she recorded were unanimous on the fact that Diyāb's origin was different from the other major characters. See p. 65.

15. H. M. Chadwick and N. K. Chadwick, *Growth of Literature* III, pp. 763–764.

16. See Howard R. Bloch, *Etymologies and Genealogies,* pp. 94–96; see also Jean Frappier, *Les Chansons de geste du cycle de Guillaume d'Orange,* Vol. I (Paris: Sociétés d'Edition d'Enseignement Supérieur, 1955), p. 67.

17. Isidore Okpewho, *The Epic in Africa* (New York: Columbia University Press, 1979), p. 88.

18. J. R. Patterson, *Stories of Abu Zeid the Hilali in Shuwa Arabic;* on the life cycle pattern of this series of tales, see B. Connelly, "The Structure of Four Banī Hilāl Tales: Prolegomena to the Study of Sīra Literature," *J. of Arabic Literature* 4 (Leiden: Brill, 1973):18–47.

19. The name is pronounced variously in different dialects: Dhiyāb in Tunisia; Ḍiyāb in Shuwa Arabic; Diyāb in Egyptian and Sudanese.

20. Baker, pp. 70–71.

21. Baker, pp. 80–83.

22. On Zāziya, see Baker, pp. 641–645, esp. p. 642, for citations of the rāwīs.

23. Guiga, *La Geste hilalienne,* p. 26.

24. Baker, p. 397, Arabic text; p. 163, English translation and notes.

25. Baker, p. 552, Arabic text; p. 351, English translation. In the two passages cited, I have made minor stylistic changes in Baker's translation to make it parallel the Arabic more literally.

26. Baker, pp. 296, 505–507, Arabic text; pp. 162, 297–299, English translation and notes.

27. Baker, pp. 126–127, for English and Arabic text.

28. Feeding and conflict are so intimately related in the African concept of the *Hilaliyya* that even the birth episode contains it. Guiga's Tripolitanian narrator has the future mother make a sacrificial offering of a plate of couscous (the Tunisian "national dish" if there is one) to the birds. His version suppresses any notion of conflict between the birds. Ḥājj ʿAbd al-Salām in the Baker collection presents sparrows fighting with a raven over some grain (Baker, pp. 361, 562). The Shuwa Arab mallam's [*sic*] version from the Bornu region similarly highlights food as the source of conflict among the birds on which the fateful wish was made and on which the Hilālī heroes will be modeled; in the Shuwa version, the rapacious birds are fighting over a piece of meat or a carcass. The Shuwa Abū Zayd/Ḍiyāb, as twin heroes (following the local Nigerian tale oicotype), will be a vulture of sorts and his tribe will fear he will cannibalize them (Patterson, p. 3, Arabic text; p. 23, English translation).

29. Baker, pp. 57–59.

30. Baker, pp. 31, 32.

31. Ibn Khaldūn, *Prolegomènes d'Ebn Khaldoun,* Texte arabe publié d'après les manuscrits de la Bibliothèque Imperiale, vols. 16–18, ed. Quatremère (Paris: Imprimerie Imperiale, 1858), vol. 18, 362–388. See also, Ibn Khaldūn, *Kitāb al-ʿIbar* (Būlāq, 1284), 7 vols., VI, p. 18.

32. See Baker, p. 91, for a description of the game.

33. For versions, see Bel, *La Djazya, chanson arabe,* and Baker, pp. 82–107.

34. Micheline Galley and Abderrahman Ayoub analyze the tale pattern similarly; see *Images de Djazya* (Paris: Editions du CNRS, 1977), pp. 14–16. For additional texts, the reader may refer to: Hans Stumme, *Tripolitanische-tunisische Beduinenlieder* (Leipzig, 1894), p. 107; V. Loubignac, *Etude sur le dialecte berbère des Zaïan et Aït Sgougou* (Paris: E. Leroux, 1924), pp. 294–297. Abderrahman Ayoub has collected extensively in Beja. For three recently collected oral texts, see Micheline Galley and A. Ayoub, *Histoire des Beni Hilâl et de ce qui leur advint dans leur marche vers l'ouest* (Paris: Classique Africaines, Armand Colin, 1983).

35. M. Masmoudi has written extensively about the Tunisian reverse glass painting tradition, which illustrates the heroic subjects of the various siyar told in Tunisia under the French Protectorate. Many of the paintings he reproduces in his book show a developed concern with framing and boundary in their cyclical composition and oppositional distribution of thematic elements. A similar tradition exists in Syria. Whether there are links between the two folk art traditions is not known. More research needs to be conducted in this area. See Mohamed Masmoudi, *La Peinture sous-verre en Tunisie* (Tunis: CERES Productions, 1972); "Une Peinture sous verre à thème héroïque," *Cahiers des arts et traditions populaires,* no. 2 (Tunis: Institut National d'Archéologie et d'Art, 1968), pp. 5–14; "Deux autres peintures sous verre à theme héroique," *Cahiers des arts et traditions populaires,* no. 3 (1969), pp. 85–98. A. Ayoub and M. Galley have published a short, limited edition, typescript monograph on two other reverse glass paintings in "Images de Djazya: à propos d'une peinture sous verre de Tunisie" (Paris: Editions du Centre National de Recherche Scientifique, 1977).

36. Ayoub and Galley, pp. 13–20ff. My description of the Jāziyah painting follows Ayoub and Galley.

37. See my "Structure of Four Banī Hilāl Tales," p. 32; and Galley and Ayoub, pp. 9–10.

38. See Bel's version for example, ll. 26–29; and Basset, "Une Episode de chanson de geste arabe," p. 143.

39. This research was made possible by grants from the Mabelle McLeod Lewis Foundation and the Social Science Research Council. My thanks to my friends Sarah and Mohamed Moussa and to all of the family Ezzine in Nabeul for information and assistance in my research.

40. Mohamed Masmoudi, *La Peinture sous-verre.*

41. This is based on conversations with Mohamed Masmoudi and Hashemi Saada; see M. Masmoudi, *La Peinture sous-verre,* pp. 23, 45–48.

42. See Baker for the story of King Harrās of Armenia, pp. 194–207, English translation; and pp. 422–432, Arabic text.

43. Lévi-Strauss explains mythic logic as a dialectical process that proceeds from the awareness of oppositions toward their resolution by a double process of opposition and correlation; myth thus provides a "logical model capable of overcoming a contradiction." *Structural Anthropology* (Garden City: Anchor Books, 1967), pp. 226, 221.

44. See Baker, p. 144.

45. Mary Douglas, *Purity and Danger,* p. 126.

46. The literature on boundaries and identity is extensive. For a summary of the literature and an inclusive bibliography of the relevant materials, the reader might refer to a recent book by Annya Peterson Royce, *Ethnic Identity* (Bloomington: Indiana University Press, 1982); the primary adherents of boundary theories of identity are Frederik Barth and Edward Spicer, cited elsewhere.

47. Sayyid Hurreiz, "Afro-Arab Relations in the Sudanese Folktale," pp. 158, 160, 161–162, 163.

48. Hurreiz, translated text in Dorson's *African Folklore,* pp. 368–386.

49. Hurreiz, p. 158. Hurreiz refers the reader to examples: Ahmed Nasr, "Writing the History of the Abdallah from Their Oral Tradition" (Arabic), *Sudanese Heritage Series,* no. 7 (Khartoum, 1969), pp. 14–25; R. C. Stevenson, "Some Aspects of the Spread of Islam in the Nuba Mountains," in *Islam in Tropical Africa,* ed. I. M. Lewis (London, 1966); Naʿʿūm Shuqayr, *The History of the Sudan* (Arabic) (Cairo, 1903), pp. 111–112; D. T. Niane, *Sundiata: An Epic of Old Mali,* trans. G. D. Picket (London, 1969), p. 2; R. S. Rattray, *Hausa Folklore,* vol. 1 (London, 1913), pp. 7–8.

50. Hurreiz, p. 161.

51. Ibid., p. 162.

52. Ibid., p. 162.

53. Baker, pp. 349–350; pp. 550–551, Arabic text.

54. Baker, p. 297, English text; p. 505, Arabic text.

55. Baker, p. 375, English translation; p. 575, Arabic text. The salutation "Peace be upon you" is the rāwī's interjection addressed to his audience by way of apology for the overt violence of the scene narrated.

56. Baker, p. 376, English; p. 576, Arabic.

57. Baker, pp. 391–392, English; pp. 590–591, Arabic.

58. See my translation of this poem in *Women Poets of the World,* eds. Joanna Bankier and Deirdre Lashgari (New York: Macmillan, 1983), pp. 88–93.

59. The reader may consult a new treatise on the rhetorical terms and processes in Arthur Quinn's *The Figures of Speech, Sixty Ways to Turn a Phrase* (Layton, Utah: Gibbs M. Smith, 1982). See also William Brandt's useful "Finding List" in *The Rhetoric of Argumentation* (Boston: Bobbs-Merrill, 1970). My thanks to Professors Quinn, Brandt, and Beloof for numerous conversations on rhetorical terminology and processes.

60. Baker, p. 272.

61. I am summarizing a lecture Dr. Ayoub delivered at Berkeley in 1983 entitled "The Hilālī Epic, Material and Memory."

62. Baker, p. 372, footnotes especially.

63. Sabra Webber, in "Living Proof: A Structure for Male Storytelling Events in a Tunisian Town," paper delivered at the Berkeley Symposium on Middle Eastern Oral Narrative, May 1980.

64. Baker, p. 269. See fn. 8, on Dhiyāb's tribal affiliation.

65. Baker, p. 290, English translation; p. 499, Arabic text.

66. Baker, p. 320, English translation; p. 515, Arabic text.

67. Baker, pp. 324–326, English translation; pp. 553–555, Arabic text.

68. Baker, p. 346, English translation; p. 547, Arabic text.

69. The association of the wolf with the tribal outcast and the outlaw dates in Arabic poetry from the pre-Islamic oral culture. See the poem of al-Shanfará particularly.

70. Baker, p. 249, English translation; p. 468, Arabic text.

71. Baker, pp. 300–302, English translation; pp. 508–510, Arabic text.

72. Baker, pp. 302–306, English translation; pp. 509–518, Arabic text.

73. Baker, pp. 309–314, English translation; pp. 516–521, Arabic text.

74. Baker, p. 329 fn.; the passages summarized refer to pp. 329–346, English translation, and pp. 532–547, Arabic text.

75. Baker, pp. 337, English translation; p. 340, Arabic text.

76. Hurreiz, p. 382.

77. G. J. Lethem, *Colloquial Arabic, Shuwa Dialect of Bornu, Nigeria and of the Region of Chad* (London: Published for the Govt. of Nigeria by the Crown Agents for the Colonies, 1920).

78. The foregoing account of an Iesiye muʿallim's rendition of the stories of Abū Zayd in four tales is taken from my analysis of the cycle in "The Structure of Four Banī Hilāl Tales: Prolegomena to the Study of Sīra Literature," *J. of Arabic Literature* 4:18–47. The analysis is based on Patterson.

79. See Connelly, p. 23, for the tribal origins of the Iesiye and their wretched economic status.

80. Alfred Bel, "La Djazya, chanson arabe, précédée d'observations sur quelques légendes arabes et sur la geste des Beni-Hilal," *Journal asiatique* 19, ser. 9 (Mar.–Apr., 1 902):289–347; 20, ser. 9 (Sept.–Oct. 1902):169–236; 1, ser. 10 (Jan.–Feb. 1903):311–366. Many of the spellings of Arabic words I use in this passage are Bel's transliterations.

81. See Bel, vol. 1, p. 311, for French translation; vol. 20, p. 169. The rhyme pattern of the poem is [ab ab], the first half of the poem rhymes in [aab/iil] and the last half in [aas/aali].

82. Bel, vol. 1, pp. 320–321, French translation; vol. 20, p. 177, Arabic text.

83. Bel, vol. 19, pp. 326–327.

84. Ibid., p. 289.

85. J. Desparmet, "Les Chansons de geste dans la Mitidja de 1830 à 1914," *Revue africaine* 83 (1939):192–226.

86. C. M. Bowra, *In General and Particular* (London: Weidenfeld and Nicolson, 1964), pp. 80–84. On the "heroic age," see also H. Chadwick and N. Chadwick, *The Growth of Literature*, vol. I (Cambridge: University Press, 1932–1934).

87. Abderrahman Ayoub used this phrase in a paper he delivered at Berkeley in 1983 entitled "The Hilālī Epic, Material and Memory."

88. Baker, pp. 71–73. See also A. Vassière, "Les Oulad Rechaïch," *Revue africaine* 36, no. 206 (1892):312–341, esp. pp. 313–314.

## 10: Etymology as Genealogy: On Generation(s) and Transmission(s)

1. On the combat myth pattern, see esp. Joseph Fontenrose, *Python: A Study of Delphic Myth and Its Origins* (Berkeley and Los Angeles: University of California Press, 1959).

2. On the history of Tunisia and the Maghrib, see Hicham Djait, F. Dachraoui, M. Talbi et al., *Histoire de la Tunisie* (Tunis: Société de Diffusion, 1960); Abdallah Laroui, *L'Histoire du Maghreb, essai de synthèse* (Paris: Maspéro, 1970; Jean Duvignaud, *Change at Shebika: Report from a North African Village,* trans. F. Frenaye (New York: Random House, 1970), originally published in French as *Chebika: mutation dans un village du Maghreb* (Paris: Gallimard, 1968); Ch. A. Julien, *Histoire de L'Afrique du Nord,* 2 vols. (Paris, 1961); Alfred Bel, *La Religion Musulmane en Berbérie* (Paris, 1938).

3. Fredrik Barth, *Ethnic Groups and Boundaries* (Boston: Little, Brown & Co., 1969); Edward Spicer, "Persistent Identity Systems," *Science,* no. 4011 (1971):795–800; George de Vos and L. Romanucci-Ross, eds., *Ethnic Identity: Cultural Continuities and Change* (Palo Alto: Mayfield Publishing, 1975); Immanuel Wallerstein, ed., *Social Change: The Colonial Situation* (New York: Wiley, 1966).

4. Gabriel Baer, *Fellah and Townsman,* Pt. IV, "Urban and Rural Revolt," pp. 223–312; *Studies in the Social History of Modern Egypt,* pp. 93–108.

5. Fatima Mernissi, *Beyond the Veil: Male-Female Dynamics in a Modern Muslim Society* (Cambridge, Mass.: Schenkman Publishing Co., 1975), p. xiii.

6. Fredrik Barth, *Ethnic Groups,* pp. 15–19.

7. Hasan El-Shamy, "Mental Health in Traditional Culture: A Study of Preventive and Therapeutic Folk Practices in Egypt," *Catalyst,* no. 6 (Fall 1972):13–28; esp. pp. 25–26.

8. Spicer, p. 799.

9. Hazel Hitson Weidman, "Cultural Values, Concept of Self, and Projection," in *Mental Health Research in Asia and the Pacific* (Honolulu: East-West Center Press, 1969), pp. 259–285, esp. 263 265.

10. See esp., Leon Grinberg, M.D., and Rebecca Grinberg, M.D., "A Psychoanalytic Study of Migration: Its Normal and Pathological Aspects," *Journal of the American Psychoanalytic Association* 32 (1984): pp. 13–38.

11. C. M. Bowra, "The Meaning of a Heroic Age," in *General and Particular* (London: Weidenfeld and Nicolson, 1964), pp. 63–84.

12. Ibid., pp. 80, 81, 82, 84.

13. Ibid., p. 84.

14. Oral communication. See also Henry N. Massie, *Childhood Psychosis in the First Four Years of Life* (New York: McGraw-Hill, 1984).

15. Margaret Mahler, "The Separation-Individuation Process and Identity Formation," in *The Course of Life: Psychoanalytic Contributions Toward Understanding Personality Development,* vol. I, *Infancy and Early Childhood* (Adelphi, Md.: Mental Health Study Center, Division of Mental Health Service Programs, National Institute of Mental Health, 1980–81) pp. 395–423.

16. Patterson, *Stories of Abu Zeid the Hilali in Shuwa Arabic;* see B. Connelly, "The Structure of Four Banī Hilāl Tales," *JAL* 4:22, 25–31.

17. Erik Erikson, *Toys and Reasons,* p. 49, citing Piaget.

18. Walter Ong, *Orality and Literacy* (London and New York: Methuen, 1982), pp. 46–48.

19. Abderrahman Ayoub, paper delivered to a colloquium of the Middle Eastern Studies Center, University of California, Berkeley, Spring 1982.

20. Gregory Gizellis, "Historical Event into Song: The Uses of Cultural Percep-

tual Style," *Folklore,* no. 83 (London, 1972):302–320.

21. Albert B. Lord, "Homer and Other Epic Poetry," in *A Companion to Homer,* eds. A. J. B. Wace and F. H. Stubbings (London: Macmillan, 1962), pp. 179–214, esp. p. 208.

22. Isidore Okpewho, *The Epic in Africa: Toward a Poetics of the Oral Performance* (New York: Columbia University Press, 1979), pp. 66–76.

23. Carol Gilligan, *In a Different Voice: Psychological Theory and Women's Development* (Cambridge: Harvard University Press, 1982).

24. K. Nelson, *The Art of Reciting the Koran,* pp. 26–27, 28.

25. See Clifford Geertz on Arabic poetry as a kind of "archetype of talk," "Art as a Cultural System," *Modern Language Notes* 91 (1976):1473–1499.

26. See M. Canard, "Dhu'l-Himma," *Encyclopaedia of Islam* 2, p. 235.

27. Harry T. Norris, *The Adventures of ʿAntar* (Warminster: Aris & Phillips, Ltd., 1980).

28. Ibid., p. 231.

29. Ibid., pp. 6, 7, 15.

30. Ibid., pp. 19, 20, 22.

31. Roger Abrahams, "The Complex Relations of Simple Forms," in *Folklore Genres,* ed. Dan Ben-Amos (Austin: University of Texas Press, 1976), pp. 193–194. Northrup Frye, *The Anatomy of Criticism: Four Essays* (New York: Atheneum, 1969), pp. 247–248. Kenneth Burke, *A Rhetoric of Motives* (Berkeley and Los Angeles: University of California Press, 1969).

32. Lane says 45 volumes; Bernard Heller says 32 in *EI* 2, p. 518.

33. See Edward Lane, *Manners and Customs of the Modern Egyptians,* p. 421; M. Canard, *EI* 2, p. 234.

34. See chap. 1 above, pp. 5–8.

35. *EI* 2, pp. 238, 520.

36. Identification of the "outsider" with the sīra seems consistent through the ages, for one cannot help but compare this Jewish convert to Islam with the Egyptian gypsy "outsiders" who transmit the Hilālī tradition today.

37. Micheline Galley described the Tunis manuscript in her talk at the Bergen International Folk Narrative Council meeting, June 15, 1984. Abderrahman Ayoub and Dwight Reynolds are preparing an edition and translation of chapter IX of the manuscript.

38. Peter Molan comments on the indications of the storyteller which still remain in the text of the *Thousand and One Nights;* see his essay, "The Oral Connection," in the *Berkeley Symposium on Middle Eastern Oral Narrative,* ed. Hickman and Connelly, for *Edebiyat,* in press.

39. Abderrahman Ayoub, "A propos des manuscrits relatifs a la geste des Banī Hilāl conservés à Berlin-ouest," *Actes du Congrès de l'Association Int. d'Études des Cultures Médit.* II (Algiers, 1978).

40. Ibid., p. 349.

41. Ayoub kindly lent me a manuscript copy of this paper entitled "*Sīrat Banī Hilāl:* Notes à propos de quelques manuscrits conservés à Berlin-Ouest."

42. Wagner, *Verzeichniss der orientalischen Handschriften in Deutschland,* vol. 17, Bk. 1.

43. See ʿUthmān Kaʿak, *al-Taqālīd wa-al-ʿĀdāt al-Shaʿbiyya wa-al-Fulklūr al-Tūnisiyya* [Tunis, 1963), p. 65.

44. Karel Petráček, "Die Lebensform der volksarabischen gedruckten Texte," *Acta Universitatis Carolinae-Philologica* 4 (1971):25–31.

45. British Museum, cat. no. 14570 a12, b31, b33. The University of California Library also possesses a copy of this same text as published by Maktabat al-Kastaliyya (Cairo, 1282).

46. British Museum copy of *al-Alfāẓ al-Ẓarīfa,* cat. no. 14570 b29.

47. Abnoudy, *La Geste hilalienne,* pp. 16, 17.

48. James T. Monroe, *The Art of Badīᶜ az-Zamān al-Hamadhāni as Picaresque Narrative* (Beirut: American University, 1984).

49. Del Hymes, "Breakthrough into Performance," in *Folklore: Performance and Communication,* eds. Dan Ben-Amos and Kenneth Goldstein (The Hague, 1975), pp. 11–74.

50. ᶜAbd al-Ḥamīd Hawwās's paper contributed to the Hammamet Hilālī conference to be published in the Proceedings of the International Mediterranean Studies Association in *Cahiers des arts et traditions populaires.*

51. Baker, p. 35.

52. Ibid., pp. 22, 46.

53. Ibid., p. 46, fn.

54. Kristina Nelson, *The Art of Reciting the Qur'an* (Austin: University of Texas Press, in press). See also Jacques Jomier, "La Place du Coran dans la vie quotidienne en Egypte," *Revue de l'Institut de Belles Lettres Arabes,* no. 58 (Tunis, 1952):131–165.

55. E. Shouby criticizes his native language for its very oralness from the perspective of an upper-class Western-educated man. See "The Influence of the Arabic Language on the Psychology of the Arabs," in *Readings in Arab Middle Eastern Societies and Cultures,* eds. Lutfiyya and Churchill (The Hague: Mouton, 1970).

56. Pierre Cachia, "The Egyptian Mawwāl," *Journal of Arabic Literature* 7 (1978):85.

57. Pierre Cachia, "Social Values Reflected in Egyptian Popular Ballads," in *Studies in Modern Arabic Literature,* ed. R. C. Ostler (Warminster: Aris and Phillips, Ltd., 1975), p. 86.

58. Ibid., p. 86.

59. Abnoudy, *La Geste hilalienne,* pp. 13–14.

60. See the bibliography for a listing of the Abnoudy cassettes as well as others available commercially.

61. Ṣafī al-Dīn al-Ḥillī, *Die vulgärarabische Poetik: Kitāb al-ᶜĀṭil al-Ḥālī wal-Muraḫḫaṣ al-Ġālī,* ed. W. Hoenerbach (Wiesbaden, 1956), p. 7.

62. P. Cachia, "Egyptian Mawwāl," p. 79.

63. George Herzog, "Music of Yugoslav Heroic Epic Folk Poetry," *Journal of the International Folk Music Council* 3 (1951):62–64. See also Bose, "Law and Freedom in the Interpretation of European Folk Epics," *Journal of the International Folk Music Council* 4 (1958):29–34. See also Amnon Shiloah, "Le Poète-Musicien et la creation poético-musicale au moyen orient," *IFMC Year Book* (1974), pp. 52–63.

64. Cachia, "Egyptian Mawwāl," p. 89.

65. Faiq A. Mukhlis, *Studies and Comparison of the Cycles of the Banī Hilāl Romance,* Ph.D. diss., University of London, 1963.

66. Bridget Connelly, "The Oral-Formulaic Tradition of Sīrat Banī Hilāl," Ph.D. diss., University of California, Berkeley, 1974.

67. Joseph J. Duggan, "Formulas in the *Couronnement de Louis,*" *Romania* 87 (1966):315–344; *The Song of Roland: Formulaic Style and Poetic Craft* (Berkeley, Los Angeles, London: University of California Press, 1973).

68. Jihad Racy, "Record Industry and Egyptian Traditional Music, 1904–1932," *Ethnomusicology* (Jan. 1976), pp. 23–49.

69. Albert B. Lord, "The Influence of a Fixed Text," in *To Honor R. Jakobson,* vol. 2 (The Hague: Mouton, 1967), pp. 1199–1206.

70. J. Schliefer, "Hilāl: The Saga of the Banu Hilāl," in *EI* 1, 2, p. 387.

71. On the aşık, see Ilhan Başgöz, "The Epic Tradition among Turkic Peoples," in *Heroic Epic and Saga,* ed. Felix J. Oinas (Bloomington: Indiana University Press, 1978), pp. 310–335; "The Tale-Singer and his Audience," in *Folklore: Performance and Communication,* eds. Dan Ben-Amos and Kenneth Goldstein, pp. 143–203.

72. Penny Williams, "Through a Glass Brightly," *Aramco World Magazine* 29, no. 4 (July–Aug. 1978):2–5.

73. See B. Connelly, "*Sīrat Banī Hilāl* and the Oral-Epic Technique of Poesis," Cahiers des arts et traditions populaires (Tunis, in press).

74. Baker, p. 44.

75. Muḥammad Moussa told me of this phenomenon in his own village on the island of Kerkenna.

76. This idea developed from a conversation with Christopher Knipp. See his essay, "The *Arabian Nights* in England: Galland's Translation and its Successors," *Journal of Arabic Literature* 5 (1974):43–54.

77. Lecture delivered to the Berkeley faculty seminar, Friends of Oral Literature, in May 1982. See also Connelly, "The Structure of Four Banī Hilāl Tales," *JAL* 4 (1973), for a similar pattern.

78. C. Bremond, *La Logique du récit* (Paris: Editions du Seuil, 1973).

79. Fatima Mernissi uses the word *fitna* to mean woman; see *Beyond the Veil,* p. 4, and "Glossary," p. 125.

80. I have developed this idea about name puns elsewhere in "The Structure of Four Banī Hilāl Tales," *JAL* 4:18–47.

81. David Bynum, *Daemon in the Wood: A Study of Oral Narrative Patterns* (Cambridge, Mass.: Center for the Study of Oral Literature, 1978), p. 325.

82. See my essay on the women's voice in medieval Arabic poetry in *Women Poets of the World,* pp. 88–99.

83. See also William Bright, "Literature: Written and Oral," in *Analyzing Discourse,* ed. D. Tannen (Washington D.C.: Georgetown University Press, 1982), pp. 272–273.

84. Michael Meeker, private communication.

85. See Michael N. Nagler, *Spontaneity and Tradition* (Berkeley, Los Angeles, London: University of California Press, 1974).

86. See Wallace Chaffe, "Integration and Involvement in Speaking, Writing, and Oral Literature," in *Spoken and Written Language,* ed. D. Tannen (Norwood, N.J.: Ablex, 1982), pp. 35–54.

87. Robert Scholes and Robert Kellogg, *The Nature of Narrative* (New York: Oxford University Press, 1966), pp. 55–56.

88. Jack Goody, *The Domestication of the Savage Mind* (Cambridge: Cambridge University Press, 1977); "The Consequences of Literacy," *Comparative Studies in History and Society* 5 (1963):304–345 (with I. P. Watt); *Literacy in Traditional Societies* (Cambridge: Cambridge University Press, 1968). Eric S. Havelock, *Preface to Plato* (Cambridge: Harvard University Press, 1963); *Origins of Western Literacy* (Toronto: Ontario Institute for Studies in Education, 1976); and *Prologue to Greek Literacy* (Cincinnati: University of Cincinnati Press, 1971). David R. Olson, "From Utterance to Text: The Bias of Language in Speech and Writing," *Harvard Educational Review* 47, no. 3 (1977):257–281; Margaret Rader, "Context in Written Language: The Case of Imaginative Fiction," in *Spoken and Written Language,* ed. D. Tannen (Norwood, N.J.: Ablex, 1982), p. 194.

89. Chaim Perelman and L. Olbrechts-Tyteca, *The New Rhetoric: A Treatise on Argumentation* (Notre Dame: University of Notre Dame Press, 1969), trans. John Wilkinson and Purcell Weaver; first published by Presses Universitaires de France (1958), as *La Nouvelle rhétorique.*

90. Chaffe, pp. 49–52.

91. Further fieldwork in Egyptian villages is needed to explore in greater detail what this study proposes as the essence of the oral epic performance; that is, the conscious awareness both poet and patron have of etymological allusions and the ways in which each uses puns to interpret the epic event.

92. Baker, p. 619.

93. Baker, pp. 619–622; A. Laroui, *L'Idéologie arabe contemporaine: essai critique* (Paris: Maspéro, 1970), p. 66; Baker elucidates what she calls the "tawwa phenomenon"; *tawwa* is an adverbial participle that means right away, at once, immediately, just now, this very minute. As Baker points out, however, the phrase "tawwa yijiy" or "he'll be right here" can mean a great variety of things: "here he is approaching," or "he'll be here in a few minutes," or "he does not know he is supposed to be here, but someone has gone to tell him" [or "we intend to send someone to tell him"], or "we have no idea when he'll come," or "he won't be here until this evening, several hours from now," or "he's not coming, but we don't want to be the ones to tell you and disappoint you."

94. Carol Gilligan, *In a Different Voice.* Linda Dégh also points to the adult-child continuum in Hungarian folk communities; see *Folktales and Society: Storytelling in a Hungarian Peasant Community* (Bloomington: Indiana University Press, 1969).

Gilligan's female developmental model is part of the ongoing dialogue between men and women current in the United States. Her study offers a truly "human" model of psychological development (at least for Americans); it derives from Gilligan's reaction against the moral developmental sequence postulated by her mentor and teacher, Lawrence Kohlberg, on which women always measured out as somehow deficient or immature or not fully "moral." As Gilligan's title suggests, she asserts that women have a separate and different model of moral development and she offers hard evidence from her own research data base.

95. Lawrence Kubie, "The Drive to Become Both Sexes," *Psychoanalytic Quarterly* (1974):349–426.

96. Mernissi, *Beyond the Veil,* pp. 81–87.

97. Mary Douglas comments on the conflicts that arise from female seclusion

as an ideal that is not observed in actual practice in *Purity and Danger*.

98. Wayne Booth, *Modern Dogma and the Rhetoric of Assent* (Chicago: University of Chicago Press, 1974). Booth discusses the scientismic versus irrationalist mentality of contemporary American and European post-Cartesian dichotomizations.

99. Isidore Okpewho, "The Anthropologist Looks at Epic," *Research in African Literatures*, vol. 11, no. 4 (Winter 1980):429–448.

# BIBLIOGRAPHY

## A NOTE ON SĪRA SOURCES

Fine bibliographic essays are available. The scholar may refer to Giovanni Canova, "Gli Studi sull'epica popolare araba," *Oriente Moderno* 57, nos. 5–6 (1977):211–226. Canova's bibliographic essay surveys sīra literature as a whole. Claude Breteau, Micheline Galley, and Arlette Roth survey the Hilālī epic in "Témoignages de la longue marche hilalienne," in *Actes du 2e Congrès International d'études des cultures de la Méditerranée occidentale* (Algiers: SNED, 1978), pp. 329–346. Udo Steinbach's book, *Dhāt al-Himma: kulturgeschichtliche Untersuchungen zu einem arabischen Volksroman* (Wiesbaden, 1972), contains an extensive bibliography of sīra materials. I also refer the reader to two Ph.D. dissertations: Cathryn Anita Baker, "The Hilālī Saga in the Tunisian South," Indiana University, 1978, available through University Microfilms, no. 7900678; and Peter Heath's dissertation, which treats in depth the manuscript tradition of *Sīrat ʿAntar,* "The Thirsty Sword: Structure and Composition in *Sīrat ʿAntar ibn Shaddād,*" Harvard University, 1981.

## MANUSCRIPTS

Major sīra manuscript collections are contained in the following libraries:


1. Berlin: W. Ahlwardt, *Verzeichniss der arabischen Handschriften* VIII, Bk. 20 (Berlin, 1896), nos. 9188–9361, 155–462 (189 Hilālī MSS alone).
2. Gotha: W. Pertsch, *Die arabischen Handschriften der herzoglichen Bibliothek zu Gotha* IV (1883), nos. 2569–2577, 380–383.
3. Tübingen: Universitätsbibliothek Tübingen, *Verzeichniss der arabischen Handschriften* II (Leipzig, 1930), no. 52, 4–5. See also, Wagner, *Verzeichniss der orientalischen Handschriften in Deutschland,* vol. 17, Bk. 1.
4. Halle: H. Wehr, *Verzeichniss der arabischen Handschriften in der Bibliothek der Deutschen morgenländischen Gesellschaft* (Leipzig, 1940), nos. 118–119, 43–44, in *Abhandlungen für die Kunde des Morgenlandes* 25, 3.
5. Paris: Bibliothèque Nationale, *Catalogue des manuscrits arabes des nouvelles acquisitions* (1894–1924), E. Blochet (Paris, 1925), no. 4726, 10.

6. Manchester: A. Mingana, *Catalogue of the Arabic Manuscripts in the John Rylands Library* (Manchester, 1934), nos. 623–627.
7. Vatican: G. Levi della Vida, *Elenco dei manoscritti arabi islamici della Biblioteca Vaticana-Vaticani Barberiani Borgiani Rossini* (Vatican, 1935), no. 287, 20, and no. 1264, 197.
8. London: Charles Rieu, *Supplement to the Catalogue of the Arabic Manuscripts in the British Museum* II (London, 1894), esp. p. 743.
9. Tunis: National Library of Tunis; one 500-page Banī Hilāl MS dated A.H. 1256/A.D. 1840.
10. Cairo: *Dār al-Kutub al-Miṣriyya.* Two Banī Hilāl MSS listed in catalog: *Fihrist al-Kutub al-ʿArabiyya al-Mawjūda bi-Dār al-Kutub* (Cairo, 1924).
11. Bahrain: ʿAlī Abā Ḥusayn, *Index of Bahrain Manuscripts,* vol. I (Beirut, 1977), pp. 253–255.

## PRINTED EDITIONS (Kutub ṣafrā')

This is a list of printed editions that I used in my research. Such editions of "kutub ṣafrā'" are available in bookstalls and markets throughout the Arab Middle East. Most Arabic book collections in American university libraries also contain a few exemplars. See, for example, the University of Utah Catalog. See especially the *British Museum Catalogue of Arabic Printed Books* (1894–1935) by A. G. Ellis, vol. I, pp. 638–642; with *Supplementary Catalogue of Arabic Printed Books* (1926), pp. 428–429.

*Sīrat al-ʿArab al-Hijāziyya, al-Mushtamila ʿalá al-Ālfāẓ al-Ẓarīfa fī Riḥla al-ʿArab wa Ḥarb al-Zanātī Khalīfa.* Cairo, n.d.

*Sīrat al-ʿArab al-Hilāliyya, al-Riyāda al-Bahiyya al-Āṣliyya al-Kubrā.* Cairo, n.d.

*Sīrat Banī Hilāl wa Hiya Tashtamil ʿalá Kitāb al-Uns wa-l-Ibtihāj fī Qiṣṣat Abū Zayd al-Hilālī.* Cairo, n.d.

*Sīrat Fāris al-Yaman . . . al-Amīr Sayf ibn Dhī Yazan,* 17 fasc. in 4 vols. Cairo, 1885.

*Sīrat al-Ẓāhir Baybars.* Cairo, n.d.

*Sīrat ʿAlī al-Zibaq al-Miṣri.* Beirut, n.d.

*Sīrat al-fāris al-humām . . . al-Amīr ʿAntara ibn Shaddād.* Cairo, 1925. 32 vols.

*Sīrat al-Amīra Dhāt al-Himma.* Cairo, 1959.

*Sīrat al-Amīra Dhāt al-Himma wa-l-Amīr ʿAbd al-Wahhāb wa-l-Amīr Abū Muḥammad al-Baṭṭāl wa ʿUqbá Shaykh al-Dallāl wa Shūmadris al-Muḥtāl.* Cairo, n.d. (1909?)

*Sīrat al-ʿArab al-Ḥijāziyya, al-Durrat al-Munīfa fī Ḥarb Diyāb . . . .* Cairo, n.d.

*Dīwān Miṣr al-Kabīr . . . wa Mā Jarā li-l-Amīr Diyāb wa-l-Amīr Abū Zayd.* Cairo, n.d.

*Ḥarb al-Basūs al-Kabīr.* Cairo, n.d. (*Sīrat Banī Hilāl*).

*Kitāb al-Ālfāẓ al-Ẓarīfa fī Riḥlat al-ʿArab wa Ḥarb al-Zanāta Khalīfa.* Cairo, n.d.

*Kitāb ʿAntara ibn Shaddād.* Beirut, 1890.

*Kitāb ʿAntara ibn Shaddād.* Beirut, 1883. 6 vols.

*Kitāb ʿAntara ibn Shaddād.* Beirut, 1902. 6 vols.

*Kitāb al-Riyāda al-Bahiyya wa Mā Jarā li l-Amīr Abū Zayd wa-al ʿArab al-Hilāliyya.* Cairo, A.H. 1282.
*Kitāb al-Sabaʿ Tukhūt . . . Sultan Diyāb wa Abū Zayd.* Cairo, n.d.
*Sayf ibn Dhī Yazan.* Cairo, 1967.
*Mughāmarāt Sayf ibn Dhī Yazan.* Cairo, 1964.
*al-Muhalhil, al-Zīr Sālim (Sīrat Banī Hilāl).* Cairo, 1957.
*Taghrībat Banī Hilāl ilá Bilād al-Gharb.* Beirut, n.d.
*Taghrībat Banī Hilāl wa Raḥluhum ilá Bilād al-Gharb wa-Harubhum ma ʿa al-Zanāta Khalīfa.* Cairo, n.d.

## PUBLISHED ORAL SOURCES

Abnoudy, ʿAbd al-Raḥmān. *Al-Sīra al-Hilāliyya.* Performed by Jābir Abū Ḥusayn. 6 cassette recordings. Cairo: Nijmat al-ʿAtaba, 1983.
Alexandru, Tiberiu. *Anthology of Egyptian Popular Music.* Sono Cairo. EST 52, 53, 1967.
Canova, Giovanni. *Egitto: Epica.* I suoni di musica di tradizione orale, Italy, 1980. 33 records with 28 pp. booklet. Italian with English translation by Linda Lappin and musicological notes by Habib Tuoma.

Commercial recordings of sīra performances by professional musician-poets are available through Nijmat al-ʿAtaba and Nefertiti. Dwight Reynolds has compiled a discography of titles.

## SOME TRANSLATIONS FOR THE GENERAL READER

Abnoudy, ʿAbd al-Raḥmān. *La Geste hilalienne.* Trans. by Tahar Guiga. Cairo: General Egyptian Book Organization, 1978.
Ayoub, Abderrahman, and Dwight Reynolds, in progress. An edition and English translation of the Tunis manuscript of the Banī Hilāl epic.
Baker, Cathryn Anita. "The Hilāl Saga in the Tunisian South." Ph.D. Diss., Indiana University, 1978.
Bel, Alfred. "La Djazya, chanson arabe, précédée d'observations sur quelques légendes arabes et sur la geste des Beni-Hilal," *Journal asiatique* XIX, ser. 9, pp. 289–314; XX, pp. 169–236; I, ser. 10, 311–366 (1902, 1903).
Blunt, Sir Wilfred Scawen, and Lady Anne Blunt. *The Romance of the Stealing of the Mare.* London: Reeves and Trabner, 1892. Reissued as "The Stealing of the Mare, an Arabian Epic of the Tenth Century," in *Poetical Works,* by Wilfred Scawen Blunt, vol. 2. London: Macmillan, 1914. Pp. 129–217.
Davis, Russell G., and Brent Ashebranner. *Ten Thousand Desert Swords: The Epic Story of a Great Bedouin Tribe.* Boston: Little, Brown, 1960. (For children.)

Devic, L. M. *Les Aventures d'Antar: roman arabe.* Paris: M. Poujoulat, 1868–1869.

Galley, Micheline, and Abderrahman Ayoub. *Histoire des Beni Hilâl et de ce qui leur advint dans leur marche vers l'ouest.* Classiques Africaines. Paris: Armand Colin, 1983.

Guiga, Abderrahman. *La Geste hilalienne.* Trans. Tahar Guiga. Tunis: Société Tunisienne d'Edition et de Diffusion, 1968.

Hamilton, Terrick. *ʿAntar: A Bedoueen Romance.* London, 1820.

Hurreiz, Sayyid. "The Cycle of Abu Zeid," in *African Folklore,* ed. Richard Dorson. Bloomington: Indiana University Press, 1972. Pp. 371–385.

Mercier, G., and C. Starkweather. "Ahmed el Hilalieu and El Redah." One of "Five Berber Stories" in *The World's Greatest Literature,* vol. 49, *Moorish Literature.* New York: The Colonial Press, 1901. Pp. 176–180.

Norris, Harry. *The Adventures of ʿAntar.* Warminster: Aris and Phillips, 1980.

Patterson, J. R., and P. G. Butcher. *Stories of Abu Zeid the Hilali in Shuwa Arabic.* London: Kegan, Trench, Trubner, 1930. Preface by H. R. Palmer. Introduction and translation by editors.

Richmond, Diana. *ʿAntar and ʿAbla, a Bedouin Romance.* Rewritten and arranged. London: Quartet Books, 1978.

Rouger, G. *Le roman d'ʿAntar d'après les anciens textes arabes.* Paris, 1923.

# INDEX


Abbasid period, 8
ʿAbd Allāh, Naṣr b., 198
ʿAbd al-ʿAzīz, Fārūq, 60, 61, 62, 63, 66, 67, 70, 72, 255, 260, 267; on audience, 189; on Bedouins, 119; "Birth of Abū Zayd" of, 81, 91, 127, 130–131, 144, 145, 176, 180–181, 256; decorum of, 80; dichotomies of, 101; epithets used by, 105; as gypsy, 160, 164; identity with hero by, 164; on literacy, 180; melody used by, 91; opening of, 88–92; performance by, 57–58, 80; puns of, 116, 138; repetitions used by, 105; rhymes of, 106, 253; on social values, 179, 180–181; style of, 81–82, 96, 97, 101, 102, 105, 116
ʿAbdel-Meguid, 20
ʿAbd al-Salām al-Muhadhdhabī, Ḥājj, 195, 196, 208, 210–211, 212–213, 214, 216–217, 218, 224, 259; "Birth of Abū Zayd" of, 199–200, 215, 246
al-Abnoudy, ʿAbd al-Raḥmān, 50, 51, 57, 63, 66–67, 93, 116, 254, 259; as audience, 184–185, 186–187, 189, 251; audience of, 186, 261; on hero, 244; on *Hilāliyya* as history, 149; on *Hilāliyya's* compilers, 249–250; on key, 74; on peasant-poet relationship, 157–158, 250; as poet, 251; on poet, 148, 184–185, 186, 187; radio program of, 49, 62, 184, 185–186, 250, 260; records poets, 48–49, 109, 185–186, 187, 246, 250; on slave motif, 177; as transmitter, 187, 267; on yellow books, 249–250, 252, 253
Abraha, 235, 236
Abrahams, Roger, 236
Abū Ḥusayn, Jābir, 50, 64, 67, 70, 71, 80, 81, 106, 133, 150, 180, 185, 186, 187, 252, 255, 260; ancestry of, 166; audience and, 111–112, 114, 115–116, 120, 131, 134; on Bedouins, 119; "Birth of Abū Zayd" of, 72–73, 97–103, 104, 109–110, 111, 112, 114–115, 125, 126, 127–129, 131–132; epithets of, 105; formulaic lines of, 103–104; on Khaḍrā, 125, 134–135, 136–137, 144; language of, 103; on literacy, 172; music of, 82–84; on name meanings, 143–144; opening of, 97–103; puns of, 107, 108, 111, 114–115, 116, 120, 131; recording by, 48–49, 109, 261; rhymes of, 113, 120; on Rizq, 113, 136; on sacred and profane, 125; on society, 179; style of, 82–84, 101, 102, 114
Abū ʿUbayda, 8
Abū Zayd al-Hilāli, 26, 33, 57, 63, 64, 65, 264; as black, 77, 78, 92, 102, 103, 131–132, 144, 172, 195, 196, 209–210, 234; death of, 208; epic of, 5, 18, 35, 40, 91, 92, 176 (*see also* "Birth of Abū Zayd," *Hilāliyya*); as hero, 28, 48, 184–185, 198, 244; kills his teacher, 77,

Hamilton, Terrick, 18
Ḥanafī, ʿAbd al-Ḥamīd, 28
al-Ḥarīrī, 244
al-Harrās, 206
Hartmann, Martin, 28, 32–33, 42, 240
Ḥasan, Muḥammad, 61, 264
Hawwās, ʿAbd al-Ḥamīd, 66, 187, 246, 261
Heller, Bernard, 9
Hero, 3, 6, 230; Abū Zayd as, 24, 48, 184–185, 198, 244; ʿAntar as, 18; biography of, 229, 264 (see also *Hilāliyya*; Sīra); birth and childhood of, 197–198 (*see also* "Birth of Abū Zayd"); black slave, 235–236; Dhiyāb as, 197, 198, 210–211; fellah as, 187, in glass paintings, 204–207; identification with, 146, 164, 180, 215, 243–244; missing, 185, 244; prints of, 206; twin, 198
Heroic age, 228–229
Herzog, George, 252
al-Hijjawī, Zakariyya, 66
Hilāli tribe, 23–24; migrations of, 28, 256; saga of (see *Hilāliyya*)
Hilāliyya, 4, 23, 26–51, 188; Algerian, 6, 29, 30, 194, 198, 202, 210, 215, 220–223, 225, 238, 246; appeal of, 162; assignment of blame in, 215, 231; authorship of, 28, 34, 242, 243, 249–250; as autobiography, 225; Berber influence in, 220, 221; as biography of hero, 229, 264; boundary transgression in, 203, 206, 207, 217; as chanson de geste, 29; chronicles settling of Africa, 193–224; class hostility expressed in, 171; compared to epic, 33, 34–35, 36; cycles of 28, 33, 131, 134, 140, 194, 217 (*see also* "Birth of Abū Zayd"; Maghribī episode; Taghrība episode); date of, 8; Egyptian, 6, 25, 28, 32, 225 (*see also* "Birth of Abū Zayd"); as episodic, 36; as fixed text, 259–261; fluidity of, 25, 47, 236, 248, 256, 261, 263; function of, 174–175; 262; as genealogy, 182, 194, 196, 216, 246; in glass paintings, 206; hidden meaning within 223–224; as history, 149, 173, 194, 220, 256–258; for identity, 167, 209–210, 217–218, 220, 224, 225, 226, 236; as illiterature, 168–169; influence of, 17, 168; on inside/outside, 139–140, 141, 225, 263; Iraqi, 25; Jordanian, 6, 194, 232, 246; Lebanese, 32, 241; library holdings of, 27–28, 29, 48, 239, 242, 243, 253; Libyan, 32, 194, 198, 232; licit and illicit in, 134–135; as literature, 32; as local, 193, 195, 215; marriage in, 218–219; migration in, 28, 201; multiple versions of, 28, 29–31, 32, 36, 47, 48, 193–224; as musical, 40–41, 70–75, 82, 251–252; as myth, 173; name meanings in, 219, 264, 265; Nigerian, 6, 194, 195, 198, 210, 219–220; as nonfiction, 194; opening in, 88, 244; as oral, 24, 31, 32, 35, 36, 37, 48, 236, 237, 238, 239–240, 241, 242–243, 250; as origin myth, 147–148, 162, 264; origin of, 29–30, 31–32, 33; Palestinian, 194, 232; parallelisms in, 77; poet of (*see* Rāwī; Shāʿir al-rabāba); prose, 246–247; puns in, 224, 225, 262, 265; as relevant, 193; as romance, 181; situation conflict in, 220–221; as social commentary, 160, 161; story pattern in, 78–79, 203; structure of, 33; Sudanese, 194, 198, 209, 210, 219, 225, 246; Syrian, 25; translated, 34, 35–36; transmission of, 185–186, 193, 242–243, 254, 256–261; transpositions in, 170; Tunisian, 6, 25, 194, 195–197, 198–202, 203, 207, 208, 210–213, 214, 215–219, 225, 246; verse in, 40; women in, 198, 199–201, 207–208 (*see also* Jāziya/Zāziya; Khaḍrā);

ished, 77, 132, 133, 134, 142, 144, 196; childlessness of, 73; clothing epithets for, 124–125, 133–134; fertility pilgrimage by, 77, 112, 131–132, 195; on licit and illicit, 134, 143; name pun for, 265; and Rizq, 77, 121–123, 124, 142, 161, 196
Khurshīd, Fārūq, 188
*Al-Kitāb*. *See* Koran; Sīra
*Kitāb ʿAntara ibn Shaddād, 9*
*Kitāb al-Riyāḍa al-Bahiyya,* 8, 28, 253
Knowledge, 62, 67; audience's, 91, 92, 97, 105, 114, 115, 138, 232–233, 263, 269; connects past and present, 271–272; as memory, 233–234, 248, 249; in oral culture, 232–234; shāʿir's, 15, 148–149, 262, 271–272
Koran: chanters, 248; classical language of, 16; condemns listening, 14; fluidity of, 13; as oral, 10–11, 13, 14, 233–234, 248; recitation of, 13–14; on stories/storyteller, 14–15, 16; transmitted, 13–14, 248; written, 10, 248
Koranic schools, 7, 148, 172, 233
al-Kurtī, 5

Lamartine, A. de, 5, 18, 21
Land tenure, 153, 154, 155, 177–178
Lane, Edward, 5, 10, 31–32, 237, 256; on Abū Zayd legend, 40, 176; on café poets, 6, 24, 48, 49, 65, 241; on rabāba, 24, 40, 65
Language, 103; classical, 16; colloquial/vernacular, 8, 26–27, 37, 176, 234; meaning within, 137–138
Largeau, V., 5, 29, 30
Laroui, Abdallah, 22, 271
al-Laṭīf, ʿAbd, 17, 168
Lebanon, 32, 241
Lethem, G. J., 219
Lévi-Strauss, Claude, 181, 207
Libraries, 27–28, 29, 48, 237, 239, 242, 243, 253
Libya, *Hilāliyya* in, 32, 194, 198, 232
Licit. *See* Illicit and licit
Literacy, 10–11, 13, 14, 172, 175, 180, 269–270
Literature: classical Arabic, 8, 9–10, 12, 19; folk, 15–16, 18–21, 22–24, 30–31, 55, 187–188 (see also *Hilāliyya*; Sīra); official, 169, 188, 243, 244; oral, 267–268, 269
Lord, Albert B., 69, 72, 78, 258; on fixed text, 256; formulaic analysis of, 41, 44, 47, 50, 79, 232, 253–255; on history as memory, 232; on oral composition, 37, 41–43, 47; on performance as transmission, 47–48

MacDonald, Duncan B., 20
MacKail, J. W., 34–35
Maddāh. *See* Poet, café
Maghrib (region), 26, 197, 217, 223, 225–226
al-Maghribī, Samawʾal b. Yaḥyá, 5, 238
Maghribī episode, 201–204
Mahler, Margaret, 229
Mamluks, 4, 174, 176, 177, 235, 236
Marriage, 78, 136, 143, 218–219
Massie, Henry N., 229
Maurice, Sir Cecil, 229
Mawwāl tradition, 249, 251, 266
Māzin, Yūsuf, 63–64, 65, 66, 67, 69, 160, 166
Meaning. *See* Etymology; Name meanings/puns
Melody, 70, 71, 81–82, 91, 252. *See also* Music
Memory: history as, 232; knowledge as, 233–234, 248, 249; and past and present, 231–232, 271–272
Mernissi, Fatima, 174–175, 183, 226, 227
Migration, 207, 228, 256; motif, 4, 23, 28, 201, 235
"Mīlād Abū Zayd." *See* "Birth of Abū Zayd"
Monroe, James T., 47, 244
Muḥaddithīn. *See* Poet; Rawi; Story-

al-Zayyāt, Aḥmad Ḥasan, 17, 149, 168
Zāziya. *See* Jāziya/Zāziya
Zeid, Abou A. M., 123, 125–126
Zein, Tam, 219
Zwettler, Michael, 46, 47

| | |
|---|---|
| Designer: | U.C. Press Staff |
| Compositor: | Prestige Typography |
| Text: | 11/13 Sabon |
| Display: | Sabon |
| Printer: | Bookcrafters, Inc. |
| Binder: | Bookcrafters, Inc. |